Quests and Kingdoms
A Grown-Up's Guide
to Children's Fantasy Literature

Books by K.V. Johansen

Nightwalker
The Cassandra Virus
Torrie and the Firebird
Torrie and the Pirate-Queen
Highlights in the History of Children's Fantasy (e-book)
Pippin and Pudding
Pippin and the Bones
Pippin Takes a Bath
The Serpent Bride: Stories From Medieval Danish Ballads
Torrie and the Dragon

www.pippin.ca

Quests and Kingdoms
A Grown-Up's Guide
to Children's Fantasy Literature

K.V. Johansen

SYBERTOOTH INC
SACKVILLE, NEW BRUNSWICK
Litteris Elegantis Madefimus

For my nieces and nephews

First published 2005 by Sybertooth Inc.
59 Salem St.
Sackville, NB
E4L 4J6
Canada

This book is printed on acid-free paper.
ISBN-10: 0-9688024-4-3   ISBN-13: 978-0-9688024-4-1

Library and Archives Canada Cataloguing in Publication

Johansen, K. V. (Krista V.), 1968-
Quests and kingdoms : a grown-up's guide to children's fantasy
literature / K.V. Johansen.

Includes bibliographical references and index.
ISBN 0-9688024-4-3

1. Children's stories--History and criticism. 2. Fantasy fiction--
History and criticism. I. Title.

PN1009.A1J56 2005   813'.08766099282   C2005-903485-8

Table of Contents

Acknowledgements

I would like to thank the Eileen Wallace Children's Literature Collection at the University of New Brunswick in Fredericton, which awarded me the Eileen Wallace Research Fellowship in Children's Literature in 2001, enabling me to undertake the research for this book. The collection itself provided me with access to much of the material I needed. Particular thanks go to Catherine Hoyt, then the collection's librarian, whose aid was invaluable, as well as to the rest of the staff at the collection and its home, the Harriet Irving Library. A grant from the New Brunswick Arts Board further facilitated the writing of the work. Thanks are owed as well to Victoria Pennell, editor of *Resource Links*, for her support in seeing a series of essays drawn from the *Quests* research into print.

A number of people helped me along the way by lending books: Lee and Alice Whitney, Rob Cupido and Karen Bamford, Lynne Hawkes and Janet Geier, librarians of Salem Elementary and Marshview Middle Schools respectively, Amanda Leaman, and April Johansen-Morris all gave me access to their collections. Paulette Durant was responsible for bringing the Eileen Wallace Fellowship to my attention. Ellen Pickle of Tidewater Books, HarperCollins Canada, and Penguin Canada provided review copies of some recent works. Noreen Johansen and Norma Paul read and commented on the manuscript from the elementary school teacher's perspective; Norma also brought a keen proofreader's attention to it. Thanks are owed as well to Paul Marlowe, my insightful and demanding editor, for his rigorous criticism and constructive witticisms, and to my cover models, Marina and Susanna Cupido. And particularly to Tristanne Connolly of St. Jerome's University, for advice, Blake expertise, encouragement, and long friendship – *micel þancword*.

I
Introduction: Why Fantasy?
(And what is it, anyway?)

Fantasy has been an increasingly popular genre in adult fiction over the last half of the twentieth century, ever since the university students of the sixties discovered *The Lord of the Rings*, the first volume of which had been published in 1954. As *The Lord of the Rings* captured the popular imagination and became part of it, other writers were creating books specifically for children which shared that interest in the mythical, the magical, and the 'other' – other times, other worlds, other ways of being.

With the explosive popularity of J.K. Rowling's *Harry Potter* series in the late nineties, and to a slightly lesser degree, of Philip Pullman's *His Dark Materials* trilogy, children's fantasy was suddenly news, appearing at the top of bestseller lists in national newspapers, beating out adult 'literary' fiction, sometimes to the loud dismay of critics and reviewers. Whereas books like Lloyd Alexander's *Prydain* series or *Over Sea, Under Stone*, the first of Susan Cooper's *The Dark is Rising* books, were simply made available as fiction when they were first published in the late sixties, children's fantasy has in recent years suddenly been noticed as a genre, labelled as such on school and library shelves. Older works back in print or those classics that have never ceased to be available are repackaged, marketed now as belonging to a distinctive genre, while some publishers rush highly derivative, poorly-conceived and -written fantasies into print to capitalize on the current hunger for the fantastic.

All this can leave those teachers, parents, or librarians who do not read much fantasy themselves a bit lost, when looking for something to recommend to a young reader who has finished the latest book by Rowling or Jacques and is prowling the shelves for something more. This book will provide a basis from which an adult unfamiliar with the genre of children's fantasy literature may explore it. It is not an encyclopaedia, nor a critical history heavy with theory, but merely a tour through the history of fantasy for children, calling attention to the highlights. The aim, in short, is to give those adults concerned with bringing children and books together, and who cannot themselves sit down to read two or three hundred books over the summer, a nodding acquaintance with the children's fantasy genre and its history.

As in any such work, the selection is partly governed by the status of acknowledged classics, and partly by personal choice. Rather than provide comprehensive lists of books by significant authors, several representative works for each author chosen are discussed, although where the author is of central importance to the history of the genre, their entire body of work may be included. This generally non-encyclopaedic approach, with emphasis on the actual story, will better enable a teacher or parent to get a 'feel' for the sort of story which that author tells, their approach to plot, characters, and themes, their particular concerns, and thus provide a better introduction than a mere list with one-sentence plot summaries. The synopses, therefore, are detailed, and contain, as people are fond of warning on websites, spoilers. The intent, as already stated, is to increase the awareness of teachers, librarians, and parents regarding the traditions of fantasy for children, familiarize them with the significant works of those traditions, and to encourage them to make fantasy literature more readily available in the classroom and at home. It may also, with any luck, introduce lovers of fantasy, both children and adults, to authors they have not previously discovered, and lead readers to seek their stories out.

But, what is fantasy? Ask a group of ten-year-olds and they will likely reply, 'Stories that aren't true,' an answer that reveals a certain confusion about the definition of fiction, but has some logic to it. Fantasy has in it elements that could not be 'true', things that are not possible, as opposed to say, a tale of daring ten-year-olds foiling desperate smugglers, also not true and highly unlikely, but at the age of ten you can at least imagine yourself foiling smugglers. However, you know, deep-down, no matter what you hope and wish, that you will never walk through a wardrobe into another world or discover a boggart infesting your computer. C.S. Lewis distinguished two types of realism in fiction; what he called 'realism of presentation' and defined as 'the art of bringing something close to us, making it palpable and vivid, by sharply observed or sharply imagined detail' (*An Experiment in Criticism* 57) and 'realism of content' which occurs in fiction '... when it is probable or "true to life"' (59). What children mean when they say that fantasy is not 'true' is that, although it may have 'realism of presentation' (and most of the best fantasy does), it does not demand 'realism of content'.

Fantasy takes in a broad swathe of children's books. Anything with talking animals could be and is often called fantasy, even political allegory like *Animal Farm*. Stories about animate toys are a type of fantasy. Anything involving ghosts, time-travel by means of magic objects, or ESP should be, even when it gets labelled science fiction instead. The term 'speculative fiction' is coming into more frequent usage to cover fantasy and science fiction together. Science fiction itself is sometimes used as a label to encompass fantasy, although the definition of science fiction can be narrower, meaning stories dependent on the possibilities of science and things extrapolated from current knowledge. Science fiction and fantasy are close cousins, but this book deals (more or less) with fantasy alone.

The kind of fantasy generally considered here will be stories that involve magic or the supernatural in some way, and/or what are called 'secondary worlds', i.e., invented worlds, places, times, or histories. Generally, outright science fiction, and fantasy that involves humanly-intelligent, talking animals in an otherwise realistic setting, such as Richard Adams' *Watership Down*, have not been included. Time-travel stories in which the time-travel is purely a device to facilitate a story about history are omitted. Fantasy involving animate toys has been left out as well. That said, A.A. Milne's *Winnie-the-Pooh* and Kenneth Grahame's *The Wind in the Willows* have been included, although they are about toys and talking animals in a setting that is realistic (although not for those animals), because both are classics that are in many ways about the wonders of the imagination; both create worlds that are manifestly not our world, even though, at the same time, they seem almost more real.

With an eye to the non-fantasy-reading buyer of children's books, whether teacher, librarian, or parent with a fantasy-reading child, the book will also consider the question 'why fantasy?' before embarking on its (mostly) chronological journey, since some will ask that question. Why make this genre available to children? What does it do to prepare them for the real world? *What good is it?*

Beowulf, one of the oldest works of fiction in English, is fantasy. The only manuscript of *Beowulf* (Cotton Vitellius A.xv) dates from around 1000 A.D., but the poem itself was most likely composed in the eighth century. In fact, the oldest fiction in the world, far older than the Old English *Beowulf,* is fantasy: *Gilgamesh* (probably composed between 3000 and 2000 B.C.), the *Iliad* and *Odyssey* (800-700 B.C.), and the folktales of every people on earth. These are the stories every culture has held dear since its birth, the ones that tell of gods and heroes and demons, order and chaos, creation and destruction, good and evil. They are part of humanity's attempt to make sense of its place in a chaotic and perilous world; they tell us how to live, how to be human.

Fantasy contains within it all that is in fairy-tale and legend. At its greatest, as in the works of Tolkien, it may achieve myth. Yet, a popular perception of fantasy is that it is 'mere' genre fiction, something fluffy, lacking real substance, a fit pastime for an idle hour and nothing more. Worse, an enjoyment of fantasy is sometimes seen as a desire to retreat from reality or an inability to cope with the real world, a symptom of some underlying character flaw or failure to understand the difference between real and imagined. However, C.S. Lewis argues that 'Admitted fantasy is precisely the kind of literature which never deceives at all' (*Experiment* 67) and goes on to suggest that true deception of the reader is more likely to occur in some examples of realistic fiction '... where all appears to be very probable but all is in fact contrived to put across some social or ethical or religious or anti-religious "comment on life"' (68).

'Children', Lewis writes, 'are not deceived by fairy-tales' (67). Tolkien discusses the reception of the fantastic by child readers as well, in his essay 'On Fairy-Stories'. He observes that although children may, while they are still developing their understanding of the world, need some guidance in judging '... between the fantastic, the strange (that is, rare or remote facts), the nonsensical, and the merely "grown-up" (that is ordinary things of their parents' world, much of which still remains unexplored)', they recognize the different classes (*Tree and Leaf* 38). Of his own reading of as child, he recalls, 'I never imagined that the dragon was of the same order as the horse. And that was not solely because I saw horses daily, but never even the footprint of a worm. The dragon had the trademark *Of Faerie* written plain upon him' (40).

Tolkien has an even more important point to make about fantasy, when one is considering the question of 'What good is it?' In 'On Fairy-Stories' he calls fantasy (the artistic product of the activity he referred to as 'sub-creation', distinct from mere daydreaming), 'a natural human activity' (51). He stresses the necessity of the action of the rational mind in reading and writing fantasy:

> Fantasy ... certainly does not destroy or even insult reason; and it does not blunt the appetite for, nor obscure the perception of, scientific verity. On the contrary. The keener and the clearer is the reason, the better fantasy will it make. If men were ever in a state in which they did not want to know or could not perceive truth (facts or evidence), then Fantasy would languish until they were cured.
>
> (*Tree and Leaf* 51)

Thus, the greatest writer of fantasy, a scholar and academic trained in the humanist traditions, identified the ability to imagine things not seen and known and experienced, as vital to the reasoning mind.

As though being perceived as potentially a font of deceit and a refuge for the socially maladjusted were not enough of a disability under which to labour, fantasy has even come to be regarded by a few (mostly American religious fundamentalists), as a lure for unbalanced minds, and a taste for it as the first step on the road to Satanism and mass-murder. When *Harry Potter* began attracting media attention, some schools were urged to ban it. Fantasy, according to an article in *The Philadelphia Trumpet* entitled 'Harry Spells Danger', leads to an interest in the supernatural and the occult. The fantasy world 'increasingly can assume a sense of reality' (Anderson 26). 'Otherworldly novels' and 'occult interests' can 'promote violent tendencies in the real world!' he writes. This author goes on to cite examples of teenage murderers and suicides inspired by an interest in the super-natural, and eventually arrives at the conclusion that the danger in regarding fantasy as 'just another genre of literature' lies in that 'There is, in fact, a real world of evil spirits!' (The exclamation marks are Anderson's.) The article then moves into a prediction of death and damnation for those who do not share the author's religious beliefs and who refuse to abandon 'abominable acts such as sorcery and the worship of pagan deities' (27). The argument that *Harry Potter* in particular and fantasy literature in general contains within it the seeds of evil thus seems to be founded on a belief in the literal reality of demons and sorcery. The children who define fantasy as 'stories that aren't true' are wiser.

The views expressed in the *Trumpet* article are not an isolated phenomenon; this attitude towards fantasy, with *Harry Potter* as the favourite example, is common to the religious right, both Christian and Muslim. The books have been banned from some public schools in the United States, private religious schools in Great Britain and Australia, banned (by the government), from private schools for foreign children in the United Arab Emirates, burned in New Mexico, and shredded in Maine (BBC News). The attempted public school bans have often been overturned by legal challenges. But all the rational arguments in favour of fantasy, by all the readers and scholars and critics and children in the world, are unlikely to overthrow or even moderate the beliefs of those who eagerly await the day when all who do not share their religious beliefs will perish.

What place does fantasy have in schools and libraries these days? Budgets are so small that every book purchase must be justified, and the concern too often is more with instruction than recreation. Every book must have a stated purpose. Review journals aimed at teachers and librarians frequently discuss the curricular applications of the book, because that is the way to justify its presence in the classroom. This seems to have led to an emphasis on providing books which can easily be identified with some purpose: the story illustrates an historical event, or deals with some perceived 'real-life' crisis facing children, or teaches a 'life lesson'.

Even much that is ostensibly fantasy or science fiction falls into that instructional category, especially in North America: Joey and her brother go back in time and land on a harvest excursion train heading for Saskatchewan; Alexa finds a magic bracelet which whisks her to another world, where she has mild adventures and returns able to cope with her parents' divorce; Gary's adventure with the invisible goblins in the backyard teaches him about the wrongs of bullying. It can sometimes seem as if only books which have an obvious didactic purpose, easily distilled for back-cover blurbs and publishers' catalogues, are worthy of an educator's attention. Can we really condone the belief that the only virtues in a work of fiction that can be justified in the classroom are those that also belong to history texts and fables or parables?

Against the charge that fantasy is 'mere' escapism, one can counter that escape is important. Why else do people go on holiday, take cruises, or buy cottages? Escape is not denial of reality, nor an inability to cope with the real world. Healthy escape does not confuse fiction and reality. To remain healthy and balanced, the spirit needs to refresh itself: the mind needs to play, the imagination to stretch. Recreation implies restoration, renewal.

If recreation were all fantasy literature had to offer, that would be justification enough, but fantasy has always contained so much more. Fantasy has always done subtly what fables and parables have as their express purpose; fairy-tales do remind us, over and over, that there is much to be gained by the overlooked virtues of kindness, personal integrity, and fair dealing. Fantasy, perhaps more than any other genre of literature, still contains ideals.

Ideals may never be attainable, but without them, against what can we judge ourselves? The abilities to choose between right and wrong, to aim for what is good rather than what is expedient, to consider actions and consequences rather than to follow blindly the choices made by those around us because that is easier, are something the hero in much of fantasy literature learns. These may not be virtues that suit us especially well for our business-driven society, but that should not make them an undesirable trait. Far from it.

Personal independence and fulfilment within a just society are often the ideals striven for by the heroes of fantasy. They may fight tyrannical sorcerers or invading armies. They may find

13

and restore lost treasures or people. Their quests may be on the scale of a kingdom or a world, or happen within their own suburban neighbourhood, their own home, their own mind. But always, in good fantasy as in all good literature, the heroes emerge from their adventures changed. They have grown. Very often, their society has been changed for the better as well.

Fantasy, in the end, says that an individual does matter. It teaches us that heroes are not born, they become. Choices have consequences. It is necessary to act rather than acquiesce if the world is to be changed, or saved, or renewed. It is necessary to believe in ideals so as to recognize wrongs and to strive for what is right.

And of course, sometimes a bit of escapism does more good than all the real-life, problem-themed books in the world.

II
Old Tales Retold, part one

Modern fantasy has roots in many streams of literature. Mythology is one, medieval Romance and legend another. The fairy-tale is a third, which has remained an important aspect of fantasy in its own right, especially for children, down to our own time.

'Fairy-tale' is a difficult term to define. It does not necessarily mean a tale about fairies, although as David Luke points out in the introduction to his Penguin translation of selections from the Grimms' fairy-tales, the Grimms' stories, noticeably fairy-free, actually used the French for fairy, *feé*, in their first edition, and later replaced it with *Zauberin*, witch or sorceress, in an effort to make the language more German (Luke 9). The German *Märchen* means something like 'tales', not necessarily about magic. *Kinder- und Hausmärchen*, the German title of what in English is usually called some variant of *Grimms' Fairy-Tales*, means stories told for children and in the household. The French *contes* similarly means stories or tales, not necessarily having anything to do with fairies or magic. Generally, though, when we think of fairy-tales, we think of tales involving wonder or enchantment, and these are the ones with which this discussion is concerned.

Although the types of tales told in European households, which became what we now call 'fairy-tales' in English, were not told solely for children, children were an important part of the audience. Some fairy-tales did exist in print from the sixteenth century to the nineteenth in chapbooks: small, cheap books sold by their printers or by travelling pedlars. They were often illustrated with woodcuts and drew their stories from many sources, including folk- and fairy-tales, heroic legends and stories from medieval Romance, and later on, from popular novels, as well as religious material, ballads, and recent events. Similar books existed in France's *Bibliothèque bleue* and Germany's *Volksbücher*. Chapbooks were popular with children and adults alike, but the fairy-tales we know best today were given their enduring form not in these, but in literary collections aimed, initially, at adults. Among the first collections of this sort were those published in Italian by Giovan-Francesco Straparola in the mid fifteen-hundreds, and in a Neapolitan dialect by Giovan-Battista Basile between 1634 and 1636. It was in France, though, that such literary retellings achieved their greatest form.

Literary reworkings of fairy-tales, or stories in a fairy-tale mode, became extremely popular in French upper-class salon society beginning in the late seventeenth century. Fairy-tales of this type were written and published primarily as adult enter-tainment, although critics tended to dismiss such works as not worthy of serious literary men. At that time, conversation was a fashionable art among upper-class circles, and literature was one of the popular topics in the salons which society ladies would host. The telling and discussion of fairy-tales became a popular pastime, but these were not tales as told around the kitchen fire. They were retold, or newly invented on a foundation of tradi-tional motifs, for their courtly audience. The French literary fairy-tales by various authors were collected in a series called *Le Cabinet des feés* beginning in 1785, and eventually filled forty-one volumes. The two best known authors of fairy-tale collections in French lived at the end of the seventeenth century, and are names still known today. They were the Comtesse d'Aulnoy and Charles Perrault.

Madame d'Aulnoy (c. 1650-1705)

Madame d'Aulnoy, as she is usually called, was Marie-Catherine le Jumel de Barneville de la Motte, Comtesse d'Aulnoy. She lived a colourful life, with a dramatically failed marriage and six children. It was alleged she and her mother plotted unsuccess-fully to frame her husband for treason; possibly as a result of this, she spent time in retreat from society at a nunnery and per-haps in Spain as well. She wrote a romantic novel which con-tained a fairy-tale told by the hero, an early instance of the liter-ary fairy-tale, as well as other novels and books about Spain, which may or may not have been based on personal experience. Her greatest contributions to literature, however, were her twenty-five fairy-tales, which appeared in *Contes des fées* (1697) and *Contes nouveaux, ou Les Fées à la mode* (1698). These stories were partly original and partly based on folktale traditions, probably gleaned largely from servants and from stories she had heard in her childhood in Normandy.

Many of d'Aulnoy's stories lack the simplicity of plot we think of as natural to fairy-tales. They do not necessarily follow a single character from start to finish, relating only what is important to his or her adventure, as those collected by the Grimms, for instance, usually do. Her stories can be convoluted and rich in detail, mingling the elegant and the comic, with numerous characters. Included among d'Aulnoy's tales are some still very well known, such as 'Beauty and the Beast', and others now less familiar, such as 'The Blue Bird' or 'The White Cat' (to give them their common English titles).

'The Blue Bird' is typical of d'Aulnoy's elaborate style of fairy-tale. It incorporates such traditional motifs as the substitution of the bride, the overcoming of magical barriers by means of gifts from a fairy or animal helper, and the winning of the right to spend nights near the estranged beloved. Even a synopsis of it shows its complexity:

Princess Fiodelisia is locked in a tower by her stepmother when King Charming is courting her, so that the queen's own daughter Turritella can attempt to win him. The king carries Turritella off in a chariot pulled by flying frogs, believing he is rescuing Fiodelisia, but when he finds out he has been tricked, he refuses to wed her and is turned into a blue bird by Turritella's fairy godmother, Mazilla, a spell that will last seven years.

Fiodelisia is made to believe her stepsister has married Charming, and is left locked in her tower in despair. King Charming comes to her, tells how he was tricked, and visits her often with gifts. When the queen finds out that the princess is being visited by her beloved, she lays traps for the bird-king. Wounded as he flies to her tower, Charming believes Fiodelisia has betrayed him and resigns himself to death. The enchanter who gave him the frog-chariot comes looking for him, heals him, and takes him home.

Meanwhile, Fiodelisia's father dies, and the kingdom rises up against her stepmother, making the princess queen. She sets out to find the blue bird. The enchanter has asked the wicked fairy to take the spell off King Charming, which she has done on condition that Turritella stay with the king for several months – if he does not marry her at the end of that time, Charming will be changed into a bird again. Fiodelisia encounters a good fairy who gives her four eggs to break when she needs help. Two of the eggs contain items that help her past various barriers on her way to Charming's kingdom, a common element in many traditional tales. Disguised as a servant, she lurks about the palace, and sells various of the king's gifts to Turritella in return for being allowed to spend the night where she can speak to the king – but he does not hear either her reproaches or her words of love. The final two eggs contain wonderful toys that Fiodelisia also trades for the same privilege. In the end the king hears her, all the misunderstandings are explained, and the wicked fairy's curse is overcome by the united efforts of the enchanter and the good fairy.

Another example of this type, 'The White Cat', is similarly long and complex in its plot. In it a prince is aided by a white cat in the various quests his father sets him. The cat eventually tells her own story of fairy captivity, a daring escape attempt that failed, the death of her first beloved and her own magical transformation. When she is at last freed from her enchantment by the prince, the white cat is revealed as a princess and a worthy bride for the prince.

It is the simpler stories such as 'Beauty and the Beast' that continue to appear in illustrated fairy-tale collections or as single-story picture books today, yet Madame d'Aulnoy's more convoluted stories have a great deal in common with modern fantasy. They take traditional motifs and expand on them, combining several into longer stories which follow the independent adventures of hero and heroine through their individual trials and quests, where each small victory is offset by a new obstacle until the very end. By the time that end is reached, both have been tested and can, sketchy though their personalities may be, be seen to have experienced some growth. Both have shown they are worthy of the good fortune that is finally theirs. D'Aulnoy's tales have much in them to appeal to 'middle readers' and teens, in just that similarity to modern fantasy novels.

Unfortunately, it can be difficult to locate English translations of Madame d'Aulnoy's stories, other than those commonly found as picture books for younger children, even though her stories entered the English literary tradition very swiftly. Translations appeared in 1699 and 1707, although this was roughly the period of the War of the Spanish Succession (1702-1713), during which France was at war with much of Europe, including England. At that time, in England as in France, the tales were offered for adult enjoyment. It was only in 1773 that a selection of d'Aulnoy's stories was published in an English translation specifically for children, under the title of *Mother Bunch's Fairy Tales*. These days, the most readily-available English retellings of Madame d'Aulnoy are to be found, as they were a century ago, in the *Fairy Books* of Andrew Lang (see below).

Charles Perrault (1628-1703)

The other most-celebrated writer of courtly fairy-tales in France was Charles Perrault, who trained as a lawyer and was a civil servant in the government of Louis XIV. His first venture into fairy-tales was the retelling in verse of three traditional stories. The first of these, in 1691, is not really a fairy-tale but a version of the dreadful 'Patient Griselda' story, in which a husband tests his uncomplaining wife through years of cruel lies and rejection; she is eventually rewarded for her passive endurance with restoration to his side. The story is found in Boccaccio's mid-fourteenth-century *Decameron*, but is best-known in English from Chaucer's *Clerk's Tale* in *The Canterbury Tales* (written in Middle English in the late fourteenth century). Perrault's next verse tale, 'The Foolish Wishes', in which three wishes are squandered by a husband and wife in bickering, appeared in 1693. 'Donkeyskin', about a princess who flees from the father who intends to marry her himself, was published in 1694.

Perrault's collection of eight fairy-tales in prose, published in 1697, was entitled *Histoires, ou contes du temps passé, avec des Moralitéz* or *Contes de ma mère de l'Oye* – Tales of Mother Goose. There is some question as to whether it was Perrault or his teenage son Pierre who wrote this second collection, but scholarly opinion generally holds that Charles Perrault was the author. The occasional attributions to his son that appeared early on may have been an attempt on Charles' part to avoid the criticism for indulging in such a non-scholarly pursuit, which was levelled at him by fellow members of the Académie française following publication of his first three verse tales.

The eight stories contained in *Histoires* are 'Sleeping Beauty', 'Little Red Riding Hood', 'Bluebeard', 'Puss-in-Boots', 'The Fairy' or 'Diamonds and Toads', 'Cinderella', 'Riquet With The Tuft', and 'Hop O' My Thumb or 'Little Thumb', to give them their common English titles. 'Cinderella', 'Little Red Riding Hood', and 'Sleeping Beauty' need no summary, although Perrault's 'Sleeping Beauty' goes on after the princess' awakening, the point at which modern retellings usually stop, through two years of marriage, two children, and the foiled plotting of the prince's ogre-mother. 'Puss-in-Boots', once just as popular but now somewhat neglected, is the story of how a miller's son marries a princess with the help of his cat, who outwits (and eats) an ogre, and recreates his master as the Marquis of Carabas. 'Riquet with the Tuft' is interesting for the fact that the heroine is the eldest, rather than the youngest daughter, and is a beautiful princess cursed with stupidity, who longs to be intelligent. She wins the heart of an ugly prince whose fairy birth-gift is to be able to give intelligence equal to his own to the person he loves. Her gift is to make the person she loves handsome, although as Perrault says, it may be simply that Riquet's kindness, wit, and intelligence made him handsome to the eyes of love. 'Bluebeard', not so popular now as it once was, tells of a girl married to a man who keeps his murdered wives hanging on the wall in a locked room. 'Little Thumb' is, like the better known 'Hansel and Gretel' from the Grimms' collection, the story of poor parents who try to leave their children in the woods. The youngest saves them from this abandonment and then from an ogre, whom Little Thumb tricks into killing his own daughters, in the end stealing a pair of seven-league boots and carrying riches back to his family. 'The Fairy' is about a widow's two daughters, the disdainful eldest and the sweet youngest, and the curse and blessing they receive from a fairy at a well: from the mouth of the good sister, jewels and flowers drop, while from the mouth of the bad one fall toads and snakes.

Perrault was first translated into English in 1729 by Robert Sambar, and often appeared in bilingual editions for use by students studying French. The name 'Mother Goose' came into English from Perrault's fairy-tales, and was often used as the title of the collection.

The sources of the stories in *Histoires* are debatable. One theory holds that Perrault used stories from oral folk tradition; another, that they came from earlier French and Italian literary versions and the French equivalents of chapbooks. Five of the stories are very similar to printed tales that would have been available to him; three have no known literary antecedents but are analogous to other European folktales. All, however, contain traditional folk motifs, and once published, Perrault's became the definitive versions of these tales. They entered or re-entered the oral tradition in his versions and spread throughout Europe, to be re-collected by later folklorists. The Brothers Grimms, for instance, included a German version of 'Puss-in-Boots' in their collection of German fairy-tales in 1812, but left it out of the second and later editions because of the identifiably French origins.

Today, versions of the more popular Perrault stories are found in innumerable picture books, but collections that are close translations of Perrault's originals are also available; a few even include his somewhat sardonic rhyming morals at the end. In their original form, Perrault's stories are elegant and still very readable for today's children; they lack both the occasionally excessive elaboration of Madame d'Aulnoy's and the baldness of narrative that the Grimms' stories sometimes retain from their oral sources. Whether he reworked them from written sources, from oral tales, or a combination of both, it was Perrault's literary skills that set these stories in the forms we know, and it is to him we owe what are among the most enduringly-popular fairy-tales: Cinderella and Little Red Riding Hood, Puss-in-Boots and Sleeping Beauty.

Jakob and Wilhelm Grimm (1785-1863, 1786-1859)

A century after Madame d'Aulnoy and Perrault, the Brothers Grimm in Germany began to collect folk or fairy-tales from oral tradition, with scholarship rather than entertainment as their primary aim. Jakob (frequently anglicized as Jacob) and Wilhelm Grimm were born in Hanau and grew up in Steinau and Kassel in Hesse, then an independent German state. They studied at

Marburg University, where they became interested in philology, the study of the history of languages. As liberal intellectuals of the time, they were concerned with questions of national identity, and saw the native literary traditions as an important part of German cultural history. Their lives and careers were frequently disturbed by politics as the Napoleonic Wars rearranged Europe. Both taught at Göttingen University in the kingdom of Hanover but lost their jobs for protesting the Elector of Hanover's suspension of the constitution. They ended up in Berlin in Prussia, engaged in the prodigious task of writing a German dictionary, which was not completed until a century after their deaths. Of the two, Jakob was more concerned with language (he is the Grimm of Grimm's Law regarding the correspondences of consonant sounds in Germanic and other Indo-European languages), while Wilhelm was the more literary, eventually assuming most of the responsibility for revising later editions of the *Märchen*.

The Grimms collected most of their stories from middle-class friends and neighbours. The idea that their sources were unso-phisticated peasants living in cottages, like the poor parents of so many of the fairy-tale children, persisted for a long time, despite the fact that they noted scrupulously their source for each story – although they did edit and amend according to their own agenda. The work went through seven editions in the brothers' lifetimes. There was also a smaller illustrated collection of selections from it published in 1825, intended for children. The first volume of the two-volume first edition of *Kinder- und Hausmärchen*, pub-lished in 1812 (the second volume appeared in 1815), told the stories in a simple, unadorned style and contained scholarly notes. As they added to the collection in later editions, Wilhelm became the main editor. The stories were revised by the addition of more dialogue and more detail. They were also made to sound what might be called 'folksier', with the addition of proverbs and through changes in vocabulary, while words of French origin were replaced with German equivalents. The motivation for some of this revision was the shaping of the stories to demon-strate a German way of life; like many German intellectuals of the time, the Grimms believed in the ideal of a unified German nation, and wanted to illustrate a German cultural heritage.

The stories were also changed to suit middle-class *mores* and an audience of children by blunting some of the family estrangements and by alteration of the sexual content. In the first edition of *Kinder- und Hausmärchen* (1812), some of the women we now know as evil stepmothers were the heroines' real mothers, for instance, while in 'Rapunzel', after many visits by the prince the girl naively (but pardonably) asks why her dresses no longer fit. Thus the fairy (who became a witch in later editions as the Grimms replaced French words with German) discovers the existence of both Rapunzel's lover and her pregnancy. By the final version (1857), Rapunzel seems much less intelligent, revealing her secret wooer by asking why the witch is heavier than the prince in climbing up her hair. In general, though, most of what was changed in the tales was done to expand the stories into a more polished literary form, to suit them to the Grimms' *Märchen* ideal.

Not all the stories in the Grimms' collection are 'fairy' tales having to do with enchantment, although these remain the most popular. There are stories such as 'Marienkind', in which religious figures take the role of magical friends and foes. In 'Marienkind' a girl is adopted by the Virgin Mary but is punished for curiosity and lying by expulsion from heaven. She marries a king, but continues to be punished for refusing to confess. The Virgin takes away the queen's own children and her voice. The heroine is on the verge of being burnt by her husband the king, for supposedly murdering the children, before she finally confesses. Other tales feature clever young men who outwit the devil, or virtuous girls who are rewarded while wicked ones are punished, but by saints rather than elderly sorceresses or fairies. Still other stories are simple fables or jokes, or instructional tales where disobedient or stupid children come to gruesome ends.

The most popular tales, however, remain the ones involving enchantment of some sort: 'Snow White', 'Rapunzel', 'Hansel and Gretel', 'Rumpelstiltskin'. There are dozens of these, many of which are not nearly so well known as they once were. In 'The Six Swans', six princes are turned into swans by their stepmother. Their sister searches for them, but must go six years without speaking while making shirts from flowers for them. A king marries her despite her silence, but his wicked mother convinces the court that the young queen is a cannibal who has eaten her own children. On her execution bonfire the heroine finishes the shirts (all but one sleeve of the last), restores her brothers, and reveals her mother-in-law's lies, whereupon the missing children are returned and the king's mother executed instead of the queen. This story exists in many other forms, often with seven brothers and shirts of nettles. 'Little Brother and Little Sister' tells of children cast out by a wicked stepmother, an enchanted spring which transforms Little Brother into a fawn, and of how Little Sister marries a king. She has a child and is murdered by her stepmother, but returns by night as a ghost to nurse her baby. When the king witnesses this and finally speaks to her, Little Sister is restored to life. Once the stepmother is killed, the fawn resumes his own shape as well. Another, 'Snow White and Rose Red', is about two sisters (both loving and kind, a change from the usual contrast of good sister and bad sister), a man transformed to a bear, and his enemy, a bad-tempered dwarf. A search through the Grimms' collection will unearth a number of such less-familiar stories, which still appeal to those looking for the fantastic today.

The Grimms' fairy-tales appeared in English in 1823 with the title *German Popular Stories*, translated by Edgar Taylor. There are now many editions of the Grimms' fairy-tales available. These range from scholarly translations of the work in whole or part, such as Jack Zipes' *The Complete Fairy Tales of the Brothers Grimm* (Bantam, 1987) or David Luke's *Jacob and Wilhelm Grimm: Selected Tales* (Penguin Classics, 1982), to collections of tales selected and retold specifically for children, to single tales retold as picture books. Selections from the Brothers Grimm aimed at children are usually retellings rather than translations faithful in every detail. Since the first collections there has been an urge to lessen the unpleasantness in many fairy-tales. Even the Grimms themselves altered stories to do so, as mentioned above. In recent retellings of tales from the Grimms intended for children, Snow White's stepmother is no longer executed by being forced to dance in red-hot iron slippers (a change that actually appeared in Taylor's translation nearly two centuries ago), and Cinderella's stepsisters no longer have their eyes pecked out by pigeons. Other stories, with racist themes or elements, frequently but not exclusively anti-Semitic, are simply not included at all in collections aimed at children.

With so much in the Grimms to choose from, only the most

satisfying survive as stories that 'everyone' knows. However, as movies come more and more to determine the fairy-tale 'canon', it seems that the number of familiar stories becomes smaller and smaller. If a story has not been animated, the average child will not know it, which seems a sad diminishment of the richness of children's stories.

Andrew Lang (1844-1912)

If one had to choose a single collection of fairy-tales for a library, the twelve *Fairy Books* assembled by Andrew Lang would be the only choice. To Lang, more than any other, belongs the credit for bringing the fantastic tales of the world to twentieth-century English-speaking readers, particularly children. Tolkien was first gripped by the story of Sigurd and the dragon Fafnir, from *Völsungasaga*, when he found it in the *Red Fairy Book*; more recently, fantasy author and fairy-tale reteller Robin McKinley's back-cover biographical notes mention Lang's *Fairy Books* among the significant reading of her childhood.

Lang grew up in the border region of Scotland, studied Classics at the University of St. Andrews, Glasgow, and Oxford, and lived most of his life in London as a book reviewer, journalist, poet, and translator. More than a century after his *Fairy Books* first began appearing, they are still in print, available in facsimile editions from Dover Books, or, being out of copyright, are also available in electronic form from Project Gutenberg on the Web.[*] Though Lang's introductions now seem dated, with their use of phrases such as 'Red Indian children' and the like, they invariably point out the universality of fairy-tales and the common humanity we all share. The stories in the collections themselves are still as fresh and readable as they were to our great- or great- great-grandparents. Knowing fairy-tales only through picture books for small children, many modern readers miss the grandeur and mystery that is as much a part of them as the comedy, the magic, the peril, and the romance. Lang's anthologies preserve that sense of another, greater possibility,

---

[*] Works by other authors, such as Nesbit, Barrie, Carroll, & MacDonald, now out of copyright in the US, are also available on Project Gutenberg.

greater in both wonder and danger: a world of enchantment just visible out of the corner of the eye.

Andrew Lang was the editor rather than the author of the *Fairy Books*. The selection was his, but the translations and re-tellings were by many others, in particular his wife, Leonora Alleyne. His sources were scholarly collections of folktales from all over the world. Each of the *Fairy Books* contains stories from a number of collections, and so each covers a wide cultural range. Lang chose his tales from the Grimms, Andersen, Perrault, Madame d'Aulnoy, the Norwegian collection of Peter Christen Asbjørnsen and Jørgen Moe, and many other volumes of world folktales, published mostly in English, French, and German. There are European, Japanese, Indian, North African, native North American, Turkish, and Armenian stories, among others, all retold in beautiful clear prose, with very fine illustrations in a pre-Raphaelite style by H.J. Ford. They were published originally by Longmans, Green, and Co., and the Dover facsimiles contain the original illustrations.

It is an interesting cultural note that in the nineteen-forties and fifties an American edition of the first four books was issued by the publisher David McKay, with greatly inferior illustrations. The rather condescending new foreword to these editions suggests that girls will read Lang's selection of tales for love-stories and boys for adventure, and that while girls will move on to 'real romance' in life, boys will turn to 'science and invention'. The Victorian Lang, in his introductions, certainly never discussed the stories as providing separate patterns of behaviour for girls and boys. On the contrary, he emphasized how they show our shared humanity.

The stories in the *Fairy Books* feature princes and princesses, poor youths and maidens, benevolent animals, wicked enchantments, heroism, love, betrayal, and honour: all the elements of the best fantasy. And, as in many folktales, it is as likely to be the heroines as the heroes who set out on the quests.

The first of the series was *The Blue Fairy Book* (1889). The others, named for their cover colours, were *Red* (1890), *Green* (1892), *Yellow* (1894), *Pink* (1897), *Grey* (1900), *Violet* (1901), *Crimson* (1903), *Brown* (1904), *Orange* (1906), *Olive* (1907), and *Lilac* (1910). Lang's simple intent is set out in the opening sentence of the preface to the first: 'The Tales in this volume are intended for children, who will like, it is hoped, the old stories that have pleased so many generations.'

A few stories, summarized here, will give an idea of the range of the twelve-volume collection. The earliest, *The Blue Fairy Book*, contains many of the better known tales: stories from the German and French traditions, from Scotland and England, from Asia Minor, from Jonathan Swift's *Gulliver's Travels*, and Greek mythology. Here readers encounter Aladdin, Gulliver, Dick Whittington and his cat, Rumpelstiltskin, Ali Baba and his maid-servant the brave and intelligent Morgiana, Hansel and Gretel, the Goose-Girl, Beauty and the Beast, Sleeping Beauty, Cinderella, and under the title 'The Terrible Head', the myth of Perseus, along with many others less familiar.

Among these now lesser-known tales is 'East of the Sun and West of the Moon', a Scandinavian story of the Cupid and Psyche type in which a girl is forbidden to look on her bridegroom. In the Scandinavian story, a girl is married to a white bear; persuaded by her mother to try to see him at night, she drips candlewax on the handsome prince the bear is revealed to be, whereupon he vanishes, telling her she has ruined his chance of breaking the curse placed on him by his troll-stepmother. The young wife sets out to seek him, east of the sun and west of the moon. Her quest is a long one, but she is aided by various old women and their magic horses, and by the Winds. In the end, she is able to break the curse and free her husband from both his captivity and his pending marriage to his stepsister, the princess with the nose 'three ells long'.

'The Bronze Ring', another folktale which still has great appeal, is drawn from a French collection of stories from Asia Minor. In it, a princess falls in love with the gardener's son. The young man wins her despite her father's efforts to favour a well-born rival; he is aided by those he meets along the way, winning a wish-granting bronze ring in return for curing another king by means of a beggar-woman's advice. After the marriage of princess and gardener's son, this ring leads to further adventure, which takes the hero to an island of mice. The story continues with the adventures of the three mice, one blind, one lame, and one with her ears cropped, in pursuit of the ring.

The Pink Fairy Book contains stories from Andersen and the Grimms, and from Danish, Swedish, Japanese, Sicilian, Catalan, and African folktales. 'Here, then,' Lang writes in the Preface,

> are fancies brought from all quarters: we see that
> black, white, and yellow peoples are fond of just the
> same kinds of adventures. Courage, youth, beauty,
> kindness, have many trials, but they always win the
> battle; while witches, giants, unfriendly cruel people,
> are on the losing hand. So it ought to be, and so, on
> the whole, it is and will be; and that is all the moral
> of fairy tales. We cannot all be young, alas! and
> pretty, and strong; but nothing prevents us from being
> kind, and no kind man, woman, or beast or bird, ever
> comes to anything but good in these oldest fables of
> the world. So far all the tales are true, and no further.

Here readers will find Andersen's 'The Snow Queen', the Danish folktale 'King Lindorm', which tells of a prince born as a serpent, and another snake in the Japanese story of 'The Cat's Elopement', in which a cat saves a princess from a serpent and is finally reunited with his long-lost love. Another Japanese story in this collection is 'Uraschimataro and the Turtle', well-known in Japan; it tells of a fisherman's son who spares a turtle and is later saved by it in turn, to be carried on its back to the palace of a princess under the sea, while in his village, three hundred years pass. 'The Sprig of Rosemary' is a Catalan story of the Cupid and Psyche type again, about a young woman who opens a forbidden chest, causing her husband's palace to vanish, and him with it. She sets out on a quest to find him and restore his lost memories of her.

The Olive Fairy Book of 1907 contains stories from Denmark, Turkey, India, Armenia, and the Sudan, many of them unfamiliar to modern readers. 'Samba the Coward' is a Sudanese story about a king's cowardly son who flees his country in shame after failing to lead a party of warriors to avenge an attack on his people. In a distant country a princess marries him. The princess, though, believes him to be as brave and valiant as he is kind and charming. When Moors attack, Samba hides in the cellar, and there his wife finds him. She takes his armour and his horse and leads the pursuit of the raiders herself, never letting on that she is not Samba. The princess' youngest brother is not fooled, and wounds the leader in the leg. The princess wounds Samba in the same place, but the youngest brother remains suspicious.

Samba's wound is treated, but the princess, who of course cannot reveal her own injury, does not recover so quickly, and when the Moors attack a third time she is unable to ride. Samba still will not do his duty and risk battle, but she tricks him into riding out, and in the thick of battle he finally finds courage. When his father-in-law the king praises his valour, Samba gives all the credit to his valiant wife.

Also in *The Olive Fairy Book* is 'Kupti and Imani', a beautiful story from the Punjab. When Imani, the king's youngest daughter, boasts she is capable of making her own fortune, her father sends her to be the servant to an old lame fakir, to prove it. Imani soon earns a fortune for herself and the holy man by her spinning and weaving. When the king goes abroad, he asks both daughters what he can bring them. The servant sent to ask Imani what gift she would like misunderstands her request for him to wait while she untangles a knot in her thread, and tells the king Imani desires 'patience'. In the foreign country, a servant seeking to buy 'patience' in the market draws the attention of its king, Subbar Khan, and the name Subbar, says the story, means patience. Subbar Khan sends the visiting king home with a magical fan, which can summon him and return him home. Imani, Subbar Khan, and the fakir become great friends, and Subbar Khan often visits, having his own room in their house. But the king's elder daughter Kupti is jealous, and sprinkles poisoned glass in Subbar Khan's bed while visiting her sister. When Subbar Khan fails to answer the fan's summons due to his resulting illness, Imani sets out, disguised as a young fakir, to find him. When she does, he is on his deathbed, but she is able to save him, having overheard some monkeys discussing the cure. She requests his ring and his handkerchief in payment, and returns to the old fakir. When next Subbar Khan visits them, Imani shows him the ring and handkerchief. He recognizes her as the young fakir who saved him, and takes back the magical fan, saying no-one is going to send him home unless she will come with him as his wife. Imani and the old fakir go with Subbar Khan, and they all live happily ever after.

'The Story of Zoulvisia', an Armenian tale in the same volume, falls into two parts, as many traditional folktales do. Adventures do not end with marriage for the hero and heroine. In this one, a young king first wins the amazonian enchantress

Zoulvisia, who has slain many men, including, possibly, his brothers; then, after their marriage, he must find her and rescue her, when a cunning witch infiltrates their household and steals her away for another king.

The *Fairy Books* are full of such tales, both familiar and utterly new to the average young reader. Every child should have an opportunity to spend a long, lazy summer wandering through them.

In addition to the *Fairy Books*, Lang edited other collections of stories for children, including a version of *The Thousand and One Nights* under the title *The Arabian Nights Entertainments*. It appeared in 1898, and like the *Fairy Books*, is still available from Dover. It was translated, by various people who worked on the *Fairy Books* with him, from the eighteenth-century French version of Monsieur Galland. Lang's preface, aimed at children, gives an historical background to the tales. He discusses their roots in oral tradition, their passage into Arabic literary culture and transformation into a written work for adults, and how they came to be popular in the West. He has, he says, left out the poetry and the dull bits, and '... omissions are made of pieces suitable only for Arabs and old gentlemen', by which he means that all the sexually explicit passages, and the scatological ones, of which there are a good few, are left out.

Included in Lang's *Arabian Nights* are the stories of Sindbad's seven voyages, Aladdin, and others less familiar, such as 'The Story of Two Sisters Who Were Jealous of Their Younger Sister.' This is a story spread over two generations, most of the adventures being had not by the younger sister who marries the Sultan of Persia, but by her three children, two princes and a princess raised in ignorance of their true parentage. These siblings embark on a quest for the Talking Bird, the Singing Tree, and the Golden Water. Prince Bahman and Prince Perviz both fail and are changed into black stones. Finally Princess Parizade sets out herself, achieving the quest and freeing her brothers, along with many other knights who had also failed. Through the agency of the Singing Bird, the royal siblings are reunited with their parents, and their mother is finally restored to the Sultan's favour, from which she was cast out by her sisters' lies.

Lang reads aloud very well; his collections also provide an ideal middle ground for older children between unadulterated scholarly collections of traditional tales and the picture book format in which such stories are most often retold these days.

W.B. Yeats (1865-1939)

Numerous other worthy collections of traditional stories retold for children were published in the nineteenth and early twentieth centuries. Many of these focus on the legends and folktales of a particular country. W.B. Yeats put together one such book, *Irish Fairy Tales* (1892), of stories collected from contemporary sources, having to do with the fairy lore of Ireland. This was intended for children from the start, and was meant to be a companion to his more scholarly *Fairy and Folk Tales of the Irish Peasantry* (1888).

William Butler Yeats is, of course, far better known as a poet and dramatist than as a writer for children. He was born in Dublin; as a young man he lived for a time in England, returning to Ireland in the nineties. He had an abiding interest in mythology, mysticism, and the occult, not limited to the traditions of his homeland; he believed firmly in the ability of his wife, Georgie Hyde Lees, to serve as a conduit for the supernatural through automatic writing.

Irish mythology and folklore remained of profound, almost spiritual, importance to Yeats' imagination and art throughout his life. He was far from an otherworldly dreamer though, and took an active part in politics. He was very influential in the Irish nationalist movement and served in the senate of the newly-formed Irish Free State (now the Republic of Ireland) in the nineteen-twenties. In 1923, Yeats was awarded the Nobel Prize for literature. He is one of the greats among the Modern poets, whose work ranges from the wistfully romantic of 'The Lake Isle of Innisfree' and 'The Stolen Child', through political passion as in 'The Municipal Gallery Revisted', to the symbolically and spiritually complex of 'Sailing to Byzantium' or 'The Tower'.

Always, even when passing a wry couplet on some current affair, Yeats wrote with beauty and passion and meticulous craftsmanship; his versions of Irish fairy-tales were given equal care. The fairy-tales he chose to retell were generally from the collections of other Irish folklorists before him. Unlike the German *Märchen* as offered by the Brothers Grimm, the fairy-tales Yeats chose for his attention were stories about fairies and other supernatural beings.

Among these stories are some that share very familiar European motifs, such 'The Twelve Wild Geese', in which a princess goes in search of her twelve brothers, transformed to wild geese, and must restore them by remaining mute while spinning and weaving shirts for them, in this case, of bog cotton-grass. She does this, even though she is married to a king whose stepmother makes it seem she has killed and eaten her own children, finishing the last shirt as her execution pyre is lit. Even in this, the details are distinctive: the wolf, actually a disguised good fairy, which carries off the mute queen's children, and the old woman who shows up to rebuke the girl's mother for her wickedness in saying she would trade all her sons for a daughter.

Other stories will seem less familiar. The merrow, an undersea being who has both a fish's tail and scaly legs, is rarely come across in fiction. In 'The Soul Cages' the wreck-salvager Jack Dogherty is befriended by Coomara the merrow and often joins him beneath the sea with the help of a magic hat. When he discovers his drinking companion has captured the souls of drowned sailors, innocently believing he is helping them by giving them shelter, Jack gets the merrow insensible on poteen and frees the souls. Sympathetic giants are not come across in stories very often; the tale of how the giant Fin M'Coul, with the help of his wife Oonagh, overcame his enemy Cucullin while disguised as a baby will still delight children with its comedy.

'Jamie Freel and the Young Lady', on the other hand, is a romantic fairy-tale with an appealing human hero, a poor young man who goes riding with the fairies when they steal a wealthy girl. He steals her in turn, to save her, but the fairies curse her with dumbness so that she cannot tell where to find her home. The young lady, Gracie, adapts herself willingly to life with the impoverished Jamie and his mother, and after he braves a night with the fairies again to learn her cure, Jamie and Gracie make a long journey to return the latter to her family. Only with difficulty are her parents persuaded she is in fact the daughter they believe dead. It is Gracie who insists on marrying Jamie, having fallen in love with him during the time she spent with him and his mother, a satisfying end to the story but one in which the reward of the young lady's hand is not presented as Jamie's automatic right.

Yeats' fairy-tales are distinguished by their rich, but never overblown, language and their vivid imagery. The familiar elements of traditional tales are present, in characters like the poor but clever and virtuous Jamie Freel, the cunning Jack Dogherty, or the loyal and persevering sister of the transformed princes, but there is much that will be unfamiliar to today's children as well. Such creatures as the merrow and even the giants Fin M'coul and Cucullin are now strange and exotic to most young readers, while the Irish fairies, neither godmotherly benevolent and wish-granting nor so glamorous and terrible as those of Scots ballads, humorous, capricious, and sometimes dangerous, will broaden their imaginative horizons.

Yeats' *Irish Fairy Tales* can be very difficult to find. However, various collections of selections from it and from *Fairy and Folk Tales of the Irish Peasantry* have been published over the years. One excellent recent Yeats' collection aimed at children is *Fairy Tales of Ireland* (Collins 1990). It contains nineteen stories, including those discussed above, as well as the poem 'The Stolen Child', and is appealingly illustrated by P.J. Lynch.

Joseph Jacobs (1854-1916)

Another collection in similar vein to Yeats' is *Celtic Fairy Tales* (which appeared in two volumes, in 1892 and 1894) by Australian-born folklorist Joseph Jacobs, who was also an English professor at the Jewish Theological Seminary in New York. *Celtic Fairy Tales* presents stories from Scotland, Ireland, and Wales, told in a simple, straightforward style, with little elaboration and complication in the plots. The effect is very like an oral rendition. Some of the stories, like 'Jack and his Comrades', render dialogue in dialect: "'O musha, mother," says Jack, "why do you ax me that question? sure you know I wouldn't have your curse and Damer's estate along with it."' Others convey a grander, but still oral, style, as in 'The Wooing of Olwen': 'In his hand were two spears of silver, well-tempered, headed with steel, of an edge to wound the wind and cause blood to flow, and swifter than the fall of the dew-drop from the blade of reed grass upon the earth when the dew of June is at its heaviest.' Jacobs wrote other similar collections, including *English Fairy Tales* (1890) and *More English Fairy Tales* (1894), which were also intended to preserve the illusion of a story told rather than read.

Arthur Ransome (1884-1967)

Another way of retelling old stories is to give them context within a framing narrative. An outstanding example of this approach is found in *Old Peter's Russian Tales* (1916) by *Swallows and Amazons* author Arthur Ransome. Ransome was in Russia as a newspaper correspondent during the First World War and the Russian Revolution. He taught himself Russian and was a first-hand witness to the Revolution. He played chess with Lenin and lived with Trotsky's secretary, Evgenia Petrovna Shelepina, who returned with him to England and whom he married in 1924 when his first wife finally granted him a divorce.

Old Peter's Russian Tales was Ransome's first really successful children's book. In it, he retells a number of traditional Russian fairy-tales, such as 'The Cat Who Became Head Forester', in which a cat marries a vixen, whose boastful stories of her husband's ferocity, apparently confirmed by a mutually terrifying encounter between the cat and the wolf, lead the animals of the forest to offer him tribute. 'The Fire-Bird, the Horse of Power and the Princess Vassilissa' tells of a young archer who sets out on a quest aided by his wise, talking horse. 'The Fool of the World and the Flying Ship' is the story of a simple youngest son who tries to find a flying ship and win a princess, with the aid of a number of companions of extraordinary abilities whose friendship he wins by his kindness. There are also stories of Baba Yaga, the Russian witch whose house has hen's feet, and of the girl married off by her murderous stepmother to Frost, among others little-known in English.

Ransome sets the tales up within a portrait of Russian peasant life, as Old Peter tells these traditional stories to his grandchildren, Maroosia and Vanya, in their hut in the forest. He thus creates for his audience of readers the atmosphere in which such stories would have been told in earlier times, with questions and interjections from the children, and pleas for favourites. Although there is no plot in the framing story, Old Peter and his grandchildren, while only sketches rather than deeply-developed characters, become familiar friends to the audience which is eavesdropping on them, and the evocation of the woodcutter's daily life through the seasons of the Russian forest is as vivid as is the fantastic in the tales Old Peter tells. There is also a second collection of Russian traditional tales by Ransome, published posthumously. This is *The War of the Birds and the Beasts*, which was assembled by Ransome biographer Hugh Brogan from Ransome's notes and published in 1984.

Padraic Colum (1881-1972)

Other writers presenting traditional stories may choose to string them together within a single narrative. An example by the Irish-born American Padraic Colum is *The King of Ireland's Son* (1916), a series of linked stories retold from Irish myth and legend.

In this, the King of Ireland's Son wins Fedelma, the Enchanter's daughter, after performing various impossible tasks with Fedelma's secret help. She is then carried off by the King of the Land of Mist, but to prevent his marrying her, Fedelma ensures that she will sleep for a year and a day, to be wakened by a lock of her hair being cut off by the Sword of Light, which is also the weapon that can kill her abductor. Fedelma writes a message in ogham letters to let the sleeping King's Son know who has taken her. The King's Son wanders in and out of other stories, hearing of other adventures and having them as he seeks the Sword of Light and the King of the Land of the Mist. This cross between a novel and a collection of folktales works very well. It is an enjoyable story, well-written and very readable, which contains all the humour, drama, romance, and heroism of the folktale world, while the heroes who persist from story to story give it a sustaining narrative. The structure, one tale leading into another, also creates an atmosphere of suspense; just when it seems one story is resolved, its effects spin off into further problems for the heroes. Colum also retold stories from the Welsh *Mabinogion*, Homer, and the Norse myths.

Even though television has filled the cultural niche that two or three centuries ago might have been held by oral folktales in many households, providing through stories a common set of references and anecdotes, such tales have never gone away. The great collections of the eighteenth and nineteenth centuries are still out there (including countless volumes from the nineteenth century, a golden age of nationalistic and ethnographic folklore collecting, that have not been mentioned here). They can be found in libraries or are even still in print, in whole, in part, or as selections revised for young readers, as well as in unnumbered picture book versions. Through collections such as those edited by Andrew Lang, or retold by writers of the calibre of Yeats and Ransome, fairy-tales and folktales from around the world remain available, chosen and presented specifically for a young audience.

Sadly, since children, even keen readers, no longer come across collections such as Lang's *Fairy Books* as a matter of course, the great corpus of fairy-tales is for many still an undiscovered country, to which some passer-by should point the way. These tales offer a world of heroism, comedy, and romance waiting to be explored just the other side of those few stories that have been retold to triteness in recent decades.

III
The Victorians, part one

In the sixteenth and seventeenth centuries, fiction, especially the fantastic, was regarded by many adults as somewhat dangerous so far as children were concerned. Books relating stories of enchantment, stories from medieval Romance and legend or the epic romances of the sixteenth century, might unduly influence young minds and distract them from the serious business of caring for their immortal souls. In the eighteenth century, children's books often emphasized moral and religious instruction.

Children, however, claimed as their own imaginative works of literature not originally intended for them, such as John Bunyan's *The Pilgrim's Progress* (1678), Daniel Defoe's *Robinson Crusoe* (1719), and Jonathan Swift's *Gulliver's Travels* (1726), all of which have been read, in whole or in abridged forms, by generations of young people looking for stories of adventure and imagination. Although *Pilgrim's Progress* was most definitely meant to provide religious instruction, being an allegory of the soul's journey to salvation, it at the same time offered a broad and fantastic landscape for the imagination, as well as a number of metaphors for the struggles of daily life and faith. (In the nineteenth century, it still shaped the imagination; the girls in *Little Women* (1868) make frequent reference to it, while in *What Katy Did* (1872) it provides the imaginative fuel for games of adventure. In John Buchan's spy thriller *Mr. Standfast* (1919) it is still a living presence in the narrator's imagination and provides the agents with not only their code names, but a metaphoric way of viewing their own actions.) Chapbooks, as mentioned in the previous chapter, were also an eighteenth-century source of stories of enchantment.

In the nineteenth century, as literacy among children increased (although it was far from universal) and printing became cheaper, children's books became a recognized, separate form of literature. Many of these were still meant primarily to instruct, often through alarming examples of wickedness and disobedience, or through stories in which young protagonists learn to correct their sinful errors and live pious lives. There was, however, an opposing interest in allowing children to explore and learn naturally. This trend had begun in the eighteenth century under the influence of philosophers such as Jean-Jacques Rousseau (1712-1778) and John Locke (1632-1704). Locke, in *Some Thoughts Concerning Education* (1693), recommended that children be taught without bribing reward or threat of punishment, and that reading for children should be entertaining, enticing, and appropriate to their understanding. This attitude gradually led to works that sought to entertain as well as to provide instruction or example.

By the time the young Victoria came to the throne in 1837, the landscape of children's books was changing. Perrault, d'Aulnoy, and the Brothers Grimm were available in translation. Childhood was regarded differently than it had been in earlier centuries, in part due to the influence of thinkers such as Locke. It was now a phase of life with its own value, rather than merely a preparation for the grave business of adulthood. Life, except in the strictest versions of Protestantism, was not solely a preparation for death and judgement, as it had seemed at times to be in the preceding centuries. Children, at least middle and upper class children, were meant to play as well as learn, to be delighted as well as taught. In this attitude, the fantastic found a foothold. By the end of the century fantasy would be an essential component of many of the most popular children's books. Initially, though, the most common form it took was the literary fairy-tale.

Hans Christian Andersen (1805-1875)

Hans Christian Andersen, Hans Andersen in some translations and H.C. Andersen in his native Denmark, was a prolific writer of short stories with appeal to both children and adults. Andersen was born in Odense, the son of a poor cobbler. He had a minor talent for singing and acting and went to Copenhagen at the age of fourteen to pursue a career on the stage. This venture was not a success, but in his early twenties he began to make a living as a writer. Andersen was already a well-established author when in

1835 his first collection of the tales that would earn him his un-dying reputation, *Eventyr fortalte for Børn* (*Tales Told for Children*), was published.

Andersen was a socially awkward man, always conscious of his working-class origins. He believed in a personal myth of aristocratic ancestry, which critics find to have coloured such stories as 'The Ugly Duckling' (1844), with its changeling cygnet reared among ducks. He achieved fame throughout Europe and travelled a great deal, becoming a friend of the Grimms and of Charles Dickens. In the course of his life Andersen had several unrequited passions, the most notable of which was for the Swedish opera singer Jenny Lind. She inspired his contrast of natural and artificial art in 'The Nightingale' (1845), but his reaction to rejections by other women he had loved can be detected in the theme of devoted adoration scorned, unrecognized, or proven misplaced, which recurs in many of his stories, such as 'The Little Lovers', in which a ball and a top are the main characters. Others of a similar bent, like 'The Steadfast Tin Soldier', feature love that ends only in death.

In his lifetime Andersen wrote 190 tales; his other works in-cluded six novels, five books about his travels, and three autobiographies. Not all Andersen's tales are fairy-tales; *Eventyr*, like the German *Märchen*, does not necessarily mean a *fairy* tale. However, his more literary fables and the realistic stories are not so well-known in English and do not concern us here. Despite the designation 'told for children' Andersen intended his stories for a wide audience. He dropped *fortalte for Børn* from the title of a later series of tales and eventually began to use the word *Historier* (story or history), rather than *Eventyr* (tale, adventure, or fairy-tale), to describe them. Most of his stories were written to be enjoyed on different levels by children and adults, both in elements such as the humour, in stories such as the folk-tale-based 'Big Klaus and Little Klaus', where a priest's assistant is caught 'visiting' a farmer's wife, or in the darker themes of death and loss which so concerned him.

Some of Andersen's stories, such as 'The Princess on the Pea' and the 'clever peasant' type 'Big Klaus and Little Klaus' men-tioned above, were based on traditional Danish folktales. Many, however, were his own inventions, using folktale motifs. Even in the stories he adapted from traditional material, Andersen's personal touch is evident. He had an eye for details of a type not generally found in folktales in their raw form, as when he describes the plants growing around the duck's nest on the edge of the water, and the blue powder-smoke rising like clouds from the guns of the hunters, in 'The Ugly Duckling'. Andersen was writing literature, not recording an oral tradition in which all superfluous matter has been pared away by repeated tellings. He described with simple elegance landscapes, characters, and weather, which rooted his stories in a particular moment and place, creating a vivid and richly-textured world.

Andersen's most popular stories have entered the fairy-tale canon. 'The Tinder Box' (1835), 'Thumbelina' (1835), 'The Emperor's New Clothes' (1837), 'The Ugly Duckling', 'The Little Mermaid' (1836), and 'The Princess on the Pea' (1835) are often found in fairy-tale collections. Many of his tales can be found retold in Andrew Lang's *Fairy Books*, but the first English translations appeared in 1846. Andersen's most popular stories continue to be retold from earlier translations or re-translated into English, appearing in anthologies of fairy-tales, in collections devoted solely to his work, and as picture books.

Andersen's fairy-tales take the fantastic for granted, allowing children to be born from flowers and toys such as balls and tops to speak and feel. He frequently makes such inanimate objects his characters; 'The Fir Tree' and 'The Steadfast Tin Soldier' are other examples of this type, of which the last is probably the most familiar, although 'The Fir Tree', about a small tree's fate as a Christmas tree, tends to resurface at Christmas-time. Other stories, such as 'The Ugly Duckling', 'The Nightingale', or the rather bleak 'The Storks', in which a boy who teases young storks is punished by their bringing him a dead baby brother, are about animals. When he wrote of human characters, Andersen frequently used the types found in traditional folktales: the princess, the clever soldier or peasant, the poor but kind and clever youth.

The two of Andersen's stories which have captured the imaginations of English readers more than any others are 'The Little Mermaid' (1837) and 'The Snow Queen' (1846). The first of these is well known, at least in a soft and fuzzy version. Mer-folk are not uncommon in Scandinavian folklore. Andersen wrote a dramatic poem, *Agnete og Havmanden* (Agnes and the Merman) in 1833. It is based on the medieval Danish ballad of the same title, about a woman who marries a merman. In his later fairy-tale it is the mermaid who leaves the sea for the land, but the impulse is not, as in many later retellings of his story by others, solely love for a human. Andersen's original Little Mermaid does not want to become mere foam on the sea when she dies, the fate of the inhuman merfolk; she wants to have an immortal soul, as humans do.

The Little Mermaid's fascination with the human world begins when she saves the prince from drowning after a shipwreck, but her love for him and her desire for a soul are always linked. Her bargain with the water-witch trades her voice (the witch cuts out her tongue) for human form, but every step she takes will cause her pain as though she is walking on knives, and she will only gain a soul if the prince loves and marries her. If he marries another, her heart will break and she will die and turn to foam on the water, achieving neither love, nor an immortal soul, nor even a mermaid's three-century lifespan.

The prince does love the mute girl whom he finds on the shore, but only as a friend or a child, and he weds another. The mermaid's older sisters attempt to save her, trading the sea-witch their hair in return for instructions. They bring their unhappy sister a knife from the witch, with which she must kill the prince to regain her mermaid's form. The mermaid refuses to do this, and feels herself dying. However, instead of seafoam she is transformed to a daughter of the air. These are ethereal beings who live in the wind and, although soulless, are able to earn souls through works of benefit to humanity. As one of these, the Little Mermaid will at last be able to gain the immortal soul she desires.

Andersen's longest fairy-tale, 'The Snow Queen' (1846), was once part of the common literary heritage of children, but it is little known today. It shares much with the Scandinavian ballad and folktale tradition in featuring a heroine who sets off in search of her missing beloved. The story begins when Gerda's playmate Kay gets pieces of a magic mirror in his eye and in his heart. English translations describe the maker of the mirror variously; sometimes he is a sorcerer, sometimes a goblin. Andrew Lang in the *Pink Fairy Book* uses 'hobgoblin'. The Danish original is actually *trold*, a troll. (Medieval Scandinavian trolls, the tradition with which Andersen was familiar, are not necessarily the ugly, slow, stupid creatures the word suggests to modern English readers. They are magic-users and shapeshifters, clever and dangerous enemies.) The piece of mirror in Kay's eye makes him see only the bad and ugly in everything; the piece in his heart turns it into a lump of ice, so that he abandons his friend Gerda and all the pleasures they used to share. He is taken away by the Snow Queen, a passage which had its influence on C.S. Lewis, in the image of the icily beautiful queen and the sour-minded boy who is invited into her sledge and wrapped in a fold of her white fur mantle.

Gerda sets out in search of Kay, having numerous adventures on the way. The most memorable of these is her capture by a hideous old robber queen and her bandits. From these she escapes with the help of the belligerent Little Robber Girl, who sends her off with a reindeer, to pursue the Snow Queen into Lapland and Finland. In the north, Gerda is helped by two women, one of whom, in an unforgettable detail, writes a letter to the other on a dried codfish.

The Snow Queen is a rather ambivalent figure; she is not actively evil, and her abduction of Kay seems merely a whim or even a test; she has nothing to do with the mirror that has changed him. It was he, after all, who followed her out of town. She has even given him the means to free himself and become his own master, if only he can spell the word 'love' out of shattered pieces of ice. However, it is Gerda's hot tears which free Kay in the end. As she weeps on his neck they thaw the ice in his heart, and his own tears wash the shard of mirror from his eye. The pieces of ice spell out the word 'love' of their own accord, and Kay and Gerda set out for home. On the way they meet the Little Robber Girl again, who pointedly asks Kay if he really deserves to be run all over the world for.

'The Snow Queen' is arguably Andersen's greatest work. It certainly shows him at his best. It is a story rich with symbolism and the themes that preoccupied Andersen, but is also as simple as an evolved fairy-tale. In it Andersen creates a living world, full of detail, humour, and peril, incorporating elements of nineteenth-century life and ageless folktale motifs. Andersen rarely set his stories 'long ago and far away'; he made the everyday world he knew the starting point for an exploration of the possibilities of the fantastic, as many later fantasy writers were to do.

John Ruskin (1819-1900)

In England, various authors contemporary with Andersen turned their hands to writing fairy-tales or fairy-tale pastiches, under the influence of Andersen's tales and the collections of the Grimms, Perrault, and d'Aulnoy. None, however, made the form so much their own as Andersen had, although this is not to say they failed to write good fairy-tales. It is simply that none produced anything like Andersen's volume of work.

The art critic John Ruskin wrote a short fantasy using traditional fairy-tale motifs. *The King of the Golden River* (1851) was the first really successful such English tale. It is his only fantasy and his only non-didactic work for children. The story is very much influenced by the German folk-tradition as codified by the Grimms, but the quest story is interspersed with a great deal of humour in such details as the South Wind, Esq., who has a nose shaped like a bugle. This detail, however, was changed in some later editions to a less fantastic, merely bulbous nose.

The story is even meant to sound as though it is German; the three brothers are named Schwarz, Hans, and Gluck. The elder two are of course miserly, bad-tempered, and dishonest, while the youngest, Gluck, is kind and generous. Their land is stricken with drought after the elder two annoy the South Wind, but learning from the King of the Golden River, a golden dwarf, that a nearby river could run with gold, they each set out on a quest to bring this about by sprinkling three drops of holy water into the river from the top of the mountain. The first two fail due to their dishonesty and selfishness, and are turned into black stones. Gluck completes the quest, though he believes he has failed since he gives most of his water to an old man and a thirsty child, and the last few drops to an apparently-dying dog, who is revealed as the king. The golden dwarf-king tells him, '... the water which has been refused to the cry of the weary and dying is unholy, though it had been blessed by every saint in heaven; and the water which is found in the vessel of mercy is holy, though it had been defiled with corpses.' The river, metaphorically, turns to gold: it changes its course and restores fertility to Gluck's land.

The King of the Golden River has all the familiarity and the novelty of an unknown fairy-tale, and as such, still has much appeal even to younger children if read aloud.

William Makepeace Thackeray (1811-1863)

Ruskin took the fairy-tale very seriously in his one venture into the form, but the literary fairy-tale that has fun with fairy-tale conventions became common in the mid-nineteenth century and after. One of the earliest examples is *The Rose and the Ring* (1855), written and illustrated by William Makepeace Thackeray in nineteen brief chapters. Thackeray was an important novelist of the nineteenth century, author of such enduring books as *Barry Lyndon* (1844) and *Vanity Fair* (1847-48). His flair for telling a good story full of comic social interactions and satire is given full rein in *The Rose and the Ring*. Fairy-tales had reached a level of popularity and even cliché by this time; an author could assume his audience was familiar with the genre's 'rules'. *The Rose and the Ring* is a tongue-in-cheek epic of an usurping uncle and diffident prince, a lost royal heiress raised by lions who becomes a maidservant, a crotchety fairy godmother, an excess of betrothals, a magic ring which causes a great deal of trouble by making its wearer beautiful to the opposite sex, and a warming pan as instrument of royal vengeance.

This story of Princess Rosalba of Crim Tartary and Prince Giglio of Paflagonia, both of whom are given 'a little misfortune' by their fairy godmother and have been denied their rightful thrones by usurpers, set the tone for later works in the same vein, such as those by Andrew Lang, A.A. Milne, and more than a century later, M.M. Kaye. All of these writers acknowledge Thackeray's influence in various ways, from outright references to his geography and characters as part of the 'history' of their own kingdoms, to similar comic names (the noble families of the Spinachi, the Broccoli, the Articiocci, and the Sauerkraut in Thackeray, and Kaye's Grand Duke of Rubarbary, for instance), as well as the stolidly middle-class royalty that Thackeray made almost mandatory in such tales. Although the literary style may make the story too remote from the familiar patterns of prose for many children, others, particularly older children and teens familiar with both fairy-tales and later humorous literary treatments of their conventions by writers such as M.M. Kaye, Patricia C. Wrede, or Terry Pratchett, will be able both to enjoy the story in its own right, and for its place in the history of the lighthearted, self-referential fairy-tale.

Charles Kingsley (1819-1875)

'The Snow Queen', *The King of the Golden River*, and *The Rose and the Ring* are what we might now call novellas. The first major novel of children's fantasy, a work great in both ambition and achievement, is *The Water-Babies: A Fairy-Tale For a Land-Baby* (1863), by Charles Kingsley. Its author called it both a fairy-tale and, in his concluding moral, a parable, not disguising his intention to convey a message.

Kingsley, a Cambridge-educated priest of the Church of England, was greatly concerned with social issues such as poverty and child labour. He was Regius Professor of Modern History at Cambridge, and history tutor to the future Edward VII. Kingsley also had a great interest in natural history and a respect for science, and his fascination with all aspects of the natural world and human understanding permeates the book. *The Water-Babies* may be the only 'fairy-tale' in existence to have a nine or ten page parable illustrating the workings of evolution, in the story of the Doasyoulikes and their ages-long change into apes, through the women's desire for hairy husbands and hairy children who could live in their cold, damp climate.

The story of *The Water-Babies* is that of Tom, a little chimney sweep with an abusive master. Mistakenly hunted as a thief, he falls into a brook, drowns, and is reborn as a gilled, four-inch-long water-baby, leaving the soot-stained shell of his human body behind. This is the beginning of a long series of adventures, which takes Tom from the becks of northern England, down a salmon-river, and out to the sea. He meets and learns from all sorts of water-creatures, good and bad, and is far from a saintly hero. Tom, who initially aspires merely to be a master-sweep with a string of boys of his own to bully, teases and picks on creatures smaller than himself. It takes more than one lesson, interspersed with much backsliding, to effect his spiritual growth. He learns from the results of his thoughtless actions as well as from active teaching, and is rewarded and punished by the fairies Mrs. Bedonebyasyoudid and Madame Doasyouwould-bedoneby, and the sea-spirit Mother Carey. These are not small, twinkly fairies but wise spirits, aspects of the creative principle of the divine. He is also taught by the example of a little (apparently dead) girl, Ellie, who is helping him as part of her own process of spiritual growth.

Tom matures through the long quest on which the fairies send him; he is despatched to aid in beginning the redemption of his former master, Grimes. The cruel master-sweep died by violence and has been spending the beginning of his purgatorial learning stuck in a chimney. At the end, somewhat disconcertingly, since the reader by this time is convinced Tom and Ellie are both dead, the two children grow up, and Tom becomes 'a great man of science'.

The Water-Babies is an important book, but one now less likely to find an audience among children. It expects a greater vocabulary than the average modern child possesses, as well as a greater knowledge of topics that were the popular discussion of Kingsley's day, such as the writings of Charles Darwin and Thomas Huxley. The plot unfolds at a leisurely pace, and the morals and lessons are explained, something that has long gone out of fashion. Most children find it tedious going.

This datedness is in many ways a loss to the children of today. Kingsley's book is richly imaginative, packed with fascinating creatures both invented and natural. Kingsley uses his story to comment on many aspects of mid-Victorian society. The treatment of the labouring poor and children such as Tom is a major concern, but he also satirizes the dry-fact-cramming style of education in books he attributes to authors such as 'Cousin Cramchild' and 'Auntie Agitate'. He mocks American political philosophy, and draws attention to what we would today call environmental concerns, such as the pollution of shorelines with raw sewage. However, his dry irony is now more likely to be appreciated by adults.

The Water-Babies remains an outstandingly imaginative and original work of fantasy, and although it has less appeal to the average reader than it once did, there will always be a few children who will explore it with all the enthusiasm of its first readers, especially if they chance across an illustrated version.

Jean Ingelow (1820-1897)

Jean Ingelow began publishing poetry and stories under the pseudonym 'Orris' when she was a girl, but her first book, *A Rhyming Chronicle of Incidents and Feelings*, published anonymously, did not appear until she was thirty. She went on to write a number of novels and collections of poetry popular in her day but now regarded as sentimental and affected. She wrote fiction for children as well as for adults; one of these, *Mopsa the Fairy* (1869), is both typical of writing for children at that time (rather than exceptional, as was Carroll), and still quite readable today.

Children's stories about fairies of the small, winged variety (Andersen wrote some of these) were very popular by the mid to late Victorian era, and these fairies were often drafted to serve an instructional purpose. *Mopsa the Fairy* appears more 'modern' than *The Water-Babies* because the instruction in it is conveyed by example or discussion within the story, rather than in an authorial voice as in Kingsley's book, where the narrator often addresses remarks to 'my little man'. *Mopsa* tells the story of Jack, who one day finds a nest of fairies in an old hawthorn and, putting them into his pocket, enters a hollow in the tree. From there an albatross carries him off to the borders of fairyland, where he sails up a fairy river in an enchanted boat. Among other adventures, he meets clockwork people who care for ill-used horses after they have died in the human world, and ravens who eat one of the fairies he has been carrying. This causes him only passing regret and is quickly forgotten. He discovers that one of 'his' fairies, Mopsa, is a fairy queen, who must go to a fairy kingdom currently lacking one. Their arrival breaks a curse, the heir to the kingdom assumes Jack's form and personality so that Mopsa will not miss him, and Jack returns home. His absence has not been noticed, and he begins to forget the whole thing.

Although *Mopsa* is occasionally compared to *Alice* (which was published a few years before Ingelow's book), it lacks the appeal of Carroll's story. The characterisation is shallow, while the story itself is without humour or strong emotion of any sort.

Its most interesting and original details are the depiction of fairyland as, not a place, but the time before Time, Jack's brief dream of a primeval river, and the idea of fairy queens being born, like queen bees, from among the general mass of infant fairies. Although it cannot compete with the great classics among its contemporaries, works such as *Alice* or *The Princess and the Goblin*, *Mopsa* is a pleasant and readable story which is still capable of entertaining.

George MacDonald (1824-1905)

George MacDonald remains one of the most important writers of fantasy for children, both for his original works and for the influence he had on later practitioners of the genre. As a child, Tolkien enjoyed what are generally called the 'Curdie' books, *The Princess and the Goblin* and *The Princess and Curdie*, with their mine-dwelling goblins beneath the mountains, while as an adult, C.S. Lewis esteemed MacDonald's more spiritually-concerned stories highly, and was greatly influenced by them in his own writing for children.

MacDonald was raised in a Calvinist Congregationalist family. He married Louisa Powell in 1851 and became a Congregationalist minister, but was criticized for being too liberal in his doctrine and was pushed to resign from his parish. He eventually joined the Church of England and turned to writing to make a living for his family of eleven children. MacDonald did not call his stories dealing with spiritual growth and the soul's passage through life and death to eternal life 'allegory', but tales like 'The Golden Key' and elements of *At the Back of the North Wind* are open to readings in which direct equations can be made between elements of the story and an author-imposed meaning.

MacDonald was a prolific author for both children and adults. The literary fairy-tale 'The Light Princess' is an example of the more humorous side of his fantasy. It was first published in the adult novel *Adela Cathcart* (1864) and later reprinted in the collection of stories *Dealing With the Fairies* (1867). It features a princess in a situation typical of literary fairy-tales: she is cursed. In this case, she is deprived of gravity by an aunt, which makes her not only light-hearted no matter how terrible the situation, but weightless. Like Thackeray's *The Rose and the Ring*, the story plays with the conventions of the genre, and features a degree of social satire. Another of MacDonald's fairy-tales built around the traditional conventions is 'Little Daylight', which is told in chapter twenty-eight of the novel *At the Back of the North Wind*. Penguin Classics has published MacDonald's hard to find shorter fantasy stories, including 'The Light Princess', 'Little Daylight', 'The Golden Key,' and *The Wise Woman*, in one volume under the title *The Complete Fairy Tales* (1999).

'The Golden Key' first appeared in *Dealing With the Fairies* (1867) and displays another facet of MacDonald's use of fantasy. In this story, the boy Mossy searches for and finds the golden key at the rainbow's end in fairyland. He and the girl Tangle set out to find the lock which it opens. After growing old, losing one another, and meeting the Old Man of the Sea, the Old Man of the Earth, and the Old Man of the Fire, they find one another again, young and beautiful, at the foot of the rainbow. Turning the key in the lock there, they climb the rainbow into the 'land whence the shadows fall'. It is an allegorical story about dying and passing into eternal life.

MacDonald's first enduringly popular novel-length children's fantasy was *At the Back of the North Wind*, which was serialized in 1868 in the magazine *Good Words For the Young*, and published in book form in 1871. The hero is Diamond, a coachman's son named after his father's favourite horse, and a wise innocent even before he begins his adventures. Diamond goes travelling at night with North Wind, a great and beautiful lady, as she performs her necessary tasks. These range from the frightening of a drunken nurse by blowing into a house and appearing as a wolf, to sweeping the smog out of London, to sinking a ship. Later, while he lies deathly ill, Diamond journeys with North Wind as far North as one can go, stowing away with her help in several different ships tacking north, since she herself can only travel south (not that this has stopped her carrying him away and home again on other occasions, or circling round and round London). He completes the last part of his journey floating on an iceberg, and then must pass through North Wind herself as she sits on her doorstep, to reach the land at the back of the North Wind. This is a glimpse of heaven, a great green pleasant land. When he returns, he carries away an elusive memory of the songs the river sang there.

While Diamond has been ill his father's employer has lost his money, and, unable to find new employment, his father buys the horse Diamond from his former master and sets up as a cabman. Further adventures follow for Diamond the boy in London: a fistfight in defence of Nanny the crossing-sweeper, a period of driving the cab himself while his father is sick, and the rescue of Nanny from her gin-swilling grandmother. His friendship with the gentleman-poet Mr. Raymond eventually leads to a bettering of the family's circumstances as his father becomes Mr. Raymond's coachman. First, though, the worthiness of Diamond's father goes through a period of harsh testing by both Mr. Raymond and an angel-horse. At the close of the book, Diamond dies, or goes to the back of the North Wind, as the narrator says.

The main impulse of the story is to show how Diamond affects those around him, including the nameless adult narrator who meets Diamond near the end of the boy's life and is told his story. The book is replete with spirituality, but rarely didactic. The acceptance of a Providence that can destroy a shipload of people so that one of the few survivors can change his values shows a residue of MacDonald's Calvinist upbringing, a suggestion that all the world is arranged for the spiritual salvation of an elect few. However, most of the religious message of the book is the necessity of charity, *caritas*, love of one's fellow human beings. Diamond exemplifies this over and over.

At the Back of the North Wind is a significant work of children's literature, and of fantasy, but one whose audience may have changed. It once engaged children's fancies fully, with its images of city poverty and the precariousness of life without any sort of state-run 'social safety-net', and that grand lady, North Wind, with her swirling black hair. The narrative style of *At the Back of the North Wind* is less unfamiliar to the child of today than Kingsley's; it sticks to its main story more than *The Water-Babies*, with fewer digressions or long excursions into secondary topics. Nevertheless, like *The Water-Babies*, it is now more likely to be appreciated by the adult reader than by the average child, but, as with all great books, it still will seize the imaginations of some.

A later MacDonald book with a moral purpose no-one could miss is the novel which has at various times been titled *The Wise*

Woman or *The Lost Princess: A Double Story* (1875). C.S. Lewis thought highly of it, but it is little known, most likely because no-one these days likes being lectured quite so pointedly in a work of fiction.

The story tells of two girls, Princess Rosamond and a shepherd's daughter, Agnes. Both are spoiled terribly in different ways by their parents. Rosamond is given everything she wants and never reprimanded. Agnes is repeatedly told how clever and wonderful she is. Both are carried off by the wise woman, to try to mend their faults. Rosamond, after living for a time with the wise woman and a time with Agnes' parents, does learn to better herself, but Agnes never changes, and her wilful certainty of her own rightness leads her to grow more and more conceited and contemptuous of those around her. She ends by getting her parents arrested and nearly executed by the king.

The moral of *The Wise Woman* is writ rather large, and although the two ways of spoiling a child are probably practised just as much today, the story may seem heavy-handed for modern taste. It has some captivating elements. One of these, Rosamond stepping through a painting into the northern hills, seems to be an idea that stuck with Lewis and was used by him in *Voyage of the Dawn Treader*. As a story, though, most will find *The Wise Woman* decidedly lacking when compared to *At the Back of the North Wind*, or to MacDonald's most enduring work, still as readable as when it was written, *The Princess and the Goblin*.

The Princess and the Goblin (serialized in the children's magazine *Good Words for the Young*, 1870-1871, and published as a book in 1872) remains one of the great works of children's fantasy. Part of the reason it will seem less dated to the average child of today than *North Wind* is that it is set in a familiar landscape. This is the vaguely medieval fairy-tale world of kingdoms and magic, rather than a Victorian London of cabbies and crossing-sweepers.

The story tells of Princess Irene, who is being raised in a remote castle in the mountains. Under the mountains live cunning, grotesque goblins. In a tower of the castle the princess discovers a beautiful old lady spinning, her great-great-grandmother. No-one else in the castle believes in the grandmother's existence and even Irene cannot always find her. Irene meets the miner

51

boy, Curdie, one evening when he saves her and her nurse from goblins. Curdie later discovers a two-fold goblin plot to kidnap the princess as a bride for their prince, and to flood the mines. Imprisoned by the goblins, he is rescued by Irene, who discovers him by following the magic thread the old lady in the tower has been spinning. When the castle is invaded by goblins, Curdie leads the guards in fighting them, but the princess disappears. Following her magic thread, Curdie discovers her and reunites her with the king. Curdie then saves the inhabitants of the castle when the goblins' flood, blocked from the mines, flows down their invasion tunnel to the castle instead.

The Princess and the Goblin contains everything needed to satisfy young readers, as much so now as when it was written. Curdie and the princess are courageous and intelligent, while their enemies the goblins are comically grotesque as well as malevolent and frightening. Unlike the fairy-tales, where wicked folk need no motivation for their wickedness, these goblins have plausible reasons for their enmity with the human king's family and are well-developed characters in their own right. The invention throughout the story is thoroughly appealing, from the details of goblin culture, such as the fad among women for wearing shoes (due to the goblin-king's first wife having been human), to the grandmother's elusive tower with its cleansing fire of roses and its pigeons and mysterious moon-like lamp.

The Princess and the Goblin's sequel, *The Princess and Curdie*, was serialized in the magazine *Good Things* in 1877 and published as a book in 1883. It is a darker story, in which the pessimism of MacDonald's later life is very apparent. In it, Curdie has ceased to believe in Irene's grandmother, or to pay much attention to things beyond his daily living. Thoughtlessly wounding a pigeon shocks him into a renewed sense of the value of living things. Irene's grandmother gives Curdie much instruction, leading him into better ways of looking at the world. She gives him the ability to tell a creature's true nature by taking its hand (or paw) and sends him to the city. With him goes the goblin beast Lina, whose paw to Curdie feels like the hand of a child. However, there are many in the royal city whose greed and wickedness have given them, to Curdie's perception, the paws of beasts. The king is ill, and many in his court plot against him. Curdie and the princess, with Lina and other good beasts, a very few faithful servants, and Irene's disguised great-great-grandmother, save both king and land from treachery and invasion. The people with the most irredeemable beast-natures are driven out. The princess and Curdie eventually wed and Curdie becomes king, but MacDonald concludes the story by telling us that after they died, the greedy man chosen to succeed them literally undermines the royal city in search of wealth. It collapses and the land returns to the wild.

Although it tells a story with its fair share of intrigue, suspense, and action, *Curdie* is not so evenly-paced a story as *Goblins*. The first part, especially, has overmuch lecturing on the part of the grandmother and little actually happens. Once Curdie reaches the city of Gwyntystorm, though, the pace picks up, and there is much to enjoy. The creepiness of the poisoning physician, whose hand feels to Curdie like the underbelly of a snake, the army of misshapen good beasts who are nearly all that remain to defend the realm, the mysterious housemaid who is always where she is most needed, all make for a memorable story. However, *The Princess and the Goblin* remains with cause the best-loved and best-known of all MacDonald's works among young readers.

Andersen showed what could be done with new stories using fairy-tale motifs; by mid-century Thackeray found fairy-tales so familiar to his audience he could write comedy within their outlines. With writers typified by Ingelow and Kingsley, the fantastic found a place within children's novels. It entertained, instructed, provided whimsy, cultivated the imagination, and provoked thought. It created new worlds, and showed up unfamiliar aspects of the real. The possibilities of the fantastic for whimsy and instruction, for beauty and terror, began to be realized. George MacDonald, with *At the Back of the North Wind*, created a world of enchantment woven through the real, and with *The Princess and the Goblin*, a vivid secondary world in which fully-realized characters could live. He told great stories that were dependant on the fantastic for their fulfilment, but in which the story remained paramount. All these trends would continue through the rest of the nineteenth century, and indeed throughout the history of children's fantasy.

IV
The Victorians, part two

As the nineteenth century progressed, the instructional content of children's literature became less overt. Fewer morals were made explicit by authors; more invention and playfulness entered children's stories. The possibilities of enchantment, as allowed in fairy-tales, entered fiction that was not presented as a fairy-tale. Fairy-tales of the sort involving magic or the fantastic are often vague in time or place, a little removed from the teller's 'here and now', and the characters are generally mere sketches of certain types. However, throughout the Victorian era enchantment became more common in novels about contemporary children, and also appeared in stories set in secondary worlds with a detailed invented history or geography, with more fully-developed characters than in fairy-tales. This trend can already be seen in *Mopsa*, which moves between the real world and an invented one where the fantastic is possible. In *The Water-Babies* and *At the Back of the North Wind*, the fantastic and the real co-exist, one layered on the other. All these stories use enchantment, not as it existed in folktales drawn from an oral tradition, but as it had appeared in medieval romances such as *Sir Gawain and the Green Knight* or those of Chrétien de Troyes, and in renaissance epic romances like Ariosto's *Orlando Furioso* or Spenser's *Faerie Queene*. It was fantasy in a conscious, literary form.

Increasingly, novels were written for children in which the fantastic played an important part; many of these, like MacDonald's, were fantasy novels telling new stories, not fairy-tales or retellings of folktales, legends, or myths, although there were numerous retellings of traditional material as well. The literary fairy-tale, especially in its comic mode, also continued. Near the end of the nineteenth century a story in that sub-genre would appear, as clever and entertaining as *The Rose and the Ring*, written by none other than that master purveyor of children's fairy-tales, Andrew Lang. However, the first halcyon summer of children's fantasy was in the eighteen-sixties and eighteen-seventies. It was truly a golden age for the genre, when in the space of few years were published not only *Water-Babies, North Wind* and the two *Curdie* books, but also *Alice*. In fact, *Alice's Adventures in Wonderland* appeared before either *At the Back of the North Wind, The Princess and the Goblin,* or *Mopsa,* although in some ways it seems more modern than any of them.

Lewis Carroll (1832-1898)

Lewis Carroll was the pseudonym of Charles Lutwidge Dodgson, who was a lecturer in mathematics at Oxford and a deacon in the Church of England. He had become a deacon, not out of any particular religious feeling, but to retain his Studentship at Christ Church at Oxford. This gave him the right to live there indefinitely, so long as he did not marry.

As a child, Carroll had written family magazines with his siblings; as an adult, he wrote and published verse, much of it comic. He was also an accomplished photographer, acquainted with Tennyson and a friend of the family of George MacDonald. However, his most significant friendship, from the literary point of view, was with the children, the three daughters in particular, of the man who became Dean of Christ Church in 1855, Henry Liddell. Carroll greatly admired the beauty of young girls. He formed close friendships, and the private intensity of his affection does seem to have exceeded the bounds of propriety. However, there is no evidence he ever acted inappropriately towards them.

In 1862, during an excursion up the river with various of his relatives and friends, including the Liddell sisters Lorina, Alice, and Edith, Carroll told a story which he wrote down, illustrated himself, and gave to Alice Liddell for Christmas in 1864 as *Alice's Adventures Under Ground*. Encouraged by the MacDonald family, Carroll expanded it for publication by Christmas 1865 as *Alice's Adventures in Wonderland*.

Wonderland is a book that offers illustrators wonderful opportunities. The original illustrations for both it and *Looking-Glass*, done by John Tenniel under Carroll's nit-picking supervision, have become inseparable from the story for many people, but a number of other notable artists have also illustrated *Alice*. Some of these alternate visions have recently been reissued, and are well worth seeking out. Mervyn Peake, the author of the *Gormenghast* adult fantasy novels, illustrated both *Alice* stories in black and white for editions published in 1946. These two pleasing little volumes were reissued by Bloomsbury in 2001. Arthur Rackham illustrated *Wonderland* in 1907; his version, with both colour plates and black and white line drawings, was reissued in 2002 by North-South Books. A very beautiful, lively series of colour illustrations for *Wonderland* was done in 1908 by the New Zealand-born artist Harry Rountree; this one was republished by Random House's Derrydale imprint in 2001. It has pictures on nearly every page, which will add to its appeal for younger readers.

Critics were at first unsure what to make of *Alice's Adventures in Wonderland*, in part because it had no obvious moral point. However, it had an immediate, although moderate, success, and its popularity continued to rise without faltering. An operetta based on it appeared in 1886 and it has been reworked into a number of plays and movies. In 1871 (although the title page is dated 1872), *Through the Looking-Glass and What Alice Found There* was published. The two books frequently appear in one volume. In 1889, Carroll published a simplified version of *Wonderland* for young children, called *The Nursery Alice*, but it has a rather condescending style of narration, 'talking down' to young listeners, unlike his original.

The two *Alice* books tell stories that have achieved the familiarity of fairy-tales; we all think we know them, even if we have never read them. In *Wonderland*, Alice, sitting bored and drowsy on the riverbank with her sister, sees the White Rabbit, with waistcoat and pocket-watch, and follows him into a hole which is rather more like a well, down which she falls for a very long time. At the bottom she finds a tiny door and, on a table, a golden key which opens it. Beyond is a beautiful garden. The main impulse driving the rest of the book is Alice's desire to reach that garden. First she cannot fit through the door. Then, when she shrinks after drinking from a bottle labelled 'drink me' (carefully checking to be sure it is not also labelled 'poison', since she has read all the appropriate cautionary tales), she finds that the door is again locked and the key once more on the table, out of reach.

All through the book Alice continues to change size alarmingly, usually through eating or drinking various things. She and a number of other creatures, including the poetic mouse and the Dodo, nearly drown in a pool of the tears she shed while a giant. She finds herself, grown large again, trapped in the White Rabbit's house, a foot up the chimney and an elbow against the door. She is mistaken by the Rabbit for his housemaid, by a bird for an egg-devouring serpent, has a squalling baby foisted off on her by the Duchess and her Cook, only to see it turn into a pig and run away, and stumbles into a chaotic meal with the Mad Hatter, the March Hare, and the Dormouse. She also meets the Cheshire Cat and a hookah-smoking caterpillar, who are almost the only people to offer her any advice on the chaotic world into which she has fallen. There are rules and etiquette, but Alice does not know them and is a stranger lost in a foreign land. She must reason things out as she goes along, but is always finding herself making faux pas, such as talking of cats and terriers to the mouse and birds in the Pool of Tears. All the creatures she meets seem very easily offended by remarks made in all innocence. When she recites poetry it comes out quite other than the proper words she thinks she should know.

When Alice does reach the garden, it is only to find herself swept into a croquet match by the Queen, in which the mallets are flamingos, the balls hedgehogs who keep wandering off, and the hoops the Queen's guards. She meets the Mock-Turtle and the Gryphon, endures more quizzing and nonsensical poetry, and in the end finds herself witness at the Knave's trial for tart-stealing. Unfortunately Alice has begun growing again and is threatened with eviction from the court; in the midst of the ensuing arguments, as she grows bolder in contesting the illogic of the proceedings, she recognizes all the participants as a pack of cards, and finds herself waking from her dream.

Through the Looking-Glass contains similar situations. Alice, musing on whether the part of 'Looking-Glass House' she cannot see in the mirror over the mantel is really identical to her own, finds she can step through into it, into a world populated by her chessmen. When she leaves the house for the garden, she is interrogated and criticized by the flowers. As in *Wonderland*, many of the creatures she meets react to her as to an uncouth stranger, who does not know the rules. Many are kinder, though, and more willing to explain the world to her, although they tend to retain rather a superior air while doing so.

Alice soon finds out, from the Red Queen, that she is in a chessboard landscape. The Queen invites her to play as the White Queen's pawn. Alice then makes it her goal to reach the eighth square and become a queen herself. Each passage through a new square brings a new adventure. She travels by train and boat, but mostly on foot, encountering insects such as the Rocking-Horsefly, and passing through the wood where things have no name. She meets the quarrelling twins, Tweedledum and Tweedledee, and Humpty-Dumpty, all of whom ask her thought-provoking questions and riddles; she watches the Lion and the Unicorn fighting for the crown. Like Tweedledum, Tweedledee, and Humpty-Dumpty, these heraldic beasts are figures of nursery-rhyme, not inventions of Carroll's, and would have been as familiar to his original readers as they are to Alice when she encounters them. One of the most memorable encounters is with the White Knight, who battles the Red Knight for her. He travels prepared for all contingencies, from mice to shark attacks, but Alice finds herself his protector, having to continually prevent him tumbling off his horse.

When she finally becomes a queen, Alice faces an examination by the Red and White Queens, and, that trial overcome, a feast in her honour as nonsensically-logical as the tea-party in the first book, with a pudding which objects to being sliced. As she tries to make a speech the world dissolves into chaos around her, guests and utensils flying about, and she wakes up as the Red Queen turns into her kitten.

Alice's Adventures in Wonderland and *Through the Looking-Glass and What Alice Found There* are far from being a mere patchwork of nonsense and whimsy. In each, Alice, an intelligent, curious, and considering girl, undertakes a journey or exploration with a definite destination in mind. To reach it, she must find her way through obstacles thrown up by the landscape through which she passes, mostly in the form of its inhabitants or the rules which govern its nature. These she must interact with or deduce, so as to continue. However, she learns no obvious moral lessons along the way; often Alice seems to be the only courteous and rational being in the company. The effect of this is to cast a wry light on the real world, where social interactions and conventions can often seem equally foreign, if we stand back and look at them from the perspective of an alien traveller – or a questioning child. The books are full of deeply-imaginative invention, riddles, and nonsense-poems with a good deal more 'story', internal sense, and whimsy to them than the average modern attempt at such verse. The landscape and characters remain as real to the reader long after the book has been finished, as they are to Alice in her dreams. Carroll, in the two *Alice* books, his greatest works, created a new world of possibilities in children's fiction.

Carroll's next book for children was *The Hunting of the Snark* (1876). It is a long narrative in the form of a nonsense poem about a sea-voyage taken by the Bellman and a crew of others all starting with 'B', in pursuit of a Snark, which, in the end, proves extremely elusive. It is told in good bouncing verse, and remains quite entertaining.

Carroll's final children's books do not bear comparison to *Alice* at all, and are fairly unreadable from a modern child's point of view. These are *Sylvie and Bruno* (1889) and *Sylvie and Bruno Concluded* (1893). In 1904 the two books were published together, in somewhat abbreviated form, as *The Story of Sylvie and Bruno*. Sylvie and Bruno are fairy children, observed by a human narrator, whose story is also told. There are some imaginative details and incidents, but little plot to hold a young reader's attention. Bruno speaks an excessively irritating baby-talk, and the children lack Alice's ready wit. They are all sugar and no spice. The overall impression of *Sylvie and Bruno* is that it is an exercise in the soppiest sort of Victorian sentimentality: imagine the book as the unfortunate offspring of Carroll and P.G. Wodehouse's character 'Madeline Bassett'. It is the two *Alice* books and the *Snark* that have earned Carroll his place among the undying greats (and founders) of children's fantasy.

Dinah Maria Mulock Craik (1826-1887)

Dinah Maria Mulock Craik was the author of a number of both children's and adult books. Craik, who published as both 'Miss Mulock' and 'Mrs Craik', or as simply 'The Author of *John Halifax, Gentleman*', was a successful writer before her marriage to a partner in the publishing firm of Macmillan, and was most famous for an adult work, *John Halifax, Gentleman* (1856).

Of her two fantasy books for children, the earlier, *The Adventures of a Brownie, As Told To My Child* (1872), is rather less exciting than the later, but is still of some interest nonetheless. The Brownie is a stay-at-home elf, who lives in the coal-cellar. The servants are bad-tempered, but the and the children of the house are friends. His attempt at revenge on the hostile gardener gets the children in trouble, but he makes amends to please them. In contrast to the usual trends in such stories even today, the Brownie is an amoral creature incapable of understanding that he has done wrong, and is not represented as in any way learning or reforming; he does not need to. Nor does he long for a human soul, as does Andersen's Little Mermaid. He remains a Brownie, an inhuman fairy creature, refreshingly true to his nature. *Brownie* is an enjoyable little story which may still entertain, but it is not so likely to please today's action and excitement-demanding children as *The Little Lame Prince*.

The Little Lame Prince and his Travelling-Cloak (1875) is Mulock Craik's best-known and most enduring work. The story follows the life of Prince Dolor of Nomansland, who is crippled through being dropped as a baby. When he is left an orphan, his uncle usurps the throne, exiling the little prince to an isolated, stairless tower, with a convicted criminal, previously sentenced to death, as his nurse. Once a month, a deaf-mute man brings provisions and a ladder with which to deliver them. He also brings books, and through these Dolor learns of the outside world. His loneliness is alleviated by a visit from his self-appointed, magic-working godmother. She gives him a magical flying cloak on which he can ride, 'like a frog on a water-lily leaf', to travel and see the world. Dolor finds out he is a king from his nurse, who has been reformed by her care for him, and determines to learn more about his kingdom through his travels.

When his uncle dies, Dolor's nurse has the mute servant take her out to testify that the rightful heir lives. Dolor works hard to be a just king. One of his reforms, brought about by his relationship with his nurse, is the banning of capital punishment. He never marries, but adopts one of his cousin's sons as heir. Eventually, Dolor leaves the kingdom to that prince, flying away forever on his travelling cloak, with his godmother keeping him company in the form of a lark. *The Little Lame Prince* is never overly-sweet despite the many opportunities such a story affords for that (not solely Victorian) vice.

This is not the sort of fairy-tale where all is perfected by the fairy-godmother. The travelling-cloak is no compensation for the prince's disability; it does not solve either his inability to walk or his loneliness. Along with books, though, it does allow him to see the world and to develop as a human being. In the end it is Dolor's own strength and resolve that enables him to walk on crutches, his own virtues that keep his people's loyalty, and his own wisdom that raises his adopted heir to be a worthy successor. Young readers looking for satisfying stories in the fairy-tale mode will find that this short novel still has much to offer.

Andrew Lang (1844-1912)

The colour *Fairy Books* would be glory enough to have achieved in the field of children's literature (see Chapter II), but Andrew Lang also wrote fairy-tales of his own. The earliest of these was *The Princess Nobody* (1884). Lang's next fairy-tales were *Prince Prigio* (1889) and its sequel *Prince Ricardo* (1893). These two were issued together as *My Own Fairy Book* in 1896, as *Chronicles of Pantouflia* in 1932, and as *Prince Prigio & Prince Ricardo* in 1961. The related collection, *Tales of a Fairy Court*, appeared in 1906. The best of these are the first two *Pantouflia* books, *Prince Prigio* and *Prince Ricardo*. Another outstanding original work by Lang, not a fairy-tale but a fantasy steeped in Scots legend and ballad, is *The Gold of Fairnilee* (1888).

The Princess Nobody was Lang's venture into the fairyland of the small and twinkly, but it is a well-crafted confection for all that. The story revolves around the usual sort of mistaken bargain kings from Agamemnon onwards have been making. Princess Niente is promised to a frog-riding dwarf, then rescued and married by a prince. The prince loses her through speaking her true name aloud, which she has expressly warned him not to do. Finally, he finds her. She is rather annoyed with his carelessness, but he wins her around, and all ends well. It was actually written to go with existing illustrations by Richard Doyle, which had already been published with accompanying verse by William Allingham under the title *In Fairy Land* (1870).

Much superior are Lang's *Pantouflia* books. *Prince Prigio, Prince Ricardo*, and *Tales of a Fairy Court* are firmly in the tradition of the comic and self-aware literary fairy-tale. He places his kingdom of Pantouflia in the world of Thackeray's *The Rose and the Ring*. These stories are built not upon raw folktales but on the literary, courtly fairy-tales which grew from the hybridisation of folktale and medieval Romance. They have fun with the conventions of the courtly fairy-tale as written by Madame d'Aulnoy, but with great affection.

Both stories are set in Pantouflia sometime in the early eighteenth century. Prince Prigio has the misfortune to have a Prussian mother, who does not believe in fairies and forbids their invitation to his christening. They show up anyway, with all the fairy wonders out of tales: magic carpets, seven-league boots, the sword of sharpness, the water of life, caps of wishing and of darkness. However, one fairy curses him: 'My child, you shall be *too* clever!' And he is. Prigio, like his mother, does not believe in the irrational, but he can tell anyone how best to do anything, excels at his studies, and he is always right. Everyone naturally detests him. The king, who much prefers Prigio's younger brothers, Enrico and Alphonso, finally decides to get rid of Prigio by sending him on a quest to kill the firedrake that threatens the kingdom. Prigio does not believe in such things. He refuses to go, pointing out that as the eldest son, he is doomed to fail on the quest, so King Giglio had better begin by sending Alphonso, his youngest brother, first, since the third son is fated to succeed. Alphonso and Enrico both perish, to Giglio's grief, but Prigio believes they have simply set off to see the world. In disgust, the entire court moves to another city, leaving the prince alone in the castle.

There, Prigio discovers his long-forgotten christening gifts. Even when he makes use of the seven-league boots and the cap of darkness, he refuses to believe in them, until, invisibly gate-crashing a ball, he sets eyes on Rosalind, the daughter of the English ambassador. She is the only one there who has a kind word to say about the disgraced crown prince. He falls in love on the spot, and with that, he suddenly comprehends the irrational.

He understands the fairy gifts he has been using, and realizes that all the histories of his family which he has read and disbelieved (Sleeping Beauty and the like), are true. And then, the prince realizes the terrible fate to which he sent his brothers.

Prigio succeeds in overcoming the firedrake, and survives various complications following that triumph. He restores his brothers with the water of life, and marries Rosalind. At the very end of the book, Rosalind suggests that to get on better in life, Prigio might use the wishing cap to become no more clever than other people. Prigio, wisely reflecting that everyone must keep one secret, even in marriage, wishes instead '... to SEEM no cleverer than other people'. And because of this he becomes the most popular king Pantouflia has ever had.

The sequel, *Prince Ricardo*, shows the dangers of leaning too much away from reason and study. Prigio and Rosalind, like most parents, overreact to the mistakes of their own. Their son Ricardo is raised on a diet of fairy-tales; he is forever charging about the world, rescuing princesses, slaying monsters, and neglecting his studies. One of these princesses, Jaqueline, lives at the palace with them, and is a powerful magician herself. 'Jack' and 'Dick' are great friends, but although Jaqueline loves Ricardo, he has never settled down long enough to fall in love with anyone.

King Prigio, worried by his son's dependence on the fairy christening gifts, has non-magical duplicates made for many of them, to teach Ricardo that he needs to develop his own knowledge and skills. This gets Ricardo into dangerous situations several times, despite his father's watchfulness, and it is only the fact that Jaqueline can transform herself into animals, and secretly accompanies the prince, that saves him.

On one adventure, Jaqueline is captured by a giant while saving Ricardo. The giant hands her over to the sleeping Earthquaker in South America for safekeeping, and Ricardo must enlist his father's aid to save her. Prigio works out how to do this, with reference to Ariosto's great renaissance epic *Orlando Furioso* (in which the moon is a repository of lost things and a flying horse is used to get there). There is also some sharp irony directed at literary criticism, as the heaviest weight of stupidity that Prigio can think of. The Earthquaker is accordingly destroyed with a great weight of stupidity. Jaqueline and a number of previously-sacrificed maidens are rescued, and Jaqueline revealed as the daughter of the Inca. Ricardo finally realizes that he loves her, and they are married, once in South America, and once in Pantouflia. In a final comic touch, the Inca converts his nation to Lutheranism, so that no more maidens will have to be sacrificed.

Lang writes with all the ease and readability one would expect from the editor of the *Fairy Books*. The *Pantouflia* novels, with their rapid-paced plots and witty asides, should be as fresh and enjoyable as when they were written, at least for children well-versed in the traditions of fairy-tales, even if some of the satire goes over their heads. For those who have never been exposed to the real fairy-tales, the stories should still be an exciting adventure, and the concept of such things as caps of darkness and seven-league boots will be new and unexpected, an eventuality that Lang would never have anticipated.

Tales of a Fairy Court contains several stories set in Pantouflia. The first is an adventure that begins with Prince Prigio's father meeting a cyclops around the time of the prince's birth. The others, a visit to the time of James VI of Scotland (a keen witch-burner and golfer, as Prigio finds out), the tale of the enchanter who always wanted more, and the rescuing of assorted princesses, arise as Prince Prigio tries to pass the time before his marriage. These are pleasant stories, but not of the calibre of *Prince Prigio* and *Prince Ricardo*, and Lang seems to have forgotten details of his first two *Pantouflia* books, contradicting established events in several places.

Lang's 'serious' fantasy novel, *The Gold of Fairnilee*, is very different from his comic literary fairy-tales. It is set on the River Tweed in the border regions of Scotland in the sixteenth century, a time of war and cattle-raiding. Randal is the son of a laird who dies at the battle of Flodden (1513). Later, during a raid into England, some of his mother's men carry off a young English girl, Jean. Randal and Jean grow up together, until, when he is around thirteen and she ten, he decides he wants to see the fairy queen, and is taken by her. This is not a fairy-tale; these are the old, cold fairies of the Scots and Scandinavian ballads, the ones whom Thomas the Rhymer went away with. They live in the fairy mounds and ride out to ensnare the hearts and souls of Christian men and women, who escape them years later, if ever.

Seven years after Randal's abduction, famine looms. Jean believes that in this significant seventh year, she may be able both to get Randal back and gain the legendary gold of Fairnilee of which their nurse used to tell them. (Fairnilee is a real place and the legend of its gold real; Lang grew up near the ruined castle, and as a boy dreamed of finding the gold himself.) Like the maidens and knights of the traditional ballads under similar circumstances, Jean frees Randal by remaining firm in her purpose and making the sign of the cross over him three times, when he rides out with the fairies and appears to her in a frightening form.

Lang brings original touches to his fairy otherworld. In the mound, when Randal anoints himself with the water that destroys the glamour of the fairies, he sees them as the melancholy pre-Christian dead of the region, dressed in their ancient burial robes or the clothes or armour they died in. Their feasts are of the foods left for the dead in those times.

Between the glamour-destroying water and a systematic excavation, Randal, Jean, and the nurse find the treasure: a hoard of early British coins, a Roman iron chest filled with gold, silver, glassware, and a golden image of Fortune. It is the treasure of some legion, plundered by the tribes beyond the Wall, buried and never retrieved. Randal and Jean make judicious use of the treasure, selling it in France and Rome to buy corn and cattle to save their people.

The Gold of Fairnilee deserves to be better known than it is. Although even the most important characters, Randal, Jean, and the nurse, are not deeply characterized personalities, this is in keeping with the ballad tradition from which they spring. Viewed as quick pencil sketches by a master artist, they lack for nothing. The story captures the air of that place and time flawlessly, introduces an intriguing but not overwhelming amount of real history and archaeology. In its return to the roots of fairy legend, *Fairnilee* is a refreshing foil to the fluffier, twinkly fairies of so much Victorian and later writing for children. It is, in fact, one of the first fantasies of its type: an historical fantasy set in a realistic past true to historic fact, but containing as 'real' some supernatural elements consistent with the beliefs of the setting. An earlier Scottish writer, Sir Walter Scott, attempted the same mingling of historical fiction and the presentation of historical supernatural beliefs as real in *The Monastery* (1820), but, he writes in the 'Introduction' to the edition published as part of the complete *Waverley Novels* in 1832/1833, he found the concept did not appeal very much to his audience; the time was not yet right for such a blend of fantasy and historical fiction.

The Gold of Fairnilee, The Princess Nobody, and *Tales of a Fairy Court* are all fairly short. They were last reissued in 1967, in one volume, as *The Gold of Fairnilee and Other Stories* in the Gollancz revivals series edited by Gillian Avery, and are now out of print. *Prince Prigio* and *Prince Ricardo* are likewise unavailable in any recent editions. This is a shame, since they deserve to be counted among the classics. It is to be hoped that the current interest in children's fantasy, which is resulting in the reissue of many previously unavailable nineteenth- and early twentieth-century books, will see Lang's original writings once more available. He has certainly remained very readable for the modern child; the tendency of earlier Victorian authors to use fantasy stories primarily for didactic purposes has been left far behind. There are plenty of morals to be drawn, as there are in any story, whether the author has made that the point of the work or not, but illustrating and explaining them is no longer the primary driving force behind the plot. The story exists to unfold, to entertain, and if it also makes a point, readers are left to consider it for themselves. Lang writes purely to transport his readers to another time and place, and to delight.

Oscar Wilde (1854-1900)

Oscar Wilde was born in Dublin and educated at Trinity College Dublin, and at Oxford. He was a proponent of the Aesthetic Movement, which believed art should exist for its own sake. He was a flamboyant personality, famous first as a public speaker and then as a playwright. Wilde, a bisexual, became notorious when he was convicted in 1895 for his affair with Lord Alfred Douglas and condemned to hard labour for two years. Before this, though, he wrote two collections of fairy-tales for his sons. These are *The Happy Prince* (1888) and *A House of Pomegranates* (1892). Among the stories contained in these is 'The Happy Prince', about the statue of a prince and the bird which sacrifices itself for him. Another is 'The Selfish Giant'. This, probably the best-known, is about a giant's garden into which children are forbidden to enter. Spring never comes, and the giant's heart is finally changed by the little Christ-child. It has been made into a play which is sometime performed in schools. Both these stories also exist in modern picture-book versions. They have a certain elegiac quality, and certainly owe much to the tradition of Andersen.

Howard Pyle (1853-1911)

Howard Pyle was an American author and illustrator, best known for his retellings of traditional stories, especially the Arthurian matter and Robin Hood. He taught illustration to such notable artists as Maxfield Parrish, Jessie Wilcox Smith, and N.C. Wyeth. Pyle wrote three collections of fairy-tales and several historical novels for children, as well as his more famous and idiosyncratic retellings of legendary material (for which see Chapter X). His only novel-length original fantasy work is *The Garden Behind the Moon* (1895), which seems like a story from at least a generation previous. It has more in common with *The Water-Babies* and *The Golden Key* than *The Gold of Fairnilee*.

The hero of *The Garden Behind the Moon* is David, who travels to the moon on the moon-path, the silver light that makes a path across the water at night. There he witnesses the cruelties of the slave-trade and is allowed to polish stars alongside the souls of unborn children. He is sent on a quest to find the Wonder-Box and the Know-All Book, which were originally given to Adam and Eve by the Moon-Angel. The box and the book have to be taken from the Iron Man and returned to earth. David, who has grown up by passing through the Moon-Angel or through death, captures and tames a winged horse and fulfils his quest, returning a princess' wits to her as well. As in Lang's *Prince Ricardo*, the influence of Ariosto is obvious, since in *Orlando Furioso*, Orlando's lost wits are on the moon, and are recovered by a friend who uses a flying horse. In the end, David leaves the village, where he is regarded as a simpleton, and marries the princess.

Like much of Pyle's other writing for children, *The Garden Behind the Moon* has many authorial asides to the reader, which take a very condescending tone and sound old-fashioned by comparison to his contemporaries. The novel is not couched in so artificially archaic a style as Pyle's *King Arthur* and *Robin Hood* stories, but is still somewhat grating. In subject matter, it is a parable of spiritual growth, redemption, and death, although it is not so successful at this as is MacDonald's *The Golden Key*, seeming less poetically inspired, and more stiffly contrived. However, it continues to have its readers, and was a probable influence on Tolkien's posthumously-published children's novel *Roverandom* (1998), in which a path of moonlight on water also links earth and moon. In the United States, *The Garden Behind the Moon* was reissued by Tor's young adult fantasy/science fiction imprint Starscape in 2002.

By the end of the nineteenth century, fantasy had come into its own as an important form of children's literature. New fairy-tales, utterly invented or built on traditional motifs, abounded. Literary fairy-tales could lovingly spoof the material they were founded on, as well as provide a vehicle for social satire. The enchantment of the fairy-tale world, the magic of medieval and renaissance Romance, could enter into a novel without apology. Writers such as Kingsley and MacDonald could use fantasy in telling a story with a specific intent. Children such as Jack in Ingelow's *Mopsa* could encounter a magic of fancy and whimsy in the everyday countryside. The traditional supernatural elements, such as Mulock Craik's Brownie or the old Scots fairies of the mounds in Lang's *Fairnilee*, could take centre-stage in a story of the 'real world'. And the world of Romance flourished again, in stories like *The Princess and the Goblin* or *The Little Lame Prince*, set in pre-industrial worlds where magic, for good and ill, could be allowed to exist and play its role in a history. Perhaps most notably of all, the nineteenth century saw fantasy take its most unexpected leap, into the logical, dreaming chaos of *Alice*. All later generations of children's fantasy writers have followed the paths marked out by these pioneers.

V
Before the War

The period between the turn of the century and the First World War saw a proliferation of books for children. Childhood had, in the later Victorian era, become a more important period of life, one meant for enjoyment as well as learning and moral development, while at the same time printing and book manufacture had become cheaper, thereby making books more available to children in less affluent families. Children's magazines proliferated as well, and elementary education became, during the last decades of the nineteenth century, much more common.

In Great Britain, where most children's fantasy was being written and published, the Education Act of 1870 gave locally-elected school boards the right to levy rates (a local tax on property value) in order hire teachers and establish schools in areas not served by church-run institutions, with fees being waived if parents could not afford them. This was intended to place an elementary education within the reach of all children.[*] In that year, books for children formed the second-largest category of works published (Ensor 159). In 1880, school attendance became compulsory in England and Wales, although again, only for the poor were fees waived.[**] Conflicts between church-run systems and those run by elected school boards limited the effectiveness of mandatory education, but nevertheless the literacy rate began to increase substantially. In 1891, fees for elementary schools were abolished by Parliament; in the same year, a Factory Act raised the minimum age at which children could be employed in factories to eleven. Thus, by 1901, when Victoria died and was succeeded by her son Edward VII, childhood, in theory, and in practice for all but the poor (who received a bare minimum of

---

[*] For an in-depth discussion of the various nineteenth-century Education Acts, see Woodward, *The Age of Reform*, and Ensor, *England: 1870-1914*.

[**] Scotland had a separate system which had put elementary education within reach of most of its population much earlier in the century.

education before taking on adult earning responsibilities, or slipped between the cracks altogether), was a time for play and learning both, and a much larger percentage of the population than previously was functionally literate as a result.

Books written in the early twentieth century generally allow children's imaginations full rein. Most authors assume their young readers to be well-educated and middle-class. They take for granted at least a passing acquaintance with history and geography, as well as a wide exposure to the fiction of the century past. One aspect shared by many children's books of this era is a concern with childhood as a time for young people to experience a degree of freedom from the cares of adult life. Even 'realistic' books such as Frances Hodgson Burnett's *The Secret Garden* (1911) and *A Little Princess* (published as *Sara Crewe* in 1887 and revised under its present title in 1905), or L.M. Montgomery's *Anne of Green Gables* (1908), exalt the imagination and show childhood as a state of existence to be experienced fully and revelled in. It is a state out of which truths may be revealed and virtues may grow; attributes of value in adulthood are shown to have their roots in childhood. Mary Lennox's curiosity and wonder at growing things leads her to initiate change in herself and in her cousin; Sara Crewe's empathy for others and her imagination get her through her time of impoverished suffering; Anne Shirley's imagination helps her endure early life as an unwanted drudge and in an orphanage, while her unquashable zest for the world around her transforms the lives of the couple who adopt her and paves the way for her adult success as teacher, university student, and mother. In *The Story of the Treasure Seekers* (1899), E. Nesbit's Bastables cope with their father's impoverishment by embarking on a number of comic but largely unsuccessful money-making schemes, which show them imaginatively engaged with and influenced by literature as much as modern children are by television. They do not, as a similar situation might have demanded in an earlier generation of books, actually do anything practical to support the family, but they effect a reconciliation between their father and his uncle.

All through this period, fictional children are shown living intensely as children, engaged with the world but with a child's perspective, maturing through the course of the stories, not so much by bitter experience, but through building on the virtues of childhood: curiosity, imagination, wonder, enthusiasm. The books of this era, more so than those that had gone before, celebrate the state of childhood on account of these virtues. Writers such as Nesbit wrote about children, whether the 'realistic' Bastables or the fantasy-encountering Robert, Cyril, Anthea, and Jane of *Five Children and It* (1902), simply being children.

However, despite the portrayal, in much of the fantasy written at this time, of childhood as more a separate state of existence than part of a continuum of experience, books were also written that used fantasy in a more traditional manner. As in the world of medieval Romance, heroes embarked on quests to achieve some goal, and in the process, grew and changed. As in works of the mid nineteenth century, stories were written that used the possibilities and freedoms of fantasy to teach. Neither of these elements has ever been lost to the genre, though the strength of their presence waxes and wanes.

E. Nesbit (1858-1924)

One of the most important children's writers, of fantasy or otherwise, in the period before the First World War was E. Nesbit. As a child, Edith Nesbit had hated the various schools to which she was sent, but enjoyed a great deal of freedom at home with her brothers and sisters; she celebrated that liberty to roam, explore, and pretend in her writing. Nesbit married journalist Hubert Bland in 1880. Both were very involved in the intellectual socialism of the day. They were founding members of the Fabian Society (1884), and their circle included H.G. Wells, Karl Marx's daughter Eleanor, and George Bernard Shaw.

Nesbit's marriage was a difficult one. She and Bland had five children, although two were stillborn. Another died under anaesthetic during a minor operation. She also adopted as her own at their birth the daughter and son of her husband's mistress, Alice Hoatson, who lived with the Nesbits. Nesbit herself had several affairs, often with the admiring younger men who were a fixture of the Blands' gregarious household. The archaeologist and Keeper of Egyptian and Assyrian Antiquities at the British Museum, E. Wallis Budge, who helped her with research and ideas for *The Story of the Amulet*, was another of her romantic interests, as was George Bernard Shaw. Not a whiff of this unconventionality in her personal life leaks through into her writing for children; at the time, any public scandal could have ruined her career, at least as a children's writer.

Nesbit wrote numerous magazine stories and several novels for adults, but these have not endured as have her books for children. Hubert Bland died in 1914, and in 1917, Nesbit married Thomas Tucker, a retired marine engineer; this second marriage was, by all accounts, one of contentment and mutual support, in sharp contrast to her first. However, by that time her popularity was ebbing and all of her greatest works had been produced.

For most of her life, E. Nesbit was an extremely prolific writer, who often had one book coming out as a novel while another one or two were being serialized in magazines. Her first children's works were mere potboilers, history and Shakespeare for children or things with titles such as *Pussy Tales* and *Doggy Tales* (both 1895), but in 1898, she wrote a series of stories for the magazines *Windsor* and *Pall Mall*, which became chapters in a children's novel published in 1899 as *The Story of the Treasure Seekers. Treasure Seekers* and its sequels, *The Wouldbegoods* (1901) and *The New Treasure Seekers* (1904), and the unconnected book *The Railway Children* (1906), are realistic stories about children who, although there are external difficulties affecting their families, have adventures caused by their own actions. Nesbit's fantasies follow the same pattern. They invariably take ordinary, although well-read and imaginative, middle-class Edwardian children, bring them into contact with some magical device or creature, and relate the difficulties that ensue from the children's use of the magic. This plot device now sounds rather trite, but when Nesbit did it, it was original and exciting. She was in fact the pioneer of this type of story.

Her greatest works in this vein are the three that could be called the 'Psammead' stories, although the Psammead itself only takes a central role in the first and third of them. They feature the siblings Robert, Anthea, Jane, Cyril, and their baby brother the Lamb. The first of these, *Five Children and It*, came out in book form in 1902, followed by *The Phoenix and the Carpet* (1904), and *The Story of the Amulet* (1906). *Five Children* begins when the four elder children of the family dig up a Sand-fairy in a gravel pit while staying in the country. The Sand-fairy, or

Psammead, is an ancient, cantankerous beast, brown, furry, and fat, with eyes on stalks like a snail. It is capable of granting wishes, but very peevish about doing so; to placate it the children agree to limit themselves to one wish a day. These wear off at sunset, which turns out to be a very good thing. Their wishes, both the heedlessly-uttered and carefully-considered, have disastrous consequences: their heaps of gold get them handed over to the police as suspected thieves, wings are worse trouble, while being in a besieged castle is terrifying. To undo the potential disaster of a final, thoughtless wish that could ruin the life of an innocent man, they persuade the Psammead to give them several wishes at once to sort things out, in return for their promise to ask nothing more of it.

The Phoenix and the Carpet sees the same family back in London, where an old carpet purchased for the nursery turns out to be a wishing one. Rolled up inside it is the Phoenix's egg. This hatches in the fire, and the vain, grandiloquent, and occasionally wise Phoenix is their companion through many carpet-facilitated misadventures. The Psammead does not appear in person, but as a friend of the Phoenix it nonetheless manages to figure in the action at several crucial points.

The Story of the Amulet begins with their rediscovery and rescue of the Psammead, now a captive in a pet-shop. In gratitude, it tells them where to find what turns out to be half of an ancient amulet, which will take them anywhere they want, to look for the other half. The entire amulet will bring a land peace and fertility, and can grant one's heart's desire. Their quest for the missing half takes them travelling in time. Time-travel by means of a magic object is now common and overused in children's books, especially when didactic history is the purpose, but the whole idea was quite a fresh approach when *Amulet* was published; H.G. Wells' *The Time Machine*, which probably suggested time-travel to Nesbit, had been published in 1895. The children have a great many adventures in quite a wide sweep of the past, which Nesbit took great care to research thoroughly. They also travel into a utopian future shaped by the social ideas of Wells, who in that future is revered as a great visionary. One vividly-described episode in *Amulet* has the Queen of Babylon running amuck in London. This had a very obvious influence on C.S. Lewis' description of Empress Jadis' goings-on when

Digory and Polly bring her to London in *The Magician's Nephew*. (Lewis makes direct reference to *The Story of the Treasure Seekers* in the opening paragraph of the same book.) Nesbit's Queen attacks neither policemen nor cabbies, but does try to reclaim all the Babylonian artefacts in the Museum, magically floating them out the door in a great procession of massive stones, bringing mayhem to the streets.

The Enchanted Castle (1907) is similar in spirit to the 'Psammead' stories. In this, siblings Gerald, Kathleen, and Jimmy meet Mabel, niece to the housekeeper at Yalding Towers. There they discover what appears to be a wishing ring. They suffer through various misadventures with it, but most terrifying for them is the affair of the Ugli-Wuglies, dummies the children have made to be an audience to a play they stage. The Ugli-Wuglies come alive due to an unconsidered wish and roam the town and the grounds. The castle itself is full of secret rooms and tunnels; the many statues of Greek gods and dinosaurs in the grounds live at night when the moon shines on them. The children's attempts to smooth the course of romance for a French schoolmistress and the impoverished Lord Yalding result in difficulties and in the end it is the statues of the gods who must resolve things, by revealing the mystery of the castle and the origins of the ring.

The device of time-travel by means of magic features again in *House of Arden* (1908) and *Harding's Luck* (1909). In the first, Elfrida and Edred live with their young aunt in her boarding house. Their father and her fiancé are missing, presumed dead, in South America. When old Lord Arden dies, Edred learns he is the new lord and that there is a prophecy that a Lord Arden of Edred's age can find a lost treasure if he recites a particular spell on Arden Knoll. The children try it and summon the Mouldiwarp, the white mole whose image is their family crest. They move into the family castle and have various adventures with the irascible mole. These mostly involve travelling into the past, where they live the lives of other children of the family and encounter various dangers, some of which are caused by their lack of caution regarding their knowledge of the future, as when Elfrida is imprisoned in the Tower of London for knowing too much about the Gunpowder Plot against James I. They meet the witch Betty Lovell, and Cousin Richard, who like them moves around in time. In the end, with the Mouldiwarp's and Cousin Richard's help, they rescue their father and uncle-to-be from captivity in a South American Shangri-La. Their father's eventual return to England is the treasure they receive.

Harding's Luck is the story of Cousin Richard, or Dickie Harding, who begins his life in the slums of London at the end of the nineteenth century and ends up in the early sixteen-hundreds, which is where Elfrida and Edred met him in *House of Arden*. It is he who discovers the actual Arden treasure, and he who is rightfully Lord Arden, rather than Edred's father, but Richard dislikes the state of the society into which he was born and elects to live in the past. This story, more than some of Nesbit's others, displays the awareness, and condemnation, of contemporary social conditions which one would expect of a Fabian Society founder.

Other Nesbit fantasies include the novels *The Magic City* (1910), *The Wonderful Garden* (1911), and *Wet Magic* (1913). The latter in particular has some original elements in its portrayal of underwater society. It starts with the discovery of a mermaid, which leads to adventures in a submarine kingdom at war. Nesbit also wrote a number of fantasy short stories, which, like her novels, usually appeared first in magazines. *The Book of Dragons* (1900) has been republished as *The Complete Book of Dragons* (Hamish Hamilton, 1972) and *The Last of the Dragons and Some Others* (Puffin, 1975), with the addition of the story 'The Last of the Dragons' from Nesbit's posthumously-published *Five of Us – and Madeleine* (1925). *Nine Unlikely Tales* (1901) is another collection of whimsical fantasies, many in a fairy-tale mode.

All of Nesbit's books fling her characters from adventure to adventure, difficulty to difficulty. The children always need to rely on their wits to get them out of the situation their magical encounter has created, or at least, to stop it getting any worse before the magic wears off. One of Nesbit's great strengths lies in giving careful consideration to the practical effects of the magic, and from this arises much of the comedy in her books. Another is her ability to portray characters who, while not very deep or distinct as individuals, sparkle collectively with a realistic enthusiasm, and have plausible fears and worries, daydreams and aspirations, with which young readers can identify, even after a hundred years. The children must frequently wrestle with moral conundrums of their own making, and thoughtless acts are shown to have far-reaching consequences, as when the game-keeper in *Five Children* is the only apparent culprit for the theft of jewellery that was effected by the Psammead's magic, a charge that would destroy the innocent man's life and the happiness of his fiancée, their maid. Nesbit's magical creatures, such as the Phoenix, Mouldiwarp, and especially the Psammead, are where she truly excels in creating memorable characters. By off-setting their powers with their prickly dispositions, Nesbit creates personalities that remain in the reader's memory and prevents her magic coming to the children too easily; it is really the Psammead and the Phoenix we remember, when we cannot recall any definite individual details of Robert, Anthea, Cyril or Jane.

Although many of the literary references which her well-read protagonists make will pass today's children by, the experience of reading Nesbit is not too much diminished by that, and her stories have as much power to entertain as they ever did. They will stretch the imaginations of young readers (and perhaps their vocabularies as well), and give them a glimpse of some aspects of Edwardian life truer than what twenty-first century historical fiction can offer. Many are still in print from one or more publishers, particularly Penguin/Puffin, Wordsworth Classics, and Random House's Red Fox Classics.

J.M. Barrie (1860-1937)

Sir James Matthew Barrie was a writer, journalist, and playwright, who, like Nesbit and Kenneth Grahame, kept a close emotional connection to childhood throughout his life, or to be less charitable, remained emotionally immature. Barrie in fact characterized himself as a boy who never grew up. His marriage to actress Mary Ansell in 1894 was unhappy and childless. He befriended other people's children, forming a close relationship with the sons of Arthur and Sylvia Llewelyn Davies in particular. Arthur died in 1907 and Sylvia in 1910, whereupon Barrie, now divorced, assumed custody of the five boys, though this was not welcomed by all of their relatives. His interest in the boys was regarded by some at the time as exceeding the bounds of normal paternalism, although, as with Lewis Carroll, there is no suggestion that he ever acted on any latent sexual interest he might have felt, if indeed his desire to possess them was ever tinged with sexuality at all. The boys were, for Barrie, primarily a way of recreating childhood for himself. As a boy he had loved stories and games of pirates and desert islands; he introduced the Llewelyn Davies boys to similar games before he wrote the play *Peter Pan*, which had its first performance in December of 1904. Barrie was made a baronet in 1913. He had other successful plays, but it is *Peter Pan*, traditional Christmas fare from its first performance onwards, on which his enduring fame rests.

The first appearance of the character of Peter Pan was actually in Barrie's 1902 novel *The Little White Bird*, which is about a childless old bachelor who befriends a poor couple's son. Some of the stories about fairies and lost children that the man tells the boy foreshadow the themes of *Peter Pan*. The story introducing the character of Peter Pan, *Peter Pan in Kensington Gardens*, was republished separately in 1906. When Barrie turned his popular play into a novel, it was initially titled *Peter and Wendy* (1911). A shorter version appeared as *Peter Pan and Wendy* (1915); that title was then applied to the full text in 1921, although now it is often merely *Peter Pan*.

The basic plot of the novel *Peter Pan and Wendy* is well known to most from the Disney cartoon and from numerous simplified retellings. It relates how Peter, the boy who never grew up, and his Lost Boys live in Neverland, as the play's Never Never Land becomes in the book, fighting pirates and Indians; Peter meets Wendy and invites her and her brothers to fly away with him so that Wendy can be his 'mother'. The original is more complex; the narration is occasionally ironic, sometimes coy, and the pirates are much more frightening and less comic. There is plenty in the story to stir the reader's imagination: several gory battles, the cruel mermaids, the underground house, the crocodile's unrelenting pursuit of Hook, and hairsbreadth escapes and rescues. The climactic episode in the book is the capture of Wendy and the Lost Boys by the pirates, just when Wendy has persuaded all except Peter to come home with her and her brothers. After Tinker Bell saves Peter from poison by drinking it herself, and is revived by people's belief in fairies, Peter rescues the boys, who are about to walk the plank; he kills most of the pirates and knocks Hook into the maw of the crocodile in the process. When they return to London, only Peter refuses to be adopted by Wendy's parents. He occasionally returns to fetch Wendy to do his spring cleaning; this chore passes to her daughter and granddaughter in turn.

Characterisation is not a strong point in the story, but that is not necessarily a major failing. However, the elements that do go into depicting character may not be that appealing to many children now. Captain Hook seems the most fully developed person in the book, and much of his characterisation, his (understandable!) hatred of Peter for his cockiness and his own obsession with 'good form', couched as it is in the schoolboy cant of the times, is going to be at best missed by the children of today, or at worst frustrate them, especially where it interferes with the action of the final duel. Tinker Bell's main attribute is an adult sexual jealousy of Wendy. The main child characters, Peter Pan and Wendy, are presented from the point of view of an adult looking back, or down, on childhood, and it is this more than anything that may make the story less engaging to the readers of today than it once was. Throughout, the narration is too self-conscious, which has the effect of never allowing the reader to forget that this is a consciously-created world; it is all made up.

The story seems decidedly lacking when it comes to Wendy's involvement. Neverland is a place where the imagination of children reigns, yet Wendy's adventures there, aside from looking at mermaids and being stolen by pirates, both passive activities, are all laundry and darning. Although Peter plays briefly at being an ordinary boy, Wendy's entire stay on the island is devoted to adult domestic concerns. Acting as mother to the boys is the most her imagination is allowed to aspire to, aside from her pet wolf, which has a couple of brief mentions and no actual presence in the story. In Nesbit's books, written around the same period, the girls may get stuck with doing the dishes when there are dishes to be done, but they take a full share in whatever adventures are afoot.

Many children are not going to be bothered by any of this. The action and adventure will carry them along. *Peter Pan* has held the attention of generations of readers, and for those expecting something excessively saccharine, the callousness of so many of the characters ('"There's a pirate asleep in the pampas just beneath us," Peter told him. "If you like, we'll go down and kill him'"), and the gleeful violence of the battles will be refreshing.

Rudyard Kipling (1865-1936)

Rudyard Kipling was born in 1865 in Bombay, India, where his father was principal of the Art School. He was educated in England, but returned to India, where he worked as a newspaper reporter and wrote short stories and poetry. Kipling married the American Caroline Balestier in 1892 and lived in the United States until 1896. They had three children, but the eldest, Josephine, the 'Best Beloved' whom the narrator addresses in the *Just So Stories*, died of pneumonia in 1899.

In 1907, Kipling was awarded the Nobel Prize in Literature, the first British writer to be so honoured, but in Britain his popularity declined after the First World War. He was criticized for his imperialism and for what was seen by many as a blindly jingoistic attitude. However, his popular appeal continued unabated throughout the twentieth century. Among his most famous works are *Plain Tales From the Hills* (1888), *Barrack-Room Ballads* (1892), *The Jungle Book* (1894) and *The Second Jungle Book* (1895) (which between them contain the seven short stories about Mowgli and the Seeonee wolf pack, as well as other animal stories), *Captains Courageous* (1897), *Stalky and Co.* (1899), *Just So Stories for Little Children* (1902), and perhaps his greatest work, *Kim* (1901).

Kipling's influence on fantasy lies mostly in his two books celebrating British history, *Puck of Pook's Hill* (1906) and its sequel, *Rewards and Fairies* (1910). These grew out of Kipling's love for the land around his house in Sussex. The two books are, in many ways, an encomium for England as he saw it, masterfully evoking a sense of the continuity of history. Kipling researched his material extensively, and for many children in the first half of the twentieth century his Puck stories planted the seed of an abiding interest in history. For children of the second half, this introductory role was taken over by one of those children in whom Kipling's Puck had awakened a fascination with the island's past: Rosemary Sutcliff.

The Puck books, which consist of stories framed by poems, are not really time-travel stories; the children, Dan and Una, do not journey to the past to watch history unfold. Instead, history is brought to them by magic. Characters, mostly invented by Kipling (although Queen Elizabeth is encountered by the children in *Rewards*), come to speak with them, generally aware of the magic by which they are present, and generally speaking of their own times from a perspective a little removed; their view is not that of an impartial outsider, but of a life that is finished and done. An exception seems to be the consumptive girl Philadelphia, who is still very much in the midst of her life when she speaks to Una in 'Marklake Witches' in *Rewards*.

The story begins when Dan and Una enact a shortened version of *A Midsummer Night's Dream* three times in a fairy-ring on Midsummer Eve. This summons Puck, the last surviving English fairy, the 'oldest Old Thing in England'. He is a small, brown, pointy-eared character in a blue cap, and is at once friendly, wise, cheerful, and personable, not Shakespeare's trouble-stirring servant of Oberon but a Puck of Kipling's own. He befriends Dan and Una, enacting for them a 'little magic'. They 'take seizin' of the land from him in an echo of a medieval custom accompanying the transfer of land, accepting cut pieces of the turf and becoming 'lawfully seized and possessed of all Old England'. And thus begin their encounters with the past. Dan and Una are not permitted to retain their memories of this magic, although during each encounter they remember the others. Kipling creates a particularly English magic even for that forgetting, as Puck steals their memories with leaves of oak, ash, and thorn. What they are allowed to take away from each meeting, one assumes, is their increasing appreciation for their region and its history.

Puck first tells them about the diminishment of the old gods of the Phoenicians, Danes, and all the other peoples who had an impact on Britain, into the fairies of folklore. Some of the other stories are told to them by Puck, some by characters such the Norman Sir Richard Dalyngridge, or Parnesius, a centurian in the Thirtieth Legion, or others with their roots in the region. The stories mostly combine elements of adventure and history, and generally illustrate not a crucial historical event, but a time of change in British society resulting from or leading to one. The characters from the ancient and medieval past usually speak with a clear formality that avoids the extremes of being too archaic to be easily comprehensible, or jarringly slangy and 'modern', which would now sound excessively dated itself.

A number of stories stand out, especially in *Puck of Pook's Hill*. 'Young Men at the Manor' is Sir Richard's tale of Hastings and its aftermath. 'The Knights of the Joyous Venture' is about Sir Richard, his Anglo-Saxon friend Sir Hugh, bearer of Weland's sword, and their voyage to Africa with a band of Danish sea-rovers. The stories of Parnesius and his friend Pertinax tell of fighting Picts and Saxon raiders, while the Jewish physician Kadmiel relates how his strange and lonely act of vengeance and courage drove King John to surrender to his barons and grant Magna Carta, and illustrates the ideals of English law which that charter had come to symbolize by Kipling's day. Each episode has at least one poem at its beginning or end, while some are framed by a poem fore and aft. The poetry itself is extremely memorable, as one would expect from Kipling: *Them that asks no questions isn't told a lie. / Watch the wall, my darling, while the Gentlemen go by!* with its chorus *Five and twenty ponies / Trotting through the dark* – ('A Smuggler's Song' from 'Hal o' the Draft'), or *What is a woman that you forsake her, / And the hearth-fire and the home-acre, / To go with the old grey Widow-maker?* ('Harp Song of the Dane Women' from 'Knights of the Joyous Venture'), or *Mithras, God of the Morning, our trumpets waken the Wall!* ('A Song to Mithras' from 'On the Great Wall').

Rewards and Fairies has never been as popular as *Puck of Pook's Hill*, although it contains some interesting stories. 'The Tree of Justice', Sir Richard's account of Harold Godwinson, not dead at Hastings but an ancient, half-mad beggar, telling his story to Henry I, is one of these. Another is 'The Knife and the Naked Chalk', about the coming of metal-working and the elevation of a man to the status of a god, although some parts of this one may be too metaphysical for many younger children. Another fine story, 'Cold Iron', may be equally confusing due to its allegorical import. There is less action in the stories in *Rewards* than in *Puck*, which also makes the first book the one more likely to engage a modern young reader's attention.

Neither of the two Puck books is as much read as they once

were. Fashions in children's stories change and in these there are too many layers of narrative between the action and the readers for the 'identification' with a child-character so demanded (one might suggest, unnecessarily) in fiction these days. Dan and Una themselves take little active part in the tales; their role is to listen and ask questions. The actual stories focus on others, who are themselves relating events in their own pasts, not experiencing them directly for the reader's vicarious participation. Despite this, there is an enduring interest in the stories. Eager readers will still find in these books, in *Puck of Pook's Hill* especially, the unfashionable romance of history. And, to balance the impression of the Edwardian view of girls that Barrie's Wendy might give, it is Una, not Dan, who shoots at Pertinax with a hand-catapult while pretending to be a Roman legionary.

Selma Lagerlöf (1858-1940)

Selma Lagerlöf was a teacher in Sweden before becoming a successful novelist with *Gösta Berlings Saga* (1891), *Antikris Mirakler* (1897), and *Jerusalem* (1901/1902). Her great work for children was the two-volume story of Nils Holgersson, *Nils Holgerssons underbara resa genom Sverige* (1906-1907). This is often found in English as *The Wonderful Adventures of Nils* and *The Further Adventures of Nils*, or with both books in one volume under the first title. Lagerlöf was the 1909 Nobel Laureate in Literature; she continued writing into the nineteen-thirties, publishing historical fiction and memoirs. Her portrait, quotations from *Gösta Berlings Saga* and *Nils*, and an illustration of Nils and Morten the goose flying over the Swedish countryside, appear on the Swedish twenty-krona banknote.

The two *Nils* books first appeared in English translation in 1907 and 1911, and remained in print in various versions through most of the twentieth century. The story has a didactic purpose, being written as a text for schools. On one level, it is a tour through Swedish geography, history, and natural history, and the English translation by Velma Swanston Howard has actually removed or condensed some of the geographical descriptions, although this may not seem obvious to a reader hefting her one-volume version of the story, which is over five hundred pages.

The title character, Nils Holgersson, is a fourteen-year-old boy who is lazy, disobedient, and cruel to animals. His parents, poor, hard-working cottagers, despair of him. One day, Nils catches an elf in a butterfly net, and when he breaks his promise to let it go, is transformed into a little elf himself. At the same time, a young gander from his parents' flock is being lured to fly away north with the wild geese. Nils ends up carried away with the white gander, Morten. The geese, especially their leader, Akka, initially want to be rid of him, but once he proves a loyal friend they treat him as such, nicknaming him Thumbietot, and each party is able to aid the other on many occasions. The rest of the book consists of Nils' many adventures with the geese, with walking, talking statues, owls, a vengeful fox, bears, kidnapping crows, a little girl, Osa, who is looking for her father, and Gorgo the eagle, among others. Nils also meets a woman writing a schoolbook about Sweden, and relates his adventures to her, providing a story for her book. The experience of being so small and vulnerable changes Nils for the better, and in the end, he returns to the farm, where he is able secretly to help his parents. He regains his own shape when, despite shame at his transformed state, he reveals himself to his mother to save Morten and his mate Dunfin from slaughter.

Although a great deal of the story is concerned with teaching geography and history, and showing the way of life among rich and poor rural Swedes and Lapps in the late nineteenth century, this does not mean the book is lacking in action. However, the long expository passages unrelieved by dialogue or drama may be off-putting for many children. The grim realism of the natural world and rural life, with its sudden deaths, may also be up-setting to younger readers less used to such a degree of reality in today's 'realistic' books, particularly the story of the ailing, elderly dog going willingly to death at his master's hand.

Nils' adventures are gripping, though. He is constantly in peril, which he survives by his own wits and the loyalty of the friends he makes. The overall message of the book, given voice by the goose-leader Akka, is one that remains relevant a century after it was written. She tells Nils, 'If you have learned anything at all from us, Thumbietot, you no longer think that the humans should have the whole earth to themselves.'

Kenneth Grahame (1859-1932)

Kenneth Grahame, whose great work provides many people with their archetype of a contented, leisurely life, was Secretary of the Bank of England from 1898 to 1908. He was also a noted essayist, who espoused a pantheism popular among some artists of the time, seeing in a renewed reverence and respect for nature an antidote to the ills of industrial civilization. Grahame's first collection of essays and stories was *Pagan Papers* (1893); this contained some fiction about a family of children which, with additional material, became the book *The Golden Age* in 1895. Its sequel, *Dream Days* (1898), contained the story 'The Reluctant Dragon', which tells of an amiable dragon, his friend the Boy, and St. George. After much persuasion of the dragon, the necessary conflict between him and the saint is staged to appease the fears of the villagers, and the story ends with the saint and the Boy helping the happily tipsy Dragon back from an evening in the village pub. A literary fairy-tale which plays with the conventions of the traditional stories of dragon-slayers for comic effect, 'The Reluctant Dragon', extracted from the novel to stand on its own, is still popular today.

Dream Days cemented Grahame's reputation, not as a children's writer, but as a writer about childhood. Grahame's own childhood, which he mined extensively for his fiction, was spent mostly at school or with his three siblings in his grandmother's strict and apparently unloving household. Grahame married Elspeth Thomson in 1899; they exchanged letters written in imitation rural dialect or in baby-talk, and had only one child, Alastair. Alastair suffered not only from being partially blind, but from his parents' belief in his utter perfection and genius, an illusion which the real world shattered when he finally had to face it at Oxford. Unable to cope, he committed suicide in 1920. The Grahames spent a great deal of their time in Italy after that family tragedy, and Grahame wrote little more of significance.

The Wind in the Willows (1908) is not exactly within the narrower definition of fantasy, being mostly a story with nothing in it of magic or the supernatural. However, despite its location firmly in Edwardian England, Grahame's River is experienced by many as a secondary world in its own right, a place created and separate and eternal. The chapter 'The Piper at the Gates of

Dawn' is the only encounter with the supernatural, offering as it does Ratty's and Mole's mystical, spiritually uplifting encounter with the god Pan and his music.

Wind in the Willows had its genesis in bedtime stories told by Grahame to his son, and it is often suggested that the character of Toad took on many of Alastair's traits. The book begins its story with the Mole, who, fed up with his spring cleaning, runs away one day and encounters the Water Rat. His new friend introduces him to the joys of 'messing about in boats', to the River generally, and to his friends, the gruff and gentlemanly Badger and the irresponsible and irrepressible Mr. Toad. Their assorted adventures are often precipitated by their feelings of responsibility for the selfish, vain, and impulsive Toad, who takes up caravaning, steals a motor-car, escapes from prison disguised as a washerwoman, and loses his ancestral home to an invasion of weasels and stoats from the Wild Wood. The epic battle to recapture Toad Hall, and the ensuing banquet, lead to a reformation on the part of Toad which it is hard to believe can last, even though he makes it to the end of the book without any backsliding.

A stage version simplifying the story, called *Toad of Toad Hall*, was written, with Grahame's approval, by A.A. Milne in 1930. Although Grahame wrote no sequels himself, animal-fantasy author William Horwood did so for the publisher HarperCollins in the nineteen-nineties. His continuations, *The Willows in Winter* (1993), *Toad Triumphant* (1995), and *The Willows and Beyond* (1996), are in prose that is a fair imitation of Grahame's style. They take the story, with an unreformed and unrepentant Toad, through to another generation of River-dwellers as in the end, Grahame's characters age, die one by one, and pass 'Beyond'. Some will enjoy these; others will be strongly resistant to the idea of an author's world and characters being carried on by anyone else, not to mention actually being *ended*. There is a certain presumption and effrontery in killing off another author's people.

The Wind in the Willows has been illustrated by various artists, but E.H. Shepard's drawings for the 1931 edition are generally the ones that people think of as the classics. Shepard (1879-1976), one of the foremost children's book illustrators of the first half of the twentieth century and most famous for his illustrations of A.A. Milne's *Winnie-the-Pooh*, managed to deal with the inconsistencies of size in the animal characters throughout the book quite well, showing them vaguely child-sized when interacting with humans, horses, and cars, without straining the viewer's belief in their animal-ness.

Ever since its publication, critics have been uncertain as to whether to call *The Wind in the Willows* a child's book or an adult's. Representatives of both readerships have claimed it, and will continue to do so. It is a book that either enthrals a particular reader or does not; there seems little middle ground. Part of the reason for this is that the characters are human adults in animal guise, living in a child's ideal and idyll of adulthood. The Mole, Ratty, and Mr. Toad are boys playing at being grown-ups, or grown-ups living life as they thought they would when they were boys. It is this very quality that so thoroughly engages the imaginations of some, and leaves others uninterested. For those who are captured by it, *The Wind in the Willows* becomes, like so much of the best fantasy, something to read over and over again, as both child and adult.

Walter de la Mare (1873-1956)

Walter de la Mare is much better known as a children's poet than a fantasist. Collections such as *Songs of Childhood* (1902), *The Listeners and Other Poems* (1912), *Peacock Pie* (1913), and *Come Hither* (1923) ensured his reputation as a poet, but he also wrote a number of adult novels. De la Mare worked as a clerk for the Anglo-American Oil Company until 1908, when he was able to devote himself entirely to writing due to a pension from the Civil List. He was married to Elfrida Ingpen in 1899, a marriage which, in contrast to that of many other great children's writers of the era, seems to have been quite happy. They had four children. His prose for children consisted of a number of story collections, including *Told Again* (1927), which was retellings of fairy-tales.

De la Mare's most outstanding contribution to children's fantasy, however, is *The Three Mulla-Mulgars* (1910), which was later retitled *The Three Royal Monkeys*. In some ways, it signalled a new direction in children's fantasy. It is not a retelling of a fairy-tale or legend, nor a game played with fairy-tale conventions like *Prince Prigio*, and it is not a story about children in the real or a secondary world, interacting with the fantastic, or supernatural, like *The Princess and the Goblin* or *The Gold of Fairnilee*. It is a heroic quest, a romance in the medieval style, set in an imagined world, one with its own peoples, languages, culture, and mythology, and as such, it has a place among the headwaters of one of the most significant streams of modern fantasy. It is also one of the earliest books in a tradition of which Brian Jacques' *Redwall* is the best-known modern example: high fantasy in which the protagonists are animals.

De la Mare's imagined world is shaped on the bones of the African continent and rubs shoulders with the real, as shown by the person of Andy Battle, the English sailor, but it is not our Africa. It is the Forest of Munza-mulgar, and the Valleys of Tishnar, and the Arakkaboa Mountains. It is a world overseen by the goddess Tishnar, peopled by Mulgars (or monkeys) of many kinds, and Coccadrillos (crocodiles), Zevveras or Horses of Tishnar (zebras), leopards, witch-hares, Ephelantoes (elephants), Gungas (gorillas), Jack-Alls, and Oomgars (humans).

The hero of the story is Nod, the youngest of three brothers. His father, Seelem, was a prince of the royal or Mulla-mulgars, who left his home, married a forest monkey, and had three sons. Eventually, Seelem sets off to visit his homeland once more, and never returns. After their mother's death the three young princes decide to journey to their uncle Assasimmon's kingdom themselves. The two elder princes, Thumb and Thimble, are both protective and mocking of their little brother Nod, who, though terribly naive and trusting, is also a Nizza-neela, 'who has magic in him'. It is he who is entrusted by their mother with their father's treasure, the Wonder-stone, a powerful jewel with which he can summon the aid of the goddess Tishnar.

The brothers encounter many hardships on their journey. They run into trouble with wild pigs and a fisher-Gunga. They are captured by the mound-dwelling, flesh-eating Minimuls, from whom Nod rescues them on the very day of the feast at which they are to be the main course. Separated from his brothers, the wounded Nod is cared for by Mishcha the witch-hare, then, when he sets out again, captured by an Oomgar, Andy Battle. He lives with the English sailor as a friend, learning some of his language and his songs, and saving him from the Nameless,

Immanâla, the Queen or Beast of Shadows, before resuming his quest with Thumb and Thimble. The brothers quarrel, fall out, make up, mock one another, are tempted to give up their journey, and suffer all the friction to be expected between heroes on such a quest. They are aided in their crossing of the mountains by the Môh-mulgar, or Men of the Mountains, and begin to hear rumours that their father may have gone that way. They battle eagles and strange illusions. Nod meets a water-midden or water-nymph, servant of Tishnar, and nearly loses the Wonder-stone to her – he has already lost and recovered it several times in the course of his quest. They build rafts to sail along an underground river whose waters bring sleep, and finally reach the beautiful valleys of Tishnar and their uncle's kingdom.

The landscape of this story is strange and wonderful. The three Mulla-mulgars move in a natural world of physical dangers, of accident and illness and predators, as well as a supernatural of ghosts and spirits and magic. They are grand and heroic, foolish and endearing, and are always, underneath it all, monkeys, though they walk upright (being royal monkeys) and cook their food. The names of the various species and other words in Mulgar-language quickly come to seem natural. Most are easily deciphered, like Ephelantoes, or are explained when first encountered. The story moves with a rapid pace from event to event, magic saves them only in direst need, but never makes things easy. In the end, their courage, determination, and wits are what see the three brothers and their companions through to the Valleys of Tishnar.

It is very surprising that *The Three Mulla-Mulgars* is not better known. Unfortunately, it does not currently seem to be available in any reasonably-priced edition meant for children's reading. This is a book well worth seeking out from a library or in a second-hand book-store. It certainly deserves more recognition as a classic of children's fantasy literature.

L. Frank Baum (1856-1919)

American L. Frank Baum was an extremely prolific writer, who published a wide variety of children's fiction under at least seven pseudonyms, including 'Floyd Akers' and 'Edith van Dyne'. He was at various times an actor, playwright, journalist, and travelling salesman, and worked in his family's oil business. *The Wonderful Wizard of Oz* grew out of bedtime stories he told his four sons.

The Wonderful Wizard of Oz (1900) is, in fact, the first of fourteen *Oz* books by Baum. He also wrote other fantasies that connect with Oz in tone, geography, or spirit, such as *Queen Zixi of Ix* (1905), in which a young boy unexpectedly becomes king and his sister's wishing-cloak causes havoc in his kingdom. *The Sea Fairies* (1911) and *Sky Island* (1912) are set in California, and feature the adventures of a young girl, Trot, and her friend Cap'n Bill. Both are to some degree explorations of radical and whimsical ideas about government; as fantasies they are as engaging as the *Oz* books. Trot and Cap'n Bill find their way into Oz in *The Scarecrow of Oz* (1915). The last of Baum's fourteen *Oz* books, *Glinda of Oz* (1920) appeared posthumously, and the series was then continued by a number of writers. Ruth Plumly-Thompson wrote twenty-one more, and four were written in the forties by John R. Neill, who had been the illustrator for most of the original series. Others have written *Oz* books too, right into the nineteen-eighties.

Everyone is familiar with the plot of *The Wonderful Wizard of Oz* from the movie, although the book contains an entire second journey by the heroes to find the land of Glinda the Good, but other *Oz* books are not so well known. *The Marvelous Land of Oz* (1904) is typical in its mix of old and new characters and in Baum's continual development of the history of his world. In *The Marvelous Land*, the boy Tip runs away from his guardian, the witch Mombi. With him goes a wooden, pumpkin-headed man and a sawhorse, both animated by the Powder of Life. They arrive in the Emerald City during a revolution of girls led by General Jinjur. Eventually, with the Scarecrow and the Tin Woodman, they travel to the south to ask for aid from Glinda the Good. She is reluctant to help the Scarecrow, who inherited the throne from the usurping Wizard of the first book. Since the Scarecrow is willing to turn over the crown to the rightful heir, Princess Ozma, if she can be found, Glinda and her army of young women return to the Emerald City with Tip and his friends. Glinda's women are real soldiers, not dilettantes like Jinjur's, and quickly restore order. Glinda defeats old Mombi the witch, the true enemy, and learns from her what happened to baby Ozma: she was transformed into a boy. Tip is dismayed to discover he is a girl, and a fairy princess at that, but is eventually resigned to his restoration, and as Princess Ozma, attacks and captures the still-defiant Jinjur and her officers in the palace, ending the war and becoming ruler of all Oz.

Baum's narrative style is simple and direct, his language undemanding. His characters are always very active participants in their adventures. Dorothy, who appears in many of the books after the first, is a rather more assertive, curious, and practical young lady than the movie might lead one to expect, accepting all her adventures with little fear. By the final book, *Glinda of Oz*, she is a member of Ozma's council, and accompanies her on an important mission to negotiate a peace between two warring peoples. Many of Baum's main characters are girls. They explore, rule, lead armies, act as diplomats, and always use their heads in a crisis. There is little introspection or complexity to the personalities, but every chapter introduces some new event or invention.

Inventive is perhaps the best word for Baum's magic. Much of his magic and fantasy is not of the natural world, but of the manufactured. Creatures such as the Scarecrow, Tik-Tok, Jack Pumpkinhead, and the Sawhorse are made things given life by one means or another. Magic and technology go together in Baum, as in the Skeezer city in *Glinda of Oz*, where the mechanism to control the domed city is commanded by a magic word. There are bizarre and fantastic invented peoples, talking animals, and fairies who are more or less humans possessing inherent magic, but no nymphs, dryads, gods or demons. Magic generally does not arise out of nature in Oz, or persist from the ancient past. Oz is in this quite a contrast to most modern fantasies, which nearly always portray magic as either supernatural and connected with divinities of some sort, or arising from a spiritually-perceived natural world, or something ancient. In Oz, magic is very un-mystical and sometimes seems closer to chemistry.

As the *Oz* series progresses, more characters, both heroes and villains, are introduced. Not all the characters appear in every book, though. Adventures happen to different people, in different parts of Oz. When characters from previous books reappear, or when some event is a result of past Oz history, Baum quickly reintroduces the person or fact, so it is not necessary to read the books in order, or to be familiar with the whole series to enjoy even the last story. However, each book adds something new to the history of Oz, introducing new characters and new wonders, which may give the *Oz* books renewed appeal to series-conscious young readers.

Children's fantasy during the first years of the twentieth century encompassed a broader landscape than previously. Fantasy could be about 'real' children playing; it no longer had to have a weighty intent shaping the course of its plot, or to happen in a fairy-tale reality. Writers like Nesbit, Barrie, and even Grahame used it to explore an idealized childhood, to write about children (in Barrie's case boys, in Grahame's adult animals) freed of adult responsibilities. Even Badger, the Water Rat and Mole deal only with the ageless care of friends for a friend, in chasing after Toad. Fantasy still provided an ideal vehicle to teach by carrying protagonist and reader to a new perspective on the world, as in Lagerlöf's *Nils* and Kipling's stories about Puck, while the creation of rich and complex secondary worlds became an important part of children's fiction, with one of the early immortal secondary worlds being offered in Baum's Oz. De la Mare revived Romance, returning to the structure of the medieval quest and its underlying presentation of the maturation, education, or spiritual development of the hero. The narrative style became generally more direct, with fewer authorial digressions; the prose of this era is generally less 'old-fashioned' sounding to the average young reader now than that of the previous century. By this time, most of the types of fantasy which children's literature contains had appeared; nearly all that the twentieth century would offer was in some combination of these traditions.

VI
The Wars and Between, 1914-1950

The 'Great War' of 1914-1918 changed European and North American society irrevocably. It accelerated the pace of technological and social change, but even more than that, it changed the way people felt about the world. Society could no longer be counted on to continue in its old patterns. Many believed that those old patterns were flawed and in need of change; others found the rapid change and apparent instability of society something to regret or fear, and looked to the period before the First World War, or even before the Industrial Revolution, as a lost golden time, when the world was orderly and comprehensible.

In England, where most children's fantasy continued to be written and published, elementary education was mandatory until the age of thirteen; the 1918 Education Act raised the school-leaving age to fourteen, although it was still a two-tiered education system even at the elementary level, with private schools for those who could afford them, and at best mediocre publicly-funded schools that were often extremely over-crowded. As a result of the war, women in Great Britain gained the right to vote under certain conditions; by 1928 their right to do so was equal to that of men. Medicine, hygiene, and housing conditions improved, and average family sizes decreased, while the infant mortality rate in 1922 was half what it had been in 1900. Church attendance declined, while people left the cities and industrial towns for new suburbs, in part due to the great increase in the number of automobiles and buses. Although the number of people who could be called 'middle class' increased, class differences remained, fostered in part by the sharply-divided education system. There was, however, more social mobility, as more working class people approached a middle class lifestyle. The average family's standard of living increased. Socialism made itself felt, both in labour movements and in intellectual circles. Radio and the BBC 'voice' contributed to the standardisation of spoken English, lessening the differences between regional dialects. By the nineteen-thirties, newspaper circulation had increased dramatically and the cinema was the favourite form of entertainment. Thrillers and detective stories were the popular literature, while 'literary' writers examined themes of social upheaval and instability. The Depression caused wide unemployment and yet, for most people, the standard of living remained better than it had been before the First World War, miners being the exception; the battles between miners and mine-owners dominated the nation and the economy, providing the keynote for the decade in Great Britain just as the devastating drought on the prairies and the sufferings of farmers did in North America.

In 1939, the Second World War began, bringing terrible hardship and suffering. It also affected book publishing materially, since paper rationing was introduced in Britain in 1940 and not lifted until 1949, while the vast destruction of the Blitz damaged or obliterated many publishers' stocks and premises – the blocks from which the illustrations were to be printed, as well as some of the original drawings, for Arthur Ransome's *The Big Six* were one such literary casualty in 1940 (Brogan 373, 375). The hard times did not end with the end of the war, as rationing, shortages, and rebuilding continued through the late forties and into the fifties. Potato and bread rationing were not lifted until halfway through 1948, clothes rationing in 1949, petrol in 1950, sugar, eggs, cheese, butter, and margarine in 1953, while meat was not derationed until June 1954, almost fifteen years after the war's beginning. The Second World War effected a second great change in how people saw the world; the fifties and the thirties were very far apart, just as the twenties and the eighteen-nineties were.

In children's books, the period between the wars was a great age of realism. The most significant contribution to children's literature, other than *The Hobbit*, was Arthur Ransome's *Swallows and Amazons* (1930) and its sequels, one of which, *Pigeon Post* (1936), won the first Carnegie Medal. Ransome's extremely realistic yet idyllic books, celebrating plausible, practical, and imaginative adventures in the outdoors, inspired many to imitate him, and books of holiday adventures became standard fare, although few writers managed to keep their plots so much within the bounds of possibility as most of Ransome's. Smugglers and spies were prone to appear in many 'realistic' children's adventure stories, under the influence of adult thrillers and mysteries as well as that of current events. Enid Blyton's perennially-popular *Famous Five* series, the first of which was published in 1942, is of this latter sort of 'realism', as were many of her other books. Captain W.E. Johns' *Biggles* appeared in the early thirties and flew through both wars and 102 books, not hanging up his goggles until the seventies, joined in Johns' output by Biggles' female counterpart, 'Worrals of the WAAF', in 1941. School stories, nearly always set in boarding schools, were also extremely common through the twenties, thirties, and forties, though that genre had first become popular in the nineteenth century.

Fantasy did not fall by the wayside, though few of the children's fantasy works of this era (Tolkien excluded) are as universally familiar as *Alice, Peter Pan and Wendy*, or *The Wizard of Oz*. Nonetheless, some excellent fantasies were written, and many remain in print.

Norman Lindsay (1879-1969)

Norman Lindsay was an Australian artist, editorial cartoonist, and novelist. *The Magic Pudding* (1918) is his only children's fantasy of note. It was written in part as a distraction for himself from the war, and in part because it had occurred to Lindsay that children would rather have stories about food than fairy-tales. The feast scene in *Through the Looking-Glass,* where the leg of mutton and the pudding are introduced only to be taken away again (because it would not do to eat something to which you had been introduced), contributed its inspiration. In *The Magic Pudding*, the Puddin', Albert, is quite keen on being eaten, no matter what courtesies have been exchanged with the diner; in fact, he insults those he feels have not eaten enough.

The story begins with a young Koala, Bunyip Bluegum, who leaves home to become a wandering gentleman of leisure. He meets the human Bill Barnacle and the penguin Sam Sawnoff, both retired sailors, and joins their 'noble society of puddin'-owners'. The Puddin' itself can be steak and kidney, jam roll, plum duff, or apple dumpling. It is always a complete basin of food, no matter how many slices are cut and eaten. The threesome, with the cantankerous and truculent Puddin', wander the roads of Australia, pursued by and pursuing the puddin'-thieves, the Possum and the Wombat, masters of disguise (or so the thieves firmly believe). As they travel, the characters break into song and recitation. The Puddin' is stolen back and forth several times, runs away, and gets itself arrested, but our heroes always retrieve it in the end, with cunning and fisticuffs. Finally, realizing that the book is about to end and they will be cut off by the back cover, they decide to settle down, building a tree-house in which to live, complete with 'Puddin' paddock' to keep Albert exercised.

Lindsay illustrated the book himself, and the pictures form a large part of its charm, frequently being referred to by the narrator. However, it is not a picture book in the conventional sense, but a short novel in four 'slices', with extremely lively illustrations which form an essential part of the portrayal of character and events. An animated movie version in 2000, with John Cleese and Sam Neill among the voice actors, did not follow the plot of the original story at all (do not confuse the tie-in book with the real thing). The original book by Lindsay can be difficult to find outside of Australia. However, *The Magic Pudding* has a certain quality of eternal light-heartedness about it, which makes it worth the effort it can take to track down.

A.A. Milne (1882-1956)

Alan Milne was the son of a schoolmaster; he began writing light verse and humorous prose pieces while quite young and was Assistant Editor of *Punch* when only 24. He became a playwright and was a signalling officer during the First World War. While an army instructor, he wrote a play for performance in the camp, which he eventually turned into a comic fantasy novel, *Once on a Time*. His wife, Dorothy de Selincourt, whom he had married in 1913, played the Countess, with whom the historian-narrator appears to be in love in the book version. Their only child, Christopher Robin, was born in 1920. After the war, Milne continued to write plays, some of which were very successful, as well as two adult novels, but all his other writing was eclipsed by *Winnie-the-Pooh* and remains so to this day.

Winnie-the-Pooh is not exactly fantasy, but for many it is one of those worlds that exists, immortal and unchanging in the imagination, forever. The Pooh stories and Milne's poetry for children have been published as two or four books. The two volumes of poetry, light, whimsical, yet with a great depth of perception into a child's outlook on life and always impeccably-crafted, are *When We Were Very Young* (1924) and *Now We Are Six* (1927). They were published in one volume as *The World of Christopher Robin* (1958). The verses introduce children to a world of both nature and the imagination, and give some their first abiding love of poetry.

The stories of Pooh and his friends, the animals and animate toys of the Hundred Acre Wood, are found in *Winnie-the-Pooh* (1926) and *The House at Pooh Corner* (1928), and in one volume as *The World of Pooh* (1957). They are the sort of story that can accompany many readers, first introduced to them as young children, throughout their lives. The individual episodes are intended for reading aloud, and, while not at all overwhelming, nonetheless have a depth of character, complexity of plot, and detail of environment now rare in books meant for young children. Pooh, Piglet, Eeyore, and the rest deal with adventure and misadventure, they explore and imagine and create, in a world that is secure and familiar to them, and yet always on the edge of the unknown. The unfamiliar, in the form of flood, storm, imagined Heffalump, or new arrivals, intrudes and threatens, but is either overcome or incorporated into the Forest and made safe. The stories reassure, but they do not limit.

Both the poetry and the Pooh books have line drawings by E.H. Shepard; the landscapes are particularly beautiful and evocative. *The World of Pooh* and *The World of Christopher Robin* feature additional colour plates by Shepard. A 1991 edition of the four-volume set features 'colourized' versions of the original pen and ink drawings; the overly bright added colour detracts from the beauty of the originals, not resembling the Shepard watercolours of the nineteen-fifties in either subtlety or precision. *The World of Pooh* and *The World of Christopher Robin*, with black and white illustrations unaltered and Shepard's supplementary colour plates, happily do remain in print.

Once on a Time (1917), like Milne's plays and other fiction, has been overshadowed by Pooh and almost forgotten, although

NAL/Signet reissued it as an adult mass-market paperback fantasy in 1988. It is intended for an older audience than *Winnie-the-Pooh*, having its origins, as mentioned above, in a play for adults. It is of a type with *The Rose and the Ring* or *Prince Prigio*, being set in a fairy-tale world where the artefacts of courtly fairy-tales are taken for granted. The whole thing begins with a pair of seven-league boots acquired by the King of Barodia, whose carefully worked-out route for his daily constitutional takes him over the King of Euralia's outdoor breakfast-table, resulting eventually in a declaration of war. The war is bloodless and meticulously organized; it ends when the King of Euralia cuts off the King of Barodia's whiskers one night. Most of the story happens 'back in Euralia', where Princess Hyacinth has been left in charge. The conniving Countess Belvane takes over, mostly so that she can fraudulently obtain money to distribute largess to the masses, an occupation that gives her extreme gratification. Hyacinth asks a neighbouring prince, Udo, for help, but Belvane makes use of a magic ring's power to grant one bad wish. When Udo shows up he has the head of a rabbit and the tail of a lion, with the body of a woolly lamb in the middle. He is also intolerably self-centred and useless. Hyacinth and the man she has fallen in love with, Udo's companion Coronel, put Belvane in her place on their own; simply outwitting her once is enough for Hyacinth, who knows her father loves the Countess. On the king's return the two couples are married and a disenchanted Udo returns to his own land.

The whole story is told and commented on by a nameless narrator, an historian supposedly working from an earlier history by 'Roger Scurvilegs', which he feels does not do justice to the Countess. Some of the humour may be too dry and ironic for younger readers to notice, but older children and teens (especially girls) who do not demand their fantasy be limited to struggles against grim fate will find *Once on a Time* a light-hearted, comic, and romantic fairy-tale with an engaging heroine.

Eleanor Farjeon (1881-1965)

Eleanor Farjeon was the daughter of a largely unremembered

Victorian novelist, Benjamin Farjeon. She and her three brothers grew up in a book-filled house, and Farjeon's education consisted of what she could find there; she was never sent to school or given any formal tutoring. She was shy to the point of incapacity outside her family and was in her thirties before she overcame this enough to enter into normal social interactions. She fell in love with the married poet Edward Thomas, who remained her friend, although nothing more, until his death in the First World War; Farjeon never married.

Farjeon may be best remembered these days for the poem or hymn 'Morning Has Broken', but she was an extremely prolific writer of children's stories and poems. Her short stories are usually either fairy-tales or 'realistic' stories about children, the latter tending to be in a slightly over-sweet vein. The settings range from the world of medieval Romance, through a fairy-tale eighteenth century, to the Second World War. They vary greatly in their appeal to modern children; some, like, the nostalgic and sentimental book *Kaleidoscope* (1928), or *Perkin the Peddler* (1932), a whimsical alphabet book in which the peddler recounts short tales to explain place names, are not terribly gripping. Others contain more enduring stories. All her work, however, is equally rich in poetic language and a love of the countryside, of the rhythms of nature, and of an imaginary pre-industrial agrarian idyll.[*] This longing for an idealized rural life on Farjeon's part is despite, or perhaps because of, the fact that she lived much of her life in London and its suburbs, except for a brief period after the First World War spent in Sussex, the setting for the *Martin Pippin* books.

Martin Pippin in the Apple Orchard (1921) is an idiosyncratic book with an small but devoted following found as far afield as Japan. In it, the minstrel Martin Pippin wanders by a hedge-fenced orchard, in which six milkmaids guard Gillian the

---

[*] 'Anindustrial' would be a more apt word, since, like The Shire of Tolkien's *The Hobbit*, the Sussex of her *Martin Pippin* stories is not meant to be specifically medieval or renaissance, despite Martin Pippin's lute. Both are socially and culturally more like the late eighteenth, the nineteenth or even the pre-war twentieth century; they lack the factories and the negative effects of the Industrial Revolution, but possess its benefits of increased prosperity and, eventually and indirectly, the potential for personal freedoms.

farmer's daughter, who is locked in the well-house, pining away for love. Martin undertakes three missions for Robin Rue, Gillian's tearful and defeatist admirer, the third being to free her. The milkmaids have all quarrelled with men, but they believe Gillian can be cured of love-sickness by hearing six new love-stories, which Martin Pippin is commissioned to provide. These stories form the body of the book, with interludes of songs, games, and talk between Martin and the maids. As a story is told for each of the maids, she is reconciled to love, her quarrel with her lover is shown to be groundless, and Martin wins from her a key to the well-house. In the end, Martin, having obtained the six keys, frees Gillian to go to Robin Rue (though in fact, the locks are so rusted she must escape by swinging over the wall, as she could have at any point, had she really desired to be united with the lachrymose Robin). The six milkmaids run off into the night with their young farmhands. When Martin sets out on his travels again, he finds Robin Rue still in tears, now because he believes himself not good enough for Gillian, a judgement with which Martin is forced to agree. Gillian, meanwhile, has been waiting by the road for Martin to follow her. She tells him she wept in the well-house not for love, but for lack of it, and they set off together into the Sussex countryside.

The stories told by Martin Pippin are fairy-tales, often strange and powerful fantasies. One, 'The King's Barn', is the story of a king who has nothing in the world but a barn and horse, and who apprentices himself to the Lad, a young smith who is actually the beautiful woman the king has glimpsed bathing in a forest pool. Another, 'Open Winkins', tells of a fey woman who lures and bespells four of five brothers, but is courted by the eldest, who frees her from the evil that compels her. Martin stops each tale at the point of failure or tragedy, since the maids denounce the idea of love as an ideal ending, affecting disdain for men and for dreaming. Each time, he allows their criticism to persuade him to continue to a happier conclusion. The juxtaposition of these elegant tales with the more homely romance of Gillian and Martin, and of the six maids and their swains, creates a book that can be read straight through as a novel, or dipped into as a collection of shorter tales.

The most likely audience for *Martin Pippin in the Apple Orchard* these days would be adult fantasy and fairy-tale readers, and pre-teen or teenage girls. (It was treated as an adult book when first published.) Since the stories are more concerned with emotional drama than action, they are less likely to hold the attention of very young children, and many teenage boys are rather resistant to anything that can so obviously be labelled as 'love-stories'. *Martin Pippin* will not appeal to all tastes, but it nonetheless retains an enduring magic, and deserves to be far more widely known than it is. Martin's stories, read as romantic fantasy or literary fairy-tales, have a pre-Raphaelite air to them, while the down-to-earth characters of the milkmaids and the minstrel Martin Pippin himself, and the lovingly-depicted orchard, with its apples, wildflowers, well-house, swing, and ducks, are immortal.

A sequel, *Martin Pippin in the Daisy Field* (1937) follows the same format, as Martin Pippin talks with and tells stories to six little girls and a baby in a basket. The girls are the milkmaids' daughters; the baby, who in the end is only an imagining of his own or a glimpse of the future, is or will be his and Gillian's. The stories in *Daisy Field* are not romantic fairy-tales as in *Apple Orchard*, but stories intended for younger children, such as 'The Tantony Pig', about a pig and Saint Anthony. Though the little girls of the framing narrative lack the distinct personalities of their mothers, the six milkmaids, the stories themselves are good ones for reading aloud.

The Old Nurse's Stocking Basket (1931) is a linked collection for even younger listeners. In it, Old Nurse tells a tale to four young children every night as she darns their stockings. The stories are all quite short and simple, and each contains a touch of the fantastic. Among other tales, to all of which Old Nurse claims a personal connection, a tiny Princess of China elopes with a butterfly, a Prince of India's heart is hidden in a blue lotus, a young Duke switches places with a rag-picker's son, and Neptune's baby is won back from a sea-captain's spoiled daughter.

The tales in *The Little Bookroom* (1955) are for older readers than those in *Stocking Basket*. They are a selection of Farjeon's stories chosen by herself, and reflect a variety of types. The book won both the Carnegie Medal and the International Hans Christian Andersen Award for 1955. Many of the stories are not fantasy, but are a romantic realism, like that of the orphaned Second World War evacuee, labelled a sullen troublemaker, who finally

100

finds a new family in 'San Fairy Ann', or the sentimental 'And I Dance My Own Child', about a little girl looking after her ancient and senile great-grandmother. A few stand out as fine specimens of the literary fairy-tale. 'The Clumber Pup' tells how an orphan woodcutter, Joe Jolly, saves a pup from being drowned, takes over the job of the injured King's Woodcutter (who turns out to be a ghost), and courts and eventually marries a princess. 'Westwoods' is about the King of Workaday's search for a bride, and how he finds his love in the servant girl Selina, who shows him the magic of Westwoods beyond the fence, where all the dreams of childhood go. 'The Little Dressmaker' is about Lotta the apprentice dressmaker, who makes and models fine dresses for the three ladies a king is supposed to choose between for his bride. Each time, Lotta dances with the young king's footman before handing over the beautiful dress. In the end, she models the wedding dress and is swept off and married by the footman. Just when the reader, familiar with this sort of tale, assumes she must have married the disguised king, it turns out the king did not want to be married at all, and sent his footman to dance with his prospective brides. The king remains single, while Lotta and her footman live happily ever after.

Farjeon is not very highly regarded any more and can be very difficult to find even in libraries, which is a loss to today's readers. Her stories about children are frequently overly-sentimental, but her fantasies have more of an edge to them and are more enduring. There is always the threat of misfortune and potential disaster, there are always some shadows and darkness hovering around the edges. Despite this potential to still appeal to today's fantasy audience, regrettably little by Farjeon remains in print.

Hugh Lofting (1886-1947)

Hugh Lofting was an animal-loving civil engineer who worked in South America and West Africa until 1912, when he moved to the United States, married an American, and began making a living writing. In 1916 he joined the Irish Guards and fought in France. The sufferings of the horses in warfare were a part of what inspired his creation of the character of Doctor Dolittle, a doctor for animals who was capable of discussing his patients' symptoms with them. Another aspect of the Doctor, his frequent exasperation or even anger with human cruelty and intolerance, could also be attributed to Lofting's war experience.

Lofting wrote one largely-forgotten fantasy for children. *The Twilight of Magic* (1931) is a medieval fantasy in which twins Giles and Anne try to solve their father's financial problems with the aid of a shell that lets the listener hear whatever anyone is saying about them. They sell the shell to the king, who through it discovers his cousin's treason; as a reward Giles is knighted and goes to court. Much of the story is about his adventures as an adult, in the midst of court intrigue. *The Twilight of Magic* is neither a bad story nor a great one. It is more convincing when dealing with the adult Giles than with the young children. Giles takes on added interest as a man, in love with the bride of his friend the king, struggling with the temptation to betrayal. There is a certain lack of unity in the book; some incidents, like the haunted inn in which Giles and Anne find themselves the hosts one evening, seem to have nothing to do with the rest, and the significance of the benevolent witch Agnes and her cats never becomes clear.

Lofting's thirteen *Doctor Dolittle* books, of which he was also the illustrator, are much greater works, and can claim to be fantasy, of a sort. They contain no magic, and all their wonders are given a 'scientific' grounding, however unrealistic that science, but they have always appealed to the reader looking for an imaginative otherness. After the first book, *The Story of Doctor Dolittle* (1920), in which Doctor Dolittle learns to speak with animals from his parrot Polynesia, becomes an animal rather than a human doctor, and travels to Africa to cure an epidemic among monkeys, the books are narrated by his assistant, young Tommy Stubbins. There are travels to distant places, run-ins with pirates, a voyage inside the shell of the last Great Glass Sea-Snail, imprisonments and escapes. The most fantastic adventure, involving a trip to the moon, is spread over three books: *Doctor Dolittle's Garden* (1927), *Doctor Dolittle in the Moon* (1928), and *Doctor Dolittle's Return* (1933).

Doctor Dolittle's Garden introduces some elements that will be important in the moon story: the Doctor is studying insect languages and Chee-Chee the monkey tells his grandmother's story of Otho Bludge the prehistoric artist 'in the days before there was a Moon'. Then they play 'Blind Travel' one evening, in which the destination for a voyage is chosen by opening and stabbing at the atlas with a pencil, eyes shut. Their friend the African Prince Bumpo hits the moon. Fate seems to be conspiring to send them there, because a giant moon moth lands in the garden, sent to ask the Doctor for help. He, Polynesia, and Chee-Chee, with Tommy as a stowaway, travel to the moon on the moth's back, using flowers called moon-bells to breathe as they pass through the airless Dead Belt between the two worlds.

In the Moon begins as they land. The moon is an amazing place, peopled with giant birds and insects, and intelligent plants which communicate using scents as well as semaphore-like signals and sounds made by angling branches into the unchanging wind. All live in harmony, governing themselves in a great council. *Doctor Dolittle in the Moon* belongs to the tradition of Utopian books; it is a world imagined in intricate detail, demonstrating another way of life as a comment on our own society. Great attention is also paid to such details as differences in gravity, the effect of a nearer horizon, and how plants, without any sound-making organs, might communicate, all of which adds to the realism within the story of this fantasy moon. Long before the Apollo astronauts witnessed it for the first time, the Doctor's expedition watches the earth hanging in the sky above them. Lofting illustrated this, as had Tolkien for his story *Roverandom* (written 1925, published 1998, see Chapter VII). The imagination in both cases anticipated that moving image by a good few decades.

Tommy Stubbins is a faithful chronicler of the scientific expedition, but there is plenty of story too, as the explorers travel, secretly observed by birds and insects, unable to find out who it was that sent for them, making new and astonishing discoveries every day. They finally discover that the prehistoric artist Otho Bludge is now the giant Moon Man, in need of the Doctor's medical attention. Then Tommy is kidnapped and sent back to earth. *In the Moon* ends with Tommy, the dog Jip, and the other animals who stayed in Puddleby-On-The-Marsh watching the sky, wondering if the Doctor, Polynesia, and Chee-Chee will ever return.

The return is left for *Doctor Dolittle's Return*. After the Doctor, Polynesia, and Chee-Chee come back, the Doctor relates more of what happened on the Moon after Tommy was sent home: Otho Bludge kept them prisoner so the Doctor could treat his rheumatism. When the Moon Man fell very ill and the Doctor saved his life, Otho Bludge repented, allowing them to go home on a Mammoth Locust. The book ends with the Doctor determined to find the secret of everlasting life and the harmonious coexistence that the Moon creatures seem to enjoy.

Some elements of the earlier books are potentially offensive, such as the African Prince Bumpo in *The Story of Doctor Dolittle*, who at that point wishes he were white and is tricked, with a potion they claim will effect this, into letting the Doctor and his friends escape prison. But Lofting is not overtly racist as many writers of his day were. Bumpo's father is king of an independent country and is angry because the last white man who came to his kingdom destroyed the environment, killed elephants, and fled; the king assumes the Doctor will be like that other and so imprisons him in accordance with his law forbidding white men to travel through the kingdom. He is a short-tempered man with a just grievance unjustly taken out on the heroes. The conflict is presented as one of sovereign versus foreign trespasser rather than as a matter of race, except incidentally. In *The Voyages of Doctor Dolittle* (1922), which in 1923 won the second-ever Newbery Medal, Prince Bumpo reappears as an Oxford undergraduate and is invited to join the Doctor's voyage to the floating Spidermonkey Island, to visit the great South American Indian naturalist Long Arrow. In this book Bumpo is very much an equal among the rest of the Doctor's friends, and his comic misuse and invention of grandiose vocabulary is most likely meant to denote his status as a young university student, full of undigested information. Unfortunately for the book's acceptance today, the parrot Polynesia uses the word 'nigger' on several occasions. No other character treats the prince as anything but a friend and equal, so the derisive language applied by Polynesia to both Bumpo and the natives of the island reflects badly on the parrot, not on Lofting. (Polynesia also frequently and comically assumes a degree of knowledge she does not possess, when condescendingly lecturing Tommy, adding to the impression that she is someone who unjustly holds herself superior to the Doctor's friends.) Polynesia, in short, is abrasive and vulgar; Lofting shows this by having her speak in ways the Doctor and Tommy never would, using language which, although belittling and contemptuous even then, was not regarded as so deeply offensive in the twenties as it has come to be now. Placing language within its historical context can be an important part of reading older works of fiction, even for children. However, the three books which span the moon adventure present no difficulties of this sort, and should be more widely known than they have become.

Lofting's *Doctor Dolittle* stories, though obscured by later movies that did not do them justice (or, in the case of the later movies, which had no connection with the novels at all beyond the name and the concept of talking to animals), and despite the sprawling of the moon-story over three books, remain utterly engaging. His prose is deft, his narrative full of event, even when it is real or invented natural wonders rather than crisis and action that are the focus. Lofting's original illustrations add to the pleasure. His figures are cartoonish, but the lines of the landscapes (particularly in the lunar pictures), and the compositions, are excellent. The books have been reissued in various editions and remain fairly easy to find.

John Masefield (1878-1967)

John Masefield's parents had both died by the time he was twelve; he was sent to sea by his guardian aunt and uncle while still in his early teens. At seventeen, after more than two years in merchant ships, he had deserted in New York. He lived as a vagrant and farmworker in the United States for a time, but eventually worked his passage home to England, suffering from malaria and tuberculosis. He then worked as a clerk while pursuing his childhood ambition to write. When his poetry began to sell he turned to writing full time, becoming a book reviewer in order to support a family; he married Constance Crommelin in 1903. His most famous poem, 'Sea Fever', appeared in *Salt-Water Ballads* (1902). In addition to poetry, Masefield wrote adult adventure novels and children's historical fiction. He was made Poet Laureate in 1930.

Two of Masefield's books are fantasies for children that deserve the status of classics, though they are not as well known as they deserve to be, in part because their plots unfold in a somewhat confusing manner. *The Midnight Folk* (1927) and *The Box of Delights* (1935) both have as their hero Kay Harker, a wealthy young orphan. Kay lives at Seekings, a rambling old house full of secret passages, ancestral portraits, and stories. Seekings is to some degree inspired by reality; Masefield's grandfather's house, where he spent part of his childhood before his grandfather lost the family money and his own father died, was built in the sixteen-hundreds, and was, especially to a child's perception, a vast and mysterious place, heavy with stories of the past.

In the first book Kay is quite young. He is looked after by an unpleasant governess, Sylvia Daisy Pouncer, and two kindly servants who have told him many stories about the history of the house and the countryside, furnishing it with smugglers, highwaymen, murders, ghosts, and treasure, and both enthralling and terrifying him. The narrative in *The Midnight Folk* is complex and dreamlike; Kay passes from the waking world to what seems dream, and back, in a manner that leaves the reader uncertain of what is 'real' and what is only Kay's imagining. Even Kay has doubts, though most of his adventures have tangible results: muddy pyjamas, the discovery of part of Benjamin the highwayman's buried hoard, and in the end, the installation of Caroline Louisa, whom Kay first encounters on one of his night-time adventures, as his guardian.

The plot of *The Midnight Folk* is a search for missing treasure and the piecing together of a mystery. Kay's great-grandfather was entrusted with the treasure's safekeeping by the Archbishop of the island nation of Santa Barbara, but lost it due to mutiny. Others believe he stole it, and are conspiring to recover it. Foremost among these is a coven of witches, and prominent among the witches is Sylvia Daisy Pouncer, Kay's governess. To make matters worse, two of Kay's cats, Greymalkin and Blackmalkin, are allied with the witches, and 'the guards', who should protect the house, have set out to look for the treasure. These twenty-three guards are toys of Kay's, which he thought had been locked away lest they remind him of the past – why he should not be reminded of the past is never said, but he is an orphan, alone in the world. Whether the guards are really toys or not we are never certain.

106

Kay, with Nibbins the loyal cat and the fox Bitem, begins to piece together the history of the treasure. He discovers many secret tunnels and hiding places in and around his home, including the lair of the highwayman Benjamin, and is sidetracked for a time in seeking and recovering this lesser treasure. Kay's other friends, Otter and Water-Rat, get involved, and he comes to know Bat and Blinky the owl, as well as the seedy Rat the cellarman. Kay seems to change without comment between human and animal size. He enters portraits, talks to ghosts, birds, and mermaids, flies with bat-wings and swims with an otterskin, and borrows an invisibility potion, fox-eye spectacles to see in the dark, and one-league shoes from Sylvia Daisy Pouncer's secret closet. He meets a re-formed court of Camelot, whose knights aid the returned guards of Seekings House in searching for the Santa Barbara treasure. Piece by piece, Kay and Nibbins are able to put together the history of the treasure, which has involved mutiny, shipwreck, recovery, burial, discovery, theft, and murder. Kay and various of his allies are captured, or nearly captured, on several occasions, but he always finds a way out. They discover the treasure only hours ahead of the witches, who are led by Abner Brown. Past and present are entangled here as well, for Brown's grandfather was involved in the early stages of the hoard's story. Kay delivers the treasure to the Dictator and Archbishop of Santa Barbara, and Caroline Louisa, who appeared earlier in the story riding a flying black mare, becomes his guardian.

The Box of Delights is the same sort of rapid adventure amid uncertain realities. In it, Kay is a few years older and is returning from boarding school for Christmas. He meets Cole Hawlings, an old Punch and Judy man, who asks him to deliver a warning to a woman he will meet: 'The Wolves are running.' The Wolves that Cole Hawlings warns of are a gang of criminals disguised as members of a theological college, led by none other than the witches Abner Brown and Sylvia Daisy Pouncer of the first book. They are after a little magic box owned by Cole, who is also the medieval philosopher and wizard Ramon Lully, discoverer of the Elixir of Life. The box can make its possessor very small, transport him very quickly, and take him back in time within Europe. It was made by Arnold of Todi, another medieval philosopher, who became trapped in the past while using a similar box.

Kay, using Cole Hawling's box, has various adventures with the ancient god Herne and with a mouse, meets Britons and Romans, witnesses the aftermath of the Trojan War, is captured by pirates of a later time, and marooned on an island with Arnold of Todi. After most of his friends and an entire Cathedral, from the choirboys to the bishop, are captured by the witches, Kay sneaks into the theological college, discovering that Abner Brown intends to flood the dungeon and drown all his prisoners. Kay rescues Cole Hawlings first, and with the help of his magic, they create a boat and boatmen to rescue all the other prisoners as the flood sweeps through. Abner Brown, betrayed by his own men, is drowned, and most of the criminals are captured by the police.

The one major disappointment of *The Box of Delights* lies in the last scene of the book. All of a sudden, Kay wakes up to find the train is just arriving. Caroline Louisa greets him at the station, asking, 'Have you had a nice dream?' It seems best to simply stop reading before then, at the great Christmas celebration of the Cathedral's millennium, which ends with, 'the singing shook the whole building.' It is a closing note much truer to all that has gone before. One really wishes Masefield had made the ending of *The Box of Delights* part of the same world as the rest of the story, the way he did in *The Midnight Folk*, in which fantasy and reality blend so ambiguously and seamlessly from start to finish. The falling back on a trivializing 'it was all a dream' final paragraph is extremely jarring and disappointing, when we know that *The Midnight Folk* was 'real' (and surely the presence of Caroline Louisa herself is the proof of it).

There is a certain disregard for time between the two books, as well. *The Midnight Folk* is obviously meant to be happening at the end of Victoria's reign. 'The Queen' is mentioned several times, and people talk of things their grandfathers told them happened in the first Napoleon's day or earlier. *The Box of Delights*, though, takes place a generation later, in 1935, and rather than smugglers and highwaymen forming the remembered history of the countryside, the talk is of gangsters and Bolsheviks. The criminals use cars that transform into aeroplanes rather than the witches' brooms of the first book, though Abner Brown is still a witch. However, this kind of inconsistency is not the sort of thing most children, fairly unconscious of history, will care about, and each book has internal integrity. Readers may miss Nibbins and Bitem as characters in the second book; human friends, most notably the pistol-wielding, car-stealing little Maria, have largely displaced animals as Kay's comrades, though the shifty cellarman Rat is back from a stint of piracy, now treacherously allied with Abner Brown.

In both books, back in print after a period in which they were very hard to find, Masefield's narrative sweeps the reader into the story at once. He creates a richly-textured and complex world where history, landscape, local legend, popular culture, folklore, and the imaginings of children all combine in one dizzying and credible mosaic. In some ways it recalls *Alice*; anything is possible, within the frame of a certain wild logic. These books are wonderful. They have almost everything: pirates, highwaymen, ghosts, treasure, fairies, knights, animals, gods, witches, and the young hero who encounters them all and emerges triumphant, his world intact.

Beatrix Potter (1866-1943)

Beatrix Potter does not at first seem to belong among the writers between the wars, but rather among the Edwardians. However, her one fantasy novel was written in the late twenties, after she had otherwise given up writing much at all.

Potter was a keen naturalist and artist raised in a very strict, controlling London household. Family holidays in Scotland and the Lake District, and visits to museums and galleries, fuelled her creativity and scientific interests. Her brother escaped to become a farmer and marry, but it seemed likely that she would remain forever trapped as the dutiful middle-class Victorian spinster daughter. However, in 1901, after failing to find a publisher, Potter self-published a story she had written and illustrated for the son of a former governess almost a decade before. *The Tale of Peter Rabbit* was republished the following year by Frederick Warne and, winning immediate popularity, was followed by other stories about animals in human dress, all illustrated in beautiful and accurate detail by herself. Potter became engaged to the publisher's son Norman, despite her parents' disapproval, but he died of leukaemia before they could marry.

Potter's income from royalties was such that she was no longer financially dependent on her parents; she bought Hill Top Farm at Near Sawrey in the Lake District. Hill Top's seventeenth-century farmhouse features in several of her picture books, such as *The Tale of Tom Kitten* (1907) and *The Tale of Jemima Puddle-Duck* (1908). In 1909 she bought a second property in the same area, Castle Cottage, and in 1913 she married the solicitor William Heelis, finally becoming a permanent resident in the north. She became a promoter, breeder, and judge of Herdwick sheep, even then a rare breed, bought more land, and actively supported the National Trust in the Lake District, eventually providing it with over 4,000 acres of wood- and farm-land. (The Trust now owns Hill Top.)

Potter's novel for young children, *The Fairy Caravan* (1929 in the US, 1952 in the UK) lacks the elegant story-cohesion of her picture books, but is enjoyable none the less. It tells of a group of animal travellers in the north of England, although it starts in the Land of Green Ginger, with the guinea pig Tuppenny. He runs away from home and wife to join a troupe of animals who make up 'Alexander and William's Circus'. They travel around the farms of the Lake District, unseen by Big Folk due to the packets of fern seed they carry (fern seed being a traditional means of achieving invisibility). There is a long section, probably uninteresting to younger readers but of greater historical significance now than when it was written, consisting of Herdwick sheep telling about the properties of the breed and the traditions of sheepfarming in what is now Cumbria. There is no real plot to unify the episodic tales and adventures, but the story contains many fine comic character sketches, and the incidents are on the whole entertaining, sprinkled with the dialect of the Lake District. The urge to run away and join the circus has always been appealing. It evokes the possibility of an idyllic wandering through the world, observing the lives of settled folk but distanced from their concerns, part of a secret companionship of the road. *The Fairy Caravan* captures the longing for such a life, which every person feels at some point. Potter illustrated the novel in her characteristic style; the picture of the pig in his costume as a pygmy elephant is particularly memorable, and there are many fine line drawings of the countryside as well.

P.L. Travers (1906-1996)

Pamela Lyndon Travers was born Helen Lyndon Goff in Australia. She was a professional actor from a young age, using Travers as a stage name. At seventeen, she emigrated, working as an actor and dancer in Ireland and England. Her interest in mythology and folklore led her, in the nineteen-thirties, to become a follower of the Russian-born Greco-Armenian mystic George Georgiades, who called himself G.I. Gurdjieff; his movement still has followers today. Like many of his contemporary mystics, Gurdjieff claimed to present philosophies adhering to an Eastern tradition. However, little influence of folklore or philosophy, mystic or otherwise, is discernible in *Mary Poppins*, on which Travers' fame now rests.

Mary Poppins (1934) and *Mary Poppins Comes Back* (1935) are stories about the Banks children, Jane, Michael, the young twins Barbara and John, baby Anabel, and the vain, strict, short-tempered nanny Mary Poppins. She is described as looking rather like a doll, with smooth, glossy black hair and bright red cheeks, and is a descendant or possibly daughter of Noah (the traditional toy ark Noah of brightly-painted wood?) and a cousin to snakes, as well as being related to all sorts of other peculiar people. Mary Poppins does not so much work magic as exude it; around her, the improbable and impossible happen quite matter-of-factly. She and her beau, Bert the matchman and pavement artist, go for tea in the country through one of his pictures, for instance, and her birthday is celebrated by the animals of the zoo with a reversal of roles in which humans are caged and the animals, at peace with one another, roam free. One night she steals the golden stars the children have saved off their gingerbread, helping the older-than-the-world Mrs. Corry and her enormous daughters to paste them in the sky.

The *Mary Poppins* books are meant for younger children and read aloud well, since each chapter is a self-contained story. There is little adventure or drama, and the children have little personality. Their role is to partake of marvels, which Mary Poppins promptly denies to have happened. Sometimes they do not even partake, but merely witness. Travers wrote a number of *Mary Poppins* books, continuing into the nineteen-eighties. All make good read-aloud material for younger children.

Alison Uttley (1884-1976)

Alison Uttley was born Alice Taylor. She won a scholarship to study physics at Manchester University, where she was, in 1906, only the second female honours graduate. She became a science teacher and married, but her husband, James Uttley, died in 1930. To support herself and her son, Uttley began writing. Most of her more than one hundred books were for younger children: the *Little Grey Rabbit*, *Little Red Fox*, *Brown Mouse*, *Tim Rabbit*, and *Sam Pig* series.

Uttley's time-travel novel *A Traveller in Time* (1939) is intended for an older audience. *Traveller* is the story of Penelope Taberner Cameron, a girl of the early twentieth century staying at her great-uncle's farm, which Uttley calls 'Thackers' in the book, but which is an historical place, Dethick, the country manor of the Babington family, birthplace of that Anthony Babington who was executed in 1586 for conspiring to assassinate Elizabeth I. Unlike most time-travel fantasies, in which the time-travel seems primarily a device to make history interesting or 'relevant', Uttley's is a novel about the experience of travelling in time. The story focuses on the character of Penelope, rather than the failed plot to rescue Mary Queen of Scots.

Penelope drifts between past and present like a ghost; she makes a place for herself among her Taberner ancestors, servants of the Babington family. While in the sixteenth century, she has only the most tenuous memories of Thackers in the twentieth and its inhabitants. Over the course of several years she becomes an intimate member of the Babington household, privy to the conspiracies brewing there. At one point she tells Anthony Babington that Mary will be executed, but when she tries to warn Mary Stuart herself that the secret service is reading her letters, she is unheard, only a ghost glimpsed for a moment by the queen. Penelope is unable to effect the outcome of events; the past has happened, even though it is, for the participants, the future. She is forced to witness the slow, fateful unfolding of tragedy, knowing the doom that awaits the Queen of Scotland and Master Anthony Babington, after another failed papist plot yet to come. She also falls in love with Anthony's younger brother Francis, and recognizes the inevitable sorrow in that relationship, as indeed does he. Francis, like the mute kitchen-boy Jude, knows that Penelope belongs to another time and that their love is doomed.

A Traveller in Time is a book rich in imagery; it conveys the rural life of the first decades of the twentieth century as convincingly as it does that of the last half of the sixteenth, with an attention to detail, to the very scents of the place, that makes those times vividly real. The book is hauntingly atmospheric. There is never any hope that the tunnel, by which Mary is supposed to escape imprisonment to Thackers, will succeed, but there is the drama of its secret construction, and of Cousin Arabella's attempt to kill Penelope, believing her to be an agent of the spy-master Walsingham. The house itself is in some ways the central character of the story, a symbol of the continuity of past and present. It changes over time, but it and some of its fittings endure, linking generations of the Taberner family.

This is not a story filled with action, and as such its slow unfolding will not hold the reader who has a short attention span. There is little suspense except for the episode in which Penelope is buried alive in a disused tunnel, since even if the reader knows no history, Penelope does, and her narration leaves no doubt that all the historical figures will come to their fated ends. What this story does most strongly is re-create two pasts, over three hundred years apart, with tangible reality; it is also a wistful, elegiac love story.

Eric Linklater (1899-1974)

Welsh-born Eric Linklater lived much of his childhood in the Orkneys. He intended to become a doctor, but the First World War intervened and he joined the Black Watch. Linklater was hospitalized for several months with a head wound, but recovered fully. After the war he resumed his studies, switching from medicine to literature. He lived for a time in Bombay as assistant editor of *The Times of India*, and travelled widely. During the Second World War he worked for the War Office in public relations. He was a prolific writer of novels and travel books, and continued to travel all his life, though he and his wife had their permanent home in the Orkneys.

The Wind on the Moon (1944), which won the Carnegie Medal for 1944, was originally a story told to Linklater's daughters. It begins as though it is going to be a series of Mary Poppins-like adventures of minor consequence. A complicated chain of events begins with the sisters Dinah and Dorinda, having resolved to be 'naughty', obtaining a magic potion from a wise old witch, transforming themselves to kangaroos, and ending up imprisoned in a zoo. This leads up to the main adventure, in which Dinah and Dorinda, accompanied by two animals they free from the zoo, the Golden Puma and the Silver Falcon, and their dancing-master Mr. Corvo, set out to rescue their father, Major Palfrey, a captive of Count Hulago Bloot, the Tyrant of Bombardy.

The count is both a comic parody of the various fascist dictators in Europe, and realistically terrible. He imprisons and executes those who oppose him, is driven by hatred for all other nations, consumes chocolate peppermint creams by the pound, frequents palm-readers, and like many other fascist tyrants, keeps meticulous records of his victims. Through a combination of resourcefulness and luck, Dinah and Dorinda free the Major from the dungeon, but they are all are captured by the Count and imprisoned.

Their second escape is effected by Notchy and Mr. Stevens, a pair of elderly sappers (military engineers) who have been 'sapping' their way around Europe since the Crimean War, having gone the wrong way at the Battle of Sebastopol. When the escape party encounters the revolver-wielding Tyrant again, the Puma saves their lives, killing the Count but dying at his hand. The others escape and make their way back to England. Soon after there is a revolution in Bombardy, and the grateful people raise a monument to the Golden Puma. Life at home is very dull for Dorinda and Dinah, as they try to be good after all their adventures. One is left hoping there will be more of their carefully-considered naughtiness, but Linklater wrote no sequel.

Although the first couple of chapters seem like a succession of minor whimsies, these are nonetheless entertaining, and the main story is fast-paced, suspenseful, and often funny. *The Wind on the Moon* is a gripping tale once it gets rolling. The heroines are bright, brave, and occasionally subversive as they look at the adult world. What is right, what is expedient, and how what is

right can still be right yet cause much trouble and misunder-
standing, is a recurring theme in the book, illustrated by the case
of the Puma. She pines in captivity, yet free in the Forest of
Weal she preys on farmers' livestock. Since the girls cannot send
her back to Brazil, there is no easy solution.

When it was first published, *The Wind on the Moon* must
have seemed a lighthearted escape from the war, but the Puma's
heroic self-sacrifice is a moment of real tragedy. This is a book
well worth seeking out and bringing to the attention of children
today, as is Linklater's other children's fantasy, *The Pirates in the
Deep Green Sea*.

The Pirates in the Deep Green Sea (1949) has much in common with *The Wind on the Moon*, being a story about two
children who enter matter-of-factly into fantastic adventures.
Here the main characters are brothers, Timothy and Hew Spens,
who live on the Scottish island of Popinsay with their father,
Captain Spens. The brothers become involved in an underwater
conflict, recruited by their friends Cully the octopus and Gunner
Boles, who was killed aboard the *Royal Sovereign* at Trafalgar.
Sailors who die at sea have another life below the oceans, but
there is conflict impending between the good sailors, ruled by
Davy Jones, and the pirates. A magic oil lets Timothy and Hew
breathe under water, and they are sent to carry word of imminent
pirate attack to Davy Jones' summer court. They have many
adventures on their journey, riding basking sharks and porpoises
with the powder monkeys, being captured by pirates, escaping,
and outwitting them. Davy Jones, duly warned, defeats the
pirates in battle both in the south and at Popinsay. A final phase
of this battle has nearly the entire population of Popinsay stream-
ing out of church in pursuit of pirates, in a comic chase involving
a pirate in an ill-fitting dress, two fat old ladies with shotguns,
and a bull.

A second thread in the plot is Captain Spens' obsessive search
for the sunken ship of his ancestor Aaron Spens, an alleged pirate, which is supposed to lie with its treasure off Popinsay.
Aaron Spens is one of Davy Jones' court and no pirate, but rather
someone who took the native side against the Dutch in a colonial
war during the reign of William and Mary. The boys and their
friends retrieve the treasure. In the end the boys are to be sent
away to school. Rather like Dinah and Dorinda settling down to

be good, after all they have been through, Timothy and Hew must satisfy society's expectations. Like *The Wind on the Moon*, *The Pirates in the Deep Green Sea* is a story of rapid action and satisfying invention, just as entertaining now as when it first appeared.

It is almost needless to point out that few writers of the twenties and thirties were imaginatively unaffected by the First World War, and for those writing in the forties, the destruction and deaths of the Second World War, and its lingering aftermath of rationing and rebuilding, were equally influential, if not more so. Few children's fantasy books of the time mention either war directly; Linklater's two books, and the threat of Bolsheviks in *The Box of Delights*, are the exception. Most children's books concerned entirely with the real world never dealt explicitly with the wars or the Depression either, aside from introducing the spies necessary in children's thrillers; although the Walkers' father is in the navy, past war, present hard times, and the darkening political outlook in Europe never enter the world of Arthur Ransome's 1930 *Swallows and Amazons* or its sequels. Children's books featuring heroes living everyday lives in the midst of war or the hardships of the thirties were mostly written later, often as historical fiction intended to bring that time to life (rather than merely as dramas to which the setting is of course important, but not the motivating factor in the writing of the book). In the period during and between the wars, stories for children, especially fantasy, seemed more intent on capturing 'otherness', to create a space or time away from present difficulties, and to offer alternatives, or at least a respite, even though those alternatives might be just as fraught with political uncertainty, threat of war, and personal danger, as is the case in *A Traveller in Time*.

On the whole, fantasy during this period tended to create a golden time, a space within or outside of reality where threats, once overcome, are done with for good. It was Tolkien who returned to fantasy the darker stream of Christian teleology, of unending struggle within history, victory never complete within this world, which grew to dominate modern, post-Tolkien fantasy as a tradition that old enemies, defeated and forgotten, will return, and that evil is ever present and active, good always a besieged minority. The post-Tolkien development of the genre would be influenced as well by society's full realisation of the horrors of both World Wars, the imaginative digestion of them, so to speak, and by the long dragging-on of the Cold War; the twentieth century had, by the fifties, provided a pattern in which each war contained the seeds of the next, potentially more terrible conflict. However, even in the post-war forties, this shadow of apocalypse did not yet appear in children's fantasy, other than the shadowy hints of Tolkien's *Silmarillion* cosmology in *The Hobbit*.

For many children today, the stories of this period between and including the two World Wars seem less 'old-fashioned' than those of the nineteenth century or the pre-war era. Plots tend to be more compact, while the children seem more like 'modern' children than Carroll's Alice or Nesbit's Cyril, Anthea, Robert, and Jane, in what they know, imagine, and talk about. As well, the diction is often more familiar, as is the background knowledge that is taken for granted by the authors. For young readers who find George MacDonald or even Nesbit too hard going, Linklater or Lofting will seem less alien, though Masefield's frantically convoluted plots may leave a struggling reader lost, while delighting and enthralling those who enjoy a more complex story.

The most significant children's fantasy, or fantasy of any sort, of 'the wars and between' has been left for the following chapter. It was *The Hobbit*, the first edition of which was published by Allen and Unwin in 1937. It is quite fair to say that without it (since Tolkien's attempts to write a sequel drew in the mythology and legends he had been working on since around 1917 and became *The Lord of the Rings*), fantasy might never have become such a vast and distinctive genre as it is today.

VII
J.R.R. Tolkien

The Hobbit is one of the most significant fantasy works of all time. Without the prodding of his publisher, Allen and Unwin, for a sequel to what had become a popular children's book, it is probable that Tolkien would never have written *The Lord of the Rings*. Without *The Lord of the Rings* as an inspiration and an example of excellence in prose, imaginative depth and internal integrity, the fantasy genre would most likely never have reached the literary quality it has now, in the works of some authors, achieved. Tolkien set a high standard which others have since striven to reach.

The intent here is to introduce Tolkien as a writer read by children: what he wrote, what he wrote for children in particular, and what children may take away from reading him. It is also intended to familiarize those aware only of *The Lord of the Rings*, or perhaps only aware of Tolkien by hearsay, with the greater body of his work.

J.R.R. Tolkien (1892-1973)

John Ronald Reuel Tolkien was born to English parents in Bloemfontein in the Orange Free State (now part of South Africa), where his father was a bank manager. His years in South Africa were few. In 1896 his father died, while his mother Mabel was visiting relatives back in Birmingham with Ronald and his younger brother Hilary. The family therefore did not return to Africa, but settled in Sarehole outside of Birmingham, where Tolkien's love of the rural and natural countryside was formed. Tolkien's fascination with languages also began in those early days; the boys were initially educated by their mother, who taught Ronald Latin and French, in addition to other basic subjects. A third strong influence on his life and work was also introduced at this time: Mabel Tolkien converted to Roman Catholicism, to the dismay of many relatives on both sides of the family, though some were more tolerant. Eventually the family moved into Birmingham to make it easier for the boys to attend school. They lived in what might have been called at the time 'reduced circumstances'. Mabel Tolkien developed diabetes, and in those days before the discovery of insulin, this inevitably proved fatal. She died in 1904.

Mabel Tolkien had appointed Father Francis Morgan of the Birmingham Oratory as the boys' guardian, and he remained a friend and foster father to them throughout his life. Ronald and Hilary lived in a boarding-house in Birmingham, near both the Oratory, where they saw Father Francis daily, and their school, King Edward's. Ronald Tolkien was an enthusiastic scholar whose early interest in languages never abated. He studied Latin and Greek, usual elements of the curriculum in those days, but also Middle English, Old English, Old Norse, and even Gothic. He also began to invent languages. In later years he would discuss this as a natural expression of a creative mind educated largely in languages, in the lecture 'A Secret Vice' (reprinted in *The Monsters and the Critics*, 1983/1997). In adolescence, Tolkien also met the woman he would eventually marry, another lodger in the Tolkien boys' second boarding-house. Edith Bratt was an orphan three years older than himself. Their romance had its difficulties: Father Francis disapproved of the relationship due to the distraction from Tolkien's studies it caused and to his youth. Eventually he was forbidden to see Edith until he turned twenty-one.

Tolkien attended Oxford, where he studied philology, the history and science of languages. He became an expert on Old and Middle English and Old Norse, but he also studied Finnish on his own, which was to have an influence on some of his invented languages; he could read several other modern languages as well. Once he turned twenty-one, he re-established contact with Edith Bratt. She had become engaged to another young man, but after a meeting with Tolkien, she broke that engagement and promised to marry him.

The First World War began before Tolkien graduated. He finished his degree in 1915 while in the Officers' Training Corps, and joined the 11th Lancashire Fusiliers as a second lieutenant, becoming his battalion's signalling officer. He married Edith in March of 1916; by July he was in France, his regiment having arrived just in time for the Somme offensive of July-November, in which two of his three closest schoolfriends were killed. In the autumn he was sent back to England with trench fever, and was in and out of hospital for an extended period. He was eventually promoted to full lieutenant and had various postings in England for the remainder of the war, but was never sent back to France. The Tolkiens' first child was born in 1917; they eventually had three sons and a daughter.

During 1919 and 1920 Tolkien worked for what was initially called the New English Dictionary, which would eventually become the thirteen-volume Oxford English Dictionary. He also worked as an Anglo-Saxon tutor for some of the Oxford women's colleges. Between 1920 and 1925 he was Reader in English Language at Leeds University, where he, with E.V. Gordon, was largely responsible for the development of the linguistic course of study. In 1925 he became Professor of Anglo-Saxon at Oxford; in 1945 he was made Merton Professor of English Language and Literature there, retiring in 1959. Tolkien died in 1973.

Tolkien's first love was language. This passion was for him both scholarly calling and personal creative outlet. He spent a great deal of time, from his adolescence onwards, developing languages of his own; these achieved their most complex form in the two elvish languages found in *The Lord of the Rings* and *The Silmarillion*, Quenya and Sindarin. From these languages arose a land, a history, and a body of myth and heroic legend. This was given most polished form in a posthumously-published prose work, *The Silmarillion*, on which Tolkien had actually laboured for most of his life, and as poetry both rhymed and alliterative in *The Lays of Beleriand*. The characters of the *Hobbit*-sequel, who would eventually become Frodo and his companions, were drawn into this *Silmarillion* world as Tolkien wrote; in the revised second edition of *The Hobbit*, he gave some of its characters roots in the mythology and legends that were to become *The Silmarillion*. All the linguistic and legendary material, to which Tolkien had devoted his creative life, thus came together in *The Lord of the Rings*.

The Hobbit (1937) is the first book by Tolkien most children are likely to read, or to have read to them. It was also his first published work of fiction, although he had published poetry as early as 1913. The adventures of the tamely middle-class, middle-aged hobbit Bilbo Baggins with the wizard Gandalf and the thirteen dwarves, in pursuit of vengeance and dragon-gold, would deserve its place among the classics of children's literature even without its role as a harbinger of *The Lord of the Rings*. Like *Alice* and other classics, it may suffer from an illusion of familiarity on the part of those who have not read it.

Hobbits, Tolkien's invention, are a race of small, long-lived people, who often make their houses underground. The hobbits' land, the Shire (not actually named in *The Hobbit*), is placidly pre-industrial (or, like Farjeon's *Martin Pippin* world, 'anindustrial'), while at the same time more evocative, socially and culturally, of Edwardian England. Much of the rest of the world suggests, in culture, aspects of the medieval. Not, however, the medieval of the High Middle Ages, like Lewis' *Narnia* (see Chapter VIII), but the Early Middle Ages, the Dark Ages, of the barbarian kingdoms which succeeded Rome – societies where concepts of honour and loyalty, valour and pride, are the pre-eminent ideals and driving forces in interpersonal relationships. Bilbo's comfortable life is disrupted by the appearance of the wizard Gandalf, who inflicts a supper-party of thirteen dwarves upon him, and bustles him off on their quest to avenge the loss of their treasure and fortress-city under the Lonely Mountain to the dragon Smaug. Bilbo is proclaimed by Gandalf to be a skilled burglar, but in his first adventure, an encounter with three trolls, he fails as a pickpocket and the dwarves are captured and nearly eaten. In his subsequent adventures he does better. When the dwarves are captured by goblins and rescued by Gandalf, Bilbo is lost in the goblin tunnels. There he finds a ring and survives his encounter with the murderous Gollum through luck and wits.

This proves a significant event in Bilbo's adventures, and in Tolkien's future masterpiece, though at the time it was no more than a useful and amusing artefact for a light-hearted tale. Magic rings conferring various abilities are not uncommon in folktales and fairy-tales; invisibility, speech with animals, or control over this or that, are attributes frequently associated with such rings. In the first edition of *The Hobbit*, Gollum actually offers the ring as the prize in a riddle-contest. Tolkien revised the chapter 'Riddles in the Dark', which was published in its new version in the 1951 second edition of *The Hobbit*. This revision 'corrects' Bilbo's account of how he came by the ring, to bring it into line with the greater story as it had developed in *The Lord of the Rings*, which Tolkien had begun writing late in 1937. Development of the idea of the ring, or the Ring, in *The Lord of the Rings* made it improbable that Gollum should so easily give up his 'precious', so its loss by Gollum and discovery by Bilbo was substituted. The existence of that correction was even worked into the story, as Bilbo's first edition account of winning the ring became a lie on his part to strengthen his claim to it, early evidence of its corrupting nature even on the relatively good and innocent.

After more adventures, Gandalf leaves the party to their own devices. In Mirkwood the dwarves are captured first by giant spiders and then by their old enemies, the wood-elves; from both they are rescued by Bilbo, using sword, cleverness, and his invisibility-conferring ring. When the adventurers finally reach the Lonely Mountain, there is nothing they can do against the dragon. Bilbo steals a cup (an echo of *Beowulf*, in which the theft of a cup awakens the fateful dragon's wrath). His encounter with Smaug leads the dragon to attack Lake-town, where the monster is slain after slaughtering many of the inhabitants. When rumour of the dragon's death reaches the dwarves, as well as word that the men of devastated Lake-town and elves from Mirkwood are coming to claim the hoard, they fortify the old gates and prepare for siege, awaiting the arrival of their kinsman Dain with a dwarf army. Bilbo despairs at the thought of the coming slaughter, but his councils of peace are rejected.

Hoping to avert war, Bilbo steals the Arkenstone, a wonderful jewel that is the greatest treasure of the place, and takes it to the human leader Bard and the Elvenking, saying they can exchange it for a fourteenth share of the hoard, Bilbo's portion as originally agreed to by the dwarves. He discovers that Gandalf is there with them. Thorin, though, refuses to ransom the stone or have anything more to do with Bilbo. The besiegers are attacked by Dain's army of dwarves, but a force of goblins and wolf-like Wargs from the Misty Mountains arrives, and dwarves, men, and elves unite against them. Though they defeat the goblins, Thorin dies of his wounds after asking Bilbo's forgiveness. Bilbo, accompanied by Gandalf, returns to Hobbiton with a modest treasure and his extremely handy ring, only to find that he has been presumed dead and his possessions are being auctioned off.

The Hobbit has in recent years been relegated to a 'prequel' to *The Lord of the Rings*, and is found more often in the science fiction and fantasy section of bookstores than on the children's shelves. It is, though, a children's book, suitable, with some dramatic and frightening sections and some moving and sorrowful parts (such as the death of Thorin), for reading to many children of six or seven, those at least who are used to being read something more complex than picture books. Certainly most children of eight and up ought to be quite capable of reading it on their own, though for some it may be a vocabulary-broadening experience. *The Hobbit* also contains a great deal of comic irony which a child-reader may only discover on a later re-reading, but it is full of excitement, suspense, wonder, terror, and humour enough to satisfy any reader and make the reality of many other fantasy books seem very thin by comparison.

Part of this is due to the sense one has while reading it of a vast reach of history and geography surrounding Bilbo's adventure. The story takes place on a little, well-lit stage, while in the background mysterious movement suggests other action. The old feuds between dwarves and elves, the ancient, dwarf-made treasures like the mail shirt Thorin gives to Bilbo, the swords from the troll-hoard forged for ancient wars against evil, all evoke a sense of rich, vast, history. Even the present is mysteriously larger than what is clearly seen. There is rumour of 'the Necromancer' in southern Mirkwood, in whose dungeons Thorin's dying father was found by Gandalf; in *The Lord of the Rings* the Necromancer, driven out of Mirkwood in one of the off-stage events of *The Hobbit*, has reappeared in his old fastness in Mordor, revealed as Sauron. Moria, where Thorin's grandfather died at the hands of goblins, is likewise mentioned in passing, its stories waiting in *The Lord of the Rings* and *The Silmarillion*. Elrond, at whose hall Bilbo is twice a guest, is said by the narrator of *The Hobbit* to come into a great many other tales. What little is revealed of him and his valley of Rivendell is enticing, but no hint of these other tales enters Bilbo's adventure; in *The Lord of the Rings* Strider teases Bilbo about his presumption in making a song about Eärendil and Elwing while in Elrond's house, but only in *The Silmarillion* do readers discover that these are Elrond's parents, human and elven lovers whose story was, in an earlier age, crucial to the fate of the world dominated by Melkor or Morgoth, Sauron's lord.

This ever-receding vista of history is only a small part of the book's appeal, however. *The Hobbit* is, without reference to other works, an adventure containing ample suspense, drama, and humour. The hero, though an adult and not even a young one, is easily identified with by children. Bilbo's previous experience of the sort of life in which he finds himself is non-existent; he is thus underestimated and even looked down upon by his dwarf companions at the start, and must grow, proving his quality to both them and himself, in order not only to earn respect and self-respect, but to survive. Bilbo's most crucial quality, though, is something he has always had, the very un-epic common decency that leads him to try making peace between equally-wronged parties, even at the risk of alienating his friends. This sort of internal journey is one of universal appeal and Bilbo, viewed from outside by a fond and occasionally ironic narrator, remains engagingly childlike without being presented as in any way childish or immature. It is, deliberately, a very different narrative style from Tolkien's writing for adults, though his ability to suit his style both to his audience and to subtleties of mood and mode is often overlooked.

Another overlooked aspect of Tolkien's creative talent is his ability as an illustrator. The original editions of *The Hobbit* contained his own illustrations and had a dust-jacket designed and drawn by Tolkien, very distinctive in stark green, black, blue and white, with its forest rising into mountains and a red sun. The Unwin Hyman fiftieth-anniversary edition of *The Hobbit* returned to the original dust-jacket and featured Tolkien's illustrations, both black and white drawings and colour plates.[*] Although, as with those other author-illustrators of the period between the wars, Arthur Ransome and Hugh Lofting, human

---

[*] The current publisher of Tolkien's work, HarperCollins, has said that their 1995 hardcover edition (ISBN 0261103288) also contains the original artwork.

figures were not Tolkien's strong point, he created elegantly stylized landscapes that lead the eye on, deeper and deeper into the world. Other books illustrated by him were published posthumously, and will be discussed in due course.

Many children do go on from *The Hobbit* to read *The Lord of the Rings*, which was first published in three volumes, *The Fellowship of the Ring* (1954), *The Two Towers* (1954), and *The Return of the King* (1955), the third volume also containing the appendices and index. This division was made only to keep the cost down. Tolkien always considered it a single unified story, not a trilogy, but it was not published in one volume until 1968.

Tolkien began writing *The Lord of the Rings* in 1937, intending a sequel to Bilbo's story, but the story rapidly became something larger, grander, and grimmer, as themes and history from his then-unpublished mythology found their way into it. The book starts off with hobbits, not so diminutively or ironically viewed as in *The Hobbit*, but still on a young person's scale of experience. As the story moves farther from the Shire it expands beyond that, opening out into greater vistas, styles of narrative, themes, and motives of character that a child reading it is likely encountering for the first time, though they are old and loved in the great literary works of the heroic past. Now, many even come to the emotions and sense of what is dramatically fitting displayed in *Beowulf, Niebelungenlied*, the *Iliad*, and *Gilgamesh*, and find them familiar because they met these emotions and patterns of thought for the first time in a modern (or, as Shippey observes, a Modern) literary work. A lifelong instinct for the rhythms of the English language and its great variety of styles and moods is also to be gained by an early delight in Tolkien's prose and poetry.

The Lord of the Rings grows in what it demands from the reader as it is read, and some children may be left behind along the way, or follow through it only very slowly. Others, even though fantasy readers, will never venture it at all until teens or adults. Some relatively young children, though, will read and re-read it until the book falls apart, taking more from it on each return as their real and literary experience and understanding grow. They will miss some levels of the story. The subtler themes and ironies, the complexities and tensions that underlie the plot, will

only be understood and appreciated fully on more mature reading, as the reader's awareness and experience of life expand to
comprehend them. Yet, young readers will absorb the grand, the
formal, the passionate and heroic and archaic, without the distance that later 'learning' insists the modern reader must bring to
reading and experiencing such elements. We are taught that such
emotions or such styles may only be viewed ironically when presented in a modern work. To read *The Lord of the Rings* young is
to approach it with innocence and experience it unprejudiced. It
does not matter that some or much may not be completely understood; the same can be said of first encounters with Shakespeare,
Dickens, or Homer, all of whom have captured the imaginations
of past generations of young readers and been returned to by
those readers as adults.

The story of *The Lord of the Rings* is too polyphonic, composed of too many interweaving narrative strands and complexities, to summarize in any sort of detail here. The central journey,
though, is that of Bilbo's cousin and adopted heir, Frodo Baggins, and Frodo's friend and servant Sam Gamgee, to Mordor.
They intend the destruction of the Ring that Bilbo brought back
from his travels long before, and with the Ring, the power of
Sauron. Along the way, great suffering is endured, great heroism
is achieved, and great sacrifices made. The landscape is vast and
detailed, the lands and peoples encountered are varied and never
mere background sketches. Every single character involved in
the story goes through great changes along the way.

The plot of *The Lord of the Rings* is sometimes dismissed as
utterly unoriginal and clichéd. Many who believe Tolkien unoriginal have never actually read him or have read him shallowly,
seeing only the much-imitated surface. Others have read too
many of his imitators to see through the shadows of imitation, be
it worshipful or cynically derivative. Quests of a desperate band
of heroes comprising wise wizards, heroic, darkly mysterious
warriors, and naive village boys, hunted by monstrous servants
of a Dark Lord who is generally just an ill-defined generic evil,
abounded while the adult fantasy genre was finding its feet.
Dismissing Tolkien because of satiety on these is like dismissing
Jane Austen as unoriginal and clichéd because of a superficial
resemblance between her plots and the modern 'regency romance'.

Sauron, for example, is not the ill-defined generic evil power so used and over-used in post-Tolkien fantasy (particularly but by no means exclusively in fiction based on role-playing games), such as is satirized in Terry Pratchett's *The Last Hero* (2001) with the character of Dark Lord Evil Harry Dread, or in the entire plot of Diana Wynne Jones' *Dark Lord of Derkholm* (1998). Sauron's origins are intimately bound up with the whole history of the world. He is, to greatly oversimplify, a fallen lesser 'angelic' power, corrupted servant of a greater evil, Morgoth, whose own fall and corruption of the created world are part of the mythology of *The Silmarillion*. Morgoth's rebellion is motivated by pride and a desire to force his own shaping will into the creation of Eru or Ilúvatar, the One who made the universe. Sauron is no simple, convenient, motiveless enemy created merely for heroes to overthrow.

Gandalf, Saruman, and Radagast, staff-wielding wizards, prototypes of the vast array of staff-clutching, lightning-hurling, bearded, celibate, short-tempered wizards mocked in Pratchett's earlier *Discworld* books, are likewise ancient powers, lesser 'angelic' beings sent into the world to aid men and elves by the Valar, the greater powers equivalent to the highest angels. Gandalf's adjuration to the Balrog in Moria and his reference to being 'sent back' when he meets Aragorn, Legolas, and Gimli in Fangorn after his supposed death, are almost the only hint of this, but it adds an extra richness to a character already engagingly complex. Gandalf is wise, highly-regarded by people of awe-inspiring power and history, yet humanly irritable and short-tempered, his own power only hinted at by his actions, and those actions proving him fallible.

Characters like the wizards, the Dark Lord Sauron, and Galadriel, beautiful and serenely wise, or Aragorn, the intriguingly mysterious wanderer who can act with authority among the powerful of the world, have come to *seem* like stock characters. They have *become* archetypes for the genre (though the patterns that appeal so in them have often come from other, ancient storytelling modes). Tolkien's characters are much more than the outlines that later works have repeated – and they are repeated because they appeal, deeply, to readers; they satisfy some imaginative desire. Tolkien's characters are bound intricately into the plot and into the past on many levels; in the case of Gandalf and

Aragorn, and even Galadriel, they are also vividly-realized personalities. In contrast, Sauron, who is not a character with personality, is almost more accurately regarded as having come to be a force rather than a person, though his past is one of personality and will.

Tolkien's characters were not all destined to become patterns for future writers, and not all the characters are coloured by glimpses of his mythological writing. The characters closest in thought and temper to young readers, the main characters, are the four hobbits who leave the Shire and return to restore it in the end. Frodo begins as a thoughtful, cheerful, conscientious hobbit, capable of light-hearted foolery, recklessness, and considered bravery; his experiences wear him away to someone much more reflective and sorrowful – there is no simple happy ending for him. Merry and Pippin start off on the adventure for the sake of simple friendship, but their experiences test them and draw out unexpected reserves of courage and dedication, as well as providing military experience that is useful on the home front when they return, carrying an air of earned authority, to find the much-diminished Saruman turning the Shire into a fascist wasteland. Sam's unfaltering loyalty also reveals courage and resolve equal to Frodo's; his love of beauty and his generosity in his use of Galadriel's gift of soil from Lothlorien enable him to restore the devastated Shire in the end.

Though the plot of *The Lord of the Rings* does not unfold in the rapid series of cliffhangers more commonly written now to hold the television-addicted attention span, it is dramatic and full of event. Before the hobbits even reach the relatively nearby town of Bree and meet the wandering heir of the ancient kings, Gandalf's friend Aragorn, they have been hunted across the Shire by Black Riders, met elves, and narrowly escaped murder at the hands of a hobbit- and human-hating willow tree. They have met Tom Bombadil, the oldest being in Middle Earth, who speaks, even when his words are not typeset as verse, entirely in poetry. They have been imprisoned in deathly sleep in a barrow among the bones and grave-goods of the dead, and nearly slain by a barrow-wight, a foul spirit possessing the grave.

Frodo, a mature and active hero, is not the irritatingly passive, helpless, dewy-eyed boy of the 2001-2003 movies[*]; but despite

---

[*] The 2001-2003 movies did not do justice to the book, missing the

being an adult character, he has much appeal to young readers, as has Sam. As the main characters separate to their individual adventures, Sam remains more rooted in the ordinary, more 'accessible' to young readers, while Frodo becomes more subtle and subdued. Merry and Pippin, in Rohan and Minas Tirith, carry the 'younger', more modern point of view into the Germanic outlook of the Rohirrim and the archaic formality of the councils of Minas Tirith. Characters like Aragorn, on the other hand, are grand, even mysterious, and engage the imagination with possibilities of splendour, tragedy, or triumph on the epic scale.

The antagonism on the part of the extreme end of conservative Christianity to the modern fantasy genre, so shaped by Tolkien's world, is ironic, given that the devout Roman Catholic Tolkien took great care, in what he called his sub-creation, to remain in accord with a Christian conception of the world. Behind all Tolkien's mythology lies monotheism, the creation of the world, its corruption by a rebel servant of the one creator, the fall of mankind, and personal salvation obtainable only through grace. However, *The Lord of the Rings* is no religious allegory and is nowhere explicitly Christian. Though it is suffused with a spiritual sensibility – its heroes strive and struggle to make ethical choices, acting in accordance with a firm belief in right and wrong, and sometimes failing despite this, when the limits of divinely-unaided humanity are reached – there is no overt or underlying religious message or structure to the book. *The Lord of the Rings* is not a political allegory either, though it was proclaimed as such, usually by those trying to gloss it as an allegory of events and situations (the atomic bomb and the Cold War are favourites of such an approach) which arose after its conception and much of its composition. However, *The Lord of the Rings* is, at its most fundamental level, an epic of desperation, courage, and hope, danger and friendship, with a goodly measure of homely humour and hobbit common-sense to complement the concerns of the great and the mighty.

---

point in several places. By the third movie, distortions were being inflicted on the fundamental personalities of several characters, particularly Faramir and Frodo, which altered the meaning and inverted the significance of some key episodes, while omitting 'The Scouring of the Shire' from the theatrical release seems again to have seriously missed a crucial thematic concern.

Most fantasy-reading children will be likely to leave *The Lord of the Rings* until their teens, but nonetheless a goodly number will read it for the first time at a younger, even a much younger, age, and there is no reason why they should not. There is so much to be enjoyed in it on so many levels, that if children approach it without being told it is 'too hard', those few who are ready will devour it, and all their subsequent reading experiences will be the richer for it.

The Silmarillion (1977), in contrast, is unlikely to be read through by most younger children no matter how good their vocabularies, because it is not a novel. It reads like, and is meant to read like, a collection of mythology and legend, relating the matter of the First Age of Middle-earth. The narrative is not 'personal' in the way one expects in a novel, and a modern novel in particular; it does not take the reader deep into the emotions of a character, but simply presents that character's choices and actions, and accounts for them with less emotional immediacy than a novel usually strives to attain. The experience is more that of reading the *Iliad*, or the *Eddas*, or the *Mabinogion*. By the time someone has reached their teens, they usually have a wider exposure to different modes of narrative, and those who have enjoyed *The Lord of the Rings* and have a desire to explore Middle-earth further will find many stirring stories in *The Silmarillion*. It comprises the most-final form of the mythology on which Tolkien worked throughout his life, edited by his son Christopher. *The Silmarillion* contains an account of the creation of the world, and tales of the elves and humans – heroes, vengeance-seekers, and lovers – whose deeds shaped the past to which characters like Elrond, Gandalf, Aragorn, and even Sam refer in passing. Elrond's parents are central figures in one of the most important stories, that of the human man Eärendil and his elvish wife Elwing and the defeat of Morgoth. Galadriel takes part in the rebellion of the elves against the Valar and the wars between the elves. The story of the lovers Beren and Luthien – his quest for a gem stolen by Morgoth, her rescue of him from Morgoth's dungeon – was of deep personal importance to Tolkien, who had the names *Luthien* and *Beren* inscribed on Edith's gravestone and his own following her death in 1971. It is an enthralling tale, and perhaps *The Silmarillion*'s finest story.

Christopher Tolkien has edited over a dozen volumes of earlier drafts of *The Lord of the Rings* and the legendary and mythological material that became *The Silmarillion*, as well as unfinished pieces relating to Middle-earth, which some teens may find interesting. One of these volumes, *The Lays of Beleriand* (1985), contains versions of some of the matter of *The Silmarillion* in rhymed and in alliterative poetry, which display Tolkien's often overlooked skill as a poet. His mastery of alliterative verse in Modern English may stir some interest in Old and Early Middle English amongst adolescent readers, as may his translations of three Middle English poems, published together as *Sir Gawain and the Green Knight; Pearl; Sir Orfeo* (1975).

Aside from *The Hobbit*, Tolkien's only book specifically for children published in his lifetime was *Farmer Giles of Ham* (1949), a very short novel about a farmer who defeats a giant with a blunderbuss (an early firearm), is awarded an unfashionable sword which turns out to be a famous dragon-slaying blade, and, overawing a dragon with it, makes himself king with the dragon's aid. There are many levels of humour at work in this book, but as a fairy-tale it can be enjoyed by most children capable of reading it themselves. The clever, pragmatic hero, who bests both monsters and the stuck-up knights and courtiers who think him a country bumpkin, has a universal appeal. Farmer Giles, his phlegmatic grey mare, Garm the ebullient dog, and most of all the dragon, Chrysophylax Dives – smooth, superior, sophisticated, and put firmly in his place by Giles – are all utterly charming characters. The story of *Farmer Giles* is light-hearted but not simplistic, and the illustrations by Pauline Baynes are an added appeal.

Another very short novel, written for adults but which some teens may enjoy, is *Smith of Wootton Major* (1967). This story of a village smith's journeys in fairyland is an allegory, in part, of Tolkien's own thoughts on the creative life. In spirit, though, *Smith of Wootton Major* looks back on life from the end, and so many children find its themes too distant from their own experience for complete empathy. *Smith* and *Farmer Giles* were republished in one volume, along with 'Leaf by Niggle' and *The Adventures of Tom Bombadil* (see below), as *Tales From the Perilous Realm* (1997).

Another allegorical story on a creative life, by this writer who disliked allegory, is 'Leaf By Niggle' (1945; subsequently in *Tree and Leaf*, 1964/1988; *The Tolkien Reader*, 1966; *Tales From the Perilous Realm*, 1997). This may have a great deal of interest for teens considering art and its place in the private and public worlds, with its story of the painter Niggle and the fate of his one great and unregarded creation.

The collection of poems, some comic, some more serious, called *The Adventures of Tom Bombadil* (1962; also in *The Tolkien Reader* and *Perilous Realm*), will find some eager readers among the young, while 'The Homecoming of Beorhtnoth Beorthelm's Son' (1953 and in *The Tolkien Reader*) is a drama on the aftermath of the Battle of Maldon in 991, a contrast of the poetic ideal of glorious last stands with the realities of battle. The play has a grim beauty and will appeal to teens who have never read even a translation of the Old English poem *The Battle of Maldon*, though it may lead them to seek one out.

Tolkien wrote several works intended for children which were not published until after his death. *The Father Christmas Letters* (1976) is a selection of the letters he wrote and illustrated for his four children over many Christmases, purporting to be from Father Christmas, one of his elves, or the North Polar Bear. They recount the adventures of the North Pole community, everything from goblin raids to the Polar Bear's frequent disasters. Another posthumously-published story originally written and illustrated for Tolkien's own children is *Mr. Bliss* (1982), the tale of an accident-prone driver and a chaotic road-trip in his brand new yellow motorcar.

A third posthumous publication is another children's book, *Roverandom* (1998), which was written and illustrated in the mid to late nineteen-twenties. It is a short novel relating the story of a dog turned by an annoyed wizard into a toy, and his subsequent adventures in the sea and on the moon with wizards, dragons, and the Man-in-the-Moon, before he finally finds his family and his proper form again. It was begun in 1925 to console one of Tolkien's sons on the loss of a toy dog, but Tolkien took the expanding story seriously and worked at it through several drafts. *Roverandom* is full of allusions to material ranging from British legend and Norse mythology to E. Nesbit and Tolkien's own developing fictional cosmology. It abounds in wordplay, some of which will pass over the heads even of many adult readers unless they resort to the endnotes, but the story itself is not dependent on the puns and allusions. Rover's adventures are full of whimsy and invention, with many comic encounters on his quest to return to both his home and his proper shape. The illustrations for this are among Tolkien's finest. Like Hugh Lofting in *Doctor Dolittle in the Moon,* he imagined and painted a view of the earth seen from the lunar surface. The book's interest lies not solely in the quality of its illustrations or in the novelty value of a 'lost' Tolkien story, though. *Roverandom* is a story on solid bones, which could become an enduring favourite with young children as a bedtime read-aloud.

Bilbo's Last Song (1990) is a poem, the manuscript of which was given by Tolkien to an employee of his publisher. It was first published as a poster (1974) but later came out as a small book. The speaker is Bilbo, taking leave of Middle-earth at the Grey Havens. The full-colour illustrations are by Pauline Baynes, and contain a pictorial summation of *The Hobbit* in small vignettes, as well as larger pictures following the journey of Bilbo, Elrond, and others from Rivendell to the Havens. *Bilbo's Last Song* is not, like *Roverandom,* meant specifically as a children's story. Readers of *The Hobbit* will enjoy tracing its plot through the small illustrations, but the primary interest lies in the poem as Bilbo's last reflections on Middle-earth, a final taking-leave of earthly life and a complementary piece to the last chapter of *The Lord of the Rings.*

A large part of Tolkien's impact on fantasy lies as much in how he did it as in what he did. He told a gripping, moving, powerful story, but he created a world and a mythology vaster than that story could contain. Although fiction was not his primary 'job', throughout his life he took the creation of his art seriously, far more so than many who have identified themselves first and foremost as authors. Tolkien's attention to the internal integrity of his creation results in something capable of sustaining what he called 'literary belief' (*Tree and Leaf* 36) or Coleridge, 'the willing suspension of disbelief' (*Biographia Literaria* 442). While one is reading, it is real, and nothing incongruous, sloppy, or ill-considered jars the reader out of that conviction of reality. Even once the book is read and set aside, all the layers and threads hold together. The fantastic, in *The Lord of the Rings*, is not merely a device to facilitate the adventure, as in Nesbit, or a whimsical what-if, as in Lofting or even Baum; it is not a blurring of the possibilities of dream and wish and waking, as in Masefield. Even elements that began as whimsy in *The Hobbit* or in *Farmer Giles of Ham* were given solid roots that bound them into a complex reality. Tolkien's fantasy reaches back to myth, legend, and fairy-tale; he built worlds upon that foundation of possibilities both grimmer and grander than those encompassed in 'what-if' magic stories.

Modern fantasy, particularly secondary world fantasy, learnt from this. After Tolkien, children's fantasy took on new depth. Before him, MacDonald had approached this depth, but the kingdom of Curdie and Princess Irene remains a fairy-tale one, indefinite in form. In Baum's *Oz* the magic is still the fairy-tale one of useful devices and whimsical 'what-ifs', a new world every day but not one that gives any sense of having much past. De la Mare's *The Three Mulla-Mulgars*, like Baum's novels, offers a fully-realized created world, which unlike *Oz* evokes an impression of legend, but his book never won the popularity and influence of *The Hobbit*. Moreover, Tolkien's writing greatly influenced his friend and colleague C.S. Lewis, and between them, *The Hobbit* and *The Chronicles of Narnia* showed the way to a wider terrain for children's fantasy to explore. After Tolkien and Lewis, secondary world fantasy becomes more common, serious concerns enter into it more often, and even stories where magic enters the 'real' world take that fantastic more seriously. From the fifties onwards, there begin to be children's writers who specialize primarily in fantasy, whereas before, it was not seen as something separate – it was a preference on the part of some writers, but not a genre. By the sixties, the main stream of children's fantasy was one given shape by Tolkien's example, with writers such as Lloyd Alexander, Alan Garner, and Susan Cooper setting stories in either carefully-created secondary worlds, or a real world wound through with ancient, rooted magic. The characters in such stories find themselves on the edge of affairs with an epic or legendary component, and are drawn into them, whereas characters like Nesbit's children are in the centre of things, and the magic revolves around entertaining them.

In adult fantasy, too, Tolkien's influence was great. It first appeared as a desire to write stories like those of Tolkien. Many (though not all) of these of were undistinguished, and read like the sort of admiring near-plagiarism that children and teens generate when a desire to write fiction strikes and they are caught up in some favourite book. People were hungry for this sort of story, and not very critical, so long as they received a taste. Children's fantasy seems to have absorbed and comprehended the example of Tolkien sooner, and may even have influenced adult fantasy, as a generation of writers whose imaginations had been shaped by Tolkien-influenced children's literature began to write adult fiction themselves. In the eighties, the quality and originality of adult fantasy began a marked improvement that became more noticeable in the nineties. It has now reached a point where the influence seems to be the other way; young adult fantasy, in particular, is incorporating themes and ideas from adult fantasy, especially the concern with the creation of detailed, consistent secondary worlds, a lesson learned ultimately from Tolkien.

There are several excellent and readily available books which undertake a scholarly discussion of Tolkien's literary achievement. The depth, richness, and consistency of Tolkien's world, the complexity of his moral and spiritual concerns, his themes, his literary skill, and his vision of humanity, are examined in detail in Tom Shippey's *J.R.R. Tolkien: Author of the Century* (2000). *The Road to Middle-earth* (1982, 2nd Edn. 1992) by the same author (as T.A. Shippey) examines the philological and other scholarly roots and elements of Tolkien's creative output, while Humphrey Carpenter's *J.R.R. Tolkien: A Biography* (1977) and to a lesser extent his *The Inklings* (1978; also a vital biographical source on C.S. Lewis), look at Tolkien's work in the context of his life. Another excellent book, which examines Tolkien's experiences during the First World War and their influence on his creative life, is John Garth's *Tolkien and the Great War* (2003).

Despite the enduring impact of Tolkien's writing on the literary quality of fantasy, perhaps his greatest lesson to the authors who followed him lay not in that, but in leading fantasy back to its headwaters in myth, legend, and heroic epic, by reintroducing the type of story which has fascinated, moved, and inspired humans for millennia.

VIII
The Fifties

The nineteen-fifties was another period of rapid change for Britain. The Second World War's aftermath of shortages in food, housing, and consumer goods dragged on into the mid fifties, with food derationing not complete until 1954. In part due to the terms of American wartime loans, the British economy was slow to recover from the war, and the feeling that the nation had sacrificed itself without reward or recognition affected the national mood adversely, once the first euphoria of the war's end passed. There was no rapid return to good times, but a great deal of social change: nationalisation of some industries, the National Health Service, Social Insurance. The Empire gave way to the Commonwealth; India and Pakistan achieved independence in 1947. In response to the threat seen in the Soviet Union, Europe and North America allied in NATO in 1949. The Cold War had begun, and it found its first battleground in the Korean War (1950-1953), in which American, British, Australian, and Canadian troops fought as part of a United Nations force drawn from many countries, shattering any remaining illusions that world peace could be achieved. The threat of Communist aggression reaching even into Europe became a real one in many people's minds. The Suez Crisis of 1956, perhaps more than any other event, demonstrated that Britain was no longer a dominating world power. In the United States, meanwhile, anti-Communist paranoia was fuelled by Senator Joseph McCarthy's allegations against numerous officials, and spread to disrupt the lives of many academics, scientists, and artists. Behind all the fears of the Soviet Union, Communist fifth columnists, and Middle Eastern instability, lurked the spectre of nuclear war.

In Britain, it was not a decade of much confidence in the future, and in children's fantasy, a field in which British writers continued to play the greatest part, there was a predominance of concern with other times and places; fantasy, of course, lends itself well to reconsiderations of the past. For some, that golden past was no more distant than the period between the wars. As had always been the case, fantasy was used to examine themes and subjects of concern to the authors. The influence of Tolkien had not yet made itself strongly felt in the imaginations and work of writers other than his friend C.S. Lewis, though that was soon to change. Fantasy had, however, become a respected and common element of children's books, and much of the best children's literature of this period was fantasy. Children's books in Britain were cheap and plentiful; Puffin had been founded as an imprint of Penguin Books in 1941, and by the fifties was very influential in making affordable, well-written books available to children throughout the Commonwealth. Reading for pleasure became an activity stressed in school.

Mary Norton (1903-1992)

Before her marriage in 1927, Mary Norton was a professional actor; following her marriage, she lived with her husband Robert and four children in Portugal. While her husband was serving in the Royal Navy during the Second World War, Norton and the children lived briefly in the United States. The family returned afterwards to Britain.

Norton's first children's fantasy was published in the United States. *Bed-Knob and Broomstick* (1957) originally appeared as two short books, *The Magic Bed-Knob* (1943) and *Bonfires and Broomsticks* (1947). In the first book, the three Wilson children, Charles, Carey, and six year-old Paul, meet Miss Price, who is studying to be a witch. They are bribed with an enchanted brass bed-knob into keeping her secret. The spell will let the bed take them wherever they wish if turned one way, and whenever, if the other. Their adventures take them to London (where things go badly with the police) and to a South Sea Island. In the second book, Miss Price has given up magic. They argue themselves into being allowed a trip to the past and end up in London just before the Great Fire in 1666, bringing back an incompetent necromancer, Emelius Jones, for a visit. He spends a week in the twentieth century and falls in love with Miss Price. After his return to his own time, the children are allowed one final trip, on which they discover Emelius has been imprisoned as a witch and sentenced to burn at the stake. Miss Price rescues him, using her witchcraft to make a cloak and sword appear alive. In the end, Miss Price and Emelius Jones return to live in a little cottage in the seventeenth century, finding that era, despite the threat of the witch-hunters, more desirable than the mid-twentieth-century present.

These two stories draw the young reader in from the start. The influence of Nesbit it obvious. Miss Price recalls the crusty magical creatures Nesbit's children encounter, and the magic itself is very like Nesbit's, literal-minded and prone to unintended consequences, although it is usually Miss Price, rather than the children, who must sort things out. The books are ideal for reading aloud to younger children; the chapters are short, full of action, and contain both danger and humour. The only drawback is the stereotypical depiction of the stock 'native savage' in the South Sea Islanders of the first book.

A more substantial fantasy is Norton's *Borrowers* series, which began with the Carnegie-winning *The Borrowers* (1952). The Borrowers are tiny people who live as parasites on human society, 'borrowing' everything. In this lies one of the appeals of the stories; the idea of little people adapting our artefacts to their needs has always fascinated children. The story in the first book is told to young Kate by old Mrs. May, whose brother told it to her. This two-layered remove in the narrative serves to connect Kate's present with that of the heroine, the Borrower Arrietty Clock, and allows her to believe in the story, which is told by someone who had it from someone who should know the truth.

The Clock family, Pod, Homily, and the lonely daughter Arrietty, live under the floor in a late Victorian or Edwardian house, eating 'borrowed' odds and ends of food, using pins and string as grappling hooks to climb the tablecloths and curtains to 'borrow', and terrified of being seen by 'human beans', which would mean exile. They are in fact the last family of Borrowers in the house. Some, like their relatives, Uncle Hendreary's family, have emigrated to live in the dangerous out-of-doors, a disgraceful result of having been seen by humans, but many families have simply died out. Arrietty feels caged and dreams of escape. Eventually, she breaks the Borrowers' most fundamental rule. She is seen by a human and becomes friends with the lonely boy staying in the house. When the adults discover them, in part due to the boy's enthusiastic aid in their borrowings and their own failure to curb their desire for more possessions, the Clocks' little world is destroyed; their exits are sealed up and the rat-catcher summoned to smoke them out. The boy, Mrs. May's brother, is only able to escape the vindictive housekeeper's eye long enough to pull off a grating with a pickaxe, and his horrified expectation of the deaths of the Clock family creates an agonizing drama. Though he is being packed off to India at the time and never sees them again, Mrs. May assures Kate the Clocks survived to set up housekeeping in a badger's den, since she herself found Arrietty's memoranda-book – although the handwriting was very like her brother's.

The series continued with *The Borrowers Afield* (1955), *Afloat* (1959), and *Aloft* (1961), with a final novel, *The Borrowers Avenged*, appearing in 1982 and a collection of stories, *Poor Stainless*, in 1994. Arrietty is a likeable heroine whose desire to learn more of the world, and whose impatience with adult restrictions no matter how much intended for her protection, create a character with whom young readers can easily identify, while at the same time enjoying the experience of seeing their own world anew through her eyes. Some themes in the first book seem very relevant today, even moreso than in the fifties: Homily Clock's 'consumerism', as she creates a grander and grander home of useless possessions with the help of the boy, is a large part of what leads to the final destruction of the culture of which her family is the last remnant in the house.

Tove Jansson (1914-2001)

Tove Jansson was born in Helsinki, Finland, to an artistic family; her mother was a graphic artist and her father a sculptor. She studied art in Stockholm and Paris, and embarked on a long career as a cartoonist for the magazine *Garm* in the twenties. The first Moomintroll book, *Kometjakten*, written in Swedish, was published in 1946 and translated into English in 1951 as *Comet in Moominland*. In 1953 Jansson's comic strip *Moomin* began running in the *London Evening News*. Although best-known for the eleven *Moomintroll* books, Jansson also wrote a few adult novels. She was awarded the Finnish State Award in Literature three times.

The Moomintrolls began appearing in English not with *Comet in Moominland*, but in *Finn Family Moomintroll* in 1950; it had been published in Finland in 1948. In all, there are eleven Moomintroll books, published in English translation between 1950 and 1971, with *Moominpappa's Memoirs* appearing only in 1994. The adventures of young Moomintroll with his parents, mild and infinitely tolerant Moominmamma and impulsive Moominpappa, his friends the mouth-organ playing, goblinlike Snufkin, the 'small animal' Sniff, and assorted others, are a combination of imaginative play and strange quests. Sometimes magic comes to them, as in the adventure of the hobgoblin's transforming hat in *Finn Family Moomintroll*, and sometimes they encounter it while travelling, as in *Comet in Moominland*, when Moomintroll, Sniff, and Snufkin set off to discover if the world really is about to be destroyed by an approaching comet.

Other adventures are sought simply because a character is in the mood; Snufkin frequently takes to a wandering life, and in *The Exploits of Moominpappa* (1952) the title character tells his own story. This book is unusual for the series in being a first person narrative, with third person interruptions. Moominpappa has decided to record the story of his life. He reads his story to Moomintroll, Sniff, and Snufkin as he goes, although they do have doubts about some parts of it. The main story takes him from the time he was left as a baby in a newspaper-wrapped parcel on the doorstep of the Home for Moomin Foundlings, through his adventures with his friends, the fathers of Sniff and Snufkin, on a voyage of exploration and their formation of an outlaw colony, to the time he rescued Moominmamma from shipwreck.

Occasionally the entire family travels. In *Moominsummer Madness* (1955) the Moominhouse is washed away by a flood after an offshore volcano explodes. Along with other creatures, the Moomintrolls move into a theatre they find floating past. This inspires Moominpappa, who has always displayed a literary bent, to take to writing tragedy. The comedy of a play taken too literally by its audience is mixed with the drama of various members of the extended family getting lost or left behind as the theatre floats along; each has his or her own adventures as they all find their way back together.

The Moomintroll books are set within a vast landscape of forests, mountains, and waters, inhabited by numerous animals and fanciful creatures. There are a few towns and villages, but mostly families and individuals are found in contented isolation. It is a world where there are many dangers, ranging from the Angostura bush which nearly eats the Snork maiden in *Comet in Moominland* and the menacing Groke in *Finn Family Moomintroll*, to such forces of nature as volcanoes, floods, and comets. Jansson's invented creatures are myriad. There are the Moomintrolls themselves, who look rather like small and amiable hippos with long tails, the very similar Snorks, the obsessive Hermulens, Snufkin in his pointed hat, the mouthless, wormlike Hattifatteners, the shambling, hairy Groke, and many others. The characters' days are passed mostly outdoors and time is measured by the cycle of the seasons; the Moomintrolls' world, though not rooted to any particular era, seems born of a nostalgia for childhood's freedom. There is, however, always the potential that everything could end, not only in disasters such as comets and floods, but on a smaller scale, as people enter and leave Moomintroll's life, and friends quarrel and make up. Every adventure concludes in peace, contentment, and homecoming. The stories are written with a dry humour arising from both character and action. Jansson's illustrations enrich the books; it is far easier to understand what a Hermulen, a Groke, a Hattifattener, or even a Moomintroll is by looking at the pictures, than from any description in words.

For many readers, Jansson's *Moomintroll* books have created a world to which they return again and again over the course of their lives, not just as children. To children, the stories offer adventure, friendship, humour, and dangers and adversity overcome. For adults, they offer the ideal of a life lived with attention to the values many of us would like to think we aspire to, a life where there is time enough for family pleasures to be the most important part of the day, and where contemplation and creation free of the stresses of 'making a living' are possible.

C.S. Lewis (1898-1963)

C.S. Lewis was the son of a Belfast solicitor. He was christened

Clive Staples, but throughout his life was known as Jack. He read widely and voraciously as a child and was an excellent student, but found the cliques and bullying of the boarding schools he attended intolerable and was educated for at a private tutor's, before winning a scholarship to University College, Oxford, in 1916. Conscripted in June of 1917, he left for France in November, but was back in England, wounded, the following spring. The war seems to have made less impact on Lewis' imagination than on that of many of his contemporaries; the First World War found little place in his writings directly or indirectly, and he himself regarded it as an experience somehow separated from the rest of his life. He returned to Oxford late in 1919, studying classics, philosophy, and eventually English language and literature. In 1925, he obtained a fellowship in English language and literature at Oxford's Magdalen College, where he was to teach until being elected Professor of English Language and Literature at Cambridge in 1954.

In 1931, Lewis, who had become an atheist as a teen, returned to the conservative Protestant Christianity of his youth and rapidly became a celebrated Christian apologist. This return to Christianity was largely due to the influence of his friend Tolkien (a Roman Catholic). In addition to his writings on medieval and renaissance literature, Lewis would produce a number of books on Christianity and spirituality over the course of his life; on both literary and religious matters he was a man of dogmatic and conservative opinion. He also wrote a science fiction trilogy for adults, *Out of the Silent Planet* (1938), *Perelandra* (1943 — sometimes titled *Voyage to Venus*), and *That Hideous Strength* (1945), in which elements of religious allegory play an increasing role in the story. The experiences of his hero, Ransom — particularly in the first two books, which take place on an imagined Mars and Venus whose exotic landscapes and inhabitants are depicted in great detail — are very entertaining adventures with appeal to teens. It is not necessary to share or even be aware of Lewis' religious beliefs to enjoy the stories, even though the climax of the second novel is the successful resistance of an alien Eve to Satan's temptation. By the third book, consideration of religious issues has become dominant over plot.

For much of his life Lewis lived with Janie Moore, the mother of a friend killed in the war; whether she was in the beginning his mistress remains unknown. It is certain that for most of that time, until her death in 1951 at the age of eighty, the relationship resembled that of son and demanding mother. In 1956, Lewis married a divorced American with two sons, Joy Gresham Davidman, whom he had initially gotten to know through 'fan mail'; she died of cancer in 1960, three years before Lewis, who continued to write on both Christianity and literature until the end of his life. His book written in reaction to Joy's death, *A Grief Observed* (1961, originally published pseudonymously as by N.W. Clerk), is for many, especially Christians, a moving and though-provoking reflection on grief and loss.

Lewis' great contribution to children's literature is *The Chronicles of Narnia*, a seven-book series consisting of (in internal 'historical' order rather than that of publication) *The Magician's Nephew* (1956), *The Lion, the Witch and the Wardrobe* (1950), *The Horse and His Boy* (1954), *Prince Caspian* (1951), *The Voyage of the Dawn Treader* (1952), *The Silver Chair* (1953), and *The Last Battle* (1956). The *Narnia* books are often referred to as a Christian allegory; certainly *The Lion* and *The Last Battle* can be read in such a light, having as their central themes respectively the Resurrection, and the end of the world and Last Judgement, while *The Magician's Nephew*, with its creation of a world, the introduction of evil, and the end of Innocence, is Old Testament rather than specifically Christian. Although Lewis did not share Tolkien's dislike of allegory, he was not writing anything like John Bunyan's *The Pilgrim's Progress*, in which every aspect of plot, character, and landscape exists only to function within the allegorical intent of the author. Lewis believed a story, although containing allegorical elements, should only suggest possible allegoric meanings to the readers, not impose it on them. Thus, his children's books are capable of being read and enjoyed as stories in their own right, independent of allegoric meaning.

The Lion, the Witch and the Wardrobe was an attempt to reimagine the central Christian myth in another setting, but as story, it is an adventure drawing on many elements of the fantastic that have had enduring appeal to children. There are talking animals, fantastic creatures, heroism, pageantry, adventure, battle, and another world where, with adults out of the way, children must take responsibility for both their own fate, and that of a land and even a world. Whereas earlier fantasy writers had tended to use creatures from the French and German fairy-tale traditions such as dwarves and witches, Lewis drew on classical mythology. He peopled Narnia with fauns, dryads, nymphs, centaurs, and Greco-Roman gods such as Silenus and Bacchus, in addition to his dwarves and giants. He rarely invented his own peoples, aside from the morose Marsh-Wiggles and the goblin-like but exuberant gnomes or Earthmen of *The Silver Chair*. His Talking Beasts owe a great deal to Kenneth Grahame; they are generally larger than natural animals, and, taking the Beavers in *The Lion* as typical, live comfortably middle-class human lives. *The Wind in the Willows* was a book Lewis enjoyed throughout his life.

Each of the seven stories stands on its own, so the series does not actually need to be read following the order of its internal chronology, or, indeed, in the order Lewis wrote them. *The Lion, the Witch and the Wardrobe* is often the best introduction to Narnia, since, in addition to being the first written, it is more suited in tone to a younger audience (as well as being a shorter novel, usually set in larger type). It also works well read aloud to children before they are reading longer works on their own. All seven are illustrated by Pauline Baynes, who illustrated several of Tolkien's shorter books.

The story, as it unfolds over the course of the seven books, begins in *The Magician's Nephew*, with Digory and Polly, neighbours in London of about the year 1900, sent off into other worlds by Digory's Uncle Andrew, who dreams of riches and power to be gained. They inadvertently bring back the tyrant Queen Jadis from a dying world, whose population she has utterly destroyed. Trying to get her out of London (as she brandishes a lamp-post, braining policemen), they end up in Narnia just as it is being created by the Lion, Aslan, out of song. This is one of the many influences on Lewis of Tolkien, who conceived of the world being created in song in his mythology, with which Lewis was very familiar. There is also a trace of Nesbit, an echo of the Queen of Babylon's mayhem in London in *The Story of the Amulet*.

In *The Lion, the Witch and the Wardrobe*, ages have passed and the Queen has become the White Witch, ruling Narnia as a cruel tyrant. Since humans brought evil to the new and innocent world of Narnia, humans must defeat her, and it falls to the four Pevensies, Peter, Susan, Edmund, and Lucy, evacuated from London to the Professor's country house during the Second World War, to do so. They tumble into Narnia through a wardrobe built of the wood of a Narnian tree, grown from the core of an apple brought back by Digory – the wardrobe is no passing convenience, but is well-rooted in the logic of Lewis' creation. Edmund takes the Witch's side at first and betrays his siblings and their friends; in him one person symbolizes the fall and redemption of the human race, as well as the betrayal of Judas. Aslan ransoms Edmund with his own life, fulfilling a great prophecy that a willing sacrifice for a traitor will reverse death. Aslan returns to life and kills the Witch in battle. The four children rule as kings and queens in Narnia for long years, before returning through the wardrobe and finding themselves children again.

The third Narnia story, *The Horse and His Boy*, is the only one not to have children from our world as its heroes. It is set during the reigns of Peter, Susan, Edmund, and Lucy, mostly in the Ottoman-like country of Calormen, from which the boy Shasta flees with Bree, an enslaved Talking Horse. They are joined by a young Calormene woman, Aravis, and the Horse Hwin, also escaping to freedom in Narnia. (Narnia is used of the entire world, especially by characters from our world, but in most of the books it refers to a specific kingdom within that world.) Their journey rapidly becomes a race across the desert carrying news of Calormene treachery and invasion to the Narnian-allied kingdom of Archenland, where, after the battle, Shasta is revealed to be the heir, Prince Cor, kidnapped long before.

Prince Caspian is set many generations after the golden age in which Peter and his siblings reigned, but time in the two worlds does not flow in parallel. The Pevensies, only a few years older, are suddenly called into Narnia by the blowing of a magic horn that once was Susan's, to find themselves in the overgrown ruins of their castle. They discover that Narnia has been invaded by Telmarines (humans from a distant land, but ultimately from our own world), who conquered the Talking animals and other creatures and have ruled for several generations. The current

Telmarine heir, Prince Caspian, has fled into the wilderness and become the champion of the Old Narnians against his usurping uncle's oppressive rule. With the aid of the Pevensies, he regains his throne and becomes a good king of both humans and Old Narnians.

The Voyage of the Dawn Treader has Edmund and Lucy enter Narnia, along with their troublesome cousin Eustace Scrubb, through a painting. They find themselves on a voyage with King Caspian aboard *Dawn Treader*, sailing into the east in search of seven loyal lords exiled by his late uncle. They have many adventures among the distant islands on their voyage; Eustace is changed into a dragon for a time and gradually learns to be a better person, and Caspian falls in love with the daughter of a star. When they reach the edge of the world, the *Dawn Treader* must turn back, but Edmund, Lucy, Eustace and Reepicheep the courtly Talking Mouse go on. Reepicheep passes beyond the edge of the world into Aslan's country (more Tolkien influence on the structure of Lewis' world), but the three children meet Aslan and return to their own world through a door in the sky.

In *The Silver Chair*, Eustace and his friend Jill Pole, escaping from bullies at their experimental school, are sent to Narnia by Aslan to find the lost Prince Rilian. Accompanied by the gloomy Marsh-wiggle, Puddleglum, they end up, after nearly losing their lives among man-eating giants, in an underground land ruled by a beautiful witch who has stolen Rilian's memory and enslaved him as her Black Knight. She has also enslaved an entire race of cheerful gnomes from deeper underground, enforcing a dour, mindless obedience upon them. She very nearly succeeds in convincing the three rescuers that there is no upper earth, no sun, no Aslan, but Puddleglum's obstinate faith endures and he saves them all from the enchantment, enabling the others to slay the witch as she transforms into a poisonous serpent.

The Last Battle, which won the 1956 Carnegie Medal, is simply that, the last battle in the world of Narnia. By the end it brings in all the human characters from the earlier books, except Susan, who no longer believes. Calormen invades the kingdom of Narnia, false prophets and a false Aslan are set up, and the land is torn apart in war. Eustace and Jill aid the last king, Tirian, but they and those loyal to Aslan are overcome by Calormenes and traitors; the Calormene victory is made easier by the many

Narnians who opt to stay neutral and look out only for themselves. The captured heroes are sent through a door, sacrifices, perhaps, to the evil Calormene god Tash, and witness the end of the world as Aslan calls the stars from the sky. They, and all who were believers and lived good lives, enter a world that is all the places they loved made larger and brighter. This is not a merely Narnian afterlife; the Calormenes who lived good lives are there also – faith in godhead and virtuous actions in life, rather than what name the believer gave to the deity, are what matters. In the end, the characters learn they are all dead and in Aslan's country, the ultimate reality of heaven, to stay. Even at this point, though, the religious matter is not made explicit, and a reader does not have to share Lewis' religious beliefs to enjoy the story as a story.

Although Lewis wrote with a purpose, his *Narnia* books have endured not because of their religious affinities, but because they are excellent fantasy novels of the kind children turn to again and again. They mingle adventure, drama, humour, wonders, action-filled plots, and protagonists capable of both the childish bickering and pettiness we know we share, and of the courage and heroism of which we would like to think we could be capable. Narnia was significant as the first of many modern fantasies returning to the tradition of MacDonald, combining realistic children with fairy-tale and medieval Romance magic, in stories where serious themes of concern to the author underpin the adventure.

Edward Eager (1911-1964)

The American author Edward Eager was a playwright whose interest in writing children's books was sparked by a search for stories to read to his son. His seven books are very influenced by E. Nesbit, a fact he took pains to acknowledge, making some reference to Nesbit's works in each of his own, in the hopes that this would lead children back to her. In *Half Magic* (1954), for example, the children are reading Nesbit's *The Enchanted Castle* and wishing something of the sort would happen to them, when it very obligingly does.

Half Magic is set in the mid twenties, about half way between

Nesbit's earliest fantasies and Eager's own time. The four children discover a coin capable of granting wishes, but it only grants half the wish, or grants it half-way. The cat talks, but is barely comprehensible; their mother, inadvertently carrying the coin to a dull visit, ends up halfway home; they land in the desert rather than on a desert island; Martha becomes ghostly and transparent by wishing she were not there at a boring movie. They quickly learn they must wish for twice as much of whatever it is they want to happen, which generally works, but a trip to a Pyle-esque King Arthur's court quickly goes awry when nine- year-old Katharine defeats Lancelot in a duel, to the great glee of Mordred.

Finally, the coin will grant them no more wishes, and concluding it may still have power for another user, they drop it by a girl and a baby, who disappear on the first of their adventures. The book also tells the story of bookseller Mr. Smith's courtship of the children's widowed mother who, like Lord Yalding in *The Enchanted Castle*, believes she is going mad and must not marry, after witnessing some effects of the magic. *Magic by the Lake* (1957) is a second adventure for the same children which tells much the same sort of story, with wishes granted by lake-water thanks to a magical turtle's intervention.

Eager's other books, although about different groups of children, are in a similar vein. They are enjoyable reads, full of event, but lack Nesbit's vital spark. They seem thin by comparison with hers, too self-consciously 'made-up'. Eager never induces the same degree of suspension of disbelief, because his magic has less provenance. The children's coin that grants half-power wishes in *Half Magic* has no history; the turtle's ability to grant wishes in *Magic by the Lake* is merely attributed to the species being ancient. Neither of these is as convincing as the ancient and unique Psammead or the myth-rich Phoenix, or the Amulet so carefully examined by an eminent scholar and rooted in Babylonian history. As well, in Eager's stories there is never any real jeopardy or fear, never any danger of consequences and loss, whereas in Nesbit's books there is always the possibility that something could go wrong for ever. Eager, compared with Nesbit, never seems to free himself from a feeling of 'let's pretend'.

Although they rarely approach Nesbit's convincing reality of detail or her mastery of irony, Eager's stories do have enjoyment to offer. Many young readers now find them 'easier going' than Nesbit, simply because Eager's books do not take for granted the broad exposure to other literature and to history which Nesbit's did. Having been written closer to the present, they contain less unfamiliar language. They are simple, light fun.

In the nineteen-sixties, books in a very similar vein were written by the British author Elisabeth Beresford; the first of her many Nesbit-like stories was *Awkward Magic* (1964), which featured a treasure-seeking Griffin and, like some of Nesbit's books, an absent father restored at the end.

L.M. Boston (1892-1990)

Lucy Boston attended Somerville College at Oxford, but left her studies to serve as a nurse during the First World War. She married and had one son, but was divorced in 1935. At this time, she bought Hemingford Grey Manor (near Huntingdon, now in Cambridgeshire), which changed the course of her life. The Manor is claimed to be the oldest continually occupied house in England. It was built around 1130, and much of the original Norman structure remains. It was the house itself which inspired Boston to begin writing and which was the focus of nearly all her prose.

Boston transformed Hemingford Grey Manor to Green Knowe in a series of six books, beginning with *The Children of Green Knowe* (1954), in which young Tolly comes to stay at the house of Green Knowe, with Mrs. Oldknow, his maternal great-grandmother, in the nineteen-fifties. Green Knowe is an ancient house that has been in the same family since it was built in the twelfth century. The ghosts of the children who have lived there inhabit it. In the first book Tolly meets and plays with Toby, Alexander, and Linnet, Oldknows from the seventeenth century who all died of plague on the same day, but later books reveal not all the ghosts of the house came to early deaths, or are even dead. Tolly meets many ghost-children who lived to a ripe old age and became his ancestors. Even his great-grandmother, still living, joins him as a ghostly young girl in a meeting of all the children near the end of the last book, *The Stones of Green*

Knowe (1976).

Other books tell stories from other times. In *The Chimneys of Green Knowe* (1958) Tolly learns the story of Susan, a blind girl of the late eighteenth century, and her African friend and servant, the freed slave Jacob. Past and present intersect in a search for lost treasure. *The River at Green Knowe* (1959) happens when Mrs. Oldknow has rented the house for the summer. A girl, Ida, stays there with her aunt, as well as two 'displaced children', Polish Oskar, and Burmese-born Chinese Hsu, called Ping. The children spend most of their time exploring the river in a canoe, meet a hermit who lives in a treehouse and eats raw fish, see flying horses, and discover a real giant, Terak, whose great aspiration is to be a circus clown. They also, as seems inevitable at Green Knowe, have a glimpse of the past, witnessing a prehistoric ritual on the site where Green Knowe would someday stand. *A Stranger at Green Knowe* (1961), which won the Carnegie Medal, contains no fantasy and is very sad in tone. In *Stranger*, Ping, now living with Mrs. Oldknow, befriends Hanno, an escaped gorilla. In the end, Hanno is discovered, shot, and killed. Children vary in their ability to cope with realistic tragedy in fiction; some will find *Stranger*'s sorrowful ending more than they are ready for, but it is an excellent book.

An Enemy at Green Knowe (1964) features Tolly and Ping together and is the best of the series in terms of plot and unity of story. In it, alchemy and necromancy trouble the house in the seventeenth century and in the present. In the past, the tutor, Dr. Vogel, practices black magic. In the present, a mysterious scholar, Dr. Melanie D. Powers, tries to control Mrs. Oldknow's mind to gain possession of the house. Tolly and Ping investigate and discover two hidden books on magic, the objects of Dr. Powers' desire. Green Knowe is besieged by maggots, adders, and giant black cats, defended by birds, hedgehogs, and the spirit of Hanno the gorilla, summoned by Ping. Even the past is not safe: Dr. Powers finds a way to control Susan, the eighteenth-century girl from *Chimneys*, to get an object she desires, but the boys again destroy her magic. The attacks continue to increase in danger and horror, until Tolly and Ping find a way to defeat the evil to which Dr. Power has dedicated herself. *Enemy* is really the finest of the Green Knowe stories, gripping, beautiful, and enjoyably terrifying from start to finish. Tolly and Ping reveal themselves as courageous, resourceful heroes, and the consolidation of coincidences does not seem out of place, since Green Knowe has been established throughout the preceding books as working its own magic to bring about just such events.

The final book in the series, *The Stones of Green Knowe*, is told mostly from the point of view of Roger d'Aulneaux, who, at a time of Danish raids, watches the manor house that is Green Knowe being built, worries about its future, and meets most of the children from the intervening books who belong to it. The novel expresses a great deal of regret for the changing of the old landscape, as the standing stones by which Tolly travels to the past are hauled away to a museum.

Unlike most series, the six *Green Knowe* books lack a uniformity in approach, and so liking or disliking one is no guarantee as to whether the other five will be enjoyed or not. The first book is more concerned with atmosphere than event or characterisation, and as such, will not appeal to some readers, who may regard it as rather slow. Others may find Green Knowe, with its benevolent ghosts and family histories, a minor fantasy kingdom. In the middle books there is greater attention paid to event as well as evocation of mood; the two with least action, drama, and plot are the first and last, *Children* and *Stones*. Each book tells a separate story, but although reference is made to events in previous books, it is not done to the extent that they must all be read in sequence, or at all, for comprehension.

Margot Benary-Isbert (1889-1979)

Margot Isbert was born in Saarbrucken, Germany, attended the University of Frankfort, and worked at the Museum of Ethnology and Anthropology, where she married Wilhelm Benary. The couple and their daughter farmed in Erfurt, but fled west before the Russian advance in the closing days of the Second World War. For a time, they were refugees in the western sectors of occupied Germany, an experience which led to the books for teens for which Benary-Isbert is best known in English, *The Ark* and *Rowan Farm*, which tell about German refugees in West Germany in the immediate post-war years. Benary-Isbert's daughter emigrated to the United States and in 1952, the author and her husband followed. She continued to write in German, but oversaw the translations into English herself.

Benary-Isbert wrote one children's fantasy which was published in an English translation in the United States not long after she immigrated there. *The Wicked Enchantment* (1955) is set in the small German cathedral town of Vogelsang, at an indefinite but modern time. It has elements of both fairy-tale and political allegory, but is first and foremost an adventure in an ordinary town where the fantastic is possible and, although unexpected, not astonishing. Anemone and her dog, Winnie-the-Pooh, run away from home because of her father's housekeeper and the housekeeper's horrible son, Edwin. Aunt Gundula takes Anemone in. Gundula is an eccentric artist who keeps a beehive over her bed, is famous for her Easter eggs, real and confectionery, and has a grudge against the male half of the human race. Anemone and Winnie are soon caught up in a resistance movement against a dictator, the town's new mayor, who is ordering all songbirds killed and all eggs confiscated, just as Easter is drawing near. He has also imprisoned two of Anemone's uncles for their politically satirical puppet show. Anemone discovers that the mayor is a centuries-dead tyrant, the Wicked Owl, returned from the grave, and her father's housekeeper and Edwin are actually the cathedral's missing statues of a Foolish Virgin and a gargoyle, who are trying to win themselves souls. All three must be defeated or lured back to their proper places to save Vogelsang. *The Wicked Enchantment* has a first-rate blend of adventure, mystery, and humour, and the setting has a depth of history and legend that makes Vogelsang feel convincingly possible.

K.M. Briggs (1898-1980)

Katharine Briggs was a folklorist with a particular interest in the seventeenth century. She received a master's degree from Oxford in 1926 and her Ph.D., also from Oxford, in 1952. Her four-volume *A Dictionary of British Folktales in the English Language* (1970-71) and the smaller *An Encyclopedia of Fairies* (1976) made a lasting contribution to English folklore studies. Before the Second World War, Briggs wrote several historical stories, but her two noteworthy children's fantasies, heavily influenced by her scholarly interests, were not written until later in her life.

The one book Briggs is most often remembered for, other than her scholarly works, is *Hobberdy Dick* (1955). It blends elements of English folklore and folk-custom with historical fiction, to create what one could call a fairy-tale in which, at last, the fairy is the hero. The title character, Hobberdy Dick, is the hobgoblin of Widford Manor. He is left alone when the royalist Culvers lose their home during the Civil War. The new Puritan owners, the Widdisons, make life bleak and joyless. Though young Joel Widdison loves the land, he is intended to follow his father as a London merchant. Anne Seckar, Joel's stepmother's maid, is a relative of the previous owners, and like Joel loves the house and the old country rituals.

Dick watches over Anne and Joel, helping them to find the Culver treasure, hidden by Anne's kin before their displacement. The treasure enables them to marry, and Widford Manor becomes theirs. They acknowledge Dick's help by offering him a choice between gifts symbolic of three alternatives: a broom, to continue his guardianship of the house; a green suit, which will gain him entry to fairyland and its sustained and hollow pleasure; or, the one Dick accepts, a red suit, which seems to symbolize his choosing a mortal life and an immortal soul. In English and Scottish folklore, brownies (the most common name for the domestic elves that help out around the home), traditionally leave if offered payment or clothing.

This is a beautiful and enjoyable story, containing much folklore and history that will engage the imagination. Some children may find, though, that they simply have not been exposed to enough of the historical background to follow the story, since it takes a familiarity with the Civil War period in England for granted. Others may be inspired to find out more about it. Those with an interest in traditional folklore, children and adults alike, will find that aspect of it fascinating as well. A new generation of readers may also detect in Hobberdy Dick and his kind (as well as in Mulock Craik's Brownie) the folklore-based, literary antecedents of Rowling's 'house-elf' servants (or slaves) in *Harry Potter*.

Briggs' second fantasy, *Kate Crackernuts* (1963) is based on the Scottish fairy-tale of the same name. It tells the story of step-sisters who set out into the world together after the mother of one, jealous of her stepdaughter, has a witch cast a spell on the girl. Like Briggs' more celebrated earlier work, it is set in the seventeenth century and combines historical detail with folk traditions of magic.

A. Philippa Pearce (b. 1920)

Philippa Pearce was the daughter of a miller and grew up in the mill-house of a water-mill on the River Cam. She studied English and History at Girton College at Cambridge. Following the Second World War, she worked as a producer and scriptwriter for the BBC, and later, as an editor at Oxford University Press and at Andre Deutsch. Most of Pearce's books, such as her first, *Minnow On the Say* (1955), are realistic, but her one fantasy is much celebrated. This is *Tom's Midnight Garden* (1958), a time-travel story which won the Carnegie Medal in 1958.

Tom's Midnight Garden is often regarded as the leading example of a time-travel story; in it, a young boy, Tom Long, is sent to stay at his aunt and uncle's flat while his brother has measles. He is very bored, since he is in quarantine, and the house has no garden to play in. Tom discovers that when the old grandfather clock in the entry hall strikes thirteen he can go out into a garden. There, he is insubstantial as a ghost, but can be seen by a girl, Hatty, who is as lonely as he is. The two play in the garden, but for Hatty, Tom's visits are very far apart, and although he barely notices, she is growing up. On one visit, in the winter of 1895, they skate up the river, both wearing the same pair of skates. Tom had asked Hatty to hide them in her time, so that he could find them in his and take them with him to use in the past. Hatty grows up, falls in love, and marries, and Tom is unable to find the garden. His cries for Hatty wake all the tenants, and he discovers that Mrs. Bartholomew, the elderly widow who owns the house and lives in the top flat, is his Hatty. He has been slipping into the eighteen-nineties as she dreamed of her lonely, unhappy childhood and the ghostly friend she had.

This is a classic of twentieth century children's literature; however, aside from the melding of two times through the two children's identical loneliness, there is even less in it of the fantastic than in Alison Uttley's *A Traveller in Time*. The concern of *Tom's Midnight Garden* is not with the experience of time-travel and the impending doom of history as faced by Uttley's heroine; it is mostly a story of friendship and growing up.

A similar book, Penelope Farmer's *Charlotte Sometimes*, was published in 1969. It is about a thirteen-year-old girl sent to boarding school in 1958, Charlotte Makepeace, who wakes up to find herself still at the school, still in the same bed, but in the middle of the Great War and addressed as Clare Moby. Days in the past and present alternate as the two girls continue to switch places; Charlotte and Clare begin communicating by means of diaries in each time. Aside from the time-travel element, this later book, like *Tom's Midnight Garden*, is mostly a domestic drama, and readers who enjoy one will appreciate the other.

The fantasy books of the fifties are still enjoyed by children today; nearly all the books discussed in this chapter are still in print. In part, their continued popularity when contrasted with that of authors such as Carroll, MacDonald, or even Nesbit is due to the fact that the books were not written at such a distance in time that the language and customs in them are unfamiliar to young readers.

Many of these stories use fantasy to create a world that is more comforting, more contained, than the author's own times, or ours. Many children's writers in the fifties used fantasy as a way of looking back to another time when the world did not seem so threatening, or of creating another world, like that of Jansson's Moomins, in which the dangers were on a scale to be grappled with and overcome (with rather large exceptions, like comets and volcanoes, which nevertheless are avoided without too much terror).

C.S. Lewis' world, though, is not Moomin Valley, nor is Narnia safe and enclosing. He was heavily influenced by his friend Tolkien, who had flung open the borders of fantasy to let in vastness. Children's fantasy returned to the shadowy underpinnings of the fairy-tales, admitting legend and myth and Romance and mystery. The predominance of 'domestic' fantasy was ebbing. Stories like *The Princess and the Goblin*, *The Three Mulla-Mulgars*, *The Hobbit*, and *The Lion, the Witch and the*

155

Wardrobe were to become more common, although those like *Five Children and It* or *Tom's Midnight Garden*, stories centred on children living lives as children, would never disappear.

IX
Old Tales Retold, part two

Since the First World War, the retelling of traditional tales has taken two main forms: what could be called the 'traditional' re-telling, in which authors retell the story in their own words, but do not develop it beyond the outline of the original, and the more novelistic retelling, in which a new story is made on the foundation of the old. Fairy-tales in particular have been apt subjects for this 'novelizing' approach. Such a novelistic retelling of traditional material was uncommon in the nineteenth century, but became far more usual in the twentieth and reached its zenith in the later twentieth century. It is arguably the century's unique contribution to the telling of traditional tales.

In such books, the author takes the plot or situation of the original tale, but uses it as the basis for a story ranging beyond the limits of the source, most notably in the case of the traditional fairy-tale. Novels starting from such a source usually expand the scope of the original tale in all directions, giving the characters psychological depth and motive, pinning them through detail and complexity to a specific place and time, real or invented, making them individuals rather than types. This treatment has been used to write both juvenile and adult fiction.

In adult fantasy, an example of such an approach is the series of novels based on fairy-tales edited by Terri Windling, which was published in the United States from the late eighties through the nineties. In it, various authors were invited to write novels based on traditional fairy-tales. Patricia C. Wrede's *Snow White and Rose Red* (1989), Charles de Lint's *Jack the Giant-Killer* (1990; reissued with its 1990 sequel, *Drink Down the Moon*, as *Jack of Kinrowan* in 1995), Jane Yolen's *Briar Rose* (1993) or Tanith Lee's *White as Snow* (2001) are examples of these. The settings range from Elizabethan England to the contemporary United States, while the various stories themselves deal with a vast range of human experience and drama: love, enchantment, politics, family secrets, rape, the Holocaust. Fairy-tales, now just as much as two hundred years ago, can provide a pattern of metaphor and a template of intense emotion, a pattern which, taken as a foundation, offers the author freedom to explore to many wider horizons of experience. Although published for an adult audience, the books in this series will find a readership among teens as well; some, such as Yolen's *Briar Rose*, have in fact been reissued as young adult books. However, many novels based on fairy-tales have been written specifically for children, and these were not a phenomenon of the late twentieth century, but appeared throughout the century.

Myths and legends, on the other hand, have more often been treated in a traditional manner, adapted in form, content, or language for children, with their action and characters left in the starker style of a story honed to its essentials by centuries of re-telling, the details those sanctioned by tradition. The twentieth century has produced some great works of this sort, and yet, they do not appear as popular with readers or publishers as they once were. One cause of this may be the narrowing range of children's reading. The past is a more distant land, and young readers, perhaps in part because of the ubiquitous immediacy of television, seem to find it difficult to 'identify with' a character portrayed less emotionally, more remotely, or with a more 'alien' set of values, motivations, or beliefs, as is common in a traditional re-telling, as though 'identifying with' is the only way to partake imaginatively of a character's experiences. It sometimes seems that imagination is expected to be less involved in reading than it used to be; too often it is assumed that everything presented in a story must already be familiar, including the mindset of the characters. Some people, even those involved in education and publishing, may associate use of the imagination with effort and difficulty, and can react as though to encourage the exercise of the imagination in experiencing something other than the familiar is to impose undue hardship. Children who do explore beyond the novel-style narrative, though, may find their imaginations caught and changed by that very distance and grandeur, the very foreignness of the past, as well as by the unifying hopes and fears and struggles of the common humanity of past and present.

Numerous collections of straightforward retellings of myth, legend, and folk- or fairy-tales from around the world were published in the twentieth century, assembled, translated, or retold by numerous editors and authors. Many of these remain readily available, either still in print or in library collections.

In the eighties and nineties, Oxford brought out its paperback *Oxford Myths and Legends* series, an excellent example of the type of retelling of traditional material from around the world that many publishers produced throughout the century. Oxford's series contains collections of myths, legends, and folktales from a number of different countries retold by various writers; it numbers around twenty volumes, many of which were first published in the fifties or sixties. They are uniformly well-written. Much dialogue is used, direct speech preventing the stories becoming dry synopses. The style is formal, but not archaic: contractions, for instance, are avoided even in direct speech. This aids in imparting the universality of such stories; no descent into excessively datable idiom distracts from the experience of a story that may be centuries or a millennium old, specific to a particular culture and climate, but at the same time telling of universal human emotional experience or philosophical struggle. This traditional narrative style is suitable for older children or teens and makes an equally good introduction to the material for adults.

Barbara Leonie Picard (b. 1917) wrote original fairy-tale collections such as *The Lady of the Linden Tree* (1954) and *The Faun and the Woodcutter's Daughter* (1964). She is also the only author represented by multiple volumes in the Oxford series, which contains republications of her *French Legends, Tales, and Fairy Stories*, the *Iliad*, the *Odyssey*, *Tales of Ancient Persia*, *German Hero-Sagas and Folk-Tales*, and *Tales of the Norse Gods* (1994). The latter, which originally appeared in slightly different form as *Tales of the Norse Gods and Heroes* (1953), is an excellent example of the approach taken in the *Oxford Myths and Legends*. It contains stories from the *Eddas*,[*] following the

---

[*] The *Elder* or *Poetic Edda* is a late twelfth century Icelandic collection of poems in Old Norse composed between 900 and 1050 A.D.; it includes stories of the gods and heroes, and traditional proverbs and wisdom. The *Younger* or *Prose Edda* was written by Snorri Sturluson (1178-1244); it remains the primary source for knowledge of Norse mythology.

mythological cycle of tales from the creation of the world, through the struggles between gods and giants, to the binding of Loki and Norse beliefs about the end of the world.

The literary style of all the other volumes by other authors is similar to that which Picard made her hallmark in retellings; it is her style that seems to have set the standard for the series. Japanese, Hungarian, Russian, African, West Indian, Chinese, English, Scottish, Armenian, Scandinavian, and Indian stories are among the collections by other authors included in the series. All provide a range of mythological or folk material, some tales familiar and some less so. Typical of the material that will be less familiar to young readers is J.E.B. Gray's *Indian Tales and Legends* (1989), first published in 1961. It contains stories of a folktale type about the Buddha, animal fables, and mythological epics, including a story from the *Mahabharata*. It also contains a retelling of the *Ramayana*, the story of the demon-vanquishing hero Rama and his wife Sita, her abduction, rescue, rejection by Rama, the vindication of her virtue and fidelity, and their reunion. Each volume in the *Oxford Myths and Legends* series contains a brief discussion of the sources for the stories included, as well as pronunciation guides for names where necessary, making these a good introduction not only to the stories themselves, but to the cultures that gave rise to them. The discussion of sources can also serve as a guide to further reading for those whose interest has been piqued.

Eleanor Farjeon (1881-1965)

Farjeon, whose life and original stories are discussed in Chapter VI, had a knack for retelling fairy-tales and bringing out their comedy. Both 'Cinderella' and 'Rumpelstiltskin' were turned into children's novels by her, in a style that evokes the literary fairy-tales, the comedies on the fairy-tale world, of Thackeray, Lang, and Milne. Like Milne's *Once on a Time*, Farjeon's two fairy-tale novels had their origins in plays. Both Farjeon's stories feature strong-willed girl-heroes, but it is the whimsical supporting casts whose characters betray their stage origins: King Nollekens in *The Silver Curlew* is a particularly improbable character even in a comedic fairy-tale novel, but would be hilarious on stage.

160

The Silver Curlew (1953) illustrated by E. H. Shepard (illustrator of *The Wind in the Willows* and *Pooh*),[*] was first a play co-written with Farjeon's brother Herbert. It gives new life to the story of Rumpelstiltskin or, in English versions, 'Tom Tit Tot, and the girl who is set the impossible task of spinning straw into gold. In *The Silver Curlew*, the heroine is not the queen but her younger sister, Poll. The story is set on the Norfolk Broads, and the sea and the wind shape its atmosphere. While Doll, eldest daughter of the miller Mother Codling, is beautiful, placid, and lazy, Poll is curious, forthright, and intelligent. Through a well-meaning fib on Poll's part, Doll is forced to demonstrate herself a prodigious spinster (of linen thread, not gold) to King Nollekens and his tyrannical old Nan. Locked up to prove her speed and skill or else lose her head, Doll is saved by the Spindle-Imp, who makes the traditional bargain: he will do the spinning for her, and in a year he will come back for payment. If she guesses his name they are quit, but if she fails, she belongs to him. The flax is spun and Doll marries the king.

Farjeon's highly original addition to the story is the Silver Curlew. Poll is friends with Charlee Loon, a strange fisherman and musician, who is not exactly half-witted, but is not quite all there, either. When Poll discovers that both Doll and her baby are about to be claimed by the Spindle-Imp if Doll cannot guess the imp's name, she goes to the Witching-Wood disguised as an imp. With Charlee's help, she passes the Spider-Mother's riddling initiation test, but is revealed when her disguise slips. She and Charlee are captured, but escape with the help of the Silver Curlew, a bird Poll had earlier rescued and nursed back to health, which Charlee claims is actually the Lady of the Moon, searching for her lost husband. Poll is able to reach Doll with the Spindle-Imp's true name in time, while Charlee's lost wits are restored and he remembers himself, returning, with his wife the Curlew, to his home in the moon.

The Glass Slipper (1955) is based on a play of the same name written by Farjeon and her brother in 1944. It retells the story of Cinderella, expanding imaginatively on the framework of the traditional tale. Ella's father appears in a larger role as a timid man ashamed of allowing his second wife and stepdaughters to

---

[*] Shepard's name appears variously in the books he illustrated as E.H., Ernest, or Ernest H.

so abuse his own child, but too weak to do more than smuggle her a treat now and then. Farjeon's Ella, rather than suffering in submissive silence, does complain of her fate. The fairy godmother appears variously as a fairy, a bird, and an old crone to whom Ella is kind. At the ball, Ella and the Prince fall in love, but it is not all dancing and gazing enraptured into one another's eyes; they talk a great deal, and lead the court on a wild game of hide and seek. When the guests are summoned to the palace the next day to try on the slipper, Ella stands up to her stepmother, insisting on her right to go, but is overpowered and out-manoeuvred. The crone sees that the stepmother gets her comeuppance, and Ella finally tries on the slipper. She is not transformed again into the dazzling 'Princess of Nowhere', but remains in her rags, as the prince kisses her sooty hand. It is her he loves, not the fairy glamour. The most original addition to the tradition is the prince's mute fool, the witless and wise Zany who mirrors his moods and knows his true feelings.

Like Farjeon's original stories, her two fairy-tale retellings bring humour, romance, and the explorations of a homely landscape's poetic possibilities. *The Silver Curlew* is particularly fine. The Norfolk Broads are made a land of poetic possibility, windswept, mysterious, vast, bound together with the sea and the distant moon through the elements of wind and water, with the eerie Witching-Wood, dark, close, and claustrophobic, full of pines and spiders, as foil to the sweep of the shore and the sky.

Roger Lancelyn Green (1918-1987)

Green is one of the twentieth century's most significant retellers of traditional myths and legends for children. He was born in Norwich, grew up in Cheshire, and studied English at Oxford's Merton College. He worked as a teacher and an actor, among other things, and was for a time Deputy Librarian of Merton. Green was a friend of Tolkien and Lewis, and wrote biographies of C.S. Lewis, Andrew Lang, J.M. Barrie, and Lewis Carroll. He married a fellow Oxford graduate, actor June Lancelyn Green.

Green produced a great number of collections retelling myths and legends. His range was not so eclectic as Andrew Lang's; he concentrated mostly on European, Classical, and Middle Eastern sources. His works influenced writers of the later twentieth century, being for some their first introduction to the stories of the Classical world and of Scandinavia. Among his many books were *Heroes of Greece and Troy* (1960) and *Myths of the Norsemen* (1962), both very influential on the imaginations of children growing up in the sixties. Green's retellings are often of the traditional sort, although he did also write novels based on legends. Generally, though, he retells his material in simple but not simplistic prose, adopting a narrative style and diction suitable for a young audience without either ornate archaism or condescension, omitting the explicit sexual content found in many myths, using dialogue and adding descriptive details to create the time and place for the readers, but inventing nothing that makes any major alteration to the story. As most retellers have done, he adopts a straightforward, formal prose, not 'talking down' but not in any way artificial or difficult. Nearly every one of his collections includes a foreword providing some background on the material included, but intended just as much as the stories to be read by children.

Green's *A Book of Myths* (1965) was one of his own favourites. It contains episodes from the mythologies of ten literate traditions: Egyptian, Babylonian, Hittite, Phoenician, Cretan, Greek, Roman, Phrygian, Persian, and Scandinavian. The stories include Isis' search for slain Osiris and their son Horus' vengeance against Set, his father's killer; all of the *Epic of Gilgamesh*; the struggle of Phoenician Baal, Asthoreth, and the war-goddess Anat, against Mot, ruler of the land of the dead, in which Baal is slain and reborn, bringing agriculture and peace; Prometheus' theft of fire; Demeter's search for her abducted daughter Persephone; and Loki's treachery and the death of Baldur, among many others.

Green's *Tales of Ancient Egypt* (1967) is typical of his approach to telling a body of material from one nation. He begins with a prologue on ancient Egypt, telling a little of its culture and history and discussing the sources of the stories and the probable dates of their composition. His tales start with the mythology, the stories of the gods and goddesses – Ra, Isis and Osiris, Horus, as well as lesser-known stories about the interventions of gods in the lives of historical men and women of Egypt. He also includes stories in the folktale tradition, telling of magic, adventurous heroes, and animal helpers. He concludes with later Egyptian stories preserved in Greek, like the one about Helen of Troy's sojourn among the Egyptians, and 'The Girl with the Rose-red Slippers', in which the Greek slave Rhodopis becomes the Pharaoh Amasis' bride after the eagle of Horus brings him one of her slippers.

Green also wrote some original fiction for children, although it usually reflected his interest in myth and legend. *The Luck of Troy* (1961) is a novel telling the story of the Trojan War, mostly from the point of view of Nicostratus, Prince of Sparta, the son of Menelaus and Helen, who was carried off to Troy along with his mother. Green's story of Troy is drawn not only from Homer, but from other Greek and Roman sources; the character of Nico comes from some of these. Green begins with a 'Prologue at Mycenae' which explains, through conversation between Agemmenon's daughters and Hermione, daughter of Helen and Menelaus, how Helen was given a drug by Paris and magically enticed away against her will, and how she took two-year old Nico with her. The princesses' fathers arrive and reveal that the Greek kings are all going to war against the Trojans to get Helen back. Green introduces some discussion of Mycenaean funereal practices and architecture that seem out of place. Strangely, when it came to writing original stories, Green lacked the ability to make the past real and to introduce a different world without appearing to lecture, though in his retellings he handled the same difficulty admirably. Once this awkward explanatory preface is past, the book is essentially an adventure story set ten years later, during the final phase of the siege of Troy.

Nico has grown up among the Trojans, but as an enemy Greek, has never been at home there. He is caught between two worlds, feeling he belongs to neither. In the course of the story he comes to realize he is Greek. When Odysseus enters Troy disguised as a beggar, intending to steal the Palladion, the luck of Troy, and thus doom the city to fall, Nico becomes involved in his plans. Paris, who is a brutal thug, suspects Nico, who has many narrow escapes and plays an active part in events. There is treachery and honour on both sides, and in the end, after Odysseus' ruse of the wooden horse has been successful and the city has fallen to the Greeks, Nico meets the father he does not remember and leads him to save Helen from a vengeful Trojan just in time.

This is a different re-imagining of the story of Troy, one which may make it seem very real and immediate to young readers. Green takes great pains with the accuracy of his details, and although his explanations or descriptions of archaeological matters sometimes seem to 'smack of the lamp' they are not overly long. During the first part of the book Nico is more a witness than a participant, but as the plot progresses he becomes increasingly central to the action. The dialogue has a sometimes unconvincing quality to it, again, very unlike Green's usual style in retelling legends; the characters all sound very much like any fictional British children and parents of the fifties, which is occasionally incongruously humorous. *The Luck of Troy* should still appeal to young readers; the fact that Nico becomes such an important participant in the action sets it apart, since retellings that follow the *Iliad* closely have few younger characters that readers of a similar age can identify with, and for some, identification with a child participant in the action is an important part of engagement with a book.

In addition to his numerous collections of myths and legends, Green was also the editor of an outstanding anthology of dragon stories. In the sixties, the publisher Hamish Hamilton brought out a series of themed anthologies. Most of these were reissued in paperback by Puffin within a few years of their original publication. All will still have great appeal to young fantasy readers.

For *The Hamish Hamilton Book of Dragons* (1970 – published in paperback by Puffin in 1970 as *A Book of Dragons*, easily confused with *The Book of Dragons*, a 1901 collection of fantasy short stories by E. Nesbit), Green was the editor rather than the author, though some of the retellings are his. He chose a wide range of material. He begins with a dedication to Tolkien, whose Smaug and Chrysophylax Dives he regards as the pre-eminent modern dragons, and a scrap of alliterative verse in Modern English on dragons by C.S. Lewis, originally written to demonstrate Old English poetic form. Green's introduction discusses ideas of dragons through the ages, the possible origins of dragon tales, and why he has chosen not to include excerpts of dragons from longer modern works, instead directing readers to seek out *The Hobbit* and *Farmer Giles of Ham*, *The Voyage of the Dawn Treader*, Kenneth Grahame's 'The Reluctant Dragon', and Lang's *Prince Prigio*. The dragons Green does include are arranged by source. He begins with 'Dragons of Ancient Days', with dragons or serpents from Greek and Roman sources, and moves on to the 'Dark Ages' for dragons encountered by Sigurd, Beowulf, and Merlin, as well as a less frequently encountered Byzantine one. The dragons of the High Middle Ages are included in this section as well, with Malory and the legend of St. George. 'Folklore' dragons include everything from British folktales to Chinese stories, while 'Later Days' spans the Renaissance to the twentieth century, including pieces by Edmund Spenser, Lang, and Nesbit, as well as poems by Tolkien and Lewis. Green finishes it off with the dragon of Revelations XX, and a detailed bibliography of his sources.

Among the other volumes in this series are *The Hamish Hamilton Book of Kings* (1964) and *of Queens* (1965), both edited by Eleanor Farjeon and William Mayne; *of Goblins* (1969), edited by Alan Garner; *of Heroes* (1967) and *of Giants* (1968), edited by William Mayne; *of Witches* (1966) and *of Myths and Legends* (1964), edited by Jacynth Hope-Simpson; *of Magical Beasts* (1965), edited by Ruth Manning-Sanders, and *of Princes* (1965), edited by Christopher Sinclair-Stevenson. Like *Dragons*, all contain a wide range of material from sources both ancient and modern, and appeared as Puffins with 'Hamish Hamilton' dropped from the title. They are outstanding examples of themed anthologies, which display literary taste and scholarship in the selection and presentation of the material; they remain very readable, capable of opening new worlds of the imagination to children just as much today as forty years ago.

Roger Lancelyn Green's obvious love for the stories, his ability to make distant times and other cultures live with colour and drama for young readers, and his quiet knowledge and scholarship, make him still one of the best to introduce children to much of the material he retold. Like Andrew Lang, his influence, although not obvious, can perhaps be traced through the fiction writers of subsequent generations who count his collections among their formative youthful reading.

Rosemary Sutcliff (1920-1992)

Rosemary Sutcliff, who must be numbered among the great children's writers of the twentieth century, was born in Surrey. Her father was an officer in the navy and the family lived for a time in Malta, among other places. Sutcliff developed Still's Disease, a severe form of rheumatoid arthritis, which left her frequently ill and in pain throughout her childhood and would eventually make her dependent on a wheelchair. She studied art and became a painter of miniatures, but also began writing. Her particular loves were history and legends.

Sutcliff was almost entirely a writer of historical fiction, but her historical novels had a great impact on the fantasy writers of the twentieth century, by introducing several generations of young readers to a time other than their own. She made the past live, without making it merely a realm of modern characters, with modern values and motivations, in instructional fancy dress. She taught the importance of attention to historical detail. Through her stories linking the generations of one family from early Roman Britain to the time of the Anglo-Saxon invasions, she also made history a river of continual change rather than a series of isolated islands of significant event. She showed, through her adoption of a slightly formal but not artificial or archaic language for dialogue, the way to make a past or another language seem neither contemporary, slangy, and soon out of date and incongruous, nor artificially archaic. All these things taught the fantasy writers who read her and followed her something of their craft, and had a lasting influence on the writing of historical fiction for children.

However, Sutcliff also wrote retellings of traditional material, not fairy-tales but myths and legends, including two of the most significant stories for English, *Beowulf* and the 'Matter of Britain', the stories of King Arthur. (Her Arthurian material will be discussed in the next chapter.) The Old English epic *Beowulf* has been retold at various times for various audiences. Sutcliff's *Beowulf: Dragonslayer* (1961), is an outstanding example. Hers is not a translation, but a straightforward retelling in the clear, slightly formal prose that is a hallmark of her historical fiction. It is illustrated with line drawings by Charles Keeping (1924-1988), who also illustrated Crossley-Holland's version (see below). Sutcliff divides the story into nine chapters, imagining some aspects of the story that are not told in the original, such as word of the monster preying on the Danes coming to Hygelac's hall and the reactions of Hygelac and Beowulf to it, while omitting the Finnsburg episode, which has little directly to do with the main story. All three of Beowulf's great battles – the fights with Grendal and with Grendal's mother under the lake, and the final fateful killing of the dragon – are told in stirring style. Children have always loved the grand, bloody, and ultimately tragic heroism of *Beowulf*; Sutcliff's is an excellent prose introduction to the poem.

Sutcliff also retold Irish legend, with *The High Deeds of Finn Mac Cool* (1967) and *Hound of Ulster* (1963), and the medieval, ultimately Welsh, story of *Tristan and Iseult* (1971), as well as Greek epic. Her *Black Ships Before Troy* (1993) and *The Wanderings of Odysseus* (1995), both illustrated by Alan Lee, are beautiful books.* Nearly every page features Lee's detailed, accurate, and action-filled paintings; however, these are not picture books for little children but almost novel-length retellings of the *Iliad* and the *Odyssey* for older children and teens. Lee's artwork serves better than any description to make real the details of armour, arms, and architecture. (Lee has also provided particularly fine illustrations for editions of *The Hobbit* and *The Lord of the Rings*, HarperCollins 1997 and 1992.) An appendix has a guide to pronouncing Greek names, and a bibliography. In her distinctive way, Sutcliff chose to tell the story in a language that is dignified and formal, but not so much so as to sound artificial or stilted. She accounts for the motivations of the people involved in a straightforward manner, showing Helen a willing participant in her abduction, a young wife married to an old king who discovers passionate love for the first time on seeing Paris. Sutcliff covers the full matter of the Trojan story, from the birth of Paris, the awarding of the golden apple of discord, his elopement with Helen, the nine year's siege of Troy, through to the quarrelling amongst the Greek leaders in the tenth year and how the enmity between Achilles and Agememnon nearly lost them the war. Achilles' sullen withdrawal from battle, the subsequent death of his friend Patroclus, and his slaying of

---

* There is also a companion volume by Penelope Lively, *In Search of a Homeland* (2001) retelling Virgil's *Aeneid.* (See Chapter XII)

the Trojan champion Hector in return is dealt with non-judgementally, which can be a challenge in retelling these stories, since to modern sensibilities some of the great heroes behaved very childishly. Sutcliff presents them as they are in the original, great heroes of unchecked, even operatic, emotions. She also gives prominence to the roles of Penthesilea and the Amazons, the prophet Cassandra, Helen, and Hector's wife Andromache, who are often overlooked in shorter synopses of the matter of Troy. The disguised Odysseus entering and stealing a sacred image – the luck of Troy – from the Trojan temple is edge-of-the-seat suspense. The final battles and the deaths of the heroes, the loyalties and the petty quarrelling of men and gods, the heroism and madness, the wooden horse, and the sack of the city are all here. Like the original, Sutcliff's version of the *Iliad* moves relentlessly to its fated, tragic end. It conveys not only the story of the *Iliad*, but its spirit. Her retelling of the *Odyssey* likewise conveys the excitement and drama of the original, making Odysseus come alive as a heroic, struggling individual, his spirit unbroken even by divine enmity. As with her *Beowulf*, there could be no better introduction for the older child or teen reader not quite ready for a direct translation of the original, but hungry for the depth and power of these stories, among the greatest literary works of the human imagination preserved from our past.

Kevin Crossley-Holland (b. 1941)

Crossley-Holland studied Anglo-Saxon literature at Oxford and taught poetry at Leeds as well as working as a book editor. In the sixties Crossley-Holland began writing novels based on medieval legend; he is also a published poet and opera librettist. His children's illustrated story *Storm* (1985), about a girl and a ghostly highwayman, won the Carnegie Medal. He lives in Norfolk.

In the sixties, Crossley-Holland wrote two children's novels based on English thirteenth-century romances. The story of *King Horn* (1965) is that of Prince Horn, who is set adrift with his two friends after the kingdom of Suddenne is conquered in revenge for the Crusades. They pretend to be merchants' sons at the royal court in Westernesse, where Horn falls in love with Rymenhild, the king's daughter. Horn's friend Fikenhild betrays their love to King Aylmer, and tells him Horn plans his murder. Horn is exiled again, becomes the Irish king's champion, and returns to Westernesse with a band of Irish warriors to prevent Rymenhild's marriage to another. Having succeeded in winning his beloved, he reconquers his own kingdom of Suddenne. Rymenhild is abducted by Fikenhild, and Horn once again has to penetrate an enemy's hall in disguise to save his bride.

Crossley-Holland's *King Horn* is definitely a novel rather than a straight retelling. It attempts to bring the major characters to life as young people the audience is supposed to see as similar to themselves. To do this, Crossley-Holland makes his characters speak as though they are young people of the fifties or sixties, incongruously so, in many places, because they now sound a little comically 'old-fashioned' in a way that has nothing to do with the Middle Ages. It is an approach very different from that of Sutcliff, and one that does not always sit easily in the story. Part of the problem is that Crossley-Holland is not consistent. The narrative sometimes strives for the grandeur and sometimes the comedy of the world of medieval Romance, while the boys themselves seem to have wandered out of *Biggles*, or at least *Jennings and Darbishire*, in their patterns of speech and mannerisms. The same technique is used in Green's *The Luck of Troy*, to less disconcerting effect, because Green is at least more consistent. Crossley-Holland also tends to belabour his point in explaining what people are feeling or in describing character, which prevents the reader from ever being able to become comfortably immersed in the internal reality of the story; his habit of putting character's thoughts in italics is awkward, especially when used as frequently as he does in his early work. Very similar to *King Horn* in approach and effect is Crossley-Holland's first novel, *Havelok the Dane* (1964). This retells the late thirteenth-century romance of Havelok, a poor servant boy who is revealed to be royal and becomes king of England and Denmark.

Beowulf (1982) is a more successful retelling than Crossley-Holland's earlier works. He begins the story with a one-eyed wanderer telling Hygelac's hall of the Danes' suffering. His unfinished story inspires the young Beowulf to set out to

Hrothgar's rescue. The retelling then follows the original in events, leaving out Finnsburg and ending with Beowulf's burial. Crossley-Holland places his one-eyed Wanderer, whom readers familiar with Norse tradition should immediately recognize as the god Odin, at this final episode in the hero's life, announcing that Beowulf has now finished the story begun in Hygelac's hall. The prose is simple and the language rich and descriptive without being ornate. Sometimes Crossley-Holland retains echoes of Old English phrasing, and sometimes turns a new phrase, although he overuses sentence fragments. The dialogue is an occasionally-uncomfortable blend of formal and colloquial, reminiscent of but not so jarringly inconsistent as his *King Horn*. As in Sutcliff's *Beowulf: Dragonslayer*, the illustrations, by Charles Keeping, are impressive, although whereas Sutcliff's had only a few illustrations, in the manner of children's novels of the sixties, in Crossley-Holland's the art has a much more dominant place as an integral part of the book.

Crossley-Holland's retelling of Scandinavian mythology, *Norse Myths* (1980), is not written specifically for children but is quite accessible, being filled with dialogue and colourful detail. He recently published another book doing much the same thing but intended specifically for children, *Viking Myths of Gods and Monsters* (2002).

Robin McKinley (b. 1952)

McKinley, whose work is also discussed in Chapters X and XIV, has made a name for herself as a re-imaginer of fairy-tales for teen and adult readers. Her first book, *Beauty* (1978), was, as its name suggests, a retelling of 'Beauty and the Beast'. In it, Beauty, Hope, and Grace are loving sisters, the daughters of a wealthy merchant. Grace is engaged to one of his sea-captains, Hope secretly in love with Gervain, an iron-worker in his ship-yard, and Beauty, scholarly and horse-mad, believes herself plain and awkward. When a run of bad luck ruins the merchant and Grace's betrothed is believed lost at sea, Gervain marries Hope and the entire family heads north to a small village in need of a blacksmith. The sisters settle into their new life with determina-tion. Beauty and her powerful horse Greatheart become much in demand; the family, always loving and mutually supportive, becomes part of the community. The story follows the traditional outline: the merchant lost in the mysterious forest seeking shelter in the castle, taking a rose for his daughter, told he must send that daughter to the Beast. The father is not willing to do so. It is Beauty who insists she will go.

Beauty's life in the castle is one of leisure, scholarship, and growing friendship with the Beast, whose proposals of marriage she continues to refuse. Allowed to take her family news of the impending return of Grace's betrothed, she realizes she loves the Beast, but loses track of time and returns to the castle too late, to find it falling into ruin and the Beast dying. He is revived by her care. She tells him then that she wants to marry him, and he and the castle are transformed. Beauty, faced with a handsome stranger, first tries to leave to look for the Beast, and even after recognizing his voice, has trouble believing him when he insists on her own beauty.

McKinley returned to this same fairy-tale in *Rose Daughter* (1997). She again wrote a story of three sisters loving and loyal to one another, named Lionheart, Jeweltongue, and Beauty. This is a more magical world than that of *Beauty*, where the magic exists only in the far fringes of the world. Here it is an everyday thing, while roses are an extremely rare flower which only magic-users can grow. The sisters' mother is a glamorous and temperamental woman who dies in a reckless riding accident, the father a merchant who turns against all magic-workers. Lionheart is dauntless, Jeweltongue clever, and Beauty quiet; she heals things and makes them grow. When the father's business fails, the family is left with nothing but a small country property, Rose Cottage, willed to the girls by a mysterious woman.

The merchant, as in the earlier book, encounters the Beast's castle while lost, and takes a rose, rousing the Beast's anger. Beauty insists on going to the castle to save her father. This Beauty takes over tending the Beast's garden, making it live and flourish again. She also learns, watching her family and friends in waking dreams, conflicting versions of a mystery, a legend of a curse and a conflict between a sorcerer and a philosopher, in which a greenwitch and a simulacrum, a woman made of rose-petals, were also involved.

Beauty and the Beast are very different people from McKinley's first Beauty and Beast. This Beast is more developed as a character. Beauty discovers him to be an astronomer and an artist as well as a lover of roses and cats. As she comes to find herself comfortable in his company, her initial fear of his looks and strength turns to an attraction she does not quite admit to herself. Beauty returns home briefly, and then, having realized almost too late she loves the Beast, must go back to save his life as he lies dying. The ending is not so simple in this version, though. Her Beast was a philosopher, a sorcerer who sought knowledge for its own sake, and stirred up powers better left alone, imprisoning himself after his transformation. Other parts of the story are the ghostly greenwitch who has tried to help him, and an enemy sorcerer. The complicated magics and motives involved seem enough for a novel themselves, rather under-done as a brief explanation by the greenwitch in the last chapter.

A pleasing twist on the conclusion is that Beauty must choose whether to have her Beast returned to his human self, or to have him remain the Beast she knows. She chooses the Beast, both because that is the person she has come to know and love, and because she does not want to choose for him the power and authority over others that are offered along with human restoration. She and the Beast escape with difficulty from threatening forces and find themselves at Rose Cottage, the Beast to become an artist, and Beauty, presumably, a greenwitch.

McKinley's short story collection *The Door in the Hedge* (1981) contains, as well as two original stories, two retellings of fairy-tales, 'The Princess and the Frog' and 'The Twelve Dancing Princesses'. The princess in the first is rather humorously named Rana, the Latin for frog. She drops an enchanted necklace, which she fears is intended by her hated suitor Aliyander to control her, into a garden pool. When the frog retrieves it, the enchantment is washed away. Rana is unfailingly courteous and kind to the frog, calling him her talisman against Prince Aliyander's malevolent presence in the palace. When Aliyander discovers the frog and hurls it against the wall it turns into his own vanished brother Lian, Rana's former betrothed, but it is Rana who saves Lian and the kingdom by throwing water from the magic-dispelling pool over the sorcerer-prince. 'The Twelve Dancing Princesses' follows the original tale of the princesses compelled to enter a subterranean world every night to dance with ominous suitors.

However, it makes the nameless soldier who saves them and marries the eldest, and the king and princesses themselves, into characters whose emotions are strongly felt by the reader despite their lack of names. It is a poetic and beautiful story, beautifully and poetically told in McKinley's finest style.

Deerskin (1993) is a novel using a story found in various fairy-tale versions and perhaps best-known from Perrault's 'Donkeyskin'. The story in most versions is of a princess whose own father decides to marry her. In many versions the dying queen has made him promise to marry no-one less beautiful than herself. The daughter flees disguised in some lowly or even repulsive garb, becomes a servant in another kingdom, and by appearing three times at a ball in increasingly grand dresses, wins marriage with prince or king. McKinley's story makes the story one of terrible suffering, but also of hope and renewal.

Princess Lissar grows up very like her dead mother, her closest and almost only friend her whippet-like fleethound Ash. When she reaches womanhood more beautiful than her mother, her father announces that he will marry her. The collective opinion in the court, once the first horror passes, is that it is Lissar's fault; she has bewitched the king. Before the wedding comes to pass, the king breaks into Lissar's locked room and rapes her, leaving both the princess and the dog who tried to defend her seriously injured. Lissar flees into the autumn wilderness and eventually finds shelter in an abandoned hut; Ash learns to hunt and Lissar to prepare the game. Gradually, she comes to take pride in their survival, though she does not remember how they came to be there. Only when her pregnancy becomes obvious does memory return, devastating her. Caught in terrified nightmare, Lissar encounters the Lady or Moonwoman, a lunar and nature goddess. Lissar and Ash wake to find months have passed and it is spring. Lissar's crippling wounds are healed, her hair has changed from black to white, and she is dressed in white doeskin. She has also miscarried. She has been given a gift by the Lady, time to grow strong enough for her memories.

Lissar and Ash resume their wanderings, ending up in the capital of a very small kingdom, where Lissar, calling herself Deerskin, gets work in Prince Ossin's kennels. Hearing legends of her own death, she learns that she did not lose one winter in meeting the Moonwoman, but four years. She becomes friends with Ossin, but runs away when he reveals his love for her. When Lissar learns that her father is about to marry Ossin's sister, she returns to interrupt the ceremony, revealing to all her father's crimes. She appears as a burning white woman, a manifestation of the Moonwoman, and then as her own black-haired self, transformed by an outpouring of her own blood. Her father becomes a broken old man in that moment. Lissar runs again, and this time Ossin follows. She is finally able to tell him that she loves him and will try to stay with him as his wife.

Deerskin is not an easy book to read, since its initial crisis is a subject not often found in imaginative juvenile literature, or even in 'problem' books, and Lissar's is not the sort of suffering and heroism readers enjoy imagining for themselves, the way the sufferings of imprisonment or battle or poverty endured and triumphed over may be 'romantic'. This is one of McKinley's best, though. The growing nightmare of the king's obsession with his daughter is subtly depicted, while Lissar's retreat from herself psychologically and physically after the rape is utterly convincing, not any simple symbolic amnesia or madness but something much more complex. Her eventual reclaimings of her name, her body, and her memory are not sudden revelation, but a slow process in which the Moonwoman plays a role, but which are not imposed on Lissar by outside forces. Her healing comes from within. There are friendship and love, joy and humour in the book, as well as betrayal and suffering.

Spindle's End (2000) is based on the story of 'Brier Rose' or 'Sleeping Beauty', the princess who pricks herself on a spindle and falls asleep for a hundred years. It is set, like *Deerskin, Rose Daughter*, and some of her short stories, in a world that may be the same as that occupied by the kingdom of Damar in McKinley's two Newbery-acclaimed secondary world fantasy novels (see Chapter XIV). The kingdom in *Spindle's End* is a land where magic is plentiful and fairies are common, not twinkly flower-dwellers but people born into ordinary families and possessing a gift for magic. Katriona is a young fairy from the remote village of Foggy Bottom, who attends the princess' name-day as her village's representative. The princess is cursed by Pernicia, a powerful bad fairy who plans to destroy the kingdom in revenge for defeat by an ancient queen. Katriona

175

steals the princess, trying to protect her. On the long journey home, the baby is nursed by a variety of wild animals.

The princess grows up as Rosie, Katriona's orphaned cousin. She becomes a horse-leech or doctor and the apprentice of the blacksmith, Narl, an older man with whom she falls in love. When Rosie nears twenty-one, Ikor, a warrior fairy in royal service, shows up to warn that Pernicia's curse is about to strike and they must prepare to defend the princess. Rosie's best friend, orphaned Peony, volunteers to take Rosie's place as princess in the public eye. The fairies link the two young women magically, hoping to thus dissipate the curse, which falls, in weakened form, on Peony. Rosie, Narl, and the animals must then find and destroy Pernicia to save Peony. Rosie, kissing her friend, revives her and transfers the full mystique of 'the princess' to her, making Peony the king's heir in truth. Rosie, in addition to marrying Narl, can continue life as a horse-leech.

As in *Rose Daughter*, there is a lack of action or drama which some readers will find not compensated for by character or evocative prose alone. Even the scenes of desperate action are dreamlike and distant, lacking physical impact. There is much alluded to that seems to deserve a more prominent place in the story, such as the earlier queen's conflict with Pernicia, and the idea of fairy-smiths. The foreground story in *Spindle's End* seems a lesser, quieter tale set against a backdrop of deeper legends and more powerful histories. At the same time, it contrasts pointedly with the passivity of the heroine of the original fairy-tale of 'Sleeping Beauty', who does nothing but wake up (in some versions pregnant or having given birth, the hero not having confined himself to merely kissing her); the Sleeping Beauty often continues after her marriage to suffer with Griselda-like patience further ordeals, always a passive victim. Rosie refuses to be shaped by her destiny or to be forced to assume the role of princess and heir, to which her orphaned friend is so much better suited by her tact and diplomacy. Rosie reshapes her destiny in transferring the sometimes magically-visible glamour that is the essence of royalty to Peony.

McKinley's novels and short stories based on fairy-tales retain the originals' distance from the everyday; they take the readers to another time and place, offer possibilities of magic and poetry that free the characters, and the readers with them, to consider choices and actions to which everyday stresses and anxieties may blind them. She is one of the finest prose stylists writing for the young adult audience, and creates worlds in which the fantastic and the humbly ordinary co-exist comfortably. Strange magic and legends made flesh live among the people in McKinley, but her common folk, the farmers and the cooks and the villagers, are not there merely to acknowledge that there must be someone other than royalty or heroes in the world, as is too often the case in weak fantasy. McKinley's rural people and townsfolk are the foundations of the kingdoms in which the stories occur. She gives them depth, colour, and life. Her fantastic is that of the shadows underlying all the ordinary things, inherent in the worlds she creates and, in its strongest forms, belonging to the countryfolk and the wild places, not the academic magicians who live above the real life of the country in the courts. Legend and folklore turn out to be one with the real powers of the land. Formulated arcane knowledge usually turns out to be sterile, while the fairies, the greenwitches, the spirits of the land, experience the reality of magic and fight the real battles.

McKinley's storytelling of the later nineties became more passive; characters in these books tend to think and feel rather than grow angry or stir things up around them. They react, rather than acting for change. Her later books are beautiful worlds to enter and appreciate for a time, like a garden or a poem, but they have little tension or excitement compared to her earlier writing. They are quieter works, and appeal to a different mood. They may also not be as eagerly re-read as her earlier books. Beauty of *Rose Daughter* finds herself caught in a potentially far more interesting world than is Beauty of *Beauty*; her growing affection and passion for the Beast, and his more developed portrayal, have all the ingredients for a gripping story. However, it is the earlier Beauty whose personality endures in memory, despite her conventional concluding union with a conventional handsome gentleman of whom we know nothing except that he is kind and likes books and spicecake.

Gail Carson Levine (b. 1947)

Gail Carson Levine was born in New York City. She only began writing seriously later in her life after taking creative writing classes. Levine provides an example of a different approach to retelling fairy-tales from McKinley's, one that does not so much re-imagine the stories as invert some of the assumptions in that pattern.

In *Ella Enchanted* (1997) Levine examines the story of 'Cinderella' and the passivity and 'goodness' of the heroines of some of the best-known fairy-tales. Ella is a wealthy merchant's daughter who is given the gift of obedience by a particularly thoughtless fairy godmother, Lucinda. The result of this is that she must obey any order given her by anyone. Her stepmother and -sisters discover this and take full advantage of it. After running away from finishing school and narrowly escaping man-eating ogres who discover how easy she is to control, Ella is reduced to a scullery maid by Dame Olga, her stepmother. She and her friend, Prince Char, court by correspondence. When he asks her to marry him, she realizes what a weapon against him and the kingdom her curse would be. She leads him to believe she has eloped with another, but decides to attend a series of balls for a last glimpse of him, and does so with the help of two fairies, the cook Mandy and the gushy Lucinda, responsible for the pumpkin coach as well as the curse. When her stepsister unmasks Ella, everyone recognizes her. Her stepfamily takes advantage of her curse, ordering her to marry the prince when he asks, seeing wealth and power for themselves. Char tells her to say that she will marry him, not meaning it as an order, but because of the phrasing she knows she must obey despite the danger to the kingdom. Finally, she is able to resist the curse, made strong enough to do it for Char's sake where she could not for her own, even to save her life from ogres. The cursed gift is destroyed, and Ella, having refused Char in contravention of an order, is free to act according to her own will. She asks Char to marry her.

Ella Enchanted's first person narrative is written in an intimate, confiding, contemporary voice, full of exclamations and addresses to the reader. This style of narration became very popular in the children's fiction in the nineties; it was particularly

178

noticeable in historical fiction. Unlike Lee's *Wolf Tower* series (see Chapter XV), where the pretence of a journal makes the confessional style work, *Ella Enchanted* is not actually framed as a diary, making the confessional style seem incongruous. In addition, the fairy cook Mandy gives Ella a magic book that allows her to read other people's letters, such as Char's to his mother or Ella's stepmother's to her daughter, an invasion of privacy accepted unquestioningly as a right by Ella. This is merely a weak device to get around the limitations of a first-person narrator. That narrator seems utterly contemporary in attitude and voice, unshaped by the very loosely and vaguely conceived past setting in which she exists, one that is largely assembled from stock parts. The reader is never given much impression of being taken to another world or time, though the kingdoms are fictitious and the languages of various creatures encountered by Ella are invented. These invented languages lack any dimension of plausible reality, any illusion even of syntax or structure, and read more like the creation of someone the age of the intended audience, than something into which much thought or understanding of the functioning of language has gone. This, and the lack of a genuine impression of a distinctive place or society, or any serious attention to the working of the magic and the ethical considerations it raises, make *Ella Enchanted* a book incapable of comparison to good fantasy, despite its baffling status as a Newbery Honor book. The story often appears merely a device itself, an exercise in pointing out the excessively Griselda-like attributes of common fairy-tale heroines.

Philip Pullman (b. 1946)

A discussion of Pullman's other fantasy is found in Chapter XVI, but he has also written one of the more original stories using the Cinderella fairy-tale motif as its starting point. *I Was a Rat!* (1999) begins where *Cinderella* and its variants end. The prince is engaged to the mysterious girl he met at the ball, the newspapers print rapturous headlines, and a forlorn small boy in a page's uniform shows up at the house of Bob Jones the cobbler and his washerwoman wife Joan, announcing, 'I was a rat.' The couple take the boy in, wash him, feed him, and put him to bed. His behaviour is definitely ratty; he has no idea how to use cutlery, he tears up his blankets to make a nest, and he chews on everything. He earnestly tries to do what he is told, though, and learns quickly. Roger, as Bob and Joan name him, has a number of misadventures trying to adapt to human society. Most of the people he meets want to use him, preying on his innocent desire to be good by doing what he is told; they see in him only what suits their needs. He is kidnapped and fed garbage as a sideshow freak, rescued and used by a gang of young thieves, and tries to live like a rat again in the sewers, where he captured, proclaimed a monster, and sentenced to death by scientists who refuse to see him as a boy or admit his speech is more than mindless imitation. Bob and Joan remember Roger's insistence that the princess, Aurelia, is his friend Mary Jane. In desperation they appeal to her. As readers suspect by this point, Roger is one of the rats enchanted when Mary Jane went to the ball. He missed being restored because of running off to play. Roger is stuck as a boy, and Mary Jane, who finds her new life not all that she expected, as a princess. Both resolve to be the best they can as what they now are, and the papers print gushing headlines about how the princess transformed the loathsome monster into a boy through her love and compassion. Roger goes home with Bob and Joan, to learn the cobbler's trade.

Roger's adventures and his naive misunderstandings make for a story of both suspense and comedy. The various deceitful, self-righteous, or supercilious people who try to use him are both humorous and a commentary on how people too often see in others only that which suits their own needs or theories. Even Bob and Joan, who see in Roger a boy in need of a loving home, are fulfilling their own needs to some degree, since they have never had a child of their own, but their need and Roger's complement one another. They, and Mary Jane, are the only ones to actually see Roger himself as the person who matters most. Their search for him is long and difficult, but they never give up. Their desperation and sadness provides a counterpoint both to Roger's equal misery and loneliness, and to the comedy of the various Dickensian exploiters of Roger. Interspersed throughout the story are pages from the *Daily Scourge* newspaper, gushing about the princess, ranting against the monster, and generally telling the public what to think. Like the theories of the Philosopher, proclaimed in defiance of the evidence in a satire of blind adherence to dogmatically-held beliefs or contemporary critical theory, the newspaper's exaggerated statements, which mock the enthusiasms and vendettas of the press, are intended to be noticed as excessive even by relatively young readers. *I Was a Rat!* is both comic and thought-provoking, something too rarely achieved in writing for younger children.

In the period between the end of the First World War, and that of the twentieth century, the retelling of traditional material for children remained an important part of juvenile literature. Writers like Green, Picard, and Sutcliff continued, in the tradition of Lang, to offer folktale, fairy-tale, legend, and myth retold for young readers in an approachable manner that nevertheless expanded the horizons of those readers. That many of these retellers also put much effort into avoiding an easily datable informality means that such retellings will endure through generations much as Lang's have done, and though their popularity may diminish as the vocabulary of the juvenile 'average reader' continues, regrettably, to diminish, they will retain their claim to lasting value and readability. (And perhaps will do their part to counter that impoverishment of vocabulary.) These reworkings and retellings of traditional material will enrich not only the imaginations and historical knowledge of their readers, but their appreciation of well-written language.

Though few writers retelling legends or mythology, even those who turned the material into novels, such as Green's *The Luck of Troy* or Crossley-Holland's *King Horn*, changed the shape of the stories, some found new perspectives within that story to tell it from. On the other hand, stories reassessing the content of fairy-tales, the traditional 'happy endings', and the definitions of success and failure in them, became more common towards the end of the twentieth century. Authors often re-examined fairy-tale conventions and reworked the tales in reaction. Pullman's Mary Jane, though a minor character, finds her wish and 'happy ending' not all that she expected, and though many traditional fairy-tales have as central characters humans transformed to animals, few have considered the experience of animals transformed for some fairy or human convenience (Terry Pratchett, in *Witches Abroad*, is another who does so).

Levine's Ella has to fight for her own will; she is an extreme depiction of all the excessively good fairy-tale heroines who get what they are expected to want by meek obedience. McKinley's novels, on the other hand, find the stories hidden in the traditional tales. She does not invert the stories or deny the romance in them, but delves deeply into the underlayers, finding a human reality there. Few authors seem as concerned to retell the many fairy- or folktales which already feature bold, heroic, venturesome female heroes. Perhaps, since it is the meek and good who embody late Victorian and nineteen-fifties ideals of womanhood, it is those stories that were given prominence in our culture throughout the twentieth century, and thus those that authors felt were in most need of retelling, as well as being the most over-familiar.

X
Eternal Heroes —
King Arthur and Robin Hood

Among the most enduringly popular traditional stories of the past few centuries have been those of King Arthur and Robin Hood. Both have their foundations in the Middle Ages. They have captured the imaginations of generation after generation, and each generation of readers and writers has made their own Arthurs and their own Robins. Before discussing some of the leading examples, both of retellings of the traditional cycles of tales about Arthur and Robin Hood, and of novels based on or inspired by those tales, it may be beneficial to offer a brief overview of the material providing the foundations of these retellings, since reference may be made to this or that tradition, particularly where Arthur is involved.

The first important source for the literary (as opposed to the historical) Arthur is Geoffrey of Monmouth's *Historia Regum Brittaniae*, or *History of the Kings of Britain* (c. 1135). Also forming part of this tradition are the works based on it: Wace's Old French *Roman de Brut* (c. 1155), in which the Round Table makes its first literary appearance, and Laȝamon's Early Middle English *Brut* (c. 1200), in which Laȝamon says that the British still await the return of Arthur from Avalon, where he was taken to be healed of his mortal wounds. In Geoffrey, Arthur is simply taken to the Isle of Avalon to have his wounds tended, with no suggestion of return or supernatural survival. Geoffrey, Wace, and Laȝamon continued to influence the Arthurian legend even after romances featuring the quests of individual knights had become the dominant form of Arthurian story. There is also an important earlier body of Welsh legend about Arthur, which Geoffrey may have known, and a Breton pool of legend and lais or lays, which may have influenced Wace. Another important, related tradition contains the Old French *Merlin* of Robert de Borron (c. 1200), and Middle English variants of that, in which the sword in the stone (the sword is actually in an anvil, on an inscribed stone) is introduced. A Middle English alliterative poem about the death of Arthur, *Morte Arthure*, usually called the *Alliterative Morte* (late fourteenth century), is coloured more by the traditions of Geoffrey and Laȝamon than by Chrétien de Troyes; it concentrates on war rather than on individual adventures. The mid fourteenth-century *Stanzaic Morte*, *Le Morte Arthur*, contains much more from the French Romance tradition, such as the court of Camelot and Lancelot's affair with Guinevere. The two streams co-existed, and Malory would use both the *Alliterative* and the *Stanzaic Morte*s as sources, as well as the French romances.

In the stories drawing on Geoffrey of Monmouth and his tradition, Arthur is not the character most people think of today. Arthur's court is not one of leisured knights in late fourteenth or fifteenth-century plate armour; it does not pass its days in a search for entertainment and glory, in tournaments and quests. Instead, Arthur is a British warrior-king leading a desperate struggle against invading Saxons a generation or so after the Romans have abandoned and withdrawn the legions from the province of Britain. He is successful, makes war against various peoples on the continent (including, in the *Alliterative Morte*, Saracens), and takes on Rome itself. He is betrayed by his nephew Mordred, who seizes the kingdom and his wife in his absence. Returning, Arthur dies in battle. In the earliest literary traditions, Mordred has not yet become Arthur's son through his unwitting incest with his sister and is only his nephew, brother of Gawain, son of Lot or Loth of Lothian and of Arthur's sister. In some works, such as the late thirteenth-century *Of Arthour and of Merlin*, part of the *Merlin* tradition, Arthur has other sons, although none by Guinevere and none that entered the canonical Arthurian cast. The most important difference between the pseudo-histories (Geoffrey, Wace, and Laȝamon) and the romances adhering to this 'earlier' tradition, even those written at the same time as or later than romances of the 'later' courtly tradition, is that in the pseudo-histories and the romances related to them, Arthur, the warrior-king, is the central figure, and that his enemies are on the whole Saxon invaders and continental kings.

On the other hand, in the Old French romances by the twelfth-century French poet Chrétien de Troyes (c. 1140-1190s), who introduced both Lancelot and the Grail, by those who followed him in the thirteenth and subsequent centuries, as well as in the various romances about the Quest for the Holy Grail and in Sir Thomas Malory's fifteenth-century Middle English *Le Morte Darthur*, Arthur himself is merely the catalyst, the centre around which the court of the Round Table is formed. Once he becomes king, the focus of the stories shifts to his knights and their adventures, until the final tragedy that destroys the society of the Round Table and leads to Arthur's death in battle with the treacherous Mordred. In most of these romances, there is less attempt to tie the various stories into any sort of fixed geography or history, less emphasis in the plots on politics and the struggles of peoples. Chivalry and individual combats are the keynote of martial undertakings, not the movement of armies. Individual heroes pursue quests for spiritual gain, for glory, honour, or love, for the sake of rescue, revenge, or to prove themselves. There are numerous romances, usually written in French and dating largely from the thirteenth century onwards, which focus on the adventures of the various knights. Together, these all form a 'history', making reference to one another, incorporating events, symbolism, and themes from other stories, and creating the cycle of romances that became known as 'the Matter of Britain.'

The Arthur of Sir Thomas Malory (c. 1410?-1471) became the Arthur with whom everyone is still familiar today. Malory, a knight, rebel, and bandit, lived a wild and colourful life, wrote most of his romances in prison, and was at the time of his death quite probably imprisoned again, having supported the Lancastrian Earl of Warwick against Edward IV. His was one of the earliest books printed in England, by William Caxton's press in 1485. Malory's original manuscript, only published (edited by Eugène Vinaver) in 1954, contains eight romances based by Malory on earlier works in the tradition. Malory gathered the central episodes of the central stories about Arthur together, and wrote his eight romances in a manner that could be likened to eight modern novels in a series: two about Arthur as a young man and king, followed by ones with Sir Gareth and Sir Tristram as the respective heroes, then the account of the quest for the Holy Grail, the story of Lancelot and Guinevere, and finally the end of the 'series', the story of the death of Arthur, the end of the fellowship of the Round Table. This was in contrast to the more loosely connected and interwoven adventures of the older romances. It was Caxton who titled it *Le Morte Darthur*; Caxton's 1485 Malory, the text that has been familiar and influential for the past 500 years, is divided into twenty-one rather than eight books, but follows more or less the same order: Arthur's early kingship, the doings of his various knights, the quest for the Grail, the adultery of Lancelot and Guenevere, and the betrayal of Mordred leading to the death of Arthur. Malory wrote in a late Middle English that is fairly easily read by the Modern English speaker; the edition most likely to be encountered by the non-scholar is that published by Penguin, which, although not a translation, has modernized spelling. Malory's is a robust, unostentatious narrative, which gets quickly to the meat of the story. Most of the retellers of the stories of King Arthur for children choose to retell Malory, sometimes including stories from other works, such as the late fourteenth-century Middle English *Sir Gawain and the Green Knight*, or Chrétien's *Erec et Enide*.

There is not such a great quantity of literary sources for those retelling Robin Hood to draw upon. Poems or songs about the folk-hero Robin Hood, insouciant outlaw and champion of the poor and oppressed, were popular during the fourteenth century, as is attested by reference to them in one version of William Langland's *Piers Plowman* (c. 1362-1390). *The Gest of Robyn Hode*, which is over 450 stanzas long, was printed sometime in the early sixteenth century but was probably written around 1450. The *Gest* contains events taken from a number of separate ballads, including the aiding of Sir Richard of the Lea, who is threatened with loss of his land, the robbing and eventually the killing of the Sheriff of Nottingham, Robin's encounter with King Richard, his pardoning, and his eventual death at the hands of a treacherous prioress while being bled. Many other ballads also exist, composed or at least recorded from the sixteenth to the eighteenth centuries, telling other stories about Robin and his fellows or expanding upon already established events.

In printed form, the ballads circulated as broadsides, single sheets often sold by pedlars. In the eighteenth century, both Robin Hood ballads and fantastic stories of the fairy-tale type claiming King Arthur's time as the setting were popular material for chapbooks (see Chapter II). In 1759 Joseph Ritson published a collection of traditional Robin Hood ballads intended for a scholarly audience; an 1820 edition of Ritson was issued that was meant for younger readers as well. Francis Child published another scholarly collection of the ballads in 1888. Robin Hood appeared as a character in novels and poetry throughout the nineteenth century; writers such as Sir Walter Scott, Thomas Love Peacock, Alexandre Dumas, and even Tennyson (in a play) all turned to Robin Hood in material written not specifically for children, but often, until fairly recently, read by them. Tennyson, of course, also wrote *The Idylls of the King* (published 1859-1885), a great cycle of Arthurian poetry, as well as 'The Lady of Shalott', an earlier Arthurian poem not part of the *Idylls*, both enjoyed by young people.

The main variations in the Robin Hood legends occur in his antecedents. Some have him a yeoman's son, others a wayward nobleman, the Earl of Huntingdon. His birthplace is sometimes given as Locksley, hence he is sometimes called Robin of Locksley. There are two main settings traditionally associated with Robin Hood; these are Barnesdale in Yorkshire, and Nottinghamshire and Sherwood Forest. The time is the last decade of the twelfth century, the reign of Richard I. Both Barnesdale and Nottingham appear in the *Gest*, with Barnesdale and its environs as the primary setting, but in modern retellings Robin is largely confined to Sherwood Forest. His comrades and enemies remain the same: chiefly Little John, Will Scarlett, Friar Tuck, Maid Marian, Much the miller's son, and the minstrel Alan-a-Dale, opposed to the Sheriff of Nottingham, Sir Guy of Gisborne, and Prince John.

Over the past century or so, authors who embarked upon traditional retellings of the stories of King Arthur or Robin Hood often turned their hand to both. In novels, however, King Arthur seems a more common subject for re-imagining, particularly by authors of the later twentieth century.

Sidney Lanier (1841-1881)

Sidney Lanier was an American poet who, in 1880, published *The Boy's King Arthur*. A slightly abridged version of this was issued in 1917 with beautiful illustrations by N.C. Wyeth, and it is this edition which is best known. It has been republished many times. Lanier also adapted other traditional and historical matter in *The Boy's Froissart* (1879), a version of *Froissart's Chronicles* of the first part of the Hundred Years' War, *The Boy's Mabinogion* (1881), containing Welsh legendary material, and *The Boy's Percy* (1882), a version of *Percy's Reliques of Ancient English Poetry*, a collection of ballads originally published in 1765.

Lanier is usually described as the editor rather than the author of *The Boy's King Arthur*. His source was Malory's *Le Morte Darthur*. *The Boy's King Arthur* is, along with Howard Pyle's Arthurian retellings, the Arthur that people knew for much of the last century, the Arthur that today's popular culture thinks of, whether it is aware of the fact or not. For most, Arthur remains the Arthur of Malory and Chrétien de Troyes by way of Lanier and Pyle – knights, ladies, dwarves, jousts, chivalry, courtesy, and quests.

The Boy's King Arthur contains eight tales: *Of King Arthur*; *Of Sir Launcelot du Lake*; *Of Sir Gareth of Orkney*; *Of Sir Tristram*; *Of Sir Galahad and Sir Percival, and the Quest of the Holy Grail*; *Of the Fair Maid of Astolat*; and *Of the Death of Arthur*. This covers the ground from Arthur's birth and secret upbringing, the sword in the stone and the formation of the Round Table, through the quests of various valiant knights to Lancelot's and Guinevere's doomed affair and the treachery of Mordred.

Lanier follows his source closely, abbreviating many incidents but not altering the structure of the stories. His technique in editing was to regularize and modernize the late Middle English spelling, glossing words he felt would be unknown to his readers in parentheses and italics, while retaining the original syntax and diction. The result is language which evokes the original while being much easier for young readers to follow. Regrettably, many young readers of today, exposed to a far narrower vocabulary than their counterparts of a century ago, may decide they are bored, if not lost, by the unfamiliar sentence structure, grammar that includes the second person singular, and unfamiliar words, despite Lanier's bracketed Modern English glosses. The sentiments of Malory's day, as well, are likely to seem alien to some children – the knights and kings of today's fiction are rarely moved to tears by anything, and the impassioned emotions of Arthur's Round Table may be more alien and harder to accept as 'real' than the average television alien culture, so comfortably like our own in all but a few cosmetic points. This is *not* a reason to avoid Lanier's books, quite the contrary. If children are allowed to discover and explore Lanier at their own pace, new worlds of history and the imagination and language will open up to them. There are many young readers who take the unfamiliar in stride, absorb it and make it their own. Such readers will revel in the archaic language, and for them the magic of the story will be there as it has been since the fifteenth century. The grandeur, the excitement, the inevitable tragedy arising from conflicts of honour, loyalty, and love, as well as from treachery, will carry them away, and they will emerge the richer for it.

Howard Pyle (1853-1911)

American author and illustrator Howard Pyle's *The Merry Adventures of Robin Hood* appeared in 1883. It was the first of his books retelling old legends for young people. Pyle's illustrations evoke the woodcuts of early printing, especially so in *Robin Hood*; among Pyle's students were other great American illustrators such as Jessie Willcox Smith, N.C. Wyeth, and Maxfield Parrish. Like Lanier's *King Arthur*, Pyle's *Robin Hood* became the definitive story, the Robin Hood to which all later retellings referred, the Robin Hood everyone still knows, even if they have never heard of Howard Pyle. He also wrote stories of his own, including the historical novel for children *Otto of the Silver Hand* (1888), set in medieval Germany, and *The Garden Behind the Moon* (see Chapter IV).

Pyle begins his story by telling how Robin is forced into the outlaw's life by a quarrel with a drunken forester. The outlaw's many adventures as he encounters those who will join his band, and as they outwit the Sheriff of Nottingham along with various other nobles, prelates, and monarchs, comprise most of the book. The epilogue tells a traditional story of Robin's betrayal and death at the hands of a prioress to whom he had gone to be bled, a form of medical treatment much practised from the later Middle Ages onwards.

Among the other medieval-themed books Pyle wrote were

four about Arthur and his knights: *The Story of King Arthur* (1903), *The Story of the Champions of the Round Table* (1905), *The Story of Sir Launcelot and his Companions* (1907), and *The Story of the Grail and the Passing of Arthur* (1910). Pyle's Arthurian stories cover more ground than Lanier's. Lanier was working only with Malory, while Pyle includes material from other Arthurian romances, such as *Gereint and Enid*, from Welsh sources by way of Chrétien de Troyes' *Erec et Enide*.

Pyle, perhaps influenced by Lanier's rendering of the late Middle English of Malory, casts both his Robin Hood and his Arthur stories in what is in his case an artificially archaic English. There seems little excuse for this, since he declares himself to be retelling, rather than attempting to render an original more accessible to young readers while retaining some of the authentic language of the source. It is also less effective and pleasing than Lanier's technique, lacking the economy and poetic balance of Middle English, or of the seventeenth-century Modern English of the King James, which is what Pyle sometimes seems to be striving for. As with Lanier's language, though, so with that of Pyle: some children today will regard it as incomprehensible, off-putting, and tedious; others will find it part of what holds them in the story, an essential element that evokes for them another place and time, even though Pyle lacks any real feeling for authenticity.

Pyle's approach to narrative is another element which may deter some children, or more likely, adults. It has been fashionable for some years now to decry the presence of an intrusive narrator in children's books. Children, received wisdom would have it, find this condescending and will not tolerate it. To this it could be countered that children engrossed in a book will accept almost anything, so long as it does not bore them. (And what of the intrusive narrator in Lemony Snickett's extremely successful *A Series of Unfortunate Events* sequence, which began appearing in 1999?) Pyle's 'Preface From the Author to the Reader' at the start of his *Robin Hood* is more than a trifle pompous and heavy-handed to modern ears and likely seemed somewhat so even to the readers of the eighteen-eighties. Compare Pyle, 'You who so plod amid serious things that you feel it shame to give yourself up even for a few short moments to mirth and joyousness in the land of Fancy; you who think that life hath nought to

190

do with innocent laughter that can harm no one; these pages are not for you. Clap to the leaves and go no farther ...' with the Preface to *The Blue Fairy Book* of his contemporary, Andrew Lang: 'The Tales in this volume are intended for children, who will like, it is hoped, the old stories that have pleased so many generations.' In the story itself, however, Pyle's first-person comments serve to link the episodes together. They evoke the world of oral tale-telling to which the Robin Hood material belongs, and seem in this context a perfectly natural part of his story: 'Thus ended the famous shooting match before Queen Eleanor. And now we will hear how ill King Harry kept his promise to his Queen that no harm should befall Robin Hood for forty days ....' Here, Pyle's narrative voice is natural and effective. Like Lanier, there is much in Pyle for modern young readers to discover and enjoy, and his retellings deserve to retain their place as classics of childhood.

T.H. White (1906-1964)

Terence Hanbury White was born in India, where his father was a District Superintendent of Police. He studied English Literature at Cambridge and became an English teacher for a time, but for most of his life he lived as a recluse. White was the author of a number of novels, but is best known for the four books that make up *The Once and Future King*. The first three were published in separate volumes as *The Sword in the Stone* (1938), *The Witch in the Wood* (1939 – revised as *The Queen of Air and Darkness*, 1958), and *The Ill-Made Knight* (1940). The fourth, *The Candle in the Wind*, was only published in the revised one-volume version of the four novels, *The Once and Future King* (1958), the form the book continues to appear in today. A fifth novel, *The Book of Merlyn* (1977), was published posthumously from a manuscript found among White's papers; it was written during the early years of the Second World War but turned down for publication due to both paper shortages and its anti-war philosophy. The musical *Camelot* (1960) was based on White's version of the Arthurian story, as was the Disney movie *The Sword in the Stone* (1963).

The Once and Future King is a large and complex work.

White makes no pretence of attempting an historical Arthur, or of simply retelling Malory, although he adheres very closely to Malory in his events and in the portrayal of characters' attributes: Malory is White's template, but he views it all through a bizarrely transforming glass. In this world, there are Normans and Saxons, united under Arthur into English. Merlyn is an irascible tutor, an old man who knows the future because he experiences time backwards. His conversation is full of anachronistic references, and he is frequently confused as to what has already happened and what is yet to come. Arthur, or while he is a boy, the Wart, is naive and thoughtless. His education by Merlyn is what many young readers find most memorable about the book on a first reading – adults will find much more in it. Wart is turned by Merlyn into various creatures to learn from them. A great deal of political satire is involved, especially in his time among the ants. Their rigidly regimented society is a modern totalitarian state, complete with beloved leader and constant mind-dulling background music and public address system exhortations.

Arthur as king founds his round table to replace the rule of might with one of law, but discovers that trying to establish law, justice, or 'right' with power sows the seeds of its destruction. His ideal does not stand up to the real world. In the end he is caught in contradiction and it is all destroyed, when he is forced to acknowledge Guenever's adultery with Lancelot and sentence her to death at the stake. He cannot ignore the law and do what he wants, because then all the law will fail. It does anyway, the companionship of the table destroyed. Gawaine's desire for revenge against Lancelot, who killed two of Gawaine's brothers while rescuing Guenever, takes him and Arthur out of the kingdom, leaving as regent the weak, sly, snivelling Mordred, dominated by thoughts of Arthur's injustice to his mother. Mordred's usurpation causes Arthur's death and the final destruction of the ideal of Camelot. White uses Mordred's adoption of cannon and his railings against Saxons and Jews to symbolize the ending of Arthur's brief better world and what is at once a return to the anarchy and rule of might that existed before him, and the mass destruction and totalitarianism of might in the modern world.

White's is a strange world, peopled with characters who often seem caricatures of the types found in mid twentieth-century 'literary' novels written under the influence of Freudian psychology. They are all broadly drawn. The sons of the King of Orkney speak with Scots accents, others use bluff Edwardian heartiness, or schoolboy 'jolly goods' of mid century. Kay is a blundering, oafish enthusiast, reacting with excitement to Merlyn's ideas, but never fully comprehending them and often utterly inverting the lesson. Lancelot is an earnest, ugly schoolboy, in love with Arthur through adoring hero-worship before he ever meets Guenever. Agravaine has a severe Oedipus complex, and as does Mordred, though his obsession with his mother is less explicitly sexual than his brother's. Guenever is described as growing irrational due to her childless state as she enters menopause. White seems to both acknowledge and mock the prevalence of the Freudian interpretation of characters' driving forces that he uses, when he has Merlyn advising that the Questing Beast, stricken with love for a pair of costumed knights, be subjected to psychoanalysis and her dreams interpreted according to Freud.

The Once and Future King is thick with social and political satire, as well as outright social commentary on mid twentieth-century affairs in authorial intrusions connecting Arthur's world and White's present, many of these referring directly to events leading up to the Second World War. There are also numerous authorial digressions musing on or explaining such things as the psychology of the characters or White's extremely idiosyncratic interpretations of the facts of medieval life. All this makes it more likely to be enjoyed by teens with a broad exposure to other literature and other disciplines than by younger children, despite the Disney movie based on it having been made for the younger set.

Roger Lancelyn Green (1918-1987)

Green, who was responsible for many retellings of myths and legends for children (see Chapter IX), did not neglect King Arthur and Robin Hood. His *King Arthur and his Knights of the Round Table* (1953) is 're-told out of the old romances' as the title page says. Green organizes the many divergent Arthurian tales into a loosely chronological progression, beginning with the stories of Arthur's birth and proclamation as king following his pulling of the sword from the anvil. These are followed by the adventures of his knights in the early days of the Round Table, the adventures of various knights in the Quest for the Holy Grail, and the final failures and betrayals leading to the death of Arthur and the end of his golden age. Green's story is mostly taken from Malory, but he also uses details or stories from earlier sources, or from continental ones, that are not found in Malory. He makes slight use of Geoffrey of Monmouth's *History of the Kings of Britain* and Laȝamon's *Brut*, and of the French and Middle English *Merlins*. He includes the adventure from the Middle English *Sir Gawain and the Green Knight*, although he changes the instigator of the scheme from Morgan la Faye, motivated by hatred of Guinevere and a wish to frighten her, to Nimue, who desires merely to test the valour of Arthur's knights. There is material from the Welsh *Mabinogion* and Chrétien de Troyes, and from other French romances. Generally, though, Green's story is that of Malory. It is a world of noble deeds, proud words, and courtly manners, of honour and courtesy and quests undertaken for reasons both lofty and selfish.

Green's *The Adventures of Robin Hood* (1956) is similar, taking the story of Robin and the outlaw band through the cycle of traditional episodes. Green uses the usual late medieval and ballad sources, but his version is also influenced by the novel *Maid Marian* (1822) by the Romantic poet Thomas Love Peacock (1785-1866). Peacock's Matilda or Maid Marian crosses swords with Prince John himself in a duel, and is an archer capable of holding her own with Robin. Green, following Peacock, allows Marian a more active role in events than tradition usually permits her, an approach retellers after Green were also to adopt.

As in his retellings of myth and legend, Green writes in a very readable style, not over-ornate and artificial, but retaining a dignity and formality suggesting a little distance in time. His *Arthur* and *Robin Hood* will expand the vocabulary of most children reading them, but the language is not excessively difficult and words now less common in children's writing (such as 'unseemly' or 'amend') are easily deduced from context. The language, though formal, is natural to even the early twenty-first century ear, and not a barrier, as may unfortunately be the case with Pyle or Lanier where some weaker readers are concerned. Green's are among the best twentieth-century retellings in the traditional manner, and have remained readily available since their first publication, an ideal introduction to the worlds of Arthur and Robin Hood for younger readers.

Geoffrey Trease (1909-1998)

Trease was born in Nottingham. He won a scholarship to Oxford, but left in his second year to work with children in the East End of London. He later worked as a journalist and a teacher, and served in the army during the Second World War. Best known for his children's historical fiction, Trease was a socialist in his philosophy and this influenced his writing; he never shied away from taking a stand on what he felt was the right and wrong of any historical issue. In all his books, he showed the lives of working and rural people as well as the middle and upper classes, not treating the labouring classes as part of a stereotyped backdrop to the adventure, as so many historical fiction writers did, and still do today. He was also one of the first to write school stories about the experience of the average British child attending a state-run grammar school rather than boarding school, in *No Boats on Bannermere* (1949). Trease wrote extensively about children's literature as well.

Bows Against the Barons (1934) is Trease's Robin Hood novel, and his first book. It is now more likely to be found in the revised edition of 1966, in which Trease altered some minor points. His afterword to that edition calls *Bows* 'a young man's book', but defends his decision to let it return to print largely unaltered. Although *Bows Against the Barons* is a Robin Hood story, this is not the jolly Robin Hood of unfaltering loyalty to King Richard. It is heavily infused with the attitudes of nineteen-thirties socialism. Trease's Robin Hood is an idealist, similar to a seventeenth-century Leveller or to Karl Marx in his beliefs. He dreams of an England and indeed a Europe without lords and serfs, without distinction between Norman and Saxon, Christian, Jew, and Saracen, in which all are equal and share in the rewards of their labour equally. A few of Robin's outlaws, such as Alan and Little John, share his dream, but most are merely desperate runaway serfs, concerned only for the immediate betterment of their own lot. Although they rally around Robin's ideas, these make no lasting impression on most of them. Trease, in the 1966 afterword, notes that in 1603 Sir Walter Raleigh lumped Robin Hood in with Wat Tyler, Robert Kett, and Jack Cade, three historical leaders of peasant's revolts, thus suggesting that an identification of Robin Hood with such revolutionary heroes and martyrs existed in the popular imagination at the end of the Tudor era.

The hero of *Bows Against the Barons* is the boy Dickon, a serf on the estate of Sir Rolf D'Eyncourt, on the edge of Sherwood forest. Dickon's father has been conscripted to the crusades and the boy must do a man's labour, trying to keep his mother and brothers from starving while fulfilling the obligations of work on the lord's land. He and his fellow villagers are tyrannized over by the bailiff and robbed by the priest's demands for a tithe of their meagre produce. When Dickon is woken one night by deer devouring the cabbages in his little garden, he shoots one, realizing as soon as he has done so that he is sure to lose his ears or a hand as punishment, since the deer belong to the king. He runs away to join the legendary Robin Hood in the forest.

Dickon, taken under the wing of Alan-a-Dale, rapidly comes to share Robin's beliefs about the equality of all men and the injustice of the rule of kings, barons, and the Church. He has several adventures as a member of the band. The outlaws rescue prisoners and loot the wealthy to buy weapons for their coming uprising, which is triggered when they defend a village which helped Dickon, captured on one of his missions, escape. The serfs and townspeople of the Nottingham region rise with them. Sir Rolf's castle is successfully taken, Sir Rolf and his bailiff slain (the latter by Dickon), and they hope that their revolt will spread across England. However, the Earl of Wessex musters a large force to oppose them and the outlaws are trapped as they try to flee Sherwood for Barnsdale in Yorkshire. Robin, gravely injured, is taken by those who survive to a priory for aid. The prioress recognizes the prize within her grasp and kills Robin by bleeding him. The few survivors of the band bury him secretly and go their separate ways. Alan is dead, and only Little John and Dickon still share Robin's dream of an England without masters. They go to the Derbyshire Peaks district to continue their free outlaw life.

Dickon is an appealing young hero, quick-witted, handy with

bow and sword, and no slouch at disguise. Robin's egalitarian preaching serves as a counterpoint to much historical fiction and historical fantasy, in which the heroes are of the upper classes or aspire only to gain the privileges of those classes. The book will make young readers consider another side of the realities of medieval life – body-breaking labour, harsh and arbitrary justice, and oppression without any opposition. Though the significant peasants' revolts in England were largely events of the fourteenth century and later, it is not too incongruous an imaginative stretch to cast one back to the early thirteenth, Trease's setting. An added appeal of the story is the degree of local realism which Trease brings to his story. He makes full use of his native Nottingham's sandstone caves and the real landscape of Sherwood in his plot. The book is not as balanced as Trease's later historical fiction in its presentation of male and female heroes – his later pattern of boy and girl adventuring together, as in the Elizabethan spy thriller *Cue For Treason* (1940) is not yet established. The women in this story, even Marian and Dickon's mother, exist only dimly in the background. However, *Bows Against the Barons* is a fast-paced adventure that will carry young readers male and female along with Dickon, and in its presentation of Robin Hood as a revolutionary idealist rather than a mere outlaw, it may also give them a new way of looking at medieval life and promote consideration and discussion of ideas not so commonly found in children's books.

Rosemary Sutcliff (1920-1992)

The first book by Rosemary Sutcliff, who is also discussed in Chapter IX, was a retelling of the Robin Hood stories, *The Chronicles of Robin Hood* (1950). This follows the traditional pattern of the tales of how Robin acquires his chief companions and his feud with the sheriff. Although it is a very good retelling, it does not stand out among Sutcliff's large body of work. Sutcliff's historical novels ranged through the Middle Ages and even occasionally into the Renaissance, but it was Britain's earlier history with which she was most concerned, pre-Roman, Roman, and the centuries after Rome's decline – the early Middle Ages, also called the Dark Ages. Her Roman novels are her most outstanding achievement, and they connect with one of her re-imaginings of Arthur.

King Arthur was a story to which Sutcliff returned several times, both taking a strictly historical approach by placing Arthur in his probable time and circumstance in a novel about the Romano-British resistance to invading Germanic tribes, and retelling the later Arthur story as found in the romances and in Malory, with knights, quests, and the full panoply of chivalry.

Sutcliff's 'historical' Arthur is part of her series of books set in Roman Britain. *The Lantern Bearers* (1959) won the Carnegie Medal. It is the story of Aquila, a decurian (junior cavalry officer) born in Britain of a Romano-British family, who deserts and remains behind when the legions are recalled and the province abandoned. His home is attacked by Jutish raiders, his father killed, he and his sister separately carried off into slavery. After several years Aquila finds his way to freedom and back to Britain. He becomes a warrior in the service of Ambrosius, as they fight against Vortigern (the British king who, according to tradition, made himself supreme by Saxon mercenaries and a Saxon alliance) and the Saxon invaders. This is the terrain not so much of King Arthur, but of Merlin, the background against which Geoffrey of Monmouth tells the story of Vortigern's desire to sacrifice a boy with no human father to make his tower stand, and Merlin's prophecy before him of the two fighting dragons, the red and the white, British and Saxon. Sutcliff's is a strictly historical novel, and there is no Merlin, no magic, no prophecy, only desperate men trying to save something of civilization in the face of an overwhelming barbarian tide. Arthur, however, comes into *The Lantern Bearers* as Artos, Ambrosius' nephew, son of his dead brother Utha. He is a boy in the first part of the book and a young man of great promise by the end, but not yet a warleader. The story is that of Aquila and Ambrosius, and ends with a routing of Hengist's forces and Ambrosius crowned High King of Britain.

The Artos of *The Lantern Bearers*, which is a book for older children or teens, is the main character in Sutcliff's adult novel *Sword at Sunset* (1963). The latter can be read as a sequel to the former, though younger readers of Sutcliff will have to grow into it. It is written for an adult audience, moving more slowly, with more deliberation and reflection, than a juvenile book. It demands more of its readers in terms of an understanding of human nature and in emotional maturity. *Sword at Sunset* is narrated in the first person, a departure from Sutcliff's usual style: Artos, dying after his final victory, tended by monks, reflects on his life.

Sutcliff has with much research and skill written a novel that imagines an historically-possible reality underneath the legends of Arthur, a British war-leader leading British tribes, some still with the memory of Roman unity and Roman tactics, against the Anglo-Saxon invaders, troubled as well by factions and divided loyalties among the British tribes. There are no knights here, no tournaments, no glittering Camelot. Artos is a British war-leader, not even a territorial chieftain. His bases are smoky, wood-built hillforts, but he is always on the move, maintaining a precarious unity between the tribes and the chieftains of the west. While Ambrosius is king, Artos creates a fast-striking cavalry force. Among his Companions are Bedwyr, Cei, and Gwalchmai, all traditional companions to Arthur; not traditional but important among them is his armour-bearer, Flavian, Aquila's son. Artos' wife is Guenhumara, a chieftain's daughter married for alliance with her father; she turns against Artos after the death of their daughter, and comes to loves Bedwyr. After Ambrosius dies, Artos wins a great victory over the Saxons at Badon Hill and is proclaimed Caesar by his men. Aquila, hero of *The Lantern Bearers*, among the last survivors of Ambrosius' old Companions, dies at Badon.

Artos fights a long series of battles against the Saxons, but in the end dies fighting betrayal. Medreut is his only surviving child, a son conceived after a night with his sister Ygerna, who deliberately seduced Artos before he knew who she was. Medreut is acknowledged by Artos as his son and made one of his captains, but never his heir, because Artos recognizes in him a desire for power without service. Medreut forces knowledge of Bedwyr and Guenhumara's affair into the open, works to divide the Companions, and leads some of the British to ally with the Saxons against Artos. In the final battle Artos is mortally wounded and most of his Companions killed, though they have the victory. He recognizes that they have held back the barbarian darkness for a little time, but that the tribes, if they fail to remain united, will be overrun. He names his kinsman Constantine of

Dumnonia (Cornwall) his heir, but in an effort to keep word of his death from dissolving all the alliances, it is given out that he is wounded and being cared for by the monks, not dying. The expectation of his return, he hopes, will help Constantine to keep the tribes together. Bedwyr is to throw his sword into the marsh as a sign, so that Constantine will know when Artos has died. Thus even the traditional ending of Arthur's life, the throwing of the sword by Bedwyr into the water, and the sojourn in Avalon from which he will one day return, become part of a strictly historically-possible story, without magic or mysticism.

Sutcliff's Artos is a King Arthur to believe in. Both *The Lantern Bearers* and *Sword at Sunset* have all the strengths of this writer at her best: vividly realized history and historical possibility, meticulous historical detail, quietly compelling and powerful characters, plots both actively and psychologically dramatic. *Sword at Sunset* is more suited to the experience and expectations, real and literary, of adults and older teens; it contains much tragedy and death, sexual passion and tension. Even though Artos is not the main character, *The Lantern Bearers* on its own may give teens and older children a whole new way of considering Arthur and his time, and interest them in seeking out *Sword at Sunset* when they find themselves ready for it. *The Lantern Bearers* is also one of Sutcliff's finest novels and deserves to be read in its own right, by children and adults alike, not merely for its Arthurian content.

Sutcliff's other King Arthur is the more familiar one, though even using Malory, she gives Arthur a more detailed historical grounding than is usually found in retellings of stories from the romance sources. This Arthur was written as a trilogy for children. *The Light Beyond the Forest* (1979), *The Sword and the Circle* (1981), and *The Road to Camlann* (1981), were later republished in one volume form with the title *King Arthur Stories* (1999). Sutcliff retells Malory and uses him as her larger framework, but she also makes use of *Sir Gawain and the Green Knight* (written in the late fourteenth century) and another, shorter, Middle English work about Sir Gawain, as well as the Welsh *Mabinogion* (the individual components of which were probably composed in the eleventh and subsequent centuries based on earlier oral works, but which are preserved in manuscripts of the fourteenth and fifteenth), Godfrey of Strasburg's thirteenth-century *Tristan*, and for the beginning, Geoffrey of Monmouth's story of Vortigern's tower and Merlin's prophecy (c. 1136).

Sutcliff, in the beginning of her *King Arthur*, fixes her story to the withdrawal of Rome, Vortigern's treacherous murder of the High King, and his use of Saxon mercenaries to maintain his hold on the land; Merlin saves himself from sacrifice by Vortigern and makes his prophecy. Sutcliff then turns from Geoffrey to Malory as her source, to have young Arthur, squire to his foster-brother Kay, pull the sword from the anvil and prove himself Utha's heir while attending a late medieval tournament, even though the more historical Saxons and the Picts of Geoffrey remain the kingdom's external enemies. Merlin is in the story as advisor to the young Arthur, but then gives up this role to teach Nimue his magic and to be sunk by her into an enchanted sleep until the time comes for both him and Arthur to return. He is not the comic dotard Merlin, tricked and trapped, of Malory and other late medieval and modern versions of this ending; Merlin enters this sleep willingly, because it is his fate, and his love for Nimue is an affection returned, not the unwelcome obsession of an old man. Nimue, Merlin's love, is also the Lady of the Lake who gave Excaliber to Arthur, rather than, as in Malory, Nimue or Nenyve, merely one of many 'damesels of the Lady of the Laake.' In Sutcliff, Nimue is one of the Lordly Ones, ancient powers of the land, and Sutcliff's Merlin is half of that blood as well, accounting for his gift of prophecy. (Excaliber and the sword in the stone are two separate swords in all the original traditions regarding Arthur's swords, including Malory.)

Arthur forms the Round Table, marries Guenever, and gathers knights like Gawain and Lancelot to his service. The enmity of Arthur's sisters, Margawse and Morgan la Fay, is part of Sutcliff's story, as is Lancelot and Guenever's adulterous love. The stories of Gereint, who is accompanied on a quest to prove himself by his wife Enid, of Tristan and Iseult's doomed love, of Sir Gawain's strange compact with the giant green knight who can survive beheading, are all retold by her. So is that of Guenever's abduction by Meliagraunce, as well as the long and complex quest for the Holy Grail, which in Sutcliff's hands retains its mystic and spiritual dimensions.

The final tragedy leading to the battle at Camlann is told following Malory's version, in which Mordred uses the queen's adultery with Lancelot as part of an involved plot to destroy Arthur's fellowship and kingdom, before trying to seize it himself. After the death of both Arthur and Mordred in the battle at Camlann, the story, as in Malory, continues with the lives of some of the old knights: Lancelot and Bedivere become monks at Glastonbury, Bors and others die in the Holy Land. Guenever dies a nun.

Sutcliff brings her own touch to this conclusion, with the theme that runs through her historical fiction of post-Roman Britain, *The Lantern Bearers*, *Sword at Sunset*, and *Dawn Wind* (1961), the image of a light having been struck, capable of being remembered through the dark times to come. Though the fifteenth-century chivalry is at odds with the unifying king fighting Saxons and Picts to preserve the last embers of Roman Britain, Sutcliff stitches the two fabrics together in the books of the *King Arthur Stories* so that they sit not too-uncomfortably together. The marriage works, and gives to the traditional Malory retelling an illusion of definite place and time that Malory himself eschewed.

Sutcliff's style in *King Arthur Stories* is somewhat different from the intense, closely-focused third person narration usual in her historical fiction. It displays her skill for evocation of scene or mood in vivid and concise description of a detail that sums up the whole, but it is also written with a story-teller's cadence, and would work very well read aloud. Like Green's, Sutcliff's King Arthur must stand among the best of the traditional retellings of the standard Arthurian cycle of tales.

Mary Stewart (b. 1916)

Mary Stewart was born Mary Rainbow in Sunderland, in the county of Durham in the north of England. She studied English Language and Literature at Durham University, earned an M.A., and was a Lecturer in English at Durham. She married Sir Frederick Stewart, who held the Regius Chair of Geology at Edinburgh from 1956 to 1982. She lives in Argyll, Scotland. Most of Stewart's works have been romantic thrillers, beginning with

Madam Will You Talk? (1955). These are adult novels which will also appeal to teen-age girls, in which young women play quite an active role in their adventures, surviving peril by their wits and marrying mysterious and initially-menacing heroes with affinities to *Jane Eyre*'s Mr. Rochester.

Stewart is not primarily a children's writer, though she wrote three books specifically for children, all fantasies. *The Little Broomstick* (1971) is the story of orphan Mary Smith, who with the help of the black cat Tib discovers the magical plant fly-by-night and a broomstick. She embarks on a mission to rescue the creatures victimized by magical experiments at Endor College, a school for witches. In *Ludo and the Star Horse* (1974) the Bavarian boy Ludo, searching for his old horse Renti in the snow, finds him and accompanies him on a quest through the signs of the Zodiac in pursuit of the sun. Renti is a star horse, who wants to return to the stars. They have many adventures, meeting the incarnations of the Zodiacal symbols, some of whom are very dangerous. When they finally complete their search, Renti becomes one of those who pull the sun's chariot. *A Walk in Wolf Wood* (1980) sends two modern children travelling through time in the Black Forest. In the Middle Ages, they help a man who has been turned into a werewolf by a sorcerer. All three of these are stories that linger in the mind; Stewart writes with vivid imagery and poetic feeling.

However, Stewart's greatest contributions to fantasy are without a doubt her Arthurian books, the Merlin trilogy of *The Crystal Cave* (1970), *The Hollow Hills* (1973), and *The Last Enchantment* (1979), along with the concluding novel about Mordred, *The Wicked Day* (1983). Like Sutcliff's *Sword at Sunset*, these books were written for an adult audience. They have often been read by children, however, particularly the first two, which deal with the boyhoods of Merlin and of Arthur. Those who come to Merlin first of all through Stewart, as those who come to Arthur through Sutcliff's Roman books, form their understanding of the Arthurian matter based largely on the older sources, Geoffrey of Monmouth and his followers, and on a reasonably historical approach to the fifth and sixth centuries – and are forever after a little puzzled by all those jousting knights, with their entourages of ladies and dwarves, that are the legacy of Chrétien and Malory.

The Crystal Cave was at one point reissued under the title *Merlin of the Crystal Cave* to tie in with a BBC miniseries in 1991, but it has since reclaimed its original title. It begins in post-Roman Britain with Merlin's boyhood in Maridunum or Caer Myrddin (Carmarthen), as the illegitimate son of a Welsh princess. Myrddin Emrys, called Merlin, is educated both by tutors in the Roman manner and by the cave-dwelling hermit Galapas. Merlin has the Sight, and sometimes sees the future or prophesies, coming to understand himself as the tool of some god, perhaps the old British god of high places, Myrddin, or the Persian sun-god Mithras popular with Rome's legions, or the Christian God. He never resolves this identification in his own mind, though he inclines towards monotheism by the end of the series. His god guides him to serve the High Kings of Britain, first Ambrosius, then Uther, and at last Arthur.

After flight from a murderous uncle, abduction, and escape to Brittany, Merlin discovers he is Ambrosius' son. He aids his father and uncle in retaking Britain from Vortigern and his Saxon mercenaries, serving as spy, bard, prophet, surgeon, and engineer to first his father Ambrosius, and then his uncle Uther. The traditional elements of Merlin's story are all here. He is nearly sacrificed by Vortigern, prophesies the coming of Arthur, and arranges the adulterous night between High King Uther and Ygraine, wife of Gorlois of Cornwall, during which Arthur is conceived. Though no source claims any kinship between Merlin and Ambrosius, Merlin is called Merlinus Ambrosius in some of the oldest sources. Emrys is the Welsh form of Ambrosius; the shared name gave Stewart the foundation of her original plot, which makes her Merlin Emrys or Merlinus Ambrosius not only Arthur's prophet, but his cousin.

The Hollow Hills continues with the story of Arthur's upbringing, secretly overseen by Merlin. Even as a boy, Arthur is bold and warlike, as well as open-hearted and generous, bringing a flare to everything he does. Britain is beset by Saxon invaders and Arthur, taken to join the king's forces by Merlin, proves himself in battle; afterwards, he is invited to the bed of Morgause, Uther's bastard daughter, and Mordred is conceived. Morgause, like Merlin, has the Sight, but she hungers for power and plans to gain a hold over the next king through a child, even though she knows, as Arthur then does not, that he is her brother.

Arthur in fact has come to believe Merlin to be his father. Uther dies before he can publicly acknowledge Arthur his son and heir, and the kingdom is in danger not only from Saxons but from British kings who want to claim the High Kingship themselves. The sword in the stone plays a role in the story as the sword of the Roman general and imperial claimant Maximus, an ancestor of Ambrosius and Uther, discovered by Merlin (along with the Holy Grail) and hidden again until Arthur claims it. The sword is taken as the final proof of Arthur's right to rule as High King.

In *The Last Enchantment* Arthur's struggles to unite Britain and overcome the invaders are complicated by conspiracies against him, particularly those spearheaded by his sisters, Morgause and Morgan. His friend Bedwyr's affair with Guinevere is a part of the story, but the book remains Merlin's, the few elements of the traditional Merlin story having to do with the end of his life expanded by Stewart into a unified and gripping plot. Merlin falls in love with Nimue, a girl who first comes to him as his apprentice, disguised as a boy. Nimue has the Sight and power like his own; eventually, as his own powers wane, she becomes his successor. Morgause, who hates Merlin as much as or more than she hates her brother Arthur, poisons Merlin and he is believed dead. Nimue and Arthur have him buried in his cave in the pagan fashion, with offerings of food and wine. He wakes, and eventually is heard by a servant, who opens up the mouth of the cave. Merlin is greatly aged by this poisoning; but some power remains to him. He sees a gathering threat to Arthur and in his visions watches Morgause bringing her sons south to Arthur. Merlin travels, with great difficulty, to meet Arthur. One of the great scenes of the book is when he gives to a royal courier the dragon brooch long ago given him by his father Ambrosius, to take to Arthur with word from 'the king's cousin,' and Arthur's subsequent lone arrival at the gallop, sword in hand, as Merlin, a frail, ill man, is being set upon by thieves. After his 'return from the dead,' Merlin withdraws from the centre of power. Nimue has married another, but they remain friends; it is she who is now Arthur's prophet. The book ends with Merlin, again a hermit, living quietly in his cave, visited by the king.

The Wicked Day is not about Merlin, and is narrated in the omniscient third person rather than the first person of the first three novels. It is the story of Mordred, son of Arthur and Morgause. Tradition usually has him the youngest of the five broth-ers (the others are Gawain, Agravain, Gaheris, and Gareth), but Stewart makes him the eldest because of the sequence of events in *The Hollow Hills*. Mordred is brought up on Orkney by peas-ants, servants of Morgause. After her husband King Lot dies, Morgause has Mordred's foster-parents murdered and reclaims him. Mordred has to fight for acceptance among his half-brothers and always remains an outsider within the family, wary of Morgause and her manipulative ways. Arthur eventually takes his nephews from their mother and raises them among his own followers, telling Mordred the truth about his birth. Through continuing wars against the Saxons and conspiracies among the British, Mordred remains a loyal son. When Arthur is reported dead, Mordred, as his heir, negotiates a peace with the Saxons, but is considered by many a traitor when Arthur returns alive. It seems civil war will be averted, but the traditional mischance, the misinterpretation of a man drawing his sword to kill an adder during a parley, leads to battle and the deaths of both Arthur and Mordred.

Stewart's Arthurian world is an utterly compelling one. The people, the landscape of elusively god-touched forests and stone, the politics of the British kingdoms both warring with one an-other and united, sometimes, against external threat, make for a rich and credible world. Her late fifth or early sixth century Brit-ain is less strictly historical than Sutcliff's; it seems more medie-val, less tribal and less immediately post-Roman in social and material culture (while at the same time retaining more artefacts of Roman civilization), but it is nevertheless historically con-vincing. It never jars one's sense of historical possibility too strongly. Merlin is an absorbing character; his introspection and detailed observations on his world and himself combine, in the first two books particularly, with his personal involvement in great and dramatic events. Despite his protestations that he is not a soldier, he acquits himself well in the many physically de-manding situations he runs into, making him a satisfyingly active hero as well as a thoughtful one. The continued revelations of Merlin's identity, the workings of fate, the conflicts and the drama of the battles for Britain, and of Merlin's many private dangers encountered and overcome, make the story of the young Merlin and of Arthur's youth one with great appeal to teens and older children.

The Crystal Cave and *The Hollow Hills* are the two in the series most likely to be enjoyed by juvenile readers. They deal with themes that appeal to younger people and which are common in fantasy novels for both children and adults: youths discovering themselves and growing into their role in the world, orphans claiming a rightful high place and destiny. The later two deal more with 'adult' emotional themes in the complexities of love, desire, betrayal, and ambition, though the background of war, politics, and intrigue remains the same. These are therefore more likely to be appreciated by and hold the attention of teen and adult readers, though younger readers of the series will grow into them.

Antonia Fraser (b. 1932)

Fraser was born Antonia Pakenham, the eldest of eight children. Her father, Frank Pakenham, taught politics at Christ Church at Oxford, and both her parents were involved in politics themselves, standing unsuccessfully as Labour candidates. Her father was made Lord Longford, and her mother wrote biographies under the name Elizabeth Longford. Fraser attended Oxford and studied history. She worked for a publisher and as a ghost-writer before her marriage to Sir Hugh Fraser, a Tory MP from Scotland; they had six children. In the seventies, Fraser became involved with the playwright Harold Pinter, marrying him, after they had both divorced, in 1980. Fraser is primarily a writer of biographies. She brings a meticulous scholarship to 'popular' history, and from her first, *Mary, Queen of Scots* (1969), her biographies have been bestsellers. She has also written a mystery series, featuring the detective Jemima Shore, which has appeared intermittently from 1977 to the nineties.

Fraser has produced two books for children. *King Arthur and the Knights of the Round Table* (1970) was first published in the nineteen-fifties as *King Arthur: Retellings of Seventeen Tales About King Arthur, Lancelot, Gawaine, Tristram, and Other Knights of the Round Table,* illustrated by her daughter Rebecca. It contains retellings of the Arthurian material in the traditional manner, mostly using Malory as the source. Reprints of the 1970 edition are readily available.

Fraser's other children's work, *Robin Hood* (1955), was reissued in 1971 and again in 1993. It begins with Robin Hood's rescue of Nat the Weaver, a poor man who has killed a deer to feed his family and been captured by the Sheriff's men. Robin Hood, in Fraser's version, is the son of the Earl of Locksley, a prank-loving ward of the Sheriff of Nottingham, who covets Robin Hood's estates. His compatriot Guy of Gisborne frames Robin for an attempted assassination of paranoid Prince John. Robin and his friend Will Scarlett flee to the hidden Robber's Vale in the forest, where the minstrel Alan-a-Dale, Nat the Weaver, Much the Miller, and others join them. Little John joins after quarrelling with Robin over right-of-way on a log over a stream. In quite the reverse of the traditional version, it is Little John who is bested and ends up in the water, rather than Robin Hood. Many of the traditional episodes are worked in, but most of the plot centres on Oswald Montdragon's and Guy of Gisborne's use of Maid Marian to catch Robin Hood. The two first meet when she is rescued from a staged attack, but she does not betray the location of the outlaw's camp, having fallen in love with him. Marian's secret love is revealed by her treacherous maid, Black Barbara. She is imprisoned, and when Robin goes to rescue her, he too is captured. Marian drugs Montdragon, frees Robin, and with Much's help they escape. Robin attends an archery tournament disguised as an old man, another essential traditional element, fights and kills Sir Guy, but Marian is captured and condemned to death. Robin meets the disguised King Richard, who leads the band to Nottingham, frees Marian, and pardons them all. Robin, now Earl of Locksley, marries Marian. In old age he is bled for a fever by a prioress who is none other than jealous Black Barbara, and dies.

Fraser develops much of the conflict as that of Saxons against Normans, following Scott's lead in *Ivanhoe* (1819). She presents Robin Hood as a dashing lordling of Saxon ancestry, loyal to absent King Richard. She also develops the romantic side of the story in great detail, making the love of Robin and Marian, their loyalty and willingness to sacrifice their lives for one another, the crux of the plot in many places. Fraser's *Robin Hood* is in some ways like a novel, progressing in a sequence of events and consequences rather than disconnected episodes. However, despite shaping her story around a single long theme, Fraser's is still a fairly traditional retelling. The characters are given some motivation and complexity, but remain more ballad-like outlines with colourful surfaces than novelistically complex characters. Her Robin is bold, merry, and heedless of consequence; he retains the dashing, devil-may-care attitude of the original ballads and the turn of the century reteller Pyle.

Robin McKinley (b. 1952)

McKinley (see also Chapters IX and XIV) wrote a very original novel using the Robin Hood tradition. Like many of her other books, it appeared as a hardcover for young adults, then as adult mass-market paperback fantasy, and has recently reappeared marketed for teens once more.

McKinley's *The Outlaws of Sherwood* (1988) is, unlike the retellings of Pyle, Green, Sutcliff, and Fraser, a modern novel in approach, a re-imagining rather than a retelling. McKinley does not claim she has attempted serious historical fiction in every detail, but the story itself subtly demonstrates great attention to research. Her afterword notes that, among other historical inaccuracies in the received tradition of Robin Hood, the longbow did not come into common use in England until the fourteenth century. She gets around this by giving her Robin a father who adopted the Welsh longbow, and by observing in her afterword that it was used for hunting before it became the famous English military weapon. The longbow's novelty thus becomes in her version one of the advantages Robin Hood's band has over their enemies, a technical superiority over those using shorter bows with less power and range.

McKinley's Robin is a young forester, who runs afoul of some of his fellows, bullying favourites of the Chief Forester. In defending himself he accidentally kills one of these men. His friends Much, a miller's son, and Marian, half-Saxon daughter of a minor Norman knight, help him to hide in the forest. It is Much and Marian who see Robin as a symbol of revolt against oppressive Norman rule; Much is the dreamer, Robin and Marian the practical planners. Others eventually join Robin, either moving outright into the forest, or like Much and Marian, coming and going freely so long as their connection with the outlaws remains unknown. Robin meets Little John in the traditional way, by a hot-tempered quarrel over passage over a log bridge; in the traditional way, it is Robin who ends up in the stream. Friar Tuck is an amiable hermit with a pack of large, devoted dogs, Will Scarlet a noble-born friend of Marian's who joins them after his father undertakes to marry his sister off to a brutal lord against her will. The lutenist Alan-a-dale comes to them when his beloved Marjorie is to be married to another, as well. There are a number of others who join the band, some traditional, many others inventions of McKinley's own. They are a practical bunch, fletchers, carpenters, thatchers, farmers, and many other trades, men and women both, and not all the women spend their time doing the cooking and sewing; they are out with bows, taking their turns at hunting, hold-ups, and sentry duty with the rest. One of the most distinctive of McKinley's invented characters is Cecil, a young aristocrat who throws himself into the hardship of their life with grim determination, though all expect him to give up and leave. Cecil is quite startled to find women among the band. He assiduously avoids both Will and Marian, until Little John, who has been training him to fight, discovers he is a she, in fact, Will's sister Cecily.

McKinley works in many of the traditional adventures. Alan-a-dale's lady is rescued and married to him, and both remain with the band. Sir Richard of the Lea's mortgaged estate is saved from seizure by the sheriff through Marian's guile and the band's martial strength and stolen gold, an event that makes the sheriff's humiliation and hatred complete. There is romance in the story as well, Robin and Marian's undeclared love that goes disguised as friendship until nearly the end, Marjorie and Alan's difficult start to married life, Cecily and Little John's growing love for one another.

McKinley uses a traditional episode, in which the sheriff offers a golden arrow as an archery prize at Nottingham Fair in an attempt to expose Robin Hood, as the lead-up to the dramatic climax of the plot. Her Robin, although an excellent fletcher, is an indifferent marksman and too practical to take such a risk. Marian, one of the best archers among them, goes to the fair in disguise, motivated by a desire to further the symbolism of Robin Hood in the minds of the people, his almost mystical heroic status. It is, as she expected, a trap, but a worse one than she anticipated, and she is wounded by the mercenary Guy of Gisbourne, who was hired by the sheriff to track and kill Robin Hood. Marian is rescued in the melee by Little John and Cecily, but Guy of Gisbourne attacks the outlaws in Sherwood. There is an intense and extremely well-written battle around Friar Tuck's chapel and through the forest; a number of the outlaws are killed, deaths tragic and moving without being maudlin. Robin, in the end, kills Guy with help from Cecily. Sir Richard, summoned by Marjorie after the battle, shelters the survivors and prepares to withstand the sheriff. King Richard himself arrives, bringing news of the death of Sir Richard's son on crusade, but mostly motivated by curiosity about the stories he has heard of Robin Hood. The King pardons them, appoints Robin Sir Richard's heir, betroths him to Marian, and takes them all into his own service, to accompany him to his wars in Palestine.

The characters are given a depth of personality not found in the ballad sources; in McKinley's hands they become real people. Robin is a thoughtful, meticulous, quick-tempered yet forgiving young man. He is thrust into a terrible situation by his accidental manslaughter, and finds a way not only to survive, but to do so without compromising his own sense of right and wrong. Her Sherwood becomes a vividly real place, and her story is above all satisfyingly plausible. Robin is not flamboyant or dashing, not an Errol Flynn mocking the Sheriff and flaunting his rebellion. He is always too aware of his responsibilities, the dangers his friends and followers incur for his sake, for such bravado. He is not a leader to risk others' lives for a mere grand gesture, as the Robin of the ballads frequently does. He is a quieter hero, but a hero just the same, and one who will endure in the reader's memory.

Anne McCaffrey (b. 1926)

McCaffrey was born in Cambridge, Massachusetts, and studied Slavonic Languages and Literature at Radcliffe College. She became an actor with a particular interest in stage direction and opera. McCaffrey is a very successful science fiction author whose career began in the late sixties, when few women were finding acceptance as writers in that genre, or at least, few who wrote under an obviously feminine name. Her most acclaimed books are *The Ship Who Sang* (1969) and its four sequels, and the *Pern* series, which began with *Dragonflight* (1968) and had reached nineteen books by 2001 with *The Skies of Pern*. McCaffrey lives in County Wicklow, Ireland.

McCaffrey's Arthurian young adult novel, *Black Horses for the King* (1996) had its origins in a short story of the same title, which in her foreword to the book she says was inspired by Rosemary Sutcliff's *Sword at Sunset* and Artos' need in that for good horses. Like Sutcliff's novel, McCaffrey's is set in an historically-imagined late fifth- or early sixth-century Britain, with Arthur, Artos, as a war leader uniting the post-Roman British against Anglo-Saxon invaders. The story McCaffrey tells is of the early days of Artos' rise. It is narrated by Galwyn, who joins Artos, Comes Britanniorum or Count of Britain, as a translator and horse-handler. He helps in importing Libyan warhorses for Artos' cavalry, which the count hopes will give him the edge needed, to drive the Saxons from Britain. Galwyn's problems as a runaway from apprenticeship to his sailor uncle, his desire to serve Artos, his love of horses, his training as a farrier, and the enmity he incurs from the cruel and vengeful Iswy, provide the main story of the book, to which the horses and the preparations for war are the background. Galwyn as hero has his own development, his own crises, tragic losses, and victories. The story ends with the first great military victory of Artos and his band, mounted on Libyan horses, over the Saxons, while Galwyn, having triumphed over his own enemy in a knife fight, has grown to maturity in the count's service.

McCaffrey's story does not develop the historically possible Arthur beyond what Sutcliff has done; her Artos remains by and large an admired figure in the background to Galwyn's story. (For those who want to write strictly historical Arthurs, without Merlin or prophecy, Sutcliff's shadow is a long one.) *Black Horses for the King* is a fine recreation of Britain around 500 A.D., both an historical novel and a teen 'coming-of-age' story. It will introduce young readers, unfortunately more likely to pick up a book by a known modern name in science fiction than to take out a battered library copy of *The Lantern Bearers*, to an imaginatively-stimulating world of history and legend, and perhaps lead them back to the author McCaffrey cites as influencing her treatment of Arthur.

Kevin Crossley-Holland (b. 1941)

Crossley-Holland (see also Chapter IX) has written a non-fiction book for children about the Arthurian traditions, *The King Who Was and Will Be: The World of King Arthur and His Knights* (1999), but he has also taken a unique approach to retelling Arthurian legend in novel form in his *Arthur* trilogy. It comprises Crossley-Holland's only children's novels on original stories; his early novels were his retellings of medieval legends. The *Arthur* books are more successful narratives than Crossley-Holland's *King Horn*, because he does not make his medieval characters speak in datable slang; he adopts Sutcliff's approach to historical fiction, and uses a restrained but never artificial formal contemporary English, mixed with the bluntness usual to all social levels of English speech until the Victorians.

The first in the trilogy, *Arthur: The Seeing Stone* (2000), won the Guardian Children's Fiction Award. The book is written in the first person, in one hundred very brief chapters, few more than three pages long and some less. The premise is that the narrator, Arthur de Caldicot, is writing the story almost as it unfolds, as a chronicle of his life and his musings on family, religion, current events, and philosophy. Most are interesting for what they reveal of medieval life, Arthur's developing sense of himself, or the unfolding story of his family. Some chapters, although realistic portrayals of the sorts of things real children spend serious time on, do not make for interesting reading – Arthur's listing of words containing the element 'Jack', for instance.

The story begins in the year 1199, the year of Richard I's death. Arthur is the second son to a knight whose manor lies near the Welsh border. The book contains two stories interwoven. One is Arthur de Caldicot's life, realistically portrayed in great detail. The other is the Arthur legend, experienced by the narrator Arthur through the seeing stone of the title, a piece of obsidian given to him by the mysterious Welsh wise man, Merlin. Arthur de Caldicot's story follows the usual pattern of a boy growing up: he enjoys work and play with his siblings and friends, family love and conflict, a jealous older brother, a mischievous sister, a baby brother whose death devastates his mother, a Welsh grandmother who reminds him of the importance of the past and of stories. There are rivalries, friendships, jealousies, secret fears and aspirations. Arthur is educated by the priest and by Merlin. He is also trained in all the martial arts he will need as a knight, and though he wants to become a squire, begins to fear his father may intend him for a monk or priest, both because he is a second son, and because of his skill with book-learning.

By the end many family secrets and stresses begin to unfold. His older brother Serle has gotten his mother's servant pregnant, causing her to be turned out, homeless and without family. Arthur's father tells him he is only a foster-son. His real father is his supposed uncle, the violent Sir William. His unnamed mother was a married woman, and when her husband accused Sir William of fathering a child on her, he disappeared, presumably murdered. William sent this child to be brought up by his own younger brother. Grace, the cousin whom Arthur hoped to marry, is his own half-sister. Arthur becomes a squire to his foster-father's overlord, Stephen de Holt, to go on crusade, which delights Arthur.

The story of King Arthur that Arthur de Caldicot experiences contains elements from the traditions of both Geoffrey of Monmouth and the romances, but Arthur de Caldicot knows nothing of Arthurian legend of either school. His grandmother's Welsh tales preserve fragments of Arthurian legend, but without King Arthur's name attached. Arthur de Caldicot witnesses 'the hooded man' prophesy to Vortigern of the dragons beneath the pool, and Uther's magic-aided deception of Ygerna and the conception of Arthur. He lives episodes in Arthur's boyhood as the foster-son of Sir Ector, his rivalry with his foster-brother Kay and his desire to become a squire and perform great deeds, and as Arthur-in-the-stone he pulls the sword from the stone in the churchyard, seeking a sword for Kay. As he is proclaimed king Arthur realizes that 'the hooded man' is his own Merlin.

Arthur-in-the-stone and Arthur de Caldicot attain the first success in their journeys towards their desired futures at the same time, one as king, the other as a squire about to go on crusade. There are many parallels in their lives: the foster-father, the jealous older 'brother' outshone by the younger, the real mother who was a victim of rape, the potential of incest in Arthur de Caldicot's and Grace's desire to be betrothed, before he learns they are siblings, a parallel to King Arthur's unwitting incest with his sister. Through the parallels, events in Arthur de Caldicot's life are often foreshadowed, and he is also able to reflect on his experiences and desires.

Crossley-Holland's style is poetic, sparse, and often dense. Much occupies few words, as befits a narrative composed by a boy in stolen, reflective moments. The overall impact of the book is as historical fiction. It presents a detailed, researched picture of late twelfth- and early thirteenth-century life: hard work, justice no harsher than that of many later centuries but cruel to modern eyes, and the dominance of agriculture and religion in every aspect and level of society. The reader will come away with a greater understanding of medieval culture, society, law, folklore, religion, and martial training. Arthur's tendency to pause to consider his world as he writes about it enables the author to explain many things to the readers in the narrator's voice, without it appearing implausible that Arthur should write about them; a glossary at the end aids in understanding unfamiliar terms as well.

This will be a book eye-opening and educational for most young readers, suspenseful and even gripping, but the tale it tells is more interesting as historical fiction and as a coming-of-age story than as fantasy; the visionary experiences of King Arthur's life through the stone are interesting for Arthur de Caldicot's contemplation of them, not primarily as retellings of the Arthurian matter in their own right. The mystery of Merlin, who exists both in the world of the stone and in Arthur's present, is even stronger fantasy than visions in a stone. He is a wise man, cheerfully and rigorously debating with Arthur, the priest Oliver, and the scholars of Oxford, but at the final Christmas feast performs the 'hero's salmon leap' of Celtic legend, a mighty jump in the air; this ties him into the older heroic world in a way at once stronger and more shadowy than his identification as Merlin and the hooded man in the stone. Grandmother Nain's story of the nameless sleeping king under the hill, accidentally woken and calling out to know if it is yet the day to wake, a piece of traditional British folklore, is equally powerful magic.

Depending on what it is that readers are turning to fantasy to experience, though, it may be those seeking historical fiction for whom this series will have greatest appeal. The sequels, *Arthur: At the Crossing Places* (2001) and *Arthur: King of the Middle March* (2003), continue Arthur's story, through crusade, disillusionment with war and martial glory, and return. They continue as well the retelling of the traditional 'Matter of Britain' in Arthur's visions of the events of Arthurian romance, bringing the series to a conclusion in which thematic parallels continue, through tragedy and homecoming.

T.A. Barron (b. 1952)

Thomas Archibald Barron grew up on a ranch in Colorado, attended Oxford as a Rhodes Scholar, and became a business executive. He began writing full time in the nineteen-nineties, and lives with his wife and five children in Colorado.

Barron's five book series *The Lost Years of Merlin* was written with the intention of providing stories about Merlin's youth. It mostly takes place in the land of Fincayra, an island between the human world and the Otherworld. In the first book, *The Lost Years of Merlin* (1996), the boy Emrys and the woman Branwen wash up on the shores of Wales. She raises him as her son, but he never believes that he is. Having discovered he is from the magical island of Fincayra, he sets out for it on a raft, reaches it, encounters Rhia, a girl who has been raised by trees, and is hunted by goblin soldiers. He learns that the king, Stangmar, is his father, who turned to evil after a rather inexplicable and never-explained Fincayran law forbidding children of mixed human and Fincayran blood to be born on Fincayran soil was violated. The law demanded that Strangmar's human wife, Elen or Branwyn, be killed, for accidentally giving birth on Fincayra, and the king decided to kill his son in her place.

In the subsequent books, *The Seven Songs of Merlin* (1997), *The Fires of Merlin* (1998), and *The Mirror of Merlin* (1999), Emrys, renamed Merlin, continues his adventures. He discovers more about himself and about the threat to Fincayra from the evil but otherwise characterless power Rhita Gawr. He encounters many more of the peoples of Fincayra, is reunited with Branwyn or Elen, who really is his mother (and why he thought otherwise is never explained), discovers Rhia is his sister, and falls in love with Hallia, who can take the shape of either a woman or a deer. He overcomes dangers and enemies such as a dragon and Nimue.

By the final volume, *The Wings of Merlin* (2000), Merlin succeeds in uniting the many peoples of Fincayra. They withstand their enemies and defeat Rhita Gawr's army. As a reward for uniting, they acquire wings from the immortal Dagda, Rhita Gawr's opposite number. Merlin chooses to fulfil his destiny and return to teach Arthur, though this means giving up not only his wings and his family, but the deer-woman Hallia, who remains in the Otherworld.

Barron's stories seem heavily influenced by the writing of Mary Stewart, T.H. White, and Lloyd Alexander, without rising to their level of greatness in themes, characters, prose style, or originality. There is also an obvious lack of careful thought in his writing: in the first book, for example, a cuckoo, of all things, is used as a symbol of caring motherhood, devotedly nurturing its nestling but recognizing when it is time for the young one to fly. The cuckoo which Merlin observes caring for its hatchling in the first book is returned to, with the same symbolic import, in the final volume, as Merlin takes a final leave of his mother Branwen/Elen. The European cuckoo is a parasitic bird which lays its eggs in other birds' nests, where the hatchlings kill their foster-siblings and are raised by the parent birds of the other species. Cuckoos are thus a traditional literary symbol of cuckolding (of which cuckoo is the root word), changelings, and maternal indifference or neglect. Barron's choice of the cuckoo (presumably a European cuckoo, since it is nesting in Wales), as symbol of a wise mother is an inexplicably bizarre usage to make of that bird in particular, when nearly any other bird at all would have served the symbolic purpose he demanded of it. Merlin also somehow converts a dead oak tree into planks for a raft using neither tools nor magic – at least, what are broken limbs in one sentence become planks in the following ones, suggesting either very sloppy writing or ignorance of the definition of 'plank'.

Despite its North American popularity in the late nineteen-nineties, *The Lost Years of Merlin* does not make any significant artistic contribution to either children's fantasy or modern Arthurian stories. It is a journey through a rather lacklustre fantasy landscape, which, like a videogame, contains a plethora of plot-convenient magical objects, numerous prophecies embedded in jingles, and, in the tradition of moral tales, a large number of encounters which do little to enrich the story but each of which rather obviously teaches the hero some fact about himself or drives home a philosophical point the author wishes to make. Its fantastic elements never feel like more than window-dressing; it lacks any depth in characters or world, and is generally poorly-written.

There are as many King Arthurs and as many Robin Hoods as there are tellers and retellers of King Arthur and Robin Hood stories; it would probably be fair to say that there are as many as there are readers, for each person assembles what they want and what they need from what they find, and feeds their own imagination on what is offered. These are only a selection of the retellings and re-imaginings of both Arthur and Robin Hood for children that have been written over the past century or so. Some are retellings dedicated to introducing children to the Robin Hood of the ballads and the *Gest*, the King Arthur of Malory or the Lancelot of Chrétien, by editing content and language to varying degrees, or unifying the separate stories into a single linked plot. Others take the bare ideas underlying the legends and reimagine them to carry their own themes and present new stories. Still others combine the stories of the original sources with historical context, and reimagine Robin Hood, Arthur, and Merlin, into what-might-have-beens of history, or create historical fantasy, fashioning magic out of beliefs about the supernatural and divine of the historical period they have made their setting. All will suit different moods at different times, and enrich the imaginative lives, and even the historical understanding and the appreciation for the long history of literature, of the children and teens who read them.

XI
The Sixties

For Great Britain, which continued to be the nation with the greatest impact on the creation of children's fantasy, the nineteen-sixties was an era of greater economic prosperity compared to the decades that had gone before. Society, too, was in a period of rapid change in both Europe and North America, and the anxieties of world politics did not ebb. The Soviets sent the first human, Yuri Gagarin, into space in 1961. In the same year the Berlin Wall was built, cutting off Communist East from democratic West Berlin; the Americans sent advisers and 'special forces' to maintain the South Vietnamese government against guerrillas backed by the Communist North; and John F. Kennedy declared nuclear war survivable if one had access to a home fall-out shelter. Rachel Carson's *Silent Spring*, published in 1962, brought environmental issues to the public forum, where they have remained and grown more urgent ever since. The Cuban Missile Crisis in 1962 and the official American entry into the Vietnam War in 1965 meant that the possibility of the Cold War becoming hot was ever-present in the collective imagination of the age. In the United States, there was social upheaval as the Civil Rights movement fought for equality for all citizens, facing violent opposition from some and resorting in some cases to violence. Towards the close of the decade, there was anti-war protest as well.

By the end of the sixties, Britain's economy was again in decline. The nation was embroiled in the violence of 'the Troubles' in Northern Ireland, while student protest movements worldwide were opposing discrimination, war, pollution, nuclear arms, and totalitarianism, to name only some of the popular causes. In Communist eastern Europe, the Soviet Union sent troops to suppress attempted reform in Czechoslovakia in 1968, as they had in Hungary in 1956, keeping Cold War tensions high. The Americans sent men to the moon on Apollo 11 in 1969, and the possibilities of human endeavour were again celebrated.

To children growing up in this decade, the world was at once full of exciting possibility, as the frontiers of humanity were pushed out from the planet, and great anxiety as well, as human extinction became conceivable. Television, common in the fifties, was nearly ubiquitous in the western industrialized nations during the sixties, which exposed this generation to more of the worries of the adult world than was common earlier in the century. Then, politics and foreign affairs were discussed in newspapers with little to draw children's attention; in many families weighty issues were often deliberately excluded from juvenile awareness, though in others the opposite was true. Even in the decades when radio reigned, the news was not so vividly inescapable, as it has been since the supper-hour newscast brought pictures of disaster, violence, and tragedy into the living room or even kitchen.

Greater awareness of world events, and of young people's helplessness against them, may have had an influence on the development of a separate culture not so much of children but of 'youth', of teens, who held themselves to have a separate agenda in politics, a separate set of values and concerns. A more certain factor in this separation of adolescence from childhood as a whole was the increasing affluence of society, which meant that teens had money, from part-time jobs or parental allowances far in excess of previous generations' 'pocket-money', to spend on non-essential goods on a scale that had not been seen before. As a part of this subculture of adolescence so marked in the sixties, books aimed at children became very obviously subdivided. Previously, juvenile literature was separated only vaguely into books for older and for younger children, with the assumption that teens outgrowing children's books would move on to adult reading matter. Although books for adolescents had begun appearing between the wars, it was in the sixties and seventies that such works, for teens or as they are now called, 'young adults', focusing on perceived teen issues (puberty, sex, relationships, alienation from society/family), became plentiful, especially in North America. In this and subsequent decades such themes would find their way into fantasy works as well.

Norton Juster (b. 1929)

Architect Norton Juster's *The Phantom Tollbooth* has become a classic of American children's literature, though it can make one think of Kingsley's 'Cousin Cramchild' and 'Auntie Agitate', re-costumed for the nineteen-sixties. *Phantom Tollbooth* is an allegory of education, in which a boy, Milo, suffering from ennui, finds a mysterious tollbooth in his room. After picking a random destination from the accompanying map and driving past the tollbooth in his toy car, he finds himself in a strange countryside, on the road to Dictionopolis. On his way Milo encounters such people as the chattering Whether Man, the Lethargarians who inhabit the Doldrums, and Chroma the conductor, whose orchestral music creates colour. His companion for much of his journey is Tock the Watchdog, who has a clock in his side. Milo's and Tock's travels turn into a quest to rescue Rhyme and Reason, the princesses who kept the quarrelling rulers of Dictionopolis, the city of words, and Digitopolis, the city of numbers, in accord. The princesses have been banished by the King of Dictionopolis and his brother the Mathemagician of Digitopolis, and their absence has left the land in chaos. Enemies to Milo's mission are creatures such as the Gorgons of Hate and Malice, the Triple Demons of Compromise, Threadbare Excuse, Overbearing Know-It-All, and others, who are defeated by the armies of Wisdom. After his adventure, the tollbooth gone to those who need it more, Milo becomes aware of the exciting possibilities of the real world around him.

The Phantom Tollbooth is an allegory, leaving little to the imagination. Applicability lies not in the reader's own experience and needs but in the author's instruction; meaning is laid out and labelled. However, it contains a great deal of action, numerous puns and clever invented creatures. Several generations have found it entertaining, although it is more likely to appeal to those who do not take their reading seriously, who do not need depth of reality in their fantastic to engage in Coleridge's 'willing suspension of disbelief'.

Alan Garner (b. 1934)

Alan Garner spent his early years near Alderley Edge in Cheshire. This landscape provided the setting for many of his books, including the stories that make up *The Stone Book Quartet* (1976-78), in which Garner depicted significant moments in the imagined lives of his own ancestors in the later nineteenth and the twentieth centuries. It is also the setting for his first two fantasies. Garner studied Classics at Oxford but left without completing his degree, returning to Alderley to dedicate himself to writing. In addition to his fiction, he has edited *The Hamish Hamilton Book of Goblins* (1969) and is the author of a collection of retold English and Welsh folktales for younger children, *A Bag of Moonshine* (1986), illustrated by P.J. Lynch.

The Weirdstone of Brisingamen (1960) was Garner's first book. Its theme is a battle between ancient forces of good and evil with mythic overtones; a battle, largely unperceived by the everyday world, in which contemporary children by fate or chance become caught up. This is a theme that became much more common in the sixties and following decades, largely due to the influence of Tolkien and C.S. Lewis on the imaginations of other writers. *Brisingamen* and its sequel, *The Moon of Gomrath* (1963) show the influence of Tolkien very strongly, both in theme and style, which is not to say that Garner imitates Tolkien; he does not, not in the slavish, undigested manner of many fantasy writers (especially Americans) of the sixties, seventies, and even eighties. However, he mixes unselfconsciously the colloquial and everyday with the grand and archaic-seeming in speech, characterisation, and motive, he writes with a strong awareness of the physical landscape through which his characters move, and he offers a world in which there is above all a sense of depth and rich past, of mystery underlying the everyday, unperceived but not unconnected. All these things show Tolkien's influence. Garner is much more imitative in the presentation of his dwarves and his svart-alfar or goblins, and in characters like Angharad Goldenhair and Albanac, who, although not very developed character-portraits, are sketches which evoke very strongly the superficial impression a reader forms of Galadriel and Aragorn: beautiful and wise, or dark, grim, and mysterious.

The main characters in the two books are Colin and Susan, who, while their parents are abroad, come to stay with Gowther and Bess Mossock, farmers near Alderley Edge and the Edge, a great hill of stone, abandoned mines and quarries, and forest. Colin and Susan are the usual sort of protagonists for this sort of story: middle-class and from 'away'. It seems like the stock arrangement; before Garner, though, this type of fantasy story was not nearly so common, and few writers since have ever achieved the credibility and depth which Garner and a little later Susan Cooper brought to it. Garner makes the children's involvement in great affairs, always a weak point in this type of story, very plausible. Why should ordinary children be needed to save this powerful, ancient world? Garner's answer is that they are not needed, and not even wanted; the world of magic is hidden because it is too dangerous for humans, and everyone wants the children well out of it.

However, Colin and Susan become caught up in the ongoing battle between good and evil through chance and inheritance. Childless Bess had given their mother a family heirloom, the 'Tear', a crystal which Susan now wears on a bracelet. This stone, Firefrost or the Weirdstone of Brisingamen, is the key to great enchantments which guard a band of warriors and their mounts sleeping in a cave, awaiting a final battle in a distant time. It was taken, without the knowledge of Cadellin the guardian wizard, by an ancestor of Bess. The final battle will be against Nastrond, the Great Spirit of Darkness, who lurks in Ragnarok – in Garner a place rather than an event. The name 'Brisingamen' is taken, like 'Ragnarok' and various other odds and ends in the story, from Norse mythology, where it is the name of a fateful necklace, while Ragnarok is the battle that ends the world. The sleeping king, his knights, and their milk-white horses, along with the guardian wizard and the iron gates to the cave, are from a genuine legend of Alderley Edge, which can be found as the last item in *The Penguin Book of English Folktales* (1992). (Neither Garner nor his source claims that the sleeping king is Arthur.)

Possession of Firefrost involves the children in the conflict, since the Morrigan, a shape-shifting witch named Selina Place, attempts to steal it for her master Nastrond. Colin and Susan are hunted by the goblins or svart-alfar (another Norse borrowing, like the lios-alfar of *The Moon of Gomrath*), and by more terrifying things. They are rescued by the wizard Cadellin and befriended by the warrior-dwarves Fenodyree and Durathror. The Morrigan succeeds in stealing Firefrost. Colin and Susan steal back the stone but lose themselves in old mines and the tunnels of the svart-alfar. Durathror and Fenodyree find them and all four are hunted through flooded caves, narrow shafts and chimneys of stone in one of the most atmospheric and frightening underground chases in fiction. They learn that enemies are between them and the wizard; they have only a few days to get Firefrost to Cadellin and to do so must cross a great stretch of moor and marsh without being seen.

One of Garner's great strengths in making his magic a credible part of the real world lies in the fact that it is not something 'special' in which only children are able to believe or participate. He does not have any adult exposed to it conveniently enchanted to forget, to facilitate the action of the child-heroes. He does not play around with time, so that no adult realizes the children have been off on a desperate quest. His magic is consistent and real for all. When the dwarves and children take refuge at the Mossock farm, they tell Bess and Gowther everything. Gowther, rather than disbelieving the evidence of his own eyes or being enspelled into forgetting, joins the children and the dwarves on their desperate cross-country flight to find Cadellin and takes part in the battle which routs the Morrigan.

The Moon of Gomrath continues the story a few months later. Construction in the town has exposed an old pit; from it a formless beast, the Brollachan, has escaped. The lios-alfar, the cold, proud elves, have come from the distant lands to which human pollution of the environment has driven them, to hunt it. Susan and Colin meet new friends, a dwarf, Uthecar, and a black-clad warrior, Albanac, who is identified with the Sons of Don from Welsh tradition. They are drawn back into the world of magic, since the Morrigan has returned, seeking revenge against Susan. She is possessed by the Brollachan, which slowly consumes its hosts. Though they drive the creature from Susan's body by returning to her a protective bracelet she had lent the elves, Colin must find a magical herb growing on an ancient trackway to bring back her spirit, which has been riding with a Valkyrie-like band of women among the stars.

The second phase of the story begins with Colin and Susan unwittingly letting loose the Wild Hunt and the Hunter, creatures of the dangerous, ancient, Old Magic, of which Susan's bracelet is part. Susan, like Cadellin's ally Angharad Goldenhair and his enemy the Morrigan, has a certain kind of power now, though it is strongest in each of them at a different phase of the moon. When Colin is held hostage by the Morrigan it is Susan who leads the search for Colin and forces the reluctant elves to help. Once Colin has been rescued, only Susan insists on confronting the Morrigan and trying to defeat both her and the Brollachan, battling the witch with her own magic and then with the aid of the Wild Hunt and the nine wild women, destroying both the Morrigan and the Brollachan. The book hints that Susan, because of her experiences, has become part of the world of magic, and more specifically of the Old Magic which is now free, and may at the end of her life join the women who hunt across the sky among the stars.

One of the best elements of these two books is the way they remythologize a landscape, taking elements of English, Celtic, and Norse folklore and myth and giving them a new imaginative place. The result is stories that are rooted in their invented history, not fairy-tales of 'once upon a time in a far kingdom'. Garner's Alderley Edge books do what Kipling wanted to do in a different way with real history in *Puck of Pook's Hill* and *Rewards and Fairies*; they create an impression of deep roots. The stories told have a beginning long before the protagonists' involvement with events, and like real history, do not end when they drop out. Though Colin and Susan may have survived their involvement with the dangerous world of magic and defeated the Morrigan, Cadellin and his Sleepers still wait in Fundindelve, and Nastrond in Ragnarok; the battle between them is one which neither the young protagonists nor the readers will ever experience.

Garner's next book was *Elidor* (1965). Like his preceding works, it throws ordinary children into a world of ancient magic, but it is a more conventional story. Four children, David, Nicholas, Helen, and Roland, exploring a demolished church in a slum being redeveloped, are drawn one by one into the land of Elidor, a grim, grey place made so by the capture and locking away of four Treasures. Each sibling is sent by the man they encounter there, Malebron, into a mound. Each in turn fails until Roland. He frees his captive brothers and sister and with them brings out the Treasures which once maintained the land in peace and beauty. They are sent back to their own world by Malebron, to guard the Treasures there. One of the most entertaining parts of the book is their effort to hide the talismans, which generate power, interfering with radios and televisions, running unplugged appliances, and starting cars. In the end, as enemies break through from Elidor and hunt them around suburban Manchester, the unicorn Findhorn, who has also broken through into the city, is slain, and his dying song starts life returning to Elidor. The return of the Treasures completes the land's restoration.

Elidor lacks the poetic power both the Alderley Edge books and *The Owl Service* display. This is largely because it lacks depth. Elidor is never a very interesting place, compared with the stones, caves, and forests of the Edge, and there seems little to connect the children to it beyond Roland's vaguely mentioned psychic strength. As a magical adventure story, it lacks logical and poetic coherence, although it has some finely-done unsettling moments, as when the children flee down their suburban street crying for help and all the neighbours close their doors and turn off the lights. Little reason is given for Malebron's actions, while the background to the conflict in Elidor, like the logic for the children's involvement, is never really apparent. It seems merely typical of a particular type of shallow, formulaic fantasy (which continues to be written into this century), rather than the work of the outstanding artist in the genre that Garner's other books show him to be.

The Owl Service (1967), like Garner's critically-acclaimed but difficult novel *Red Shift* (1973), which connects the lives of several young couples across time, is a book for adolescents. *The Owl Service* is a short book with a complexly-layered plot, which has behind it a story from the collection of early medieval Welsh legends called the *Mabinogion*, that of Blodeuwedd, the woman made out of flowers by Gwydion to be the wife of his nephew Llew Llaw Gyffes. Blodeuwedd falls in love with Gronw Pebry and like Delilah, learns from her husband the only way he can be killed, so as to betray him to his rival. Llew Llaw Gyffes, though, turns into an eagle, is healed by his uncle

Gwydion, and kills Gronw, while Gwydion turns Blodeuwedd into an owl.

In *The Owl Service*, this story has been re-enacted time after time over the years in a Welsh valley, destroying the lives of the people involved. It begins to happen again with the English girl Alison, her step-brother Roger, and Gwyn, the son of the house-keeper at Alison's cottage. In the previous generation, the story came to a tragic end for Gwyn's mother Nancy, her boyfriend Bertram, and Huw, the apparently-mad gardener, descendant of Gwydion or his brother Math, and heir to wizard-like powers. Huw is also Gwyn's unknown father and inadvertently, the killer of Bertram.

In the latest generation, Alison becomes obsessed with a set of patterned plates found in the attic; she traces the pattern and makes paper owls out of it, which take on life of their own. Alison is torn between her class-conscious mother's view of the world, her feelings for Gwyn, who is only working-class and Welsh, and Roger. Gwyn fights with his bitter mother to stay in school rather than drop out to work, resents being treated as a servant by Alison's mother and step-father, resents the valley's attempts to claim him as a descendant of Gwydion, and resents most of all Roger's mockery and Alison's betrayal of some of his secret aspirations to his rival. Amidst all this, the supernatural powers of the valley begin working their pattern of anger and betrayal again. When Gwyn cannot overcome his anger at Alison's perceived treachery, it is Roger who talks his step-sister away from her owl-possession and into seeing the spirit of Blodeuwedd as flowers. However, the matter of who Alison her-self wants to be, what her dreams and aims in life are outside her mother's direction, is left unresolved.

The Owl Service, which won both the Carnegie Medal and Guardian Award, is a book that demands and rewards close reading. It is also one which is very much a young adult rather than a children's book, because so much of the story rests on the tensions between the three main characters. These are likely to be missed by younger readers, whose emotional lives, although not necessarily less complex, are less subtle and less articulately self-aware. It is an engrossing story for teens, though, which younger readers of Garner will grow into.

Garner's works are complex and poetic, spun together out of

many disparate sources. At the same time, he is able to tell stories that are at once exciting, frightening, and enthralling, with engaging characters both human and supernatural, and landscapes vividly evoked. His stories are the sort in which a reader often discovers more on a second or third reading, but they offer plenty in terms of enjoyment, thoughtfulness, excitement, and imaginative depth the first time through as well.

Madeleine L'Engle (b. 1918)

Madeleine L'Engle was born in New York City and attended Smith College and the New School for Social Research. She worked in theatre, married actor Hugh Franklin, and raised three children. In the sixties she wrote several books that were 'family' stories with a strong Christian background, *Meet the Austins* (1960) and its sequels. Her realism often carried a hint of fantasy. Her actual fantasy books about the Murry family are often called science fiction because they involve such ideas as telepathy and time-travel, beloved of at least television science fiction. One book does involve travel to other planets. However, a prominent role is played by mythological creatures and what can only be called magic.

The first book about the Murrys, *A Wrinkle in Time* (1962), won the Newbery Medal. The heroine, Meg Murry, is a very bright teenager in an odd but stable and loving family. Both her mother and her missing father are scientists, and her youngest brother, Charles Wallace, is a genius, as well as telepathic. Meg's father was doing secret government research into tesseracts, foldings of space and time, and has disappeared. Charles Wallace, Meg, and another teenage misfit, Calvin O'Keefe, are taken by the benevolently witchlike Mrs. Whatsit, Mrs. Who, and Mrs. Which to find Dr. Murry and fight a great evil darkness that is spreading through the universe. The three Mrs. W's are hinted to be angels of some sort; the supernatural in L'Engle's books is always founded on her Christianity. The children 'tesser' through space and time and are shown a 'Dark Thing', the evil that overshadows Earth and many other planets. Dr. Murry is on Camazotz, a planet that has given in to the darkness and become an utterly totalitarian society, ruled by a disembodied brain called IT. Everything is controlled; there is no individuality. When the children play, all the balls and skipping ropes strike the ground at the same time. Charles Wallace is possessed by IT, and Meg, Calvin, and Dr. Murry barely escape. There is a great deal of psychological realism in the portrayal of Meg's anger at her father for leaving her brother, at herself, and at Mrs. Whatsit and her friends. Meg eventually returns alone; she is the only one who has a chance to defeat IT, because of her closeness to her brother. Her love frees Charles Wallace and they all find themselves at home.

A Wind in the Door (1973) continues the battle against evil and darkness, although this time it is fought within Charles Wallace's body. The cells of the body in this story are like the universe, and the beings that inhabit those cells just as vulnerable as humans are to being misled or to surrendering to the darkness. The mouselike farandolae have been persuaded by evil not to mature, and so the mitochondria in which they live are failing, an element which seems possibly to have been written intending some allegorical applicability to contemporary society. Meg and Calvin are accompanied on their quest to save Charles Wallace by a cherubim, Proginoskes, all wings and eyes, and their former school principal, the ineffectual and unsympathetic Mr. Jenkins, an unlikely ally who proves to have hidden reserves of strength. Again, it is the power of love that leads the rebel farandolae back to their proper task and defeats the evil, existence-destroying Echthroi.

A Swiftly Tilting Planet (1978) sends the teenage Charles Wallace through time with a unicorn, trying to prevent the Third World War and a victory for the Echthroi, embodiment of evil. Meg is involved in the story as well through her psychic connection to her brother. The enemy this time is a mad South American dictator who is about to start a nuclear war. Charles Wallace must discover the significance of a series of events in the past when wrong choices were made, altering those events to change the ancestry of the dictator. Meg is able to help by reconciling with her bitter mother-in-law Mrs. O'Keefe, whose own family history is part of the story. Again, it is love and acceptance that show the way to fight the nihilism of the Echthroi.

A fourth book about the Murry family, *Many Waters* (1986), concentrates on the 'normal' children in the family, twins Sandy and Dennys. It is more overtly religious than the others, and, though the two things are not necessarily connected, a weaker story. Sandy and Dennys are sent back in time by their father's computer to a desert where Noah is building the ark. They witness the seduction and corruption of humanity by evil, and are themselves led into temptation to sin. They return, as the rains begin, by means of unicorns and seraphim. The book lacks the depth and interest of the earlier three, reading more like a fable, an example rather than a story; Sandy and Dennys are not very interesting characters, and have changed little by the end of the book despite the lessons to which they have been exposed, while the (technological) magic is a mere prop and convenience lacking credibility within the story.

The three books about Meg and Charles Wallace, however, are a satisfying mix of adventure, family drama, the supernatural, and considerations of right and wrong. A particular strength is in the depiction of the primary characters, especially Meg; she is likeable and believable, admirable in her strengths and very much an adolescent frustrated with herself and her world in her weaknesses.

Joan Aiken (1924-2004)

Joan Aiken was born in England, to parents who had emigrated from the United States and Canada. She began writing, and being published, while she was in her teens. She worked for several years as a magazine editor before turning to writing full-time. Aiken published numerous novels and short-story collections for children and teens, as well as gothic romances, mysteries, and thrillers for adults. Her children's books nearly all involve the supernatural, or at least a world slightly out of kilter with the real. They are perhaps best described as gothic thrillers for children; wicked governesses, lost heirs and siblings, and street-wise urchins abound. Even in Aiken's stories with modern settings, magic is apt to make matter-of-fact appearances. Her stories for young children about Arabel Jones and her mischievous raven Mortimer, which were written for the BBC and began appearing in print with *Arabel's Raven* (1972), are largely non-fantastic, if allowances are made for Mortimer, but even they include the destruction of the newly-excavated Round Table of King Arthur by Mortimer, who drops Excaliber on it.

Aiken wrote dozens of books, winning the Guardian Award three times, for *The Wolves of Willoughby Chase*, *Black Hearts in Battersea*, and *Night Birds on Nantucket*. Her most celebrated series, into which all three of the above-mentioned books fall, is often called the 'Wolves Chronicles'. These stories are set in an alternate history in which George I never came to the throne and there is still a Stuart king (with a Scots accent) ruling nineteenth-century Great Britain, continually threatened by Hanoverian conspirators. There are eleven books in the 'Wolves Chronicles', the most recent being *Midwinter Nightingale* (2003) and the posthumously-published *The Witch of Clatteringshaws* (2005), two closely-linked stories in which former waif and occasional royal agent Dido Twite and Simon, young Duke of Battersea, cope with threats to the crown from both political and supernatural sources. However, the supernatural is rarely the sole driving force in the 'Wolves Chronicles', and in some stories it puts in no appearance at all. Despite this, the alternate world of nineteenth-century Stuart England remains one where ghosts and magic, particularly dark magic, always seem imminent, and the action-packed adventures which overtake the heroes, as well as Aiken's shadow-filled, perilous world, are the sort which will appeal to fantasy readers.

The first story in the series gives it its title, although the character who would become the central hero of the series has yet to appear. *The Wolves of Willoughby Chase* (1962) is about cousins Bonnie Green and Sylvia, entrusted to the care of a wicked governess, Miss Slighcarp, who quickly takes over the estate once word comes that Bonnie's parents have been lost at sea. The girls are packed off to a school in the industrial town of Blastburn, where the 'pupils' are unpaid drudges in a laundry. Bonnie and Sylvia run away to London with their friend Simon, who lives alone in the forest with his geese and donkey. They discover the details of Slighcarp's and her friend Grimshaw's villainy, have the latter arrested, and return to Willoughby Chase with their lawyer and some constables just as Sir Willoughby and Lady Green return, having survived the sinking of their ship and a long journey in a lifeboat. This book sets the tone for the rest of the series, a world of grim factory towns, wild countryside, and bleak cities, in which the young heroes elude and foil criminals and conspirators by their wits, courage, and luck. The stories might be described as a blending of Dickens, the Brontës, and early twentieth-century boy's adventure fiction (although the heroes are more likely to be girls).

The next in the series, *Black Hearts in Battersea* (1965) follows Simon, coming to London to study art. He boards with the unpleasant Twite family, befriends the unloved younger daughter Dido, and discovers the house to be full of Hanoverian conspirators, who plan to blow up James III when he attends a feast at the Duke of Battersea's. After much action and adventure, abduction, and marooning, Simon is able to save the Duke. He is also revealed as the Duke's nephew and heir. Dido Twite, who tried to save Simon from the conspirators (including her father), is believed drowned, but in fact goes on to become the hero of many more books in the 'Wolves' series, most of which involve her foiling Hanoverian plots, as in *Night Birds on Nantucket* (1966) or chilling and foul enchantments such as those keeping the immortal queen of New Cumbria alive in *The Stolen Lake* (1981).

The Cuckoo Tree (1971) is typical of the type of adventure in which Dido gets involved. She is accompanying a wounded officer to London with urgent dispatches concerning a plot against the new King Richard IV, about to be crowned. Their coach is overturned and they find themselves trapped in a small, conspiracy-filled village. In the manor-house an elderly grandmother gambles away the wealth, the young heir Sir Tobit is kept out of touch with the world, and his twin sister Cris is not even known to exist, kept a prisoner by a witch, Mrs. Lubbage. Luckily Dido finds allies in the Gentlemen, or smugglers, of the area. Before the end there are many twists and turns, desperate escapes, and dangerous encounters, all of which Dido survives through her ready wit and courage. She manages to free Tobit and Cris from everything but their self-imposed limits, and sends them to London with the smugglers and the message, but then discovers the Hanoverians know of her plan. She follows, is captured, escapes, and pursues on a borrowed elephant. She arrives in time to warn the king and prevent the destruction of St. Paul's Cathedral. Only after returning the elephant and escorting the self-absorbed twins home does the lonely Dido discover that the Duke of Battersea, whom she has been told is looking for her, is none other than her friend Simon, and that she is not as alone in the world as she thought. Other stories in the series bring in more members of the eccentric and occasionally villainous Twite family.

An example of Aiken's short fiction is *A Small Pinch of Weather* (1969). This collection, one of many, contains darkly comic tales of the extraordinary intruding on the everyday. 'The Apple of Discord', for example, features the Armitage family. Young Mark and Harriet (who is studying 'domestic science' with an alchemist) end up possessed of the original apple of discord. The snake-haired Furies and the apple's dragon-guardian come to reclaim it, with complicated results, since the Furies also want to avenge Cain's murder of Abel on the person of the apple's new possessor, Great-Uncle Gavin. The Armitages appear in other stories in the book, such as 'Harriet's Hairloom', in which she weaves a flying carpet from an ancient druid's beard, and 'The Serial Garden', in which Mark assembles a magic garden from cut-outs on the back of cereal packets, and discovers a princess in the garden. She enchanted the garden to come to life when a tune was sung; it goes with the words of the jingle on the package. Mark's music master, Mr Johansen, wrote the tune and is the princess' long-lost love. But the ending is black humour, if not tragedy, as many of Aiken's stories are. Mark's mother throws out the cardboard garden while spring-cleaning, before Mr Johansen can join his princess there.

Aiken's stories are full of action, wild adventure, hair's breadth escapes, fateful coincidence, and tragedy narrowly averted, if averted at all. There is a somewhat frantic humour to them, and a great deal of comic caricature and slapstick. The world-view can be bleak, but the heroes are quick-witted, resourceful, determined, kind-hearted, and loyal, and in the end find enduring friends of the same qualities. The villains are usually greedy, treacherous, and motivated by lust for wealth or power over others. Aiken makes great use of regional dialects of English with the cockney Dido, the Scots Stuart kings of England, and all the people Dido meets in her travels; this does mean that children who have difficulties in reading, or have had very limited exposure to the rich variety of the English language, may find her work confusing at first, but most will quickly catch on. She portrays the darker side of nineteenth-century life; child labour, poverty and disease are not glossed over. Children die in unsafe factories or starve in slums, old folks whose working days are past are thrown on uncertain charity, orphans are warehoused and exploited. Her heroes, though, do their best to remedy the ills they encounter, and she usually gives them the means to do so by the end, at least on a local scale.

William Mayne (b. 1928)

William Mayne was born in Hull and attended the Canterbury Cathedral Choir School, which gave him the background for his four books set in a similar school, beginning with the highly-regarded *A Swarm In May* (1955). From the early fifties onwards he has worked almost entirely as a children's writer, and has over sixty books to his credit. Most of his books stand alone, rather than being part of a series about a particular character or place. He has written many books for children and teens that draw on the fantastic, too many for all to be even mentioned here, so a few examples must suffice to give an idea of the sort of fantasy he writes.

Earthfasts (1966) looks deceptively like a time-travel story. It is in fact a dense, rich, thought-provoking and somewhat demanding fantasy about two boys, David Nix and Keith Heseltine, in a small Yorkshire farming community. David and Keith hear a noise under the earth; a drummer boy, Nellie Jack John, emerges. He went into a tunnel under the castle where his regiment was garrisoned in 1742, in search of a rumoured cavern of treasure where King Arthur and his knights lay sleeping. According to local history, he was never seen again. Nellie Jack John spends a night and a day in the twentieth century, but after talking with the elderly great-grandson of his younger brother, the drummer boy re-enters the tunnel in an attempt to go back to his own time. David and Keith know he cannot have succeeded, since local legend would say so.

Nellie Jack John left behind a strange candle which burns with a physically cold, white light and is never consumed. David becomes obsessed with this. One day a black crack appears across earth and sky, and David disappears. A coroner's jury concludes that David was vaporized by being struck by lighting.

Months pass, and Keith has trouble readjusting to life without his friend. He begins to feel compelled to look into the strange candle's flame. There he sees what David saw: horses and armed men, a medieval army. Eventually he reasons out what has happened. The candle is from the legendary cavern where Arthur lies sleeping. Nellie Jack John carried it away, and that set loose the supernatural creatures of another time which have been disturbing the region.

Keith sets out to return the candle to the tunnel and find David, who was carried off by Arthur. The king and his men are not benevolent heroes. They are meant to sleep until a future time when the candle will be consumed, but they want to wake fully into the world now. If they can get the candle themselves, they will do so. Keith succeeds in preventing this and rescues David and Nellie Jack John, who are both trapped there. The dreamlike progress of the plot, Keith's growing understanding of the ancient and sometimes dangerous magic of the past that is leaking through into the world around him, and the boys' intelligent and eager approach to investigating the situation, along with the frequent quiet humour, make *Earthfasts* a book which bears more than one reading. Three decades later, Mayne wrote two sequels to *Earthfasts*. In *Cradlefasts* (1995), a sister supposedly dead at birth enters David's life, while *Candlefasts* (2000) continues David's involvement with the past.

Another interesting fantasy, which, like all Mayne's fantasies, is stimulatingly demanding of the reader, is *It* (1977). Readers have to think and pay attention while they are reading. *It* also needs a little knowledge of Christian tradition and liturgy to be fully comprehended, but a reader unfamiliar with the Church of England will find the setting as exotic as any imagined new world or culture, and no more confusing than that. *It* is the story of Alice Dyson, a Yorkshire girl who is having a strange and unhappy year. She deliberately fails a school entrance exam as a means of taking some control of her own life, and is always out of sorts, awkward and unsettled in her life, feeling that everything worthwhile has already been done, mostly by her grandfather, an Anglican priest, historian, and former missionary to New Guinea. Moping around by herself by one of four stone crosses that once warded the town, she is possessed by a spirit that she comes to think of as 'It'. Its presence shadows hers, resulting in poltergeist-like activity whenever she loses her temper.

Alice herself works out that It is some older spirit from before Christianity came to England, and finds a carving depicting how it was bound away. She decides that It is not evil, but depressed – like herself. She works out that the town's traditional St. Cuthbert parade, if it follows the forgotten traditional route around each of the four crosses, will give her mastery over It. To this end she gets the Bishop, the Roman Catholic priest, and the Baptist congregation, as well as all the choirs, involved in restoring the old route, and finds the location of the forgotten fourth cross. In doing this she discovers there are some things about local history her grandfather does not know; there is space left for her after all. Walking the route gives her the power she needs, and she chooses to send It back to Its own proper place. Alice, like the boys in *Earthfasts* and all of Mayne's main characters, is a hero who considers the world fully, and from many unexpected angles.

Mayne has also written for younger readers. *Hob and the Goblins* (1993) is one such book. Hob is a creature of the household; he looks after houses and families in return for an occasional snack, but if given clothes, must leave. This is the same folklore tradition of brownies and hobgoblins which K.M. Briggs used for *Hobberdy Dick* and J.K. Rowling for her house-elves. Mayne's story is mostly told from Hob's point of view, perennially observing. Mayne's Hob thinks and speaks of himself in the third person; Briggs' Dick was likewise observed with a certain remoteness, the narrative never entering intimately into his consciousness, and Rowling's Dobby speaks of himself in the third person.

Mayne's story begins with Hob deciding to make his new home with a bus driver, Charlie Grimes. Charlie promptly loses his job because the Gremlin living on his bus steals it and dumps it in the Thames. The Grimes family, Charlie, his wife Alice, the children Tom and Meg, Baby, and Budgie, move to a family cottage in the country, abandoned since Great-Uncle Fluellen disappeared a century before. He was a sorcerer who entered the goblin domain to steal their crock of gold. This house, called Fairy Ring Cottage, is built in a ring of great stones, not a fairy ring but a goblin one. Hob is forced to leave by the witch Idris

236

Evans, who tricks the family into giving him clothes, wanting to find the gold herself. Hob makes great efforts to break the magic compelling him to stay away, and goes to work for dwarves, forging swords and losing bits of clothing, finally able to return to the cottage, to arm his friends with stolen swords in time to prevent a goblin horde breaking out. It is the Gremlin and the bus that save the day against the goblin king, though. *Hob and the Goblins* is a great story, less dense and thickly-detailed than Mayne's books for older readers, but still rich with English folk-lore, humour, and just enough scariness, ideal for reading aloud. There is a also a sequel, *Hob and the Pedlar* (1997).

Mayne won the Carnegie for one of his early fantasies, *A Grass Rope* (1957), which features a search for a unicorn hidden beneath the fells of Yorkshire. Aside from the Hob, he rarely introduces any of the traditional elements of fairy-tale or legend, and when he does, he does not treat them conventionally – King Arthur, who appears briefly in *Earthfasts*, being a case in point. As a storyteller, Mayne is most concerned with what goes on within his characters; he creates a depth and complexity of psychological realism unusual in children's writing. His style is better suited for more advanced readers. His vocabulary is demanding (Nellie Jack John speaks a broad dialect, but this is somewhat ameliorated by David's and Keith's having to puzzle out what he means themselves), and his characters often spend time thinking, reasoning, and analysing, as well as reflecting on the motivations and actions of other characters. There is at the same time a great deal of suspense in all his stories, and the plots are usually a somewhat chilling adventure in a world that turns out not to be as limited and defined as the characters expect.

Mayne also edited two anthologies with appeal to fantasy readers, *The Hamish Hamilton Book of Giants* (1968), with stories ranging from the traditional to the modern, and *The Hamish Hamilton Book of Heroes* (1967), containing both retellings of hero-legends from around the world and extracts from classics once familiar to every schoolchild, such as Thomas Babington MacAulay's poem 'Horatius' (1842). With Eleanor Farjeon, he was co-editor of *The Hamish Hamilton Book of Kings* and *The Hamish Hamilton Book of Queens*. They were published in hardcover by Hamish Hamilton and in paperback, with 'Hamish Hamilton' dropped from the title, by Puffin.

In 2004, William Mayne was convicted of eleven charges of indecent assault against young girls (BBC News), which, particularly when it comes to introducing his books into schools, raises for some the difficult issue of how far the creation can be separated from the creator.

Lloyd Alexander (b. 1924)

Lloyd Alexander left teacher's college to join the American army when he was nineteen. He worked in intelligence, and was eventually stationed in Paris in counter-intelligence. Afterwards he studied there at the Sorbonne, where he met his wife, Janine Denni, and where his daughter was born. Back in the United States, Alexander worked as an advertising copywriter and a cartoonist, and began writing adult fiction, which he did for some years before his first book for children, *Time Cat* (1963), appeared. He is as much a writer of the seventies or the eighties as of the sixties, but his most influential series, *The Chronicles of Prydain*, appeared in that decade. Another significant contribution to fantasy by Alexander was the *Westmark* trilogy of the eighties, but through the eighties and nineties he wrote a number of stand-alone children's fantasies, as well as the historical thrillers in the *Vesper Holly* series. He continues to write into the twenty-first century, with *The Rope Trick* (2002).

The five novels of *The Chronicles of Prydain* are *The Book of Three* (1964), *The Black Cauldron* (1965), *The Castle of Llyr* (1966), *Taran Wanderer* (1967), and *The High King* (1968). The latter won the Newbery Medal for 1969, while *The Black Cauldron* was a Newbery Honor book. A short story collection set in the same world, *The Foundling*, followed in 1973. The *Prydain* books draw on Welsh myth and legend for the background of their world. Most of the names and many of the attributes of the characters have their source in the *Mabinogion*, a medieval collection of Welsh legends. Alexander's Prydain is not pre-Roman or Dark Age Wales, though, but a world of his own devising, one of small kingdoms and extensive landscape, of villages, isolated farmsteads, and dark forests. The many cantrevs of Prydain are ruled by kings, but they are threatened by Arawn of the land of Annuvin, who stole much that was good from humankind. Taran, the hero of the five books, is a foundling brought up at Caer Dallben, a remote cottage, by the ancient enchanter Dallben (whose origins the author explains in the title story of his collection *The Foundling*) and the old warrior Coll.

In *The Book of Three*, Taran's boring (as he sees it) childhood comes to an end when Hen Wen, the oracular pig, runs away. Taran, who has just been jokingly named Assistant Pig Keeper by Coll, sets out in pursuit and runs into the Horned King, a terrifying huntsman with a stag's head, who is Arawn's champion. In his flight he is rescued by the warrior Prince Gwydion, one of the Sons of Don, heroic descendants of the legendary founder of Prydain and her consort. Along with the hairy Gurgi, halfway between man and beast, Gwydion and Taran pursue Hen Wen, but are captured by the Cauldron-Born, dead men given new life as mindless slaves of Arawn by means of a magical cauldron; the cauldron that restores slain warriors to life is one of the many ancient Celtic mythological elements in the story. Taran and Gwydion are handed over to Achren, an enchantress who both serves and feuds with Arawn. Taran is discovered in the dungeon by Princess Eilonwy, a girl his own age who believes Achren is her aunt. She rescues Taran and another prisoner, Fflewddur Fflam, a bard and king of great goodwill but prone to exaggeration, whose harpstrings break whenever he stretches the truth. On the way Eilonwy also collects an enchanted sword, Dyrnwyn, from a forgotten underground chamber. They fight Cauldron-Born, meet Gurgi again, find Hen Wen in the possession of the Dwarf King, one of the Fair Folk, and continue with a bad-tempered dwarf guide, Doli. They try to reach Caer Dathyl to warn High King Math of the Horned King's coming attack but arrive only in time for the battle, which is going badly. When Taran tries to draw Dyrnwyn, which Eilonwy has repeatedly warned him not to do, he is badly burned by its power. The Horned King is killed by Prince Gwydion, who had been taken to Annuvin, escaped, and learned the Horned King's secret name from Hen Wen, thus gaining the power to destroy him. Eilonwy gives the sword to Prince Gwydion and goes to live at Caer Dallben under Dallben's guardianship.

The Black Cauldron is about an expedition undertaken to destroy the magic cauldron, the Crochan, in which the Cauldron-Born are created. It introduces the three hags of the Marshes of

Morva, Orddu, Orwen, and Orgoch, who raised Dallben and who have many mysterious powers, as well as a penchant for threatening to eat travellers. Taran and his friends eventually obtain the cauldron at great cost, only to lose it, first to a jealous prince, Ellidyr, who wants the glory of its finding for himself, and then to King Morgant, who means to use it to create his own Cauldron-Born, starting with Taran and his companions. Ellidyr flings himself into the cauldron of his own will, destroying it and himself.

In *The Castle of Llyr*, Taran escorts Eilonwy to the Isle of Mona, whose king and queen are to give her the education a princess should have. Gwydion is on Mona, disguised as a shoemaker (a nod to the *Mabinogion*, whose Gwydion, disguised as a shoemaker, tricks his estranged wife into naming their son, despite her intention to leave him nameless – another episode in the same story results in Gwydion's creation of the flower-maiden, the foundation of Garner's *The Owl Service*). Gwydion warns Taran, Fflewdurr and Gurgi that Eilonwy is in danger from Achren. Magg, the King of Mona's steward, kidnaps Eilonwy for Achren. When they find the princess, after encounters with a giant wildcat (which adopts Fflewdurr), and with a peevish giant who is really a very small man, she does not know them. Achren forces Eilonwy to read a spellbook whose contents are visible only by the light of the princess' 'bauble', a golden ball the emits light only for her. The princess destroys the book instead, remembering, due to the golden ball, her self and her friends. In choosing to destroy the spellbook, Eilonwy gives up much of her own potential to become an enchantress, the thing she thought she most wanted.

Taran Wanderer is Taran's quest for his own identity. He and Gurgi travel, learning various trades, meeting old friends and new, and encountering bandits, thieves, and dishonest lords as well as honest craftspeople and philosophers in many guises. It is the 'coming-of-age' novel of the series, as the impetuous Taran matures into a young man of strength and wisdom. By the end, Taran has learnt many new skills and gained a deeper insight into both himself, Prydain, and humanity at large.

The High King concludes the saga. The sword Dyrnwyn has been stolen by Arawn and Gwydion is badly wounded. The leaders of Prydain must attack Annuvin to get it back and forestall

Arawn's growing threat. There is treachery among the kings, and while old friends help Taran, Eilonwy and their companions on the way, old enemies cause many troubles before they finally reach their destination and nearly perish at the hands of the Cauldron-Born. Taran finds and draws Dyrnwyn unharmed, killing one of the unkillable Cauldron-Born and thus destroying all the animated dead warriors; this was why Arawn feared the sword and wanted it in his own keeping. The Sons of Don and the war-bands of all the countries of Prydain defeat Arawn's human warriors; Arawn is finally killed by Taran. Victory and the hope for peace are not the end of the story, however. The time has come for all the magical things of Prydain to pass: Hen Wen, the Sons of Don, Dallben, Fflewddur, the Fair Folk, and Orddu, Orwen, and Orgoch (now beautiful women rather than hags, the spinners and weavers of the fates of men, but as cryptic as ever), must all sail for the Summer Country. Even Eilonwy should leave, but she elects to give up the little magic that she still possesses, so as to remain with Taran. Taran is proclaimed High King of Prydain, having become the fulfilment of prophecy by acquiring and demonstrating his fitness to govern in the course of his many adventures.

Taran is reckless and impulsive, but courageous and good-hearted. Eilonwy is impatient and over-critical of those who do not think as quickly as she does, but equally bold and kind. As the series progresses, the two of them mature into good people and wise rulers. The stories themselves are rapid in pace, encounter following encounter, dangerous, humorous, and enlightening. They convey the flavour of old legend and Romance, in a society which values integrity, common sense, and honesty as well as courage in battle. Although he has written many first-rate books since, *The Chronicles of Prydain* remain Alexander's greatest achievement, and among the enduring classics of children's fantasy. More so than in any other of his works, the blend of Celtic-inspired magic, legend and Dark Age heroism is firmly rooted in the land and people of the story, making Prydain one of those worlds that remain fundamentally real long after the book has been read. However, it is not Alexander's only outstanding achievement.

The Marvelous Misadventures of Sebastian (1970) is a light-hearted and optimistic look at the themes Alexander was to explore more grimly in the *Westmark* books. Sebastian, fourth fiddle in a baronial orchestra, believes himself given the sack. He sets off through the Principality of Hamelin-Loring and runs into one trouble after another, acquiring a white cat, a cursed fiddle, and two oddly-matched comrades. These are Nicholas, who is actually the Captain, a resistance fighter against the oppression of the Regent, and Isobel, the rightful ruler, who is fleeing marriage to the Regent, pursued by an assassin. They have numerous adventures and close calls; in the end it is Sebastian's magic fiddle that saves them when they are imprisoned. He escapes and enchants the inhabitants of the castle. The music kills the Regent and would have killed Sebastian but for Presto the cat, who breaks the fiddle, freeing him from its domination. As queen, Isobel begins to make reforms, instituting a Grand Council to speak for the people. Sebastian and she intend to wed, but first he resolves to travel and make himself a true musician. He had always thought of himself as a moderately competent hack, but now, following his possession by the fiddle, is caught by the desire for true art.

The First Two Lives of Lukas-Kasha (1978) is about Lukas, called Kasha, a homeless boy well on his way to being town rogue and ne'er-do-well in the village of Zara-Petra. A conjurer comes to town offering to show wonders, but in return for his penny, Lukas gets his head dunked in a pail of water. Lukas finds himself washed up on the ocean's shore, proclaimed king of Abadan by an astrologer. Being king is a good life in Abadan, at first, but Lukas is upset by unjust laws and oppression. He overrules the Vizier Shugdad and spares Kayim, a poet condemned for making ironic verse about the Vizier's role as power behind the throne. He also befriends Nur-Jehan, a proud and warlike slave girl from the jewel-rich mountain kingdom of Bishangar in the north, which Abadan claims. When Lukas starts studying in the library, determined to make better laws, the Vizier decides to kill him. Lukas, Kayim, and Nur-Jehan flee north towards Bishangar. Shugdad proclaims himself king and heads north with an army, to crush Bishangari rebellion once and for all. Lukas and his friends have various adventures, but Nur-Jehan seems to abandon them, and Lukas ends up a prisoner of his own army as a supposed deserter, though he quickly wins the respect and loyalty of the punishment detail to which he is assigned. Nur-Jehan reappears as Queen Nur-Jehan of Bishangari, at the head of a warband. She, Lukas, and their followers pursue Shugdad, who is beheaded by an officer loyal to Lukas. The sight of the Vizier's head ends the war and Lukas ends Abadani claims to rule Bishangar. He sets out to be a good king, reforming unjust laws. When he slips on a cliff and falls, Lukas finds himself back at the wonder-worker's cart, his face wet and the crowd jeering, having found no entertainment in his ducking. A changed person, he decides to become a travelling storyteller, to look for, if not Nur-Jehan and Kayim, at least people like them.

A more recent book, *The Iron Ring* (1997), displays the same sorts of concerns as *Lukas-Kasha* in a different setting. Alexander chose for this book to create a culture based on that of India. The young king, Tamar, undertakes a dangerous quest to fulfil a vow and preserve his honour and dharma. He is accompanied by his philosopher-tutor and Mirri, a gopi or cow-herd with whom he falls in love. He is tempted to give up his quest because of love and the conflicting demands of dharma, but always returns to it, even when he becomes involved in a civil war in another kingdom. He is imprisoned and then made chandala, the lowest and untouchable caste, who burn the dead of the paupers. Through this experience, Tamar finally learns a great deal about himself and his humanity; his final confrontation with the supernatural being who bound him to undertake the quest for the sake of his honour teaches him even more about himself and about honour, self-worth, human equality, and kingship.

The Marvelous Misadventures of Sebastian, The First Two Lives of Lukas-Kasha, and *The Iron Ring* are typical of most of Alexander's stand-alone books, full of dangerous adventure and comic misadventure, featuring resourceful characters who defeat villains more powerful than themselves and who learn truths about their own failings and strengths in doing so. They are also typical in their preoccupation with governance, law, and kingship. Good stewardship on the part of a ruler in an earlier society, or democracy and republicanism in a more modern one, remain ongoing philosophical concerns in Alexander's writing. He also writes fantasies focusing more closely on the development of the individual and their interaction with society on a smaller scale. His later books, in particular, are concerned with young heroes growing into themselves within a local setting, although even in earlier ones this theme is apparent. *The Wizard in the Tree* (1974), *Gypsy Rizka* (1999), and *The Rope Trick* (2002) all show Alexander's consistent humour and thoughtfulness; they have as their heroes young orphans, strong, resourceful, intelligent, and possessed of great personal integrity, living largely by their wits on the fringes of their society, observing it with sometimes wry and ironic affection, but creating for themselves an essential role within it.

Alexander's *Westmark* books display his interest in the idea of good government and individual responsibility in a more modern society than that of *The Chronicles of Prydain*. *Westmark* (1981), *The Kestrel* (1982), and *The Beggar Queen* (1984) are set in a world similar to Europe in the later eighteenth and first decades of the nineteenth century, a time of revolution and social and technological change. They are not conventional fantasy; there is no magic, nothing supernatural, to be seen. They are, however, a secondary world, related to reality even in the language of the place-names, which is mostly French or German, but freed of any dependence on real history and thus able, within that secondary world setting, to consider possibilities and ideals that never came into being in the real world. Written for a young adult audience, the trilogy tells the story of Theo, who starts off as a printer's assistant, and of Mickle, who is many things – thief, ventriloquist, street-urchin, and the missing, presumed-dead heir to the throne. Theo and Mickle meet revolutionaries and benevolent con artists, and see both the best and worst of Westmark while on the run after Theo's master is killed by soldiers sent to destroy his press. The king's corrupt and murderous chief minister, Cabbaras, captures them, seeing Mickle's talent for mimicry as a useful tool in gaining the throne; the king is obsessed with communicating with his dead daughter. Acting as a false oracle, Mickle's long-repressed memories of Cabbaras' attempted murder of her surface, and both her parents and Cabbaras recognize her as the long-lost princess, Augusta.

In *The Kestrel*, Theo is on a tour of Westmark for the king, writing a report on the state of the kingdom and planning reform, but the king dies, Mickle becomes Queen Augusta, and Theo is attacked. The reforms are upsetting the aristocracy and the higher ranks of the military, who plot with Duke Conrad, overbearing uncle of young King Constantine of Regia, to stage a coup. Mickle runs away with some of her old disreputable friends to find Theo, who is a prisoner of some of his old repub-lican dissident friends. The Regian invasion runs into difficulties when some of the Westmark army mutinies and keeps fighting rather than surrendering, as ordered by their traitorous generals. Theo persuades the revolutionary Florian to have his people fight for Westmark as partisans, but in return agrees to support Florian's cause and push for a written constitution, even against his beloved Mickle if need be. The war is bloody and complex, with Florian working for revolution in the middle of it, Mickle hoping to make a peace profitable for both sides, and Theo be-coming a feared, single-minded commander, Colonel Kestrel. Peace, when Mickle and Constantine are able to achieve it, does not solve all their problems.

The Beggar Queen (1984) sees Westmark torn by revolution, as both Cabbaras, who has been sheltered by Duke Conrad in Regia, and the radical republicans try to seize the kingdom. Mickle escapes from the palace as the revolutionaries come to arrest her. Cabbaras and his mercenaries are the ones who seize control, though, and Mickle, Theo, and the republican Florian fight a war of guerrillas and spies to free their country. It is a nightmare for all of them, but most of all for Theo, who finds himself turning back into the bloody and remorseless Kestrel. Cabbaras, now styled Director of Westmark, eventually captures Mickle and Theo, offering her the throne again, as a puppet-ruler. When Cabbaras is killed by one of his own people, Theo and Mickle escape, and the underground and the people of the capital rise up against the mercenaries, just as Florian and his troops arrive, part of a plan made with Mickle and Theo. West-mark has won its freedom, but Mickle abdicates rather than start a civil war with her republican allies. She and Theo go into exile together, leaving Westmark to its people, for good or ill. Few books for young readers delve so deeply into the morass of poli-tics, of ideas of ruling and government and statesmanship, of the effects of war and revolution on those who are forced to face them, as the *Westmark* trilogy.

In all his writing, Alexander displays a concern with how a person ought to be the best they can be, how they should act to fulfil their potential, not only for their own sake, but for that of their society. His ideals of democracy are not something given

245

much space for discussion in many fantasies, which adopt a superficially medieval style of government without consideration of all the subtleties which provide checks and balances in even an apparently-absolute monarchy – which few European medieval states (the stock fantasy setting) were in practice. Personal sacrifice for the greater good, the conflict between ideals and reality and the need to transform one into the other, and the necessity of personal integrity in terrible times, resurface again and again in Alexander's writing, whether the dark and serious *Westmark*, the humour-filled *Sebastian*, or the classic *Prydain* books, which are, taken together, not so much about the making of a king, though they are that too, as they are about the making of a good person.

Children's fantasy in the sixties showed a wide range of styles and themes. Juster used the fantastic to dress up a fable meant to stir interest in knowledge, while L'Engle wrote adventures that incorporated it into a philosophy for living with a religious underpinning. L'Engle, Garner, and Mayne all examined the internal lives of adolescents in stories that were gripping adventures as well, rather than the mere teen navel-gazing of so much 'realistic' teen fiction. Mayne and Garner celebrated folklore and legend with roots in landscape and history, and quarried them to build new creations. Aiken wrote breathless adventure and created an alternate history, using the fantastic to open up new imaginative possibilities rooted in the social history of the past. Garner exhibited Tolkien's influence in style and scope of aspiration, as well as in teleological concerns, and was one of the first to write stories in the now-common vein of ordinary children caught up in ancient battles between good and evil supernatural forces, often through or over possession of some magical object. Alexander drew on myth and legend to create a secondary world in which the ordinary could rise into heroism, and went on to use secondary worlds to re-examine the choices and possibilities of our history, as well as to give traditional themes of maturation and self-discovery new life. Destruction and desolation of all that is good become the ultimate price of failure in stories such as Garner's, L'Engle's, and some of Alexander's, and human damaging of the natural world and of one another, witting and unwitting, is shown as strengthening the hand of evil.

Most of these elements and approaches have continued in modern children's fantasy to the present day.

XII
The Seventies, part one

The concerns of the sixties continued into the seventies, with the addition of high inflation, unemployment, and the oil crisis caused by OPEC's embargo on selling oil to countries aiding Israel. SALT I (the Strategic Arms Limitations Talks) resulted in the signing of the ABM (Anti Ballistic Missile) treaty between the United States and the Soviet Union in 1972, abrogated by the United States in 2002; the SALT II treaty, agreed to in 1979, was never ratified. In 1977, neutron bomb production was approved by the American government, postponed the next year, and resumed by Reagan in 1981. The effect of this was the continuation of an atmosphere of insecurity and instability.

Children may not have grasped that, in North America and Western Europe at least, the political situation was actually very stable and unlikely to disintegrate into war, nuclear or conventional, but they did know each side had missiles poised to totally exterminate the other, and that the treaties being discussed in the news only limited how much 'overkill' there would be. Some of the things they may have sought in their fantasy literature were reassurance, stability, and control. The prosperous post-war generations may have needed, as much or more than those growing up previously, to experience, at least in imagination, the power to confront and vanquish destructive forces, and to shape things around them for the better.

The authors writing at this time had, for the most part, grown up in the years during and immediately after the Second World War; they, too, were people for whom the world was not a stable and secure place. History had shown that the maintenance of individual freedom within a just society was a difficult and unending struggle; human societies tended to be drawn to the poles of anarchy and tyranny, or to alternate between the two. Fantasy and science fiction began consciously to examine other possibilities, both for society and for the individual. Even in children's literature, writers of the sixties, seventies, and following decades, such as Madeleine L'Engle, Ursula K. LeGuin, Lloyd Alexander, Peter Dickinson, Diana Wynne Jones, and Louise Cooper, to name only a few, can be seen exploring such themes.

The environment was threatened by acid rain and pesticides, and increasing awareness of these problems, as well as the energy crisis, contributed to an emphasis among some on return to a simpler, more sustainable way of life. In fantasy, that simpler life was often depicted as a pre-industrial agrarian culture. Others, such as Dickinson, reacted against that wistful impulse to see the past as better than modern society. Fantasy set in the real world often viewed contemporary society both as flawed, and as endangered by human ignorance, greed, and selfishness, while secondary world fantasy frequently presented the same fears externalized: the enemy opposed by the heroes can be representative of those sins which are seen to have endangered our environment and society. In such stories it is often not merely the hero's society that is threatened, but the very fabric of the world. This tendency, the raising of the stakes as it were, becomes more pronounced in both adult and children's fantasy through the eighties and nineties; it is possible to interpret this as continued insecurity, not only for our political systems, society, and civilization, but for the planetary ecosystem. Anxieties such as these do affect the *Zeitgeist*, colouring the imagination of the age.

Both individual existence and society have always been precarious; people have had to fear incomprehensible disease, epidemic, random violent death from raiders, from war, from tyrants; they have feared demons and the devil, the wrath of God or gods, the vagaries of nature. In European Medieval and later culture, with its cosmology shaped by the Judeo-Christian view of an omnipotent, omniscient God, there has always been an assurance that, although the end of the world (in Christian if not Jewish belief) approaches, it does so as part of a divine plan. Tolkien and C.S. Lewis wrote within traditional Christian cosmological parameters developed by the Medieval theologians: Morgoth and Sauron seek domination, but any end of Arda, Middle-earth, lies within Ilúvatar's will alone; Narnia suffers bloody defeat, but only as prelude to a divinely-predestined end, as Aslan calls the stars from the sky. In later twentieth-century western civilization, the belief in the end of the world as divinely predestined waned, even among conventionally-religious moderates.* Many later fantasists not sharing Tolkien's or Lewis' traditional religious beliefs but having absorbed both the idea of a fated end from Tolkien's fiction and the precariousness of continued existence (individual, societal and ecological) from their world and times, write of worlds in which all existence is threatened, especially those writing for adults. Although this begins to appear in children's writing even in the sixties and seventies, it would be in later decades that fated ends and final battles became commonplace.

Peter Dickinson (b. 1927)

Peter Dickinson was born in Africa, in Northern Rhodesia, now the Republic of Zambia, but grew up in England. He studied English at Cambridge and was an editor at *Punch* for a number of years. Most of his adult books are mysteries or thrillers, while his children's books tend towards fantasy and historical fiction. He had four children with his first wife; his second wife is the American-born fantasy writer Robin McKinley, with whom he has written the short story collection *Water: Tales of Elemental Spirits* (2002).

   The Weathermonger (1969), Dickinson's first children's book, is actually the concluding story of what has been published in one volume as *The Changes Trilogy* (1985). They were published back-to-front, as the first book in reading order, *The Devil's Children* (1970) was the last published. *Heartsease* (1969) forms the middle of the trilogy. The three books tell one story, but are not a sequence following a single character's adventures. Rather, each concentrates on a different cluster of characters caught up in the same strange event. They depict Britain at the beginning of 'the Changes', during the years in which the outside world was nearly forgotten, and at the end, as the cause is finally discovered and the restoration of normality begins.

   The premise underlying the trilogy is that the entire island of

---

* The late twentieth- and early twenty-first-century increase in fundamentalism is another matter entirely and little, if any, fantasy has been written by fundamentalists of any religion.

Great Britain has reacted suddenly and violently against technology. Machines are smashed, millions of refugees flee to France or Ireland, and those who remain become terrified, even ill, if any sort of machine is functioning near them. Society reverts to a pre-industrial level, but one without any unifying culture or central authority. Each isolated village turns inward. Some people begin to manifest strange powers, such as an ability to control the weather, and are highly regarded in their communities, while in other places anyone with such unnatural powers is executed as a witch, as is anyone regarded as different, or who seems to have some connection with machinery. Agents from outside governments sent to investigate feel the effects of the Changes and forget in terror how to run their planes, boats, and radios, or are caught and executed as witches. Unmanned planes are destroyed by violent storms, as most of the factories have been.

In *The Devil's Children*, Nicky Gore has been separated from her parents in the chaos as they flee to France during the first days of the Changes. She survives on her own in a deserted city, and then joins a band of Sikhs, who have been unaffected by the abhorrence for technology exhibited by the native British. Their travels reveal the conditions of anarchy prevailing throughout the land, the reversion to superstition and petty feudalism, the rule of the strongest, the return of epidemic disease. The Sikh extended family suffers persecution as outsiders, viewed with superstitious dread, but eventually they make a place for themselves in this new England, and find a way to send Nicky to France, where the vast network of refugee agencies and camps reunites her with her parents. In the process, the elderly matriarch of the clan helps Nicky to confront and overcome her emotional withdrawal from the world.

Heartsease tells of the flight of several teens – Margaret, her cousin Jonathan, the servant Lucy and her mentally-disabled brother Tim – after they rescue an American agent who has been captured and stoned as a witch. It is five years since the Changes began, and outside governments are still trying to find out what has happened in Britain. Margaret is quite content with her life; she has a privileged position as niece of well-to-do farmers, she abhors machines, loves horses, and has no urge even to remember how things were, unlike Jonathan and Lucy. However, the sufferings of the 'witch' force her to reassess her ideas of right and wrong, and to act for what she knows to be right against what she has lately been taught is so, even at great risk to herself.

The Weathermonger begins with a teenage boy, Geoffrey, and his twelve-year-old sister, Sally, about to be drowned as witches. Geoffrey was Weymouth's weathermonger: he controlled the town's weather. However, he was also repairing the engine of his late uncle's boat, *Quern*. When their neighbours discover this, the two are left on a rock in the bay to drown. Geoffrey, who was hit on the head when captured, has amnesia and has forgotten the previous six years, which provides a justification to explain this altered world to the reader, as Sally explains things to him. He and Sally escape in the *Quern*, crossing the Channel to France. Since they now appear to be immune to the effects, a French general sends them back to investigate the area in Wales believed to be the root of the Changes. What they find is a chemist, Mr Furbelow, who had discovered a sleeping giant of a man, Merlin, during an excavation. Merlin has the power to create and to change things around him, but Furbelow has addicted him to morphine in an attempt to control his powers. In his befuddled, dreaming state, Merlin changes Britain back to the pre-industrial world he knew. Geoffrey and Sally convince Merlin he is being poisoned and enslaved. In control of himself again, the giant returns to his original enchanted sleep, burying himself in a rocky hill. The country begins to return to normal.

The trilogy, taken together, comprises three convincing high-stakes adventures with young protagonists who must continually make ethical choices, while using all their wits just to survive in a hostile society. The premise allows a contrast to be made with much other fantasy set in pre-industrial societies and 'back-to-nature' worlds, pointing out the wearing physical labour necessary to survival, the prevalence of disease, the potential for isolation and intolerance, which were as much a part of such a life as cheerful harvest festivals and a relatively chemical-free environment.

In *The Blue Hawk* (1976) Dickinson set his story in an imagined kingdom where every aspect of life is governed by religious ritual. Tron, a boy raised in the Temple and destined for the priesthood, disrupts a serious ritual one day, believing his impulse to do so is sent by one of the gods. He steals a sacred hawk which is meant to give an omen as to whether the King should live or die. The priests take that itself as a sign, poison the King, and send Tron to the desert to try taming the hawk. He allies with the new King, who wants to break the power of the priests. Between them, they alter their society and their religion forever, overcoming entrenched religious hierarchies and external foes.

Tulku (1979) won the Carnegie Medal. It is historical fiction with only a touch of the fantastic in it, in the form of oracles and prophecies. During the Boxer Rebellion, Theo, the son of missionaries, ends up fleeing into the mountains of Tibet with a botanist, Mrs Jones, and a Chinese guide, Lung. There they become entangled in a prophecy of the birth of the Tulku, a long-awaited spiritual leader, the unborn child of Mrs Jones and Lung. They are also caught up in conflicts within the Buddhist monastery. The experience changes Theo's perceptions of the world and of spirituality. Dickinson's *City of Gold and Other Stories From the Old Testament* (1980) was also a Carnegie Medal winner.

Dickinson has written numerous other children's books, many of which contain elements of fantasy, such as *The Ropemaker* (2001). This secondary world fantasy follows a group of young people on a quest to discover why the magic which has protected their isolated community in the Valley is failing. All of his writing for children exhibits a concern with the individual's need to make their own moral choices and not to adhere without consideration to what they have been taught. His heroes are always forced to survive on their own or among strangers with whom they initially may not be in sympathy, in situations of physical danger and social upheaval. There is rarely a clear-cut case of good and evil; ordinary people do the wrong thing, believing they are doing what is right or necessary, and are sometimes forced by the actions of the heroes to re-assess their beliefs, as the heroes already have. His main characters arrive at the ends of their spiritual journeys with their understanding expanded; frequently they have, through the course of the books, changed others as well, even whole societies.

Ursula K. LeGuin (b. 1929)

Ursula K. LeGuin was born in California and studied at Radcliffe College and Columbia before teaching French at various American universities. She has written a number of fantasy and science fiction novels for adults and young adults, and is an author whose titles may be found in either the fantasy and science fiction section or the children's or young adult section of the bookstore or library, depending on the edition and the cover art.

LeGuin's Earthsea is regarded as one of the most important secondary worlds of the decade. Earthsea is a world of many islands and much magic, at least among men. Women possess little power, either in politics, law, or magical ability. The first three books give the impression that this is not a case of magic merely being forbidden to them as a career, but of powerful magic appearing to be solely a male trait; in the fourth book, written years later, this is explained in terms of ideology rather typical of the feminism of the seventies, suggesting that women and men are in essence very different types of humans. A later short story implies male and female magical abilities are not so different after all, and that female exclusion in Earthsea was a social and political development. The overall impression which these conflicting interpretations of the world give is of an author changing her mind about her world over the course of three decades, and rethinking her original conception. Although Earthsea started life as a trilogy in the late sixties and seventies, a fourth novel appeared over twenty years later, and after another decade, a short story collection and a fifth novel, all of which add to the development of the world. The first three books are often treated as intended for the young adult audience; the fourth, fifth, and sixth are sold as adult books, although teens who have enjoyed the first books will want to read them too.

A Wizard of Earthsea (1968) is about Ged, a boy who has great magical power. He eventually goes to the School on the island of Roke, where the mages train talented boys. An important part of the magic in LeGuin's world is founded on knowing the true names for things in the ancient language still spoken by dragons; mages know these names, and this is part of their power. Even common people guard their true names carefully.

Ged is a stiff, arrogant youth, over-proud and quarrelsome, and attempting a spell beyond his learning, he releases an evil creature into the world, a gebbeth that can devour men, assuming their form and powers. The archmage dies saving Ged, and he nearly dies himself. Once he recovers, Ged is a changed person, quiet, grim, thoughtful, and kinder. He travels from island to island, hunting the gebbeth and eluding enemies who want to use it to gain his powers. Eventually Ged sails beyond known lands and confronts the gebbeth, naming it with its true name, which is his own, thus attaining power through knowing himself.

The Tombs of Atuan (1971), which was a Newbery Honor Book for 1972, is set on Atuan, a part of the Kargad kingdom ruled by a man with the title Godking, a culture very different from that of Roke in the first book. There are no wizards; instead there are two competing oppressive religions, that of the Godking and that of the Nameless Ones. The heroine, Tenar, is supposed to be the reincarnation of Arha, the Eaten One, the high priestess of the Nameless Ones. She is raised in the temple, but learns as she grows how little power she really has. When a man, Ged, is caught by her in the labyrinth that only she may enter, she spares his life. Ged is there seeking part of a talisman, a broken silver arm-ring he acquired half of in the first book. When it returns to the island of Havnor, it is supposed to bring peace to the islands. Tenar realizes that she is in danger from the high priestess of the Godking, and chooses to help Ged. Together they escape the labyrinth, taking the restored ring to Havnor.

The Farthest Shore (1972) sees Ged, now archmage and a dragonlord (one dragons speak with, rather than eat), voyaging with young Prince Arren. They need to discover why magic is being forgotten on many islands. They travel into death to confront Cob, a blind mage who has discovered what he thinks is eternal life; this is somehow, although not in any clearly-explained way, connected to the forgetting of magic. Ged expends all his power to defeat Cob. A dragon carries them home, where Arren, having fulfilled a prophecy by passing through the land of death, becomes the king who finally unifies the lands. A magicless Ged returns to his home island of Gont.

The story is continued in *Tehanu* (1990), which received the 1991 Nebula Award for best novel. Tenar, now a farmer's widow, adopts an abused and horribly burned little girl, whom she calls Therru. Ged ends up working for Tenar; when Tenar is attacked in her home by Therru's family and rescued by a pitchfork-wielding Ged, she muses at length on why she did nothing to defend herself, not even scream for the neighbours. She concludes that women are made to retreat and hide, rather than to confront and attack or even resist aggressively. Her domineering son returns to take over the farm, and rather than wait on him hand and foot, she, Ged, and Therru leave; opposing him is not an option she considers. The two adults are captured by the wizard Aspen, a vicious woman-hating fanatic. They immediately fall completely under his control. When Aspen is about to make Ged murder Tenar and kill himself, Therru calls a dragon to save them. The girl is then revealed to have a special connection to dragons, and is renamed Tehanu.

Tehanu sometimes seems to have been written as an attempt to rationalize within Earthsea the genre stereotypes found in so much fantasy of the seventies: celibate wizards, women in positions of power automatically being bad people, and women's magic being lesser than men's but more 'in tune' with essential life. More so than the first three books, *Tehanu* exhibits overtones of that misogynist strain of feminism that declares all women to be helpless victims, and men and women two incompatible subspecies, if not completely alien to each other. There seems little connection between the self-possessed Tenar of *The Tombs of Atuan* and the 'I am a woman so I must be weak' Tenar of *Tehanu*, while Aspen and his psychopathic misogyny are not woven into the story in any convincing way. Rather, he and his motives seem a plot device to illustrate a point, that point apparently being that helpless women and children have been and will continue to be abused by men, and that women are inherently helpless against abuse. As a theme, this is one that might perhaps have benefited from some demonstration of resistance to it on the part of the main characters, rather than passive acceptance of it as an unchangeable fact, instant utter surrender to abuse and oppression, and a resort to *draco ex machina* at the very end.

Tales From Earthsea (2001) is a collection of stories set in the islands of the Earthsea world. It begins with a foreword containing some thought-provoking and relevant comments on the state of modern fantasy literature, and its trend towards a 'commodified' (to use LeGuin's apt word), derivative, simplified, and philosophically-shallow product. The final piece is 'A Description of Earthsea', which is just that: a detailed description of the islands, their cultures, peoples, languages, and history. Here one finds out at what point women were banned from the School on Roke and forbidden to learn the True Speech, the language of dragons and of magic, when and why wizards began forcing celibacy upon themselves and their successors, and why Ged was the last archmage.

The five stories contained in the collection are set at various times in Earthsea. The first one, 'The Finder', tells of the founding of the School on Roke. The last, 'Dragonfly', is by way of being a 'prequel' to *The Other Wind*. In it, Dragonfly or Irian, the unloved daughter of an impoverished drunken landowner, goes to Roke with a sorcerer's help, hoping to enter the School under a magical male disguise. The Doorkeeper, one of the nine Masters, sees her for what she is. The Masters debate admitting her, but refuse, though four of them befriend her, recognizing her as special. When the returned-from-the-dead would-be archmage Thorion confronts her in the magical grove that is the heart of the School, he crumples into the dead man he is and Irian turns into a dragon. She flies into the west to find her people. The story echoes what is suggested at the end of *Tehanu*, that humans and dragons were once one people, who chose different paths.

The Other Wind (2001) concludes the Earthsea story. Ged and Tenar are an elderly married farm couple, Lebannen/Arren is king, and Tehanu, now a young woman, is a dragon who has not yet taken dragon's form. The western islands are threatened both by dragons from the west, and by the dead. The sorcerer Alder dreams of the wall that marks the border of the sterile land of the dead being destroyed, and the dead haunt his sleep, pleading to be set free. Successive gatherings of characters, including the dragon-woman Irian, discuss both problems, and the king must also cope with a Kargish princess from a land bordering Tenar's homeland, who is sent to be his wife. Over the course of the book, it is revealed that in the eastern islands, Tenar's people believe in reincarnation, that all life returns to life. Only the humans of the western islands are trapped forever in the dreary land of death. This turns out to be connected to why the dragons are attacking. Immortal existence is not something humans are meant to have, and the dead are suffering in it. What is now the land of the dead was once a living, growing place to which the dragons could travel; they want it back, and the dead want to be free, so that life can return to life in its natural cycle. The wall is destroyed, Tehanu joins the dragons, and the king weds the eastern princess, perhaps thus ensuring peace throughout the islands.

LeGuin's first three Earthsea stories, the ones most often treated as young adult books, are well-written, suspenseful adventures. The system of magic, derived from the belief held in many human societies throughout history that there is power over a thing in its name, is carefully and consistently portrayed. The characters of both Ged and Tenar start off as rather unlikable and change as the stories progress and they become better human beings. LeGuin does not take the reader into the mind of disagreeable characters, which they both are initially, and show them from their own point of view. Rather, she presents them from outside, so a reader may feel little sympathy with either Ged or Tenar until they begin to change, Tenar by starting to sympathize with other people and Ged by developing more complex reactions to others than mere prickly arrogance. The narration is rather humourless, a consistent aspect of LeGuin's storytelling.

The details of the temple society on Atuan are the most thoroughly developed and original part of the Earthsea landscape, social or geographical, in the first three books. The culture is otherwise a fairly shallowly-developed pre-industrial agrarian society, with a few kings and wizards on top and none of the social complexity of a real world. For the era in which they were written, though, they were quite innovative, in that Earthsea was an original attempt at a unique world, rather than the shallow surface skim off of Tolkien's deep, rich complexity that much American fantasy of the seventies and early eighties offered. In *Tales From Earthsea* and *The Other Wind*, Earthsea has evolved in the author's mind, and the cultures are given greater depth and consideration, making the world a richer, more solid place. Those who have enjoyed the first books will find *The Other Wind* a satisfying conclusion. The apparently unalterable, grim fate of the dead is changed, as the story reassesses the Classically-bleak land of the dead travelled through in *The Farthest Shore*, declaring it unnatural. Though Ged and Tenar themselves have little to do with the events of *The Other Wind* beyond observing and advising, they are revealed by the end to have changed not only themselves, but their world at its most profound levels, both through their effect on others and through chains of events begun by their youthful actions.

Penelope Lively (b. 1933)

Penelope Lively was born Penelope Greer in Cairo and grew up in Egypt. She studied at Oxford and lived there for some years; her husband, Jack Lively, taught there for a time before becoming professor of Politics at Warwick University. Lively also writes for adults, and in 1987 won the Booker Prize for *Moon Tiger*.

Lively's first book, *Astercote* (1970), is not really a fantasy novel, though it always seems on the verge of becoming one. In the end, all the supernatural in it, the belief of the people of the modern village of Astercote in a hidden chalice which keeps off the plague, is superstition. However, the book establishes a pattern to which Lively returns in many of her fantasies; a community which rallies against outsiders when something out of the ordinary happens, and children who are at once outsiders and 'natives' as the heroes who confront and resolve the situation.

The Wild Hunt of Hagworthy (1971), Lively's next book, is a fantasy. In it, the outsider observer is teenage Lucy, who goes to spend the summer in the village of Hagworthy with an aunt. She has fond memories of holidays there as a young child, but finds her old friends, particularly Kester, have changed. The vicar recreates the village's ancient Horn Dance as a tourist attraction, but the dance brings back the Wild Hunt, and on the day of the actual performance, Kester, the village outsider, is pursued by both dancers and the supernatural hunt. It is up to Lucy, who recognizes her friend's real danger, to save him. In addition to being a good fantasy novel, *Hagworthy* touches on the subject of growing up, of friends drifting apart and changing or reforging friendships, without ever becoming excessively preoccupied with that inevitable stage of teen life.

In *The Ghost of Thomas Kempe* (1973) James Harrison and his family move into an old cottage in the village of Ledsham. Almost immediately, James discovers the house is haunted. The ghost communicates by writing, throws things around when he is annoyed, and James gets the blame. The ghost is that of Thomas Kempe, a priest-hating apothecary, astronomer, and supposed sorcerer of the time of James I. Kempe decides James is his apprentice and creates a good deal of trouble in the town, but worst of all, he believes Mrs Verity, the old lady next door, is a witch. James tries to get rid of Thomas Kempe with the help of part-time exorcist Bert Ellison, but fails. As Kempe fails in his attempts to re-establish things the way he thinks they should be, he almost seems to want James to send him away, though he is too obstinate to say so. When James can think of nothing to do to get rid of him, the ghost takes drastic action. James wakes in the night smelling smoke and sees a note written on the mirror with soap proclaiming that Kempe has set fire to the witch's house. James raises the alarm and old Mrs Verity, her cat, her canary, and all her possessions are saved. Finally, Thomas Kempe asks James to help him pass on by finding his resting place. *The Ghost of Thomas Kempe* won the Carnegie Medal.

A work similar in theme but even funnier is *The Revenge of Samuel Stokes* (1981). Tim's family moves into a brand new housing estate (subdivision), Charstock Estates, near the village of Great Maxton where his grandfather lives. He makes friends with Jane, the imaginative, reckless, disaster-prone girl next door. Almost immediately, strange things happen throughout the estate. Brick walls rise through the new lawns, box hedges come up where beans were planted, exotic cooking smells emanate from the washing machine, and a greenhouse becomes a Greek temple folly, to the acute embarrassment of the owners. Tim, Jane, and Grandpa begin to communicate, via the television and radio, with Samuel Stokes, an eighteenth-century landscape gardener on the Capability Brown scale. Long-gone Charstock Park was his finest achievement. He has removed villages before, when they interfered with a view; he will remove them again. Past and present battle it out, with everyone but the two children and Grandpa scrambling to explain it all as natural phenomena and shoddy workmanship. Finally Stokes floods a large portion of the estate, refilling the forgotten ornamental lake. Grandpa and Jane enjoy the mayhem as the suburbanites commute by boat, but Tim knows it has to end. He decides that Stokes must be given something else to do, and they divert his attention to

Phase Three of the village development, which is the playground, swimming pool, cricket pitch, and football field, convincing Stokes that the project needs the hand of a master designer. *The Revenge of Samuel Stokes* repeats to some degree the ideas in *The Ghost of Thomas Kempe*, a ghost who wants to prevent change to what he knew, but although both ghosts are arrogant, obstinate, and opinionated, the means they adopt are quite different. The ghost of Thomas Kempe is sometimes frightening, even dangerous, while that of Samuel Stokes is often comic.

Lively's books are well-crafted, well-written, full of event and action, and her heroes, especially in her later books, have a realistically imaginative and comic outlook on life. Lively tends to repeat themes and motifs, such as the persistence of the past disrupting the present, the child or children who recognize the true cause of the otherworldly goings-on and assume responsibility for sorting things out, and the determinedly rational parents, groping for mundane explanations in the face of the most decidedly arcane. Although her stories are not a series, the similar concerns and approaches in each book mean that, although they may seem repetitive if read in one orgy, those who enjoy one will enjoy them all.

Lively has also written a retelling of Virgil's *Aeneid* called *In Search of a Homeland* (2001). Like Rosemary Sutcliff's *Black Ships Before Troy* and *The Wanderings of Odysseus*, to which it is a companion volume (see Chapter IX), Lively's retelling of classical epic is intended for older children and teens, despite being lavishly illustrated, in this case by Ian Andrew. It falls short of the literary standard of Sutcliff's work, but is nonetheless a good introduction to the story of Aeneas' flight from Troy and his foundation of Rome.

Eva Ibbotson (b. 1925)

Born Maria Wiesner in Vienna, Austria, Ibbotson immigrated to Great Britain in 1933 with her father, biologist Berthold Wiesner, who took a position at Edinburgh University. Her mother, the Jewish writer Anna Gmeyner, left Austria for Britain in 1934. Even before this, Ibbotson had been shuttled back and forth between her divorced parents; like Minette in *Island of the Aunts* (1999), the young Ibbotson was sent between Edinburgh and London, trying to please both parents. Ibbotson studied physiology at London University, but found that her interests lay elsewhere and did not make a career of science. She married Alan Ibbotson, who taught ecology at the University of Newcastle; they had four children.

Although she had previously written short stories, Ibbotson only began writing novels once her children were in school. Her children's books are largely comic fantasy, while her adult novels tend to romantic realism. Her first book, *The Great Ghost Rescue*, was published in 1975. In this, ghosts, vampire bats, and other supernatural beings find themselves displaced by Progress, their traditional haunts disappearing as ruins are fixed up and modernized and the environment is polluted. Humphrey the Horrible, a friendly, pinkish ghost, his parents, the stench-producing Hag and the legless Gliding Kilt, his older siblings, Wailing Winifred and George the Screaming Skull, and Aunt Hortensia, who is always forgetting where she left her head, set out to find a new home. They end up in a dreary boarding school, where they are befriended by Rick and Barbara. Rick travels to London and successfully asks the prime minister to establish a ghost sanctuary. The man who donates the property, Lord Bullhaven, turns out to have ulterior motives. He is a hate-filled bigot who regards the sanctuary as a means to trap and exorcize the ghosts, destroying them forever. Humphrey's heroic efforts to reach Rick and Barbara, and their witch-aided disruption of the exorcism, save the day, while the villain, through his own actions, ends up a ghost himself. A very similar book published twenty years later is *Dial A Ghost* (1996), which features an agency dedicated to ghost relocation, an orphan, Oliver, befriended by ghosts sent to haunt his ancestral home in a murder attempt by his guardians, and the rescue of the ghosts by their human friend, when they are faced with destruction.

Very similar in tone is *Which Witch?* (1979), wherein a coven of witches enters a competition, the winner of which will marry the temperamental but kind-hearted dark wizard Arriman the Awful. The beautiful Belladonna, in love with Arriman, tries her best, but she is a white witch and simply cannot seem to do anything terrible or frightening. She believes the pet worm of her friend Terence, a young orphan, enables her to do dark magic, such as bringing the ghost of wife-murdering Sir Simon Montpelier back to life, but in fact it is Terence's own talent as a dark wizard that does it. Terence is eventually recognized as Arriman's successor, allowing the dark wizard to retire and marry Belladonna.

Other than Humphrey and the Wilkinsons of *Dial a Ghost*, Ibbotson's ghosts are largely cartoonishly revolting: bloodstained, filthy, foul-smelling, proud of their repulsiveness, and earnest in their efforts to be more horrible, in an *Addams Family* sort of way. Her boy heroes are earnestly tolerant and can only be described as nice, with few other distinguishing characteristics. Her witches, a class of character which reappears in several of her books and of which the coven in *Which Witch?* is typical, are often similar to the ghosts, comically competing with one another in repulsiveness and wickedness without ever really being shown doing anyone much harm. Like the ghost books, *Which Witch?* contains elements common to all Ibbotson's stories: emotionally-neglected orphans who are unfailingly polite, kind, and generous, a broad, slapstick comedy in the portrayal of purportedly wicked but generally harmless beings, and a villain depicted with the same grotesque outlines but having a genuine streak of cruelty and malice.

Some of Ibbotson's later books take on a little more depth and thematic complexity. *The Secret of Platform 13* (1994) makes more interesting use of the theme of the neglected orphan and offers a more fully-realized fantastic. It begins with an island kingdom called just the Island, reachable from everyday London by a tunnel which opens every nine years at Platform 13 at King's Cross Station and inhabited both by humans and magical creatures such as hags, ogres, wizards, and harpies, among other things both benevolent and dangerous. The baby prince's three nursemaids are humans who ran away from London, and when they travel back, overcome by a nostalgic craving for fish and chips, the prince is snatched by a wealthy woman. Nine years later, a rescue mission is sent to get him back. The rescuers are a fairy who can make plants grow and whose mother was a school gym mistress, an elderly wizard, a one-eyed, Lederhosen-wearing ogre named Hans (made invisible with fern-seed), and the young hag Odge. They find Raymond Trottle, the boy they believe to be the prince, an obese, spoilt brat, whose mother talks baby-talk to him, while he controls her through tantrums in order to satisfy his gluttony and greed for possessions. However, Ben, supposed grandchild of dying Nanny Brown, a despised, unpaid drudge who sleeps in a windowless cupboard, bonds instantly with Odge and becomes an ally to the rescuers. The rescue attempt fails, though, and the foul harpies, whose description brings Margaret Thatcher to mind even without the obvious intent in the illustration (by Sue Porter), are the ones who succeed in capturing Raymond and bringing him to the Island – where, as readers have long suspected, it is discovered that Ben is actually the missing prince. Odge's temporary feeling of resentful loneliness after her friend is restored to his family is one of the elements which adds a richer dimension to the characterisation in this book; in terms of personality Ben himself is indistinguishable from Rick, Terence, or Oliver.

Island of the Aunts (1999) is a more distinctive fantasy. Again, Ibbotson uses the motif of a magical island, but this one is firmly located in the world, off the coast of Scotland. Here three eccentric sisters (later in the book a fourth returns) care for everything from oil-spill injured mermaids to a selkie (a seal which can take human form) to a baby kraken. The sisters decide they need to train eventual successors, and by setting up an agency called 'Unusual Aunts', they get themselves hired to escort children whose guardians cannot be bothered doing so. In this way they kidnap Minette (who is being sent between the homes of her divorced parents but who is not able to be herself in either place), Brazilian Fabio (whose upper-class grandparents are trying to make a gentleman of him by sending him to a repressive boarding school), and wealthy, spoilt Lambert. Lambert is a mistake, but Minette and Fabio soon find themselves eager workers on the Island. When the kraken, guardian of the world's oceans, reawakens and prepares to make his circuit of the planet, humming a tune that reminds people of the need to respect the sea, he leaves his son at the Island in the care of Minette and Fabio. However, Lambert finds his cell phone and calls his father, a corrupt businessman; Mr. Sprott sets out with a boatload of mercenaries to rescue his son and seize the wonders of the Island. Various of the Island's stranger inhabitants are captured, though Minette, Fabio, and the Aunts put up a valiant resistance. In one of the most dramatic and suspenseful parts of the book, a rescue attempt led by Herbert, the selkie who has been transformed to a man, fails, and Sprott intends to throw them overboard to drown. The young kraken, though, is able to call his father, and Sprott's ship is smashed. Those belonging to the Island make it ashore only because the little kraken asserts his will and insists that his father rescue them, while most of the villains escape in the lifeboat. The children's problems are not over then, as policemen arrive to arrest the Aunts for kidnapping. In court, however, their defence claims that kidnapping must involve taking someone against their will, and since Minette and Fabio deny they were held against their will, the Aunts are freed. They name the two children their heirs, and in a final chapter, Herbert chooses to return to the sea as a seal, the hinted-at romance with cello-playing Aunt Myrtle not enough to hold him from accompanying the kraken. The bittersweet potential of this is made comic instead by Myrtle's inability to weep the last of the required seven tears over him to effect the transformation, due to her sudden realisation that if he becomes a seal and sets off to travel with the kraken, she'll be able to give up the swimming lessons he insisted on giving her.

Of all Ibbotson's books, *Island of the Aunts* is the one in which the fantastic is most satisfying, because the story is in every way stronger than her earlier works. The plot is more complex and not quite so predictable, the child characters have some personality and, although the adults are still cartoonish, as seems usual for her, they are also more varied and have a personality not limited to one trait. The themes with which she has shown herself concerned from her very first book – loneliness, families of choice rather than birth, environmental pollution, and cruelty to animals – become fully integrated into the plot and work together as part of the structure rather than decorative detail.

Ibbotson continues to develop more complex characterisation and themes in two non-fantasy books for children, the Brazilian adventure *Journey to the River Sea* (2001) and the story of a Viennese foundling, a false mother, and a stolen inheritance, *The Star of Kazan* (2004). In these, as in *Island of the Aunts*, she develops many of the concerns which have appeared in her earliest books in much greater depth, a maturity of style which it is possible she may carry over into future fantasies.

Ibbotson's work has had that of J.K. Rowling compared with it, sometimes in terms of detail. The conjunction of the despised orphan sleeping in the cupboard and the depiction of Raymond and his relationship with his mother in *The Secret of Platform 13*, so like the depiction of Dudley Dursley, both physically and in his relationship with his mother, in the first *Harry Potter* book, is bound to lead one to wonder if Ibbotson's books were an influence on Rowling, although such conjunctions of detail often do occur in literature simply because of the aptness of particular ideas to work together, as well as through sheer coincidence, and through things read, digested, and absorbed into another's imagination, the source of the image forgotten. There are, however, definite similarities in Ibbotson's and Rowling's approaches to storytelling, in their fondness for grotesquerie in detail, the broad rather than subtle comedy, their superimposition of a magic of witches, ghosts, and spells on an otherwise everyday world which is often oblivious to it, and their focus on emotionally neglected children as their central child protagonists. Ibbotson, like many children's fantasy writers of the seventies and eighties, is often overlooked by those newly come to a taste for the genre, but younger *Harry Potter* readers especially are likely to find her an appealing author. Her earlier books, due to their shallowness, are less likely to please those who want fantasy with some emotional depth or intensity of the created reality.

XIII
The Seventies, part two

Jill Murphy (b. 1949)

Jill Murphy, a professional artist, wrote the first of her *Worst Witch* books when she was eighteen, although it was not published for some years after that. *The Worst Witch* (1974), which Murphy also illustrated, is a short novel for quite young readers. Like Rowling's later *Harry Potter* series, *The Worst Witch* features the traditional witch's magic of potions, spells, and pointy hats in a traditional 'school story' boarding school, Miss Cackle's Academy for Witches.

The heroine, Mildred Hubble, is in her first year at the Academy, where the girls dress in black and grey with a coloured sash to show which house they are in, wear pointed hats and robes for formal occasions, have broomstick and potions lessons, and are assigned a kitten as a familiar (more fashionable schools give out owls). Mildred is a girl for whom everything goes wrong, especially in potions class. She tries to turn a bullying girl, Ethel, into a frog and transforms her to a pig instead. In revenge, Ethel lends her a broom (Mildred having had an accident with hers and mended it with tape) for the formation flying display the school is putting on at a Hallowe'en gathering of witches and wizards. The broom is enchanted and goes wild, throwing Mildred off and ruining the performance. Mildred is in disgrace, and decides to run away, but on the way down the mountain from the castle-like school she discovers a conspiracy; a band of witches led by Miss Cackle's sister plans to turn all the pupils into frogs and take over the school. Mildred casts a spell that actually goes right, turning the witches into snails, and takes them back to the school for Miss Cackle and Miss Hardbroom, her sarcastic, perceptive, and good-hearted form-mistress, to deal with. In the end Mildred is acclaimed a hero for saving the school.

Murphy has written and illustrated several further books in

the series. They are intended for children who have just begun reading novels on their own, with simple plots which nonetheless hold a reader's attention through a mixture of action, humour, and a likeable main character. The language is not difficult, but is never stilted or artificial sounding, a flaw in too many books for 'beginning readers' which Murphy avoids. A movie version of the first book, which starred Dame Diana Rigg and Tim Curry, was made in 1986, and a television show based on the series aired beginning in 1998.

Susan Cooper (b. 1935)

Susan Cooper was born in Buckinghamshire, the home of Will Stanton in *The Dark is Rising*, her most famous series of books. She studied English at Oxford and worked as a journalist for the *Sunday Times*, but following her marriage, moved to the United States in 1963; her husband, a widower with three teenage children, was a professor at MIT. She had already written an adult work as well as *Over Sea, Under Stone*. The couple had two more children, and Cooper continued to write for both children and adults. In later years she has worked as a scriptwriter on a number of television films, including *The Dollmaker* (1984), *To Dance With the White Dog* (1993), and *Jewel* (2001), as well as the film adaptation of *Foxfire* (1987), a Broadway play she co-wrote with actor Hume Cronyn, whom she married after her first husband's death.

The Dark is Rising series begins with *Over Sea, Under Stone* (1965), in which Simon, Jane, and Barney Drew, on holiday in Cornwall with their parents and honorary Great-Uncle Merry, Professor Merriman Lyon, become involved in the battle between the ancient forces of Light and Dark, good and evil. In the attic they find a crumbling manuscript and map. These immediately become objects of interest for numerous people, including a false vicar, Mr Hastings. All these people seem to expect the children to have found something, and question them closely, though they keep the map a secret, showing it only to Great-Uncle Merry. The manuscript is a copy of one from the early Middle Ages, and tells of the location of the Holy Grail, hidden in Cornwall against the time when it would be needed again in

268

the battle against the Dark. The children, choosing to become involved in the conflict, search for the grail. Their search takes all their wits and resourcefulness. Some of their enemies are human servants of the Dark; some, like Hastings, are more powerful beings, ageless and immortal. The grail, when they find it and defeat the Dark's attempts to seize it, is given to the British Museum. Barney, the lover of all things Arthurian, is the one who puts his 'great-uncle's' name together and realizes its similarity to Merlin.

The Dark is Rising (1973), which was a Newbery Honor book, can be an equally good starting point for the series to which it lends its name. The main character here is Will Stanton, seventh son of a seventh son in a large Buckinghamshire family, who on his eleventh birthday comes into his power as the youngest of the Old Ones, the immortal guardians of the Light. Guided by Merriman, his first quest is to collect the six signs, six crossed circles of various materials and symbolism, which are capable of driving back the Dark. He is opposed by the Rider, an agent of the Dark as Will is of the Light, and aided by other Old Ones. Once Will has the signs, he must keep them from the Dark, even when it uses his sister Mary as a hostage. Although the valley is paralysed by snowstorm and flooded by the Thames, the Dark is defeated in this skirmish, and the six signs are safely joined by Wayland Smith.

Greenwitch (1974) begins when the grail is stolen from the British Museum by the Dark. Simon, Jane, and Barney are invited back to Cornwall by Merriman. They believe they are to help him recover the grail, but to their horror, he has brought friends with him, and worse, the friends' young nephew, Will Stanton, who the Drews *know* is bound to be a hindrance to supernatural quests. Jane is invited to help with the making of the Greenwitch, an effigy of leaves and branches which the village women make and throw into the sea every spring. It is traditional to make a wish, and Jane, oddly moved by the somewhat disturbing figure they have created, wishes for its happiness. This kindness later convinces the Greenwitch to give up its treasure, the lost second manuscript from *Over Sea, Under Stone*, to Jane, when all the sorcery of the Dark cannot compel it. The Light thus is able to decipher the prophecy engraved on the recovered grail. By the end Jane, at least, realizes that Will belongs to Merriman's world.

The Grey King (1975) won the 1976 Newbery Medal. It features Will without the Drews, in Wales at his aunt's farm. There he meets Bran Davies, the near-albino adopted son of his uncle's hired man. Will and Bran must continue to prepare for the final battle between Light and Dark by finding a golden harp and using it to wake the six Sleepers, warriors for the Light. Their task is troubled by Caradog Pritchard, a man whose ill-nature and violence makes him useful to the Dark, and by the Grey King, a malevolent mountain-dwelling force of the Dark. They find and claim the harp, but Bran's beloved sheepdog and only close friend, Cafall, is shot by Caradog, who claims the dog was killing sheep, though the culprit was actually a shape-changing creature of the Dark. Bran's loss is deeply and movingly conveyed, and its effect on him, on the quest, and on his relationship with Will and his father realistically dealt with. Bran finally learns the truth of his parentage. He is the son of King Arthur and Guinevere, brought forward through time by Merlin, and thus an important and powerful person in the battle between Light and Dark, as his father was and is.

Silver On the Tree (1977) concludes the series. Will, Bran, Simon, Jane, and Barney are all brought together in Wales. Before they come together though, Will sees evidence of the spread of human attitudes that foster the Dark, in hatred and racism, and of the opposite, in his own family's willingness to defend the weak and oppose prejudice and cruelty. From Wales, Will and Bran journey to the Lost Land, to find, after many adventures, the crystal sword which is the last item of power needed by the Light. They are opposed by the White Rider, one of the Dark, who kidnaps Barney into the past of Owain Glyndwr's time, from which he is retrieved by Will and Bran. The final battle between Light and Dark takes place, but the Dark argues that Bran, as a person from the past, cannot take part. They choose the shepherd, John Rowlands, to judge, which is doubly hard on him, since he has just discovered his wife is the White Rider, a power of the Dark. He finally decides Bran belongs to the present, and thus, the prophesied six are able to fulfil their final task, defending Bran as he cuts the silver mistletoe flowers they have come for, throwing the Dark out of Time. Bran is free to chose whether to leave the world with the Old Ones and champions of the Light, including his father Arthur, or to return to twentieth-century Wales. He chooses to go home, and Merriman tells them all that humans are responsible for their own destiny now, without the influence of either Light or Dark. He also says Bran, Simon, Jane, and Barney must forget all that has happened.

Many readers have found this conclusion rather unfair on the children. John Rowlands, after all, was given the choice of whether to remember the truth of his wife's nature and fate as the White Rider of the Dark defeated and flung out of Time, or to forget she was anything but human; that he gave up that choice to let another choose for him does not change the fact he was offered it. Human free will is emphasized throughout the series; it seems somehow diminishing of the children's moral strength, to say they must forget all they have done in the cause of the Light, reducing them to pawns of prophecy, tools of the Light rather than truly free representatives of mortal humanity. However, Susan Cooper has said that she feels the children 'could not possibly have managed to live the lives of sane human beings' if they retained their memories of the events at the end of the last book (pers. comm.).

Cooper's decision to remove her characters' memories of the supernatural world forms an interesting contrast with Alan Garner's Susan, who is very much changed and perhaps even cut adrift from the everyday world, by her experiences in *The Moon of Gomrath*. Both authors have considered that such involvement with great struggles outside humanity must alter those who take part in them; many lesser books of the type in which children become involved in supernatural conflicts (Andre Norton's extremely undistinguished *Steel Magic*, 1965, or *Fur Magic*, 1968, for instance), in addition to having extremely weak premises for the adventure, deem it adequate if the protagonists return to everyday life unaltered, except for having taken note of an appropriate moral lesson. Susan Cooper, like Garner, takes her fantasy far more seriously and assumes her readers will do likewise.

The Dark is Rising series is rich in English and Welsh mythology, folklore, and landscape, incorporating many elements into a coherent whole: Herne the stag-headed Hunter and the Wild Hunt, the Yell Hounds, the St. Stephen's Day hunting of the wren, Arthur, the Grail, sleeping kings and champions, Wayland Smith, Celts, Romans, a ship-buried Anglo-Saxon king, all become part of one continuum of story. Cooper's young characters are always realistic children as well as heroes and champions involved in legendary matter; Simon's and Barney's initial suspicion and jealousy of Will's presence in *Greenwitch*, the outsider Bran's desire to shock with his unusual appearance in *The Grey King*, Jane's irritable, adolescent unhappiness with herself in *Silver On the Tree*, all contribute to the solidity of the story, making the supernatural and legendary more natural, because the people involved are. There is depth and complexity to the human relationships through the book, as well as to the plots and the supernatural elements.

Cooper has written other fantasies for children and teens as well. *Seaward* (1983) is a young adult book about coping with death, in which two young people, both of whom have lost someone close to them, travel through a strange land where a lord and lady representative of life and death play games with people as their pieces; one must also make a crucial decision about her selkie heritage. The Boggart books, *The Boggart* (1993) and *The Boggart and the Monster* (1997), tell of an old Scottish spirit, the Boggart, who ends up infesting a computer in Toronto rather than his highland castle, of his quest to return home and his later adventures with the castle's new owners and a struggle to save the Loch Ness Monster. *King of Shadows* (1999) is another book concerned with themes of death and loss; a modern boy actor falls ill with plague and finds himself playing in *A Midsummer Night's Dream* in Shakespeare's company. Although none of Susan Cooper's other books are steeped as deeply in legend and landscape as *The Dark is Rising* sequence, and many of them are more interested in the characters' internal struggles than in external conflicts between opposing forces, they all display her skill in creating interesting, credible young people caught up in the supernatural, who work their way towards understanding and acceptance of themselves, and understanding or alteration of their situation.

Patricia Wrightson (b. 1921)

Patricia Wrightson was born in a remote area of New South Wales in Australia. She was for a time the editor of *School*

Magazine and wrote a number of children's and young adult books in the late fifties and sixties. By the seventies she had begun to write fantasy that incorporated elements of aboriginal folklore and mythology. She received an O.B.E. in 1978.

An outstanding example of her writing for teens is *The Book of Wirrun*, actually a trilogy. *The Ice is Coming* (1977), *The Dark Bright Water* (1979), and *Behind the Wind* (1981) portray the inhabitants of Australia as being divided into three peoples. These are the People, who are the aborigines; the Inlanders, the white farmers of the interior; and the Happy Folk, the urban coast-dwellers locked into a frenzied, anxious pursuit of rarely-attained happiness.

In the first book, Wirrun, a young man of the People, notices a pattern in the unusual frosts being reported by the papers. He makes a trip to intercept the line of frosts creeping down the east coast, and meets various earth spirits while camped on a mountain. There are earth spirits in all the different regions, or different countries, to use the language of the book, that make up the continent of Australia, and only the People of a particular country know the right way to avoid its dangers, natural and supernatural. Wirrun knows the ice is caused by the Ninya, men of frost, who have come out of their caverns near Mount Conner. Ko-in, a hero spirit who lives on the mountain, sends Wirrun and a frail, wispy, rock-dwelling Mimi to find the Ninya, who are travelling underground, seeking the Eldest Nargun. This is a spirit of living rock, who defeated them long ago and who is supposed to be in the south on the edge of the sea. The Ninya want to overwhelm the land with another ice age, but they believe they must first defeat the Eldest Nargun.

Wirrun and the Mimi set out to find it, riding the wind. Wirrun's relationship with the Mimi, at first suspicious and aggravated on both parts, becomes a true friendship as they travel, encountering many earth-things, some of whom help willingly, while others are threatening but in the end helpful. On the coast, they find the Happy Folk treating the frosts as a sort of game, making up reasons ranging from UFOs to mass hysteria on the part of Inlanders. With the help of a terrifying Bunyip who owes Wirrun a debt, they find the cove where the Eldest Nargun should be. The Ninya form a glacier on the mountain above. Wirrun enlists the aid of some local men of the People, and an

Inlander farmer helps as they fight the ice with fires. Long
tensions between Inlanders and People are set aside for a time in
a common need to save the land, about which they both, in their
different ways, feel deeply. An elderly man of the local People is
able to identify the Eldest Nargun, which has been reduced by its
long ages confronting the sea from a huge and terrifying creature
capable of calling molten rock from the earth, to a stone that can
be held in one hand. It will not save them from the ice; rather,
they must save it, and trap the Ninya until men from Mount
Conner arrive with the proper songs to drive them home.

The Dark Bright Water introduces the Yunggamurra, sisters
who lure men into the water with their singing to drown them. If
a man is able to resist them, catches one, and smokes her between two fires of a particular kind of grass, she will become a
human woman, although if she enters water she can be carried
off by her sisters to become Yunggamurra again. The sisters
have no individual identities, but a single Yunggamurra has been
swept out of her river into the sea, and in trying to return has become lost in an underground river. One of the cavern-dwelling
earth-things, Kooleen, wants to make the lost and terrified
Yunggamurra his wife, but fighting between his other wives,
who have captured her, drives many earth spirits out of their
proper places and countries. Wirrun, the Ice-Fighter, is sent for
by the people of the Mount Conner area when they are troubled
with earth-things out of place and water drying up. Wirrun and
his friend Ularra seek the source of the disturbance, which takes
them across the continent from south to north, by plane, car, and
the wind.

In the country of the north-east Ularra is caught by an Abuba,
which seduces him and transforms him to a beast. Wirrun, with
help from the hunter Merv Bula, rescues him, but Ularra cannot
trust that he is completely free of the beast's nature. When the
song of the captive Yunggamurra – the cause of all the disrup-
tions – ensnares both young men, Ularra tries to save Wirrun
from her and is drowned without resisting. Despite his anger and
grief Wirrun recognizes that his friend found peace that way.
Wirrun captures the Yunggamurra, at first hating her and then
coming to pity her as a creature lost and alone. He understands
that she is not wilfully evil, but acts only according to her nature.
He inadvertently effects her transformation into a human woman

274

while trying to smoke her out of a hiding place in the marsh, and names her Murra. They set off travelling through the land, the whole continent that the hero Ko-in has told him is his country, rather than any one region.

In *Behind the Wind* the trouble is not earth spirits but a man-made thing, a judger of the dead, Wulgaru, who calls himself death and sometimes appears as a red-eyed mask. To look on any aspect of him is death for men. Murra's sisters carry her off to make her Yunggamurra again, so Wirrun is angry and sullen when Ko-in demands he find out what the red-eyed mask is. He wants only to find his wife. Nevertheless he travels around the land hunting clues to Wulgaru's nature. The People know of his quest and help him in every region he comes to.

Meanwhile, the Yunggamurra who was Murra has been changed by her experience, not by being captured and human for a time, since that is part of being Yunggamurra, but by being alone so long underground. She has a sense of herself as a separate being from her sisters. Finally she manages to escape them, but she ends up lost in dry country, burnt by the sun to something halfway between water-spirit and human. She is given an underground spring by an ancient, powerful, and kind spirit, He-of-the-Long-Grass, and lives there. Wirrun finally fights Wulgaru to confine him to his own place again. To do this, Wirrun leaves his body in the Yunggamurra's cave for her to guard, while he faces Wulgaru as spirit. The fight changes him, although he does not realize how much until he returns the cave to re-enter his body. It has become stone, but he is not dead; his spirit is alive, warm and breathing. He is now a hero-figure, like Ko-in. Wirrun and the Yunggamurra set out into the land, becoming part of its supernatural aspect.

Wrightson's books make Australia and its mythological creatures vividly real. She evokes the landscape in powerful and sometimes poetic prose, giving it life for readers who have never been there in a way that no nature documentary ever could. She writes convincingly and with respect from the perspective of her aboriginal characters, whether teens holding down service sector jobs on the fringes of white society or old men still guarding their myths. She conveys the perspective of the supernatural characters too, the heartless Yunggamurra, the frail Mimi, the Eldest Nargun patiently waiting for fish, facing down the sea.

In books written by those of colonial ancestry attempting to show something of indigenous cultures, it is easier and far more common even now for the main characters to be white children encountering some 'wise old native'; they generally have adventures involving aboriginal artefacts and mythology, meant to teach some aspect of aboriginal culture. It is far harder, more vulnerable to objections from critics on the grounds of 'cultural expropriation', to write protagonists who are modern aboriginal people and to use their mythology in a modern setting, if one is not a member of that cultural group. However, if writers and readers cannot try to imagine someone else's point of view, some experience other than their own, why bother with fiction at all? Wrightson believes that in writing of the Australian landscape, the Australian supernatural is needed and is natural. As she points out in her introductions to the books, elves, fairies, and dragons do not belong to Australia; the land already has its own spirits. The three volumes of *The Book of Wirrun* are bound to make a lasting impression, and although written for teens, could easily find an audience as adult fantasy as well, if republished today.

Patricia A. McKillip (b. 1948)

Patricia A. McKillip was born in Oregon into a large family; she has five siblings. As her father was in the US Air Force, she lived in England and Germany for several years in the late fifties and early sixties, and now lives in Oregon again. Soon after completing her M.A. at San Jose State University, she began publishing fantasy. Like Ursula K. LeGuin and later, Robin McKinley, McKillip is an author whose books can be found as both teen and adult fantasy, depending on edition. She is generally regarded now as a writer for adults, but her earlier books are often found in the children's section of libraries, though later reprints of the same works are sold as fantasy for adults.

McKillip's earliest works, such as *The Throme of the Erril of Sherril* (1973), or even the 1975 World Fantasy Award winning *The Forgotten Beasts of Eld* (1974) are not among her best, though the latter is quite good. Both show her elegant, poetically allusive prose style, but *Throme*, like much early seventies adult fantasy, is thin in conception and plot. *Forgotten Beasts* is a much better work and suffers only by comparison to her later books. The story, of the young wizard Sybel who lives surrounded by magical beasts but has little to do with humans until she is entrusted with the raising of a king-to-be, has appeared as both adult and young adult fiction in various editions over the years. It is an engaging and thought-provoking story, but McKillip had not yet achieved her mature style when she wrote it; her later worlds are deeper, richer in texture, and her later characters more complex in personality and motivation.

McKillip usually writes novels which stand alone. Her later adult works, such as the elegant and lyrical *The Tower at Stony Wood* (2000) or *Ombria in Shadow* (2002), are recent examples of the type of book she writes, stories focusing on a few characters in a world with the rich texture of a tapestry half-hidden in shadows, seen by shifting and transforming firelight. They are usually stories of solitary quests for knowledge, vengeance, or some form of salvation, within a multi-levelled landscape of the natural, social, and supernatural, but the main character will always discover conflicting impulses within him- or herself, friendships where least expected, and the resolution always arises from within the characters. It nearly always is a resolution rather than a case of simple victory for one party and defeat for another. Enemies and heroes alike are changed and transformed, ancient wrongs set right, crooked paths straightened, reconciliation effected. *The Sorceress and the Cygnet* (1991) and *The Cygnet and the Firebird* (1993) are unusual for McKillip in being two books about the same set of characters, a family which embodies aspects of powerful magic in all its members; her only other series is *Riddle-Master*. All of her more than a dozen adult fantasy books are just as likely to be read by those teens who enjoy her stories and her sometimes challengingly-poetic prose style as the ones which publishers initially marketed to the young adult audience.

The *Riddle-Master* trilogy has appeared in various forms, and used to be found on the juvenile side of the library, although it is now sold as an adult work. It deserves to retain its place as an acknowledged classic of young adult fantasy, though. Most recently, the three books have been re-issued in one volume in the United States under the title *Riddle-Master: The Complete*

Trilogy (1999) or in Britain as *The Riddle-Master's Game* (2001). The original three books were *The Riddle-Master of Hed* (1976), *Heir of Sea and Fire* (1977), and *Harpist in the Wind* (1979).

The story begins in *The Riddle-Master of Hed* with Morgon, the young farmer-prince of the island of Hed, who keeps the ancient crown of the kings of mainland Aum hidden under his bed. Morgon, who has three mysterious stars on his forehead which even the Riddle-Masters, the repositories of all the lore and history of the various known lands, cannot explain, won the crown in a potentially-fatal riddle-game with the ghost of the last King of Aum. Winning the contest also wins him the hand of Raederle, daughter of the King of An, but this is a formality; Morgon and Raederle already know and love one another.

Morgon's journey to An rapidly turns into a strange hunt; he is pursued and attacked by magic and people years dead. Morgon discovers that the wizards, thought to be gone after the destruction of their school seven hundred years before, are not, and that there are ancient conflicts still being pursued between various powerful and near-immortal beings. He travels to distant Erlenstar Mountain to ask the High One, the unseen ultimate power over the various kingdoms, about the stars on his face, since they seem to be at the root all the dangers that follow him. It is a long journey with many dangerous and mysterious encounters, and Morgon survives several murderous attacks; he is accompanied but rarely aided by Deth, the High One's harpist, and befriended, advised, and taught by the men and women who rule the various kingdoms by right of the land-law, the magic that ties rulers to their land. He becomes a shape-changer, and the dead children of the long-forgotten Earth-Masters tell him that an ancient war is not yet over, that the age of the High One is coming to an end.

In *Heir of Sea and Fire*, Morgon has been missing for a year, so Raederle goes looking for him. Her quest is as long, mysterious, and danger-filled as was Morgon's. Raederle discovers that she herself is a shape-changer and that she has many powers she does not yet fully understand. Raederle knows Morgon is travelling towards her father's chief town as a shape-changer, so she uses a long-dead king's skull to bargain with that king's ghost for a warband of the dead to escort Morgon on his journey and protect him from his enemy Ghisteslwchlohm, the wizard who de-

278

stroyed all wizards. Her father's house ends up full of the dead, who mistakenly followed Deth rather than Morgon; the ghosts of long-dead kings renew old enmities and reawaken old curses. When Morgon does arrive, it is to accuse Deth of treachery. The harpist held him prisoner for a year while the wizard Ghisteslwchlohm searched his mind for some piece of knowledge he could not find. In the process Morgon gained much knowledge of power and the magic of the land; he also experienced a death of a sort, gaining great power and understanding, but not enough to comprehend what threatens the peace of the kingdoms, or prevent it.

In *Harpist in the Wind*, Morgon and Raederle search for the true High One, as the kingdoms arm for war. Rulers, wizards, and armies gather, none fully understanding the powers that are moving. The harpist Deth turns out to be the true High One, who justifies Morgon's sufferings as necessary to awaken his powers. Morgon, the High One says, is his heir, the one who can understand, love, and rule, not only a kingdom or principality, but the whole of the land. With the aid of the dead Earth-Masters, Morgon defeats and seals away the shape-changers, who are making war on the kings and their people, ending the war Deth could not and taking Deth's place as High One. With its backdrop of ancient secrets and history that reaches out to influence the present, its two heroes each unravelling their own personal mysteries while trying to serve their land, the *Riddle-Master* trilogy is traditional secondary world fantasy with enduring appeal.

The Changeling Sea (1988) is written specifically for young adults. In it, McKillip chronicles the life of a fisherman's daughter, Peri, who hexes the sea after her father's death, more as a gesture of grief and anger than with any expectation of results, though it is her magic that is the catalyst for great change. She befriends the unhappy prince, Kir, becomes fascinated with a sea-dragon bound with a golden chain, and is drawn into the mystery that links the sea-dragon and the prince. She and the magician Lyo slowly unravel the complex story. The king had two sons, one with a human mother, and one with a woman of the land beneath the sea, who in jealousy stole the other woman's son, and from love for the king and desire to have him love their son, left that baby as a changeling in the other prince's place. Kir hates the land and longs to return to the sea, but he and Peri are falling in love. Lyo frees the sea-dragon from its chains and it becomes the human prince for brief periods. Peri begins teaching human language to him, and the half-brothers meet, each trapped in a world they were not meant for and do not want. When the king discovers he has two sons, his love for Kir and the sea-woman's own movement towards communication lead to reconciliation and forgiveness. Kir returns to the sea and the human prince who was the sea-dragon is restored to his own form and life on land, though this is only possible once Peri, who possesses very powerful magic she is not aware of, undoes her own hexes, which have thrown all the sea's magic into confusion. Peri grieves for Kir, but begins to find happiness in Lyo's love.

McKillip's fantasy draws the reader into a dreamlike world of poetic imagery, mystery, and warm humour. Her narration is not always straightforward; the reader rarely knows more than the characters, and occasionally less, so that a second reading can sometimes be required for the full ramifications of some aspects of the book to sink in. Her books always reward rereading with greater understanding and greater appreciation of the subtlety with which her tapestry is woven. Some readers, children and adults alike, will find McKillip's stories too allusive and elusive to come to grips with; quite a lot of something is going on, but they will not be sure what. Others will be pulled deeply in to the reality of the stories, finding part of their beauty to lie in just that suggestive and mysterious uncertainty as to truth, illusion, and misconception, which readers are forced to share with the characters until the final resolution of the plot.

Diana Wynne Jones (b. 1934)

Diana Wynne Jones was born the eldest of three sisters in what was, by her own account, a somewhat difficult family of emotional storms and fitful neglect. During the Second World War, she and her sisters were sent away from London because of the Blitz; she spent time in Wales, the Lake District, and Yorkshire. In 1943 her parents took jobs running a centre in Essex meant to provide further education to working teens; according to her own website autobiography, much of the hardship, neglect, and peculiarity of upbringing experienced by the four sisters in *The*

Time of the Ghost is based on her family life then. She attended Oxford, married John Burrow, who taught at various universities before becoming a professor at Bristol, and had three sons. Jones' first children's book, *Wilkins' Tooth*, was published in 1973; since then she has published more or less a book a year, all highly original fantasies and nearly all for children or young adults. *Wilkins' Tooth*, a story of a brother and sister, Frank and Jess, whose attempt to earn pocket-money with a revenge business attracts the enmity of a witch and embroils them in an effort to restore the family and fortune of two little girls, was republished in the United States as *Witch's Business* (2002).[*]

Jones is one of the most prolific and most original fantasists for children and young adults writing today, with over thirty books to her name; those works discussed below can at least give an impression of a cross-section of her work. She is uniformly excellent in her literary style, development of character, and ability to weave a complex, suspenseful plot that leads both characters and readers to discover things about themselves they had not before considered. As is the case with writers like Lloyd Alexander or Susan Cooper, Jones could just as easily be considered a writer of the eighties or nineties, since many of her significant books appeared in these decades and she has continued to produce new works into the twenty-first century. Her 2003 young adult novel *The Merlin Conspiracy*, sequel to *Deep Secret* (1997, published for adults but very appealing to teens as well), demonstrates that her story-telling and world-creating skills remain as awe-inspiring as ever. However, it was in the seventies that she first made an impact.

Jones has written many stand-alone books as well as series; many of her realities have in the background the concept of linked clusters of related worlds, of varying degrees of similarity. These cover many possibilities of human and non-human existence, and of alternate histories for our own world. The series now marketed as the *Chronicles of Chrestomanci* makes this idea of related worlds a central part of its conception (as does

---

[*] Other changes have been made to US editions of Jones' books: *Black Maria* (1991) was retitled *Aunt Maria* in the US; the 2002 American young adult reissue of *Deep Secret* has had some not-all-that-strong language expurgated, though there is also an intact 1997 US adult edition.

Deep Secret and its sequel). The *Chrestomanci* stories are not a serial in which a single plot spans several volumes; some characters reappear from story to story, but it is not necessary to read the books in any particular order.

The first 'Chrestomanci' book written was *Charmed Life* (1977), which won the Guardian Award. It is set in a world very like our own, but in which magic is relatively common. History, however, has diverged at some point, and since there was no Great War, the pace of technological and social change has been much slower. Although the stories happen in what is probably the mid to late twentieth century, English society is still very Edwardian. To prevent those with magical powers from exploiting and tyrannizing over those who lack them, there exists an important government official with the title Chrestomanci, always a very powerful, nine-lived enchanter.

In *Charmed Life*, orphans Cat Chant and his older sister Gwendolen go to live with their kinsman, Chrestomanci. Gwendolen is a powerful witch, but utterly self-obsessed, callous, and self-serving. Cat is actually a nine-lived enchanter, but believes himself without magical talent. His multiple lives are the source of most of Gwendolen's power; she uses them up in working her magic. While Chrestomanci tries to decide if Cat is a willing accomplice in Gwendolen's crimes, she and a group of disaffected witches and magicians plot against the enchanter. When Gwendolen displaces a whole series of alternate selves along the series of worlds most closely related to her own so that she can become a wealthy ruler in one, Janet, her much nicer double from our magicless world, ends up taking her place. Cat and Janet must fight Gwendolen and her allies for their own lives and Chrestomanci's.

The Magicians of Caprona (1980) tells of two feuding magical clans in the Italian city-state of Caprona, and the adventures of Tonino and Angelica, both misfits in their respective families, as they uncover and foil a plot by the legendary White Devil to destroy the city. Chrestomanci makes an appearance and lends his aid, but it is the two children who, through their friendship, resourcefulness, courage, and unrecognized talents, dominate the action.

Witch Week (1982) is about a number of witch-children in a school in one of the related worlds where witchcraft exists, but is punishable by death. Nan, Brian, Estelle, Nirupam, and Charles have to face a lot of unpleasant truths about themselves in the course of the suspicion and conflicts triggered by an anonymous accusation of witchcraft. They also find unexpected resources and strengths within themselves. Chrestomanci, inadvertently summoned by the children, attempts to fold their world back into the one from which it split, which is probably ours.

The Lives of Christopher Chant (1988) is longer and more complicated than those *Chrestomanci* books which preceded it; the boy hero, Christopher Chant, is the adult Chrestomanci of the three earlier books in the series. Young Christopher has always been able to travel among the related worlds, but he does not realize the significance of what he initially thinks are dreams. His Uncle Ralph uses Christopher's ability to travel bodily between worlds to import numerous banned or controlled magical substances, such as dragon's blood and murdered mermaids. It is a long time before Christopher begins to realize that he is involved in something not only illegal, but unethical. He is a very lonely and unhappy child, and finds it good to be needed and praised. When he revives after being killed in a sports accident at school, his father realizes he must be a multiple-lived enchanter. Eventually Christopher is sent off to the Castle to be trained as Chrestomanci Gabriel de Witt's successor. However, his work for his uncle does not end. In one world he meets the Goddess, a girl who is herself a powerful enchantress and the avatar of the goddess Asheth. He smuggles the Goddess books which seem to her the epitome of exotic freedom – particularly girls' school stories from our world. When the Goddess discovers that the avatars are sacrificed before they grow up, she flees to Christopher's world and decides to call herself Millie, after her favourite schoolgirl heroine. Uncle Ralph and his associates continue their criminal activities and Christopher loses several lives in their service. Uncle Ralph intends to kill Chrestomanci de Witt, and eventually Christopher must decide what is right and which side he is on. With Chrestomanci rendered powerless, a great battle is fought between Chrestomanci's servants and allies led by Christopher and the Goddess, and the conspirators led by Uncle Ralph.

Although still a children's rather than a specifically young adult book, *Lives* is richer and more complex in character, action, and plot than many books for the seven to thirteen age-group, and like all of Jones' novels for children, will have great appeal to teens and adults as well as to much younger readers. Christopher and the Goddess are utterly engaging and convincing characters, and Christopher, far from being a noble and perceptive hero, is troubled and self-deceiving in addition to engaging, and only slowly becomes capable of facing up to the consequences of his choices.

Another book in the 'Chrestomanci' world is *Mixed Magics* (2000), a collection of short stories. It includes 'Warlock at the Wheel', a comedy about one of the villains of *Charmed Life*, the Willing Warlock, whose Toad-like obsession with motorcars sends him on a cross-worlds spree involving car-theft, bank-robbery, and the abduction of an extremely troublesome small girl and very large Kathayack Demon Dog. Most of these short stories have appeared in earlier collections by Jones.

In 2005 Jones returned to the *Chrestomanci* world with *Conrad's Fate*, which features the teenage Christopher Chant. The hero of the story, though, is twelve-year-old Conrad, who lives in a town in the English Alps in a world where England never separated from the continent of Europe. Conrad is convinced by his uncle that he has a bad fate that dooms him to disaster and early death, which he can only avert by killing a wicked person he failed to kill in a past life. This, of course, is nonsense; like the younger Christopher in *Lives*, Conrad is being manipulated by a power-hungry relative. As part of this plan, though, Conrad becomes a servant in Stallery Mansion, where he meets Christopher, who is searching for Millie. She has run away from a horrible school and been trapped by a witch who plans to steal her power. Stallery Manor is built on a probability fault, which a small group of people is using to manipulate reality for their own financial gain, while another group, of which Conrad's uncle is a part, wants to take it over for their own benefit. Conrad's attempts to avert his fate and Christopher's search for Millie become entangled; Conrad discovers unusual talents and a strange family history along the way to the resolution, in which he takes control of his own fate at last. An additional appeal of the book for readers of the series will be encountering the vain, pompous, but endearingly self-mocking adolescent Christopher.

The majority of Jones' books are stand-alones, such as *A Tale of Time City* (1987). This begins during the evacuation of children from London during the Blitz. Eleven-year-old Vivian Smith is on a train, expecting to meet a cousin. Instead, she is abducted by two boys, the cousins Jonathan and Sam, who take her back to Time City under the mistaken belief that she is the Time Lady (who is also named Vivian) and is trying to destroy the city out of spite for her husband, its legendary founder, Faber John. Time City exists in a cycle outside Time, and its inhabitants have a responsibility to oversee History. Vivian convinces the boys that despite the similarity of names (Faber meaning smith), she is not the Time Lady. She ends up helping them try to save not only Time City, but History itself from conspiracy and treason within the city's ruling family.

Archer's Goon (1984) is in part an examination of sibling relationships, and in part a strange story of rocket ships and wizards, though that is not immediately obvious. It begins with a puzzling event and goes on being puzzling and intriguing right to the end. Thirteen-year-old Howard Sykes and his hellion of a little sister, Awful, end up with a Goon in the house, a seemingly-dimwitted, threatening, but often likeable giant, who says he is there to collect 'Archer's two thousand'. This turns out to be, not money, but words from their writer father, who has a peculiar secret arrangement, whereby he writes two thousand words on some nonsense topic every few months, in return for not paying municipal taxes. The story quickly becomes a quest to discover for whom he really writes the words, and what they do with them, since the mysterious Archer has nothing to do with it, but is bullyingly keen to find out himself. Howard and Awful discover that, as their father Quentin puts it, 'This town is run by seven megalomaniac wizards!' The quest then becomes one to find the mysterious seventh wizard who has trapped his older and mostly gangster-like siblings in the town. Repeating cycles of time, and Howard's obsession with designing spaceships, turn out to play a crucial role in both the cause and the solution.

Dogsbody (1975) is book which will appeal to both teens and adults. It begins with sentencing after a trial. The luminary of the Dog Star, Sirius, has been convicted of killing a fellow luminary and of losing a Zoi, a powerful tool of the luminaries, capable of destroying a star and many lesser things as well. Sirius is among the greatest of the Luminaries, but is nonetheless sentenced to live as a creature of Earth until he finds the Zoi that fell there, or dies. Then he is born among a litter of puppies, which are thrown into the river. Kathleen, the lonely and exploited daughter of a jailed Irish terrorist, saves Sirius from drowning and is grudgingly allowed to keep him by her exploitative guardians. Sirius only gradually recovers his memory and embarks on a mission to find the Zoi and clear his name, but he changes Kathleen's life for the better and finds himself changed by her. By the end, Sirius is able to prove that he was framed for the murder by his former Consort. Sirius' dog-body is killed, to Kathleen's great grief, and he is revealed in his vast, angel-like form. The possibility is suggested that Kathleen may eventually join Sirius in the heavens as his Companion and Consort.

Power of Three (1976) is about conflicts between three different races of people: the People of the Sun, smallish hunters, shepherds, and beekeepers who live in mounds on the Moor and work magic with words; the People of the Moon, the shape-shifting Dorig who live in halls under bodies of water on the Moor; and the People of the Earth, Giants, who are modern humans. It is a story of revenge, a curse only broken by the co-operation of the three races, and the triumph of the power of life and renewal, as well as a complex, dramatic, and suspenseful examination of heroism and self-discovery. The action is all set against the background of conflicts over a new reservoir, which is going to flood a valley important to all three races.

In *Eight Days of Luke* (1975), orphaned David's life with his horrible relatives is made more interesting by the appearance of Luke, a dangerous but irrepressible young man with a fire-obsession. Other strange people begin to cultivate David's acquaintance, while his assorted relatives plot to steal his money. The strangers are Norse gods (Luke is Loki), and David is sent on a quest for a mysterious object, which he is under an injunction to know nothing about if he is to succeed. During the course of the book, David's growing insubordination and Luke's example help his cousin's cowed wife free herself from the family's domination, to become David's ally and guardian after the rest of his relatives, fearing the law, flee the country.

Time of the Ghost (1981) is a fascinating young adult novel about family, identity, and self-discovery. It begins from the point of view of a person floating as a disembodied spirit over the road, aware only that there has been an accident. She gradually remembers that she is one of four sisters, Charlotte, Sally, Imogen, and Fenella, who live in a boys' school run by their neglectful parents. She witnesses crucial events in their past somehow connected to her present ghostly state, but cannot remember which sister she is, or what the connection might be. Only gradually do she and the reader discover she is actually the adult Sally, hospitalized after being thrown out of a car by her insane boyfriend. Her ghost-consciousness, adrift in time and unable to be seen or heard, must change the course of events in the past, so that a different sacrifice is made to the Monigan, a goddess the sisters made up in a game (embodied in a doll), but who turned out to be a real, ancient, hungry power. Otherwise, Sally's life will be the sacrifice. The mystery is enthralling, the suspense chilling, and the dark humour of the sisters' strange lives, as well as their affection for one another, leavens the story. The fact that throughout the book, the sisters take control of shaping their own destinies, rather than acquiescing to their parents' belittling expectations, gives the story added impact.

Outstanding among Jones' other works for teens are *Fire and Hemlock* (1985), in which Polly, a university student who like Sally in *Time of the Ghost* must discover a past she has forgotten, unravels the mystery surrounding her child-self and the enigmatic Thomas Lynn. This is a gripping re-imagining of the theme of the man enslaved by the fairy queen, found in the ballads 'Tam Lin' and 'Thomas the Rhymer', to which the story makes frequent reference, combining the motif of the man in the immortal queen's thrall with that of the sacrificial king whose death renews life for others. In *Hexwood* (1993), another excellent young adult book, a mysterious woods plays out the imaginings of those who enter it, sometimes fatally. Ann slowly discovers her own connection to the woods and comes to the realisation that everything she has believed to be true about her own life may be a fantasy as much as anything the woods can offer. Trapped in a reality that is not truly her own, she must discover the truth of the woods' nature in order to free herself, her family, and the man she loves. Doing so has ramifications across space and time.

Jones' *Dalemark Quartet* is a foray into traditional secondary world fantasy – related worlds do not appear and the world is not our own or a close approximation of it. *Cart and Cwidder* came out in 1975, *Drowned Ammet* in 1977, and *The Spellcoats* in 1979, but the first generation of *Dalemark* readers would have time to grow up before the conclusion of the story, *The Crown of Dalemark*, appeared in 1993.

The Dalemark of the first two books is a kingdom without a king, divided into North and South. Both North and South are ruled by many earls, but the North sees itself as free, as opposed to the tyranny with which the South is ruled. Technologically, this world at this point in its history fits loosely into a range from the late Renaissance to the eighteenth century; firearms have not entirely replaced swords, and the steam engine is a newly invented device. Its religion, which is very important over the course of the series, features various ancient gods or heroes, the Undying, who have at times lived among the people of Dalemark. The Undying seem to be born human and only over the course of their lives come to realize what they are; they have played significant roles in history and politics, and have many human descendants. The One is the greatest divine power, and the enemy is the Undying magician Kankredin, who aims to usurp the supreme position of the One.

The hero of *Cart and Cwidder* is Moril, a young Singer who inherits a magic cwidder (rather like a lute) from his murdered father, who was both Singer and secret courier for a Northern earl. The Singers are among the few who can travel between North and South. Moril and his siblings undertake to complete their father's mission, to escort a Northern earl's son, escaping captivity in the South, back to his home. On the way they uncover conspiracy and treason, and a few family secrets as well.

Drowned Ammet takes place at the same time as *Cart and Cwidder*. The hero of this story is Mitt, a self-satisfied, unthinking boy growing up with several chips on his shoulder in the Earldom of Holand in the South. Mitt has been brought up to believe it is his destiny to destroy both the earl and the Free Holander revolutionaries who oppose him, in revenge for his father's supposed death. The other main characters in the story are Hildy and her brother Ynen, grandchildren of the earl. Hildy and Ynen hate the palace life which reduces Hildy to a pawn in alliance-making; they find an escape in sailing their yacht, *Wind's Road*. When Mitt's assassination attempt fails (though another assassin succeeds), he ends up hijacking *Wind's Road*. All three young people have to reassess themselves and the sort of lives they have lived. They meet up with Mitt's father, a self-serving assassin who joins and betrays resistance groups, and Mitt is horrified to realize how like him he has become. After many dangers, Mitt and his friends escape to the North with the dangerous aid of two of the most ancient Undying.

The Spellcoats, in contrast, is set in the prehistory of Dalemark, at a time when blond 'heathen' are invading. The narration of *The Spellcoats* is interesting. Tanaqui is a weaver, who works words and symbols into the 'rugcoats' that the inhabitants of the land wear. The story is told as she weaves it into two coats; in the end, she is weaving it into the second coat as it happens. Tanaqui grows up with her brothers Gull, Hern, and Duck, and sister Robin by the River. When their father is killed while away fighting the heathen, they are driven from their village because of their foreign, blond hair. Their journey takes them down the flooded and diseased River. A meeting with a strange magician, Tanamil, warns them of the mage Kankredin, who is trapping souls at the River's mouth, searching for one in particular, and that one may be the war-shocked Gull's. Tanaqui learns that Kankredin wants to bind the River, who is also a god, the One, and supplant him. Hern eventually becomes leader of both peoples against Kankredin. It is Tanaqui who brings about the defeat of the mage, however, weaving a spell into a coat to free the River from an ancient binding. The freed One not only defeats Kankredin, but shatters the land, creating the landscape of the Dalemark of the first two books. Various of the characters in this book appear in the others as the Undying of legend.

The Crown of Dalemark returns to Mitt's story after the events of *Drowned Ammet*, but also jumps ahead to modern Dalemark and a thirteen-year-old girl, Maewen, whose father is curator at the old royal palace, now a museum. Mitt finds the North just as full of imperious earls and treachery as the South. Despite his desire to live a different life, people continue to regard him as a pawn, a violent tool to be used and discarded. Maewen, meanwhile, is of great interest to Kankredin, who is pulling together all the fragments of himself, and to her father's strange assistant, Wend. Wend sends her two hundred years into the past, to take the place of Noreth, a young contender for the crown of Dalemark who has been secretly murdered by a traitor. Mitt and Moril accompany Maewen on Noreth's intended ritual journey, but several people, including Mitt's patron, want 'Noreth' dead. Others, including the Undying Tanaqui and Duck from *The Spellcoats*, see that Kankredin is threatening Dalemark and the One again. War threatens, and Mitt, Maewen, and Moril find themselves fulfilling prophesy, although it is Mitt's fate to be the king who reunites the land, not Maewen's. Although the Undying support Mitt, he has to assert control over the earls himself.

Maewen, sent precipitously back to her own time, realizes a number of things: she loves Mitt and he has been dead for two centuries; he is the king Amil the Great who built the palace; her father's assistant Wend is one of the Undying and his motives for sending her into the past to be killed, as he thought, were confused, to say the least. Most immediately alarming, she realizes that Kankredin is still present in her time, and at that very moment is manifesting himself outside the palace. Though Maewen intends to do what she can against him, it is Mitt himself who dispels Kankredin with a powerful name and a long-laid trap. Maewen recognizes the adult Mitt; she realizes that he also must be one of the Undying, and that perhaps they have a future together after all. She even finds a way to forgive the troubled Wend and to help him restore himself.

As in all Jones' stories, the *Dalemark Quartet* books display a concern with family relationships. The characters are complex; they fail to understand one another, and themselves, sometimes almost fatally. They do wrong and even terrible things for deeply personal reasons, and find their way to doing good things for the same reasons. The heroes, as in all her books, arrive after much emotional upheaval and often-dangerous adventures at a clearer understanding of themselves, as well as of their siblings, parents, and friends. The history and legends of Dalemark, hinted at in the background or even only in the notes at the end, provide tantalizing suggestions that much more is going on – that there are other histories of this world to be revealed.

Howl's Moving Castle (1986) and its sequel, *Castle in the Air* (1990), are two of Jones' finest works. They are stories with a certain kinship to Thackeray's *The Rose and the Ring* or Lang's *Pantouflia* books. The setting is a fairy-tale world, vaguely eighteenth or even early nineteenth century in most aspects, where the magic is that of the fairy-tales – there are seven-league boots, invisibility-bestowing and shape-changing cloaks, witches and enchanters, soldiers and kings who would seem at home in Andersen's tales or in the Grimms'. The characters, however, are much more psychologically complex than in the usual literary fairy-tale, and the details of the kingdom of Ingary's politics and relations with its neighbours are likewise complex enough to give a depth of realism. The stories are also laugh-out-loud funny.

Like Lang's Prince Prigio, Jones' Sophie Hatter, eldest of three sisters, knows that it is the youngest who is fated to have a great destiny. Sophie becomes completely self-effacing and lets her job in the family hat-shop become the totality of her existence, while her sisters go off to be apprenticed to a witch and a baker. This retreat into herself seems to bear interpretation as a depression triggered by the death of her father. Her unrecognized magical ability endows the hats she makes with powers, and the feared Witch of the Waste curses her for it, transforming her into an old woman. Sophie hobbles off through the kingdom of Ingary to seek her fortune and hide from her family, and finds being a crotchety old lady very liberating. She imposes herself as a housekeeper on the vain and temperamental young wizard Howl, who, along with his apprentice Michael and Calcifer the fire-demon, inhabits a moving castle that wanders the moors. The door of the castle opens onto several different places, including Howl's own world, modern Wales.

Howl has his own problems with the Witch of the Waste, who pursues him with a far more lethal curse. The Witch is also responsible for the disappearances of the King's brother, Prince Justin, and Suliman the Royal Wizard. Sophie bargains with Calcifer to break the contract that binds him to Howl, in return for his removing the curse from her, but first she must figure out what Calcifer's contract is. These two mysteries, Calcifer's contract and the Witch's pursuit of Howl, are connected, though it takes Sophie much of the book to unravel it all, dealing along the way with the mystery of Howl's heartlessness, a man with no memory who has become a dog, the Witch's threats against the infant princess, an animated scarecrow, and her sisters' exchange of identities. It is Sophie's ability to talk life into things that saves both Howl and Calcifer, when the Witch's curse takes hold and she attacks within the Castle itself.

Castle in the Air plays with conventions from *The Thousand and One Nights* as *Howl's Moving Castle* does with the European fairy-tales. Abdullah, a young carpet seller in Zanzib, finds reality outpacing his fantasies when he is offered a tattered flying carpet. It carries him to the garden of the Sultan's daughter, Flower-in-the-Night. They fall in love and plan to elope, but a djinn carries her off and Abdullah is arrested. He escapes and sets off to rescue Flower-in-the-Night, although he has no idea where she might be. His quest takes him north to Ingary, with not only his carpet but a peevish genie in a bottle. The genie refuses to grant more than one wish a day, always tries to make the wishes cause more problems than they solve, and says that he cannot find Flower-in-the-Night because she is no place on earth.

Abdullah escapes bandits and soldiers, survives transformation into a toad, and travels through Ingary in the company of a nameless soldier of Strangia, recently conquered by Ingary's Prince Justin. On the way they acquire a dominating cat and her kitten, named Midnight and Whippersnapper by the soldier. Eventually Abdullah and the soldier capture a bandit, the original seller of the carpet. He is revealed as a powerful good djinn, Hasruel, who has been enslaved by his wicked brother and forced to steal princesses for him. Hasruel, who has a perverse sense of humour and is rather enjoying his enforced wickedness, has been trying to entice the assorted princesses' lovers and fathers into discovering them and freeing the captives and himself, with no luck except in the case of Abdullah. Princesses are not all that have been stolen. Howl and Sophie's moving castle has been taken, Howl himself is missing, and Sophie, her baby, Calcifer the fire-demon, and Prince Justin the king's brother, are none of them quite themselves for much of the book. When Abdullah, the soldier, and Sophie reach the transformed castle, they discover that the princesses, led by Flower-in-the-Night, are causing the djinns a great deal of difficulty. The wicked djinn is overcome by a resourceful group effort, Hasruel freed, and various magical transformations undone. Hasruel has all along made certain that people get what they deserve, often to their enlightenment. Flower-in-the-Night and Abdullah, united at last, become explorers and ambassadors for Ingary.

These two stories stand out for their excellence among all of

THE SEVENTIES, PART TWO

Jones' excellent books. Ingary has all the reality of the painstakingly constructed secondary world it is, and all the exuberant possibility, and potential for tragedy as well as triumph, of a fairy-tale. Sophie and Abdullah are both convincingly real people, resourceful and determined, who grow in confidence and understanding through their adventures, while the personality of Howl dominates both books and proves utterly engaging despite all his flaws of temper and vanity, probably because he is at the same time ruefully self-aware. *Howl's Moving Castle* is very popular in languages other than English, and in 2004 was turned into an anime movie, *Hauru no Ugoku Shiro*, by Japan's famous Studio Ghibli and director Hayao Miyazaki.[*]

Jones' stories and worlds are complex and imaginative, vividly and intensely realized, her characters equally complex and rich, her prose style straightforward yet literary, never awkward or forced or halting. She frequently writes about individuals struggling to make sense of difficult family situations, and the characters' struggles with their relationships are complementary to their struggles with external difficulties. Her worlds are always carefully considered, the consequences of the details of magic and created history meticulously worked out. In her stories set more or less in our reality, the reader is never jarred out of that 'willing suspension of disbelief' so important to taking fantasy seriously, as can happen very easily in lesser works that mix magic and the real world, as so many of her books do. It is rare to be able to predict the outcome of one of her stories – the end resolution, and more particularly the causes of the events, are never what one tends to expect. All her books repay repeated readings; she is without doubt among the best and most significant writers of children's fantasy of the later twentieth century.

Many of the great recent writers of children's fantasy, such as Susan Cooper, Diana Wynne Jones, and Lloyd Alexander, began producing in the sixties or seventies and continued on through the following decades. Beginning in the sixties with Lloyd Alexander and Madeleine L'Engle, American writers, who had made little impact on the genre since Baum's *Oz*, began to have an in-

---

[*] However, the 1986 Studio Ghibli movie titled variously *Laputa, Castle in the Sky*, or *Tenku no Shiro Rapyuta*, is no connection to Jones' *Castle in the Air*.

fluence on the shape of fantasy, although many who did so, people like LeGuin and McKillip, were writing secondary world stories that appealed to both adults and teens and which have more often been treated as adult works. (Fantasy and science fiction as a whole were, however, often regarded as a single genre appealing primarily to readers in their teens and twenties.)

The decade of the seventies was an era in which many authors put increasing thematic emphasis on the role of the individual, either as a hero who must grow into full potential as a person, or as a member of a society who must learn to take up mature responsibilities towards that society, even when this demands some form of opposition or revolt. Contemporary social concerns, such as sexual politics, one's relationship to a vanishing past, and humanity's place in the natural world, all played an increasingly significant part in fantasy. Another theme, particularly well-handled in Susan Cooper's *The Dark is Rising*, is the necessity of choosing what is right in a conflict between absolutes, between good and evil, light and dark, extremes that are often metaphorically illustrated outside humanity, allowing the human characters to retain aspects of both, but to one or the other of which they must in the end belong, through their actions and their moral choices. Other writers, like Jones, create worlds where nearly all good and evil is found in human action, not outside it. The vulnerability of the natural world to human activity, and the power of human greed and ignorance, are recurrent themes in the work of many writers of this decade. After the seventies, children's fantasy continued to develop along the same lines, showing increasing influence from the expanding field of adult fantasy and science fiction.

XIV
The Eighties

The eighties were a decade of worry. Children of the eighties worried about nuclear war. Their imaginations fuelled by popular culture, which was often merely looking for plot devices, they worried about computer errors starting one, or bloody-minded politicians, or fanatical generals. They were told that acid rain was killing their lakes and forests. The dangers of chlorofluorocarbons or CFCs, destructive to the earth's ultraviolet-filtering ozone layer, were recognized, and global warming first entered the realm of popular awareness, joining a list of worries which included nuclear winter. They were told about AIDS and warned off sex, while at the same time, sex was more than ever taken for granted as a teen activity. Adults, meanwhile, worried about the economy, and in 1987 the stock market crashed.

Even more so than in the seventies, the children and teens of the eighties were a significant market demographic. In North America, after-school jobs for middle-class suburban teens, often in malls where minimum wage pay could go straight to feeding the consumer culture, were common. Teens were the group catered to by many retail stores.

Politically, the eighties saw the return of conservative policies in both Great Britain and the United States. Margaret Thatcher was elected in 1979, Ronald Reagan in 1980. Social programs in both countries were cut back, making hard times harder for some. In Great Britain, central government increased, while many nationalized industries were privatized. The country went to war with Argentina over the Falkland Islands in 1982.

The Cold War had never gone away; the two superpowers, corporate capitalist and communist, fought their battles through other nations, and even when the US and USSR were not directly involved, the polarisation and the instability they created had repercussions beyond the official borders of the arenas in which they fought. In 1979, Vietnam invaded Cambodia and the genocide there was revealed; the Cambodian Khmer Rouge government that had taken power in 1975 had, by the time of the invasion, killed well over a million people, an organized horror which reminded those to whom the Second World War was only history, what humanity could be capable of. The Soviet Union invaded Afghanistan between 1979 and 1980. The United States invaded Grenada in 1983, and made aggressive 'interventions' in Nicaragua, Libya, and Lebanon as well. In 1983, the Soviet Union shot down a South Korean airliner in Soviet airspace, alleging espionage. In the United States, the highest levels of government were implicated in the Iran-Contra scandal, which saw missiles sold to Iran and the profits from this transaction used to fund right-wing rebels in Nicaragua. Reagan's proposed 'Star Wars' missile defence plan, the Strategic Defence Initiative, violated the 1972 SALT I treaty on anti-ballistic missile defence systems between the United States and the Soviet Union, a move many saw as potentially negating the 'nuclear deterrent' and escalating the arms race into space. The Chernobyl accident in 1986 reminded the world of the real effects of radiation: not superpowers and a sudden desire to dress in tights, but death and disease lingering through generations.

However, the eighties could also be seen as a decade framed in hope. In 1981, people around the world watched on television as the first reusable space vehicle, the shuttle Columbia, made its maiden flight, making regular space launches more practical. In 1989, Nelson Mandela was released from prison and reforms in South Africa's apartheid system began. The trade union Solidarity won elections in Poland. The same year, as the Iron Curtain crumbled in Eastern Europe, Berliners East and West tore down the Berlin Wall, and with that, the Cold War was, symbolically at least, over. Of course, that was also the year of the Tiananmen Square massacre of student democracy demonstrators in China. The effect of all this, as with the history of the sixties and seventies, was to make a generation saturated in the immediacy of television news – those who watched Challenger's explosion in 1986 as well as Columbia's launch, the shootings in Tiananmen as well as the crumbling of the Wall – conscious of a background level of insecurity and instability, as well as of injustice and human responsibility for disasters affecting both the natural and the social world.

Children's literature in the nineteen-eighties tended to the 'realistic' and the angstful. S.E. Hinton and Judy Blume, popular in the seventies, set the tone for what many young people were reading. Girls were rushed into emotional, well before physiological, adolescence by series like the American *Sweet Valley High*, created by Francine Pascal, which churned out volume after volume depicting the acquisition of a boyfriend as the primary function of girlhood, the measure of one's success, maturity, and female-ness (as opposed to femininity, since even a girl who disdained popular definitions of the latter could be made to feel inadequate as a woman). There were over a hundred *Sweet Valley High* books, beginning with *Double Love* in 1984; spin-off series continued to appear through to at least 2003.

Fantasy, however, endured, and some classics were written. George Lucas' movie *Star Wars* came out in 1977, and provided young people of the late seventies and eighties a fantasy on a pattern that was traditional in everything except its space opera setting. The movie reached, as few books do, a mass audience, exposing those who might never read a fantasy novel to that ancient and venerable Romance pattern of the hero's quest towards completion, a pattern of restoration both societal and personal, through a series of struggles climaxing in a symbolic death and rebirth.[*] In adult writing, at the same time, fantasy finally began to establish itself as a mature genre, moving beyond shallow imitation to true art. The migration of books between children's and adult fiction, apparent in the seventies with Patricia A. McKillip's *Riddle-Master* and Ursula K. LeGuin's *Earthsea*, continued. The eighties would see adult fantasy readers collecting Jacques' *Redwall* series (which in North America was sold as adult fantasy until into the late nineties), and children reading Pratchett's *Discworld* and Eddings' *Belgariad*. Robin McKinley's two books set in the kingdom of Damar (winners of a Newbery Medal and a Newbery Honor), published for children and then reissued as adult fantasy in mass market form, where they stayed, until the Rowling-fuelled revival of interest in children's fantasy saw new editions back in the young adult section of bookstores.

Much of the fantasy of the eighties was similar to that of the seventies in the underlying themes. It often showed the concerns

---

[*] See W.P. Ker, *Epic and Romance*, and Northrop Frye, *Anatomy of Criticism*, for discussions of Romance, which has nothing to do with Harlequin or Mills and Boone!

of authors who were young in the post-war years, and those whose imaginations had been shaped in part by Tolkien; the possibility of catastrophic devastation remains the price of failure. Often, though, the enemy is not divine, not a fallen angel of any sort, but an aggrandized mortal: we are not only the agents of our own destruction, but the prime motivators as well.

The self-aware feminism of the sixties and seventies began to make an impact on fiction, as writers who had grown up in those decades made a conscious effort to counteract imbalances they saw in the books that had influenced their imaginations as children and teens. Tolkien's warrior-maiden Eowyn is a character on the legendary scale rather than the more familiar rural-Edwardian level which co-exists with the legendary in *The Lord of the Rings*, and thus she can be more difficult for some to identify with than Pippin or Merry. Although Marphisa and Bradamante in *Orlando Furioso* (1516) and Britomart in *The Faerie Queene* (1596) had been holding their own with their brother knights in martial deeds and quests since the Renaissance, not many twelve-year-olds were reading the epic romances of Ariosto and Spenser, although those who read McKinley might go on to discover some of Aerin's literary antecedents as questing female heroes. In the books of McKinley and Tamora Pierce, the girls began to get the horses, the swords, and the fun.

The eighties were also the era when 'the series' began to be important. The concept of 'series' had always existed in children's books; Enid Blyton was responsible for any number of them. The fantasy or science fiction series, in which the world, characters, and plot continue to develop through a succession of books, had appeared early on with works like Edgar Rice Burroughs' *Tarzan* (beginning in 1914), but became nearly mandatory in fantasy and science fiction because of the three-volume form in which *The Lord of the Rings* was first published. The trilogy was briefly the dominant format, but it was during the eighties that the long series, both as one story continuing from volume to volume, as in Eddings or Pierce, and as a connected history of separate stories, like *Redwall* or the *Discworld*, really became common. Children (and even some adult readers) began to look for series title rather than author as the identifying 'brand-name', a trend which only increased in following decades, to the point where, after the release of the movies based on *The Lord of the Rings*, people would go into bookstores demanding books in 'that *Lord of the Rings* series'.

M.M. Kaye (b. 1911)

Some eighties fantasy, such as Kaye's one example, could have been written at any point in the twentieth century. M.M. Kaye is not usually considered a writer for children. She is better known as the author of *The Far Pavilions* (1978) and *Shadow of the Moon* (1979), historical novels set in India, and of a series of murder mysteries, *Death in Zanzibar* (1983) and its sequels. However, she also wrote an enduring and timeless favourite, the literary fairy-tale *The Ordinary Princess* (1980).

Kaye was born and grew up in the India of the Raj, in a family with a long tradition in British India. Her husband, an officer in the Indian army, joined the British army after the independence of India and Pakistan in 1947, and as an army wife Kaye travelled widely. *The Ordinary Princess*, though, does not grow out of this personal experience. Its roots, like those of Milne's *Once on a Time*, are in d'Aulnoy, Thackeray, and Lang, in Paflagonia and Pantouflia.

The Ordinary Princess is a simple little story about a girl's assertion of self and discovery of love. Princess Amethyst, Amy, is the seventh daughter of the King and Queen of Phantasmorania. Her godmother, the brusque old sea-fairy Crustacea, gives her the christening gift of being ordinary. Amy has mouse-brown hair, hazel eyes, freckles, a snub nose, and often climbs down the wisteria vine outside her tower to run free in the forest. Every royal suitor changes his mind once he sees her, despite her other fairy gifts of charm, wit, and courage. When the desperate king considers hiring a dragon, since if a prince kills the dragon he will be obligated to marry the princess, Amy runs away. In time, she takes a job as fourteenth assistant kitchen-maid in the royal castle of Ambergeldar. There, she becomes friends with Perry, who describes himself as a man-of-all-work. They fall in love, but an encounter with her old nurse reveals Amy to be a princess. Amy worries about her future and in her distraction is fired for breaking too many plates, but losing her job is not the disaster it seems. Perry was about to both propose marriage and reveal himself to be King Algernon. The two spend their honeymoon in a cabin they built in the woods for picnics when they were being a kitchen-maid and man-of-all-work.

Aside from Crustacea's initial gift and a bit of advice, Amy is entirely in charge of her own fate. When her clothing begins to wear out after a long sojourn in the woods and she asks her godmother for advice, Crustacea, unlike Cinderella's dress-trans-forming fairy godmother, pithily observes that the solution to the problem is to do what ordinary people must do: find a job and earn money to buy new clothes. Amy finds the job on her own, and loses it on her own – no fairy help, and no villainous perse-cution. Though her fairy godmother began it, the shape and out-come of her adventure are her own.

Throughout the book there are echoes of the literary fairy-tale tradition. The crusty fairy godmother who gave a bit of trouble as a christening gift in Thackeray's *The Rose and the Ring* is most definitely a literary ancestor of Crustacea, while the prosaic and middle-class king and queen, loving, worried about appearances, and not in the least regal, seem to figure in nearly all such stories. The comically grandiose place-names put Phantasmorania in the same atlas as Pantouflia, while references to traditional fairy-tales like 'Sleeping Beauty' having happened to ancestors of the royal family are another means by which this book is anchored in both the fairy-tale and the comic literary fairy-tale traditions. Like the stories of Thackeray, Lang, and Milne as well, *The Ordinary Princess* is written with a certain gently-wry humour, without which much of its charm would be lost.

Michael Ende (1929-1995)

German author Michael Ende was the son of Edgar Ende, a sur-realist painter whose work was banned under the Nazis. Michael Ende was conscripted into the German army in 1945, and at-tended drama school after the war. He worked as an actor, play-wright, and film critic before finding success as a children's author, beginning in 1960 with *Jim Knopf und Lukas der Loko-motivführer* (1960), which was made into a television series. In the English-speaking world, he is best known for *Die Unendliche Geschichte* (1979). This came out in English as *The Neverending Story* (1983). It has given rise to more than one movie, although only the very enjoyable first, which follows the first half of the novel quite closely, has much to recommend it.

The Neverending Story begins with fat, bullied Bastian Balthazar Bux, whose mother is dead and whose father has retreated into his work; acting on an impulse, Bastian (who has never done such a thing before) steals a strange book called *The Neverending Story* from a bookshop. Bastian hides in the school attic, where he starts to read. The story alternates between Bastian in Germany, pausing to have a snack or reflect gladly on which class he is presently missing, and the Greenskin hero Atreyu in Fantastica. Paperback editions use italics and roman type for the two narratives; the hardcovers sometimes use red and green ink. Each of the twenty-six chapters after the prologue begins with the appropriate letter of the alphabet as a full-page illustrated capital, making the book fulfil the description of the book-within-the-book that Bastian is reading.

Atreyu's quest is to find a cure for the dying Childlike Empress, who is the centre of all life in Fantastica. As her life fails, the world itself begins to be devoured by patches of Nothing. Much of Atreyu's journey is done riding the luckdragon Falkor and wearing the Empress' amulet AURYN, which makes him her representative and offers him both power and protection. Each chapter is an encounter with a new creature, a new adventure, a new deadly peril. He learns that a human must give the Childlike Empress a new name, but humans no longer enter Fantastica. The dying werewolf Gmork, who has stalked him since he set out on his quest, tells Atreyu that once they pass into the Nothing, Fantasticans become delusions, fears and fruitless desires, in human minds, used to create lies to sell products or control people's beliefs. The more real fantasy is destroyed, the more lies are accepted unquestioningly, and the more lies that are believed, the harder it is for a human to enter Fantastica. 'Admitted fantasy', wrote C.S. Lewis, ' is precisely the kind of literature which never deceives at all' (*Experiment*, 67).

With nearly all Fantastica destroyed, Atreyu returns to the Childlike Empress, believing he has failed in his quest, but she tells him he has brought a human child with him. Bastian, though he begins to believe it is himself they mean, imagines them mocking him as his classmates do and does not give the Empress her name. His failure forces the dying Empress to leave her tower, to find the Old Man of Wandering Mountain, who writes *The Neverending Story* as it occurs. They bring Bastian to them by writing Bastian's story from the moment he entered the bookshop, retracing all of Atreyu's adventures as he read them. When the story reaches the point of the Old Man telling Bastian's story, he can only repeat it all over again, because there is no more story. Bastian finally uses the name he has given the Empress in his imagination, 'Moon Child', and finds himself in Fantastica, which must now be created anew.

The second half of the book follows Bastian's many adventures with Atreyu and Falkor. From his wishes many lands and creatures are born and named, since Bastian now has AURYN. He is elated by his new power and position as the Saviour of Fantastica. With each wish, though, he loses a memory. His new friends see this happening, but he accuses them of jealousy when they try to warn him of the danger. He begins to believe he has always been in Fantastica, a strong, handsome, princely warrior. He grows more arrogant, a leader of armies estranged from his friends and under the sway of the sorceress Xayide. She persuades him that since Moon Child is gone from the Ivory Tower, he must become Emperor. Atreyu leads a rebellion to prevent the now-tyrannical Bastian's coronation. Thousands are slain in battle and Bastian, pursuing Atreyu, reaches the City of Old Emperors, where people who have tried to rule Fantastica eventually end up, having lost the memories which enable them to wish and to find their way back to their own world. They lose their pasts and so also lose their futures, the caretaker monkey Argax tells him. Bastian has only a few memories left, and so can only make a few more wishes, before he loses himself completely and ends up in the City for eternity.

Bastian's quest to find a way home takes him to Dame Eyola and her House of Change, where his lonely spirit is comforted and mothered for a while, and to Yor the miner of memories. By the end, he has lost even his name. It is only with the help of Falkor and Atreyu, to whom he willingly gives up AURYN, that Bastian is able to find the Water of Life, restore his memories, and return home, retaining the courage and self-confidence he discovered in the course of his journey. Bastian has been missing in the schoolhouse attic for over twenty-four hours; his return shatters the distance that has grown between himself and his father. He confesses his theft of the now-vanished book to the bookshop owner, who tells him that the people who can go to Fantastica and come back again are able to restore both worlds.

On one level, *The Neverending Story* is open to allegorical interpretation, as any story must be that has names like Swamps of Sadness or House of Change, or an image like the lost-memory picture Bastian discovers, which shows his mourning and distanced father encased in a block of ice. The book is not about self-knowledge gained in the course of a journey, but about a journey towards self-knowledge. Most of Atreyu's or Bastian's encounters carry some symbolism, as do many of the creatures they meet: Xadiye who is destroyed by her own empty creations, the mortar-board wearing monkey who looks after the reasonless Old Emperors, the Yskalnari who have given up all individuality and with it the ability to care about anyone. As a whole, the story is about the importance of the creative imagination, its power to restore. It is also about the dangers of losing the self, forgetting reality, and how the imagination must be anchored in reality to create. Without memory, Bastian has no wishes. Humans who enter Fantastica, the Childlike Empress tells Atreyu, learn something that they can only learn there, and return to their own world changed, able to recognize wonder and mystery. That thought has been expressed by those reflecting on the value of poetry or stories, or even the fantastic, time and again throughout the centuries, although rarely has an entire work of fiction been devoted to illustrating it.

For someone of Ende's generation, particularly a German, the idea of people accepting delusion, losing the inclination to question the lies that shape their thinking, was bound to hold particular threat. Ende clearly believed that art was a means of revealing truths, and that the imagination, in creating something far removed from the real world, could effect change in that real world, holding a mirror not only to reflect aspects of our world within fantasy, but, as archaeologists once used mirrors to bring light into dark tombs, to cast light on ignored truths and evils.

Although the main stream of children's books moved away from instructional stories through the twentieth century, *The*

Neverending Story is not likely to strike the young reader as dully old-fashioned or 'preachy'. The tendency of various characters to explain the significance of things to Atreyu and Bastian never overwhelms the adventure, and suits the actual shape of that adventure, which is, even to young readers, clearly the education of Bastian. There is more than enough story, enough mystery, suspense, action, loss, and achievement, to keep most readers completely involved, even though as a fantasy adventure the story is more in the tradition of *The Water-Babies* than *The Princess and the Goblin*.

Eiko Kadono (b. 1935)

Eiko Kadono was born in Tokyo and studied at Waseda University. An extremely popular author in Japan, she writes both picture books and novels for children; some of the former are available in English and French translations. Kadono lives in Kamakura, Japan.

Majo no Takkyubin (1985) is the first novel in Kadono's series about Kiki, a young witch. It came to the attention of the English-speaking world after Japan's Studio Ghibli and Hayao Miyazaki made an animated movie, titled in English *Kiki's Delivery Service*, in 1989. The movie proved very popular worldwide, and not exclusively with anime fans. It eventually led to an English translation of the book, although, unfortunately, no publisher has yet brought out English translations of the rest of the series of at least four books. *Majo no Takkyubin* was published in English as *Kiki's Delivery Service* only in 2003, but by then, many people were already quite familiar with a version of the story through the movie. The movie did adhere to the premise of the book, although, as seems inevitable when movies are made, many episodes were altered or replaced. The book tells of the first year of Kiki's life on her own. Tradition decrees that young witches must leave home at thirteen, to find their own place in the world. Kiki, with her black cat Jiji, bids farewell to her parents and sets out, eventually settling as the only witch in the seaside city of Koriko. Koriko is not used to witches, and at first Kiki has a hard time settling in. A kindly baker and her husband let her have a room over their shop, and Kiki comes up with the idea of running a delivery service. Her assorted errands lead to many humorous adventures and new friends, as people in the city get over their fear and distrust. Woven through the episodes is her ongoing attempt to come to terms with her identity as a witch. The thematic climax of the story is the destruction of her mother's old broom, taken by a flight-obsessed boy, Tombo, and broken when his first attempt to ride it results in a plunge down a hillside. Kiki has to make herself a new broom, but it proves very difficult to manage and breaking the new one in is a long progress. However, Tombo is added to the growing list of friends she has made. After a year away, when Kiki goes home for a visit with her parents, she realizes that the city of Koriko has truly become her home. There are elements in the book that suggest the decline in the magic of the witches and the loss of their old skills lamented by Kiki's mother will become a more central concern as the series progresses.

Kiki's Delivery Service is a very appealing book for younger children. It lacks intense drama, but its quiet humour, short episodes, and the depiction of Kiki's developing independence make it comparable to Jill Murphy's *Worst Witch* series: an engaging story about a young girl with powers out of the ordinary, intended for children newly come to reading on their own. The original illustrations, by Akiko Hayashi, are charming, although the English of the translation by Lynne E. Riggs can sometimes be stiff and lifeless.

John Bellairs (1938-1991)

John Bellairs was born in Michigan to a small-town saloon owner whose wife worried constantly about money, a situation he used for the family background of his character Anthony Monday. Many other aspects of Bellairs' childhood contributed to the landscape, actual and psychological, of his books, which appeared throughout the seventies and eighties. His hometown, with its old and potentially-mysterious houses, became the New Zebedee of the Lewis Barnavelt stories. Every child's worries about friendship, bullies, uncomprehending adults, and the inexplicable world, are given expression in all his children's writing, as are all the things one wishes for: best friends, sympathetic adult allies, creepy mysteries, and power to affect the world. Bellairs received an M.A. from the University of Chicago and taught English at a number of American colleges. He was married and had one son.

Bellairs' first books were for adults. None of these had the success of his juvenile fiction, although one, the fantasy *The Face in the Frost* (1969), is a minor gem of humour and atmospheric spookiness read by many adolescents. Its heroes are two wizards, Prospero, who lives in a whimsically gothic house with a whistling hippopotamus weathervane and a cranky and opinionated magic mirror, and his friend Roger Bacon. They find themselves the object of frightening magical pursuit by an old fellow-student of Prospero's. Trying to discover why Prospero's enemy Melichus fears him, they are hunted across several kingdoms by chilling hauntings that are the more frightening for being often intangible: atmospheres, impressions, and shadows, as well as emanations of decay and corruption. Humour mixes with the nightmare; shrunken to mouse-size, they sail a model ship down an underground river, and, not being able to find the traditional pumpkin, make a coach out of a rotting tomato. *The Face in the Frost*, although sadly difficult to find, is very likely to be enjoyed just as much by a teen audience as it is by adults.

Bellairs wrote three series of books for children, all of which are described as gothic thrillers and nearly all of which contain elements of fantasy. The first series appeared mainly in the seventies, but it was during the eighties that all three became very popular, establishing his reputation. The series have a great deal in common in terms of atmosphere, theme, setting, and character types, though they are set in different towns and feature different characters. They are usually identified by the main character's name: the 'Lewis Barnavelt', 'Johnny Dixon', and 'Anthony Monday' books.

Lewis Barnavelt is a fat, timid boy, prone to imagining disasters, whose parents have died in an accident. He comes to live with his Uncle Jonathan in New Zebedee, Michigan, in Jonathan's huge, quirky, Victorian Gothic house, which has secret passages and mirrors and windows which show images of other times and places. Jonathan is a wizard and the older lady next door is a witch; Mrs. Zimmerman even has a doctorate in magical arts. The first Lewis book, *The House With a Clock in its*

Walls (1973), was also Bellairs' first children's book. In it, Uncle Jonathan is obsessed with the noise of a clock ticking in the walls of the house, which was formerly inhabited by the evil wizard Isaac Izard and his wife Serenna. Lewis, inspired by the example of his uncle, tries to perform some magic himself to impress another boy. He lets Serenna Izard loose from her tomb; she moves into the house across the street, a malevolent presence with eyes hidden behind glasses like burning grey ice. The clock in the walls ticks louder and louder, counting down to the time when Serenna and her husband will begin a reign of sorcerous terror. Lewis, terrified that he will lose his uncle's love and be sent to the Detention House if Jonathan discovers it was he who released Serenna, nevertheless is the one who devises the magic ritual to reveal the clock's hiding place, and who destroys the clock and Mrs. Izard when the adults are frozen by a Hand of Glory. Jonathan, of course, is understanding and forgiving even of inadvertent necromancy.

At the very end of *The House With a Clock in its Walls*, Lewis announces he has made a friend, tomboy Rose Rita Pottinger. She takes part in *The Figure in the Shadows* (1975) and is herself the hero of *The Letter, The Witch, and the Ring* (1976). In this, Rose Rita goes with Mrs. Zimmerman to see a farm the latter has inherited. An old enemy and rival, Gert Bigger, steals a magic ring that was left in the house. The ring, which once belonged to King Solomon, gives its possessor the power to command the devil Asmodai. Mrs. Zimmerman disappears and Rose Rita, with a little help from a local girl, has to figure out what has happened, and save her. She is nearly sacrificed by Mrs. Bigger, but the woman, wishing to be young, beautiful, and have a long life, is changed by the devil into a tree. Rose Rita is not out of danger; she is tempted to use the ring to change herself into a 'normal' girl, interested in make-up and dating rather than Elizabethan artillery. Mrs. Zimmerman, freed from the enchantment which turned her into a hen, saves Rose Rita from this temptation. The ring has no power over Mrs. Zimmerman, who is perfectly happy with herself the way she is. She reminds Rose Rita that the great women of history were not great because they spent all their time 'powdering their noses'.

After Bellairs' death, the unfinished manuscripts of *The Ghost in the Mirror* (1993), about Rose Rita and Mrs. Zimmerman, and

The Vengeance of the Witch-Finder (1993), in which Lewis and Uncle Jonathan visit England and encounter the spirit of an ancestral enemy, were completed by Brad Strickland, who has gone on to write other books about Lewis with the approval of the Bellairs' estate.

The Curse of the Blue Figurine (1983) begins a new series. Johnny Dixon goes to live with his grandparents while his widower pilot father fights in Korea. He becomes friends with short-tempered Medievalist Professor Childermass, who keeps a sound-proofed 'fuss closet' in his house to work off his temper in. Johnny finds a blue ushabti, an Egyptian figurine, in the church. Its removal releases the spirit of murderous, black-magic-using Father Baart. Even Professor Childermass thinks Johnny is hallucinating, and he ends up having to see a psychologist, but events vindicate him. He and the professor must prevent the ghost from killing Johnny to gain a new life for itself.

Bellairs wrote eight books about Johnny Dixon. Among other adventures, he saves the Professor from an evil supernatural power in *The Spell of the Sorcerer's Skull* (1984), and Johnny, his friend Fergie, and the Professor travel in time to Constantinople, where they try to prevent an historical massacre, in *Trolley to Yesterday* (1989). Brad Strickland has also finished or written new Johnny Dixon books since Bellairs' death.

The first of the Anthony Monday books, *The Treasure of Alpheus Winterborn* (1978) is a mystery in which Anthony and his friend, librarian Miss Eells, look for a treasure hidden by the library's founder. Although there is no supernatural element to the mystery, there is the historical mystical component common to so many of the Bellairs books; the treasure is a gold statue which may have come from the Ark of the Covenant. The other three Anthony Monday books, which appeared between 1984 and 1992, do contain the fantastic and supernatural, with sorcerers and ghosts threatening the world, overcome by Anthony and Miss Eells.

All of Bellairs' stories are short, full of enticingly eccentric heroes and villains, and are suspenseful from the first chapter. They are set in the late forties and fifties, the time of Bellairs' own youth. He takes delight in evoking that setting, its radio shows, cars, and even fads, like Rose Rita's beanie. The heroes are lonely children who find friendship with an unusual and unlikely adult, who expands the horizons of their world. Their adventures, usually encounters with the supernatural, are triggered by some action or decision of their own. Often their adult friend falls prey to a supernatural threat and must be rescued by means of a combination of courage and cleverness the hero has no confidence of possessing. The conclusion reaffirms that the protagonist is already a person of wit and courage, and stresses that, although they can mature, they do not need to change what they are in order to be valued as people. Although each of Bellairs' books follows a typical pattern, the young heroes do grow in self-assurance as the series progresses; they are not static figures endlessly repeating the same mistakes. They make friends their own age, become more confident in their relationships with their guardians and adult friends, and acquire new skills. The appeal of the books is not limited to fantasy readers or those who enjoy supernatural creepiness in their stories; they are also mysteries whose heroes are very much everyday, real world young people.

Charles de Lint (b. 1951)

Charles de Lint was born in the Netherlands, but his family moved to Canada while he was still very young. Growing up, he lived in places as diverse as Turkey, Lebanon, and Switzerland; he now lives in Ottawa with his wife, MaryAnn Harris, who, like de Lint, is also a musician. De Lint started publishing fantasy short stories in the seventies, but it was in the eighties that his career as a novelist began. Although he writes horror under the pseudonym Samuel M. Key, all of his major fantasy works have appeared under his own name. De Lint is primarily a writer for adults, but his books have always had great appeal to teens; he has written a number of works specifically for the young adult audience as well. From the nineties onwards, de Lint has been one of the most significant writers of what is sometimes called 'urban fantasy', stories set in modern, urban settings realistic save for the intrusion of some element of the supernatural, often in a manner perceptible only to a special few. Celtic myths and legends, along with Native American elements, are particular influences on the fantastic he creates.

In the mid eighties, before he made the urban fantasy genre

his own, though, de Lint wrote secondary world fantasies set, like too much adult fantasy of that era, in vaguely outlined and shallowly conceived medieval-esque worlds more fit for role-playing games than for serious story creation. These worlds often have the weaknesses of such somewhat imitative creations: generic villages devoid of any wider society about them and, although allegedly agrarian, populated mostly by middle-class tradespeople, with little intimation of any government or economy beyond the village level, and geography that, one can sometimes feel, ceases to exist in any concrete fashion beyond the village boundary no matter how far the characters travel through it. De Lint, however, brought to this setting a sense of mysteries lurking barely perceived beneath the everyday reality of his characters. Although neither complex nor deeply-realized secondary worlds, those of de Lint's early works offer at least the reality of the fairy-tale, concrete in the foreground, though only dimly present beyond.

The Riddle of the Wren (1984), de Lint's first novel and an example of his secondary world fantasy, was published at a time when it was generally assumed that teens interested in genre fiction were reading adult books; it has since been reissued marketed at young adults (2002). The hero is Minda Seely, daughter of an abusive innkeeper in the town of Fernwillow. Minda is tormented in nightmares, but after a reprieve in which she meets Jan Penalurick, a small horned man imprisoned in a stone, she promises to free him from Ildran the Dream-Master, their mutual tormenter. Jan tells her it is possible to travel between worlds through gates, stone henges, and gives her a pendant which offers some protection from Ildran, so Minda leaves home and sets out. She ends up in a world of skyscrapers and rusty cars, devoid of native human life, fights giant bats with a sword she finds in a museum, and meets the loremistress Taneh Leafmoon, the tinker Markj'n, and the telepathic wizard-badger Grimbold, who are there engaged in research. With these companions, Minda's quest takes her to several other worlds. Along the way she encounters other friends and foes, and learns more about the worlds, the light and dark gods who would destroy them with their fighting, and the threat of Ildran, who slays people in dreams and imprisons their souls to augment his own power. As war breaks out between Ildran's evil creatures and her friends,

Minda must prevent her sword from possessing her and calling its divine master back into the world, before confronting and defeating Ildran, to take her rightful place as the last Wessener or Gatekeeper.

Throughout, Minda remains a character with little depth, reacting to the situations she encounters but exhibiting no real internal life; even in taking the decision to run away from her father, even when she believes her friends dead and her battle lost before it is begun, her emotions seem superficial and her encounters do not appear to change her. When threatened, she discovers new powers, but she never grows or matures as a result, remaining a callow adolescent. The various non-human races she encounters pile up, described physically but never really made distinctive for the reader's imagination (the multiple names of the various non-human races, never explained or given any foundation, quickly threaten to become a meaningless jumble themselves), while the secondary characters rarely take on any individuality or intensity of life.

The Harp of the Grey Rose (1985) is a similar type of story, set in the same cosmology as *The Riddle of the Wren*, with its ancient gods, a balance between light and dark maintained only by their absence, and the many diverse races of lesser magical folk introduced in that work. *The Harp of the Grey Rose* follows the questing of orphaned harper Cirun after a mysterious woman, the Grey Rose, who has been abducted by the evil Yarac Stoneslayer the Waster. Through his adventures, Cirun learns as much about his own heritage as he does about the woman he has come to love, who cannot remain with him in the mortal worlds. *The Harp of the Grey Rose* has the same weaknesses as *The Riddle of the Wren*; both are novels written early in this author's development, before he found his way to a type of fantasy in which he was at home. De Lint simply does not seem in his element when writing secondary world fantasy. The solid reality of Alexander's Prydain, Jones' Dalemark, McKinley's Damar, McKillip's Riddle-Master world, or even Ende's sometimes allegoric Fantastica eludes him, as it did so many other writers of adult fantasy at that time.

A stronger secondary world fantasy by de Lint is *Wolf Moon* (1988). This story of a young man, Kern, who has become a werewolf, is set in a world that, partly because it has a more localized setting, seems less vague and arbitrary in its creation, and lacks the meaningless multiplicity of designations for simplistically-conceived inhuman races. Kern is befriended by the folk of the Inn of the Yellow Tinker, but remains afraid to trust them with knowledge of what he really is. He is hunted by a mysterious and sinister harper, whose psychotically-obsessed pursuit of shapechangers and fanatical need to torment and destroy Kern is ominous and frightening, but not as well developed in motive as it could be, a flaw common to de Lint's secondary world villains, who usually appear to be evil for evil's sake, the sort of character portrayal mocked by Terry Pratchett's Dark Lord Evil Harry Dread in *The Last Hero*. Kern is a much better developed hero than Minda or Cirun, and *Wolf Moon* shows a more mature storytelling skill. Kern is a very appealing hero, sometimes bitter and adolescently self-absorbed, sometimes generous and genuinely heroic. The combination of his strength and his wildness with his desire for love, acceptance, and simple friendship, makes this a story with much continuing appeal for teen readers.

In the nineties, de Lint went on to become a master of the urban fantasy subgenre, integrating elements of folklore and mythology with modern settings and characters, and displaying his skill as a storyteller to much better effect. Most of his highly-regarded adult works fall into this category. In his young adult works of this period, he writes of contemporary teens whose stories start off in a world recognizably our own. In *The Dreaming Place* (1990), which has some elements in common with *The Riddle of the Wren*, the characters take on vivid, convincing personality, and literary belief in the Otherworld, which is both the spirit world of Native American tradition and the Celtic faerie, comes easily. The detail seems natural, felt and lived in by the author, not flatly 'made up', as characters pass from one place to another and the world shifts and changes around them.

As in de Lint's first novel, the story begins with a teenage girl suffering nightmares, who is haunted and hunted by a supernatural being. Nina Caraballo is an average, part-Native, late-eighties teen, who begins having terrifying dreams in which she finds herself inhabiting an animal's body. Initially, she is convinced her English cousin Ashley, who lives with the Caraballos following her mother's murder and who is interested in the occult, is hexing her. The narrative perspective alternates between the two girls, so readers know Ashley, a very angry, unhappy person, has nothing to do with Nina's nightmares, and is having her own problems. Taken into the Otherworld by a Native American shaman and 'street person by choice' called Bones, she becomes separated from him and meets a mysterious woman, Lusewen, who warns her that Nina is in great danger and gives her a silver-decorated pomegranate, as well as an overly-convenient magical charm bracelet which provides her with useful items for her journey.

Nina is being claimed by a winter spirit, Ya-wau-tse, who is trying to linger beyond her natural lifespan. Once Nina finds her totem animal and thus in effect comes of age, the spirit will renew her own life by taking Nina's. Added to this is the danger of Alver, a tree being from the Otherworld who wants to kill Nina to prevent Ya-wau-tse from gaining new strength, since the unending winter she creates is destroying his people. Nina and a friend manage to overcome Alver, who returns to the Otherworld, but Nina, having found her totem animal, a toad, is captured by Ya-wau-tse. Ashley tries to offer herself to the spirit in Nina's place, but Ya-wau-tse rejects her soul as withered and worthless, since Ashley does not value it herself. Ashley remembers she was told by Alver that the pomegranate was a fetish to restore balance, so she throws it at Ya-wau-tse's tower, destroying it, her, and her unending winter. A band of animal-headed totem spirits tells her that for that action to have had effect, she first had to make a sacrifice: by realizing that she was in fact willing to sacrifice herself for Nina, her old self died. Back home, the cousins, who have been thorns in one another's flesh for three years, accept one another as sisters, and set out to learn more about the spirit-world. Ashley and Nina suspect Lusewen may even be Ashley herself, although neither they nor the narrative makes this certain, leaving other possibilities open for consideration. *Blue Girl* (2004) is another de Lint novel for teens which explores themes of alienation, sacrifice, and love in a setting where the supernatural, as both a ghost and fairies, can exist within our own reality, while *Waifs and Strays* (2002) is a young adult short story collection of pieces in a similar vein.

It is the themes of de Lint's fiction, whether aimed at adults or younger readers, which give his novels, even the weak secondary world ones, such great appeal for the teen audience. His protagonists nearly always exhibit a feeling of dislocation, of being out of joint with their place or time, or even within themselves; finding and coming to terms with their identity becomes the true quest of most of his heroes. In his more mature works, this feeling of alienation becomes the driving force in the stories; although external forces may come into play, echoing the internal with an external drama and providing complexity of plot and action, the tension in the story springs initially from within the main characters and the focus remains on their feelings of emotional emptiness and unhappiness. For many readers, such feelings may echo their own adolescent uncertainties. That his stories so often start in a world recognizably our own, with the supernatural existing alongside, perceptible only to a chosen few who dare or are gifted to see, also appeals to those at a stage in their life where they feel they do not quite fit easily into the place they ought to fill, and who believe there must be something more for them, waiting to be discovered.

Robin McKinley (b. 1952)

American Robin McKinley grew up an only child in a peripatetic navy family, and attributes her love and trust of books to the stability they gave her in an ever-changing world. She lived for a number of years in Maine before marrying author Peter Dickinson (see Chapter XII) and moving to England. Many of her books are retellings of traditional material, discussed in Chapters IX and X.

When it came to traditional fantasy, McKinley wanted to write stories in which the girls had the adventures. Although her fairy-tale reworkings offer that, her two novels set in the kingdom of Damar send their female heroes off with horses and swords and kingdoms to save, doing it with rich settings, realistically complex people, and elegant prose, as well – and incidentally demonstrating that there was good secondary world fantasy with richly believable, thoroughly-created settings being written even in the early eighties.

The Blue Sword (1982) was a Newbery Honor book. The setting is Damar, a land of desert and mountain foothills, the fringes of which are occupied by a colonial power referred to only as

'Home' or 'Homeland'; it is ruled by a queen and evokes the culture of nineteenth-century England. Orphaned Angharad or Harry Crewe, tall, blonde, and awkwardly unladylike, has come out from 'Home' to be near her officer brother Richard. (The hero's name may be a nod to Anglo-Indian Sara Crewe of Frances Hodgson Burnett's *A Little Princess*, a book McKinley writes of enjoying as a child.) There are rumours of strange powers among the native 'Hillfolk', and it is said that if one goes far enough into the desert and hills, rifles cease to function, but life is peaceful and extremely boring until Harry is carried off one night by a band of Hillfolk. Her abductor, Corlath, the King of Damar, is urged to do so by his Gift, a magic of foreseeing and occasional greater powers which is strongest in the royal family, but shows up among others too, a manifestation of the power called *kelar*. Harry, too, has a degree of *kelar*; a great-grandmother was a Hillwoman. Corlath is threatened by more than the Homelander or Outlander presence on the edge of his land. Inhuman armies from beyond the northern mountains are gathering to invade. Hope is his people's greatest lack. Corlath, at first uncertain why his *kelar* inspired him to carry her off, believes Harry can be a symbol of new hope and of the return of strong *kelar*.

Harry sees a vision of Aerin, legendary hero, dragon-killer, and saviour of Damar. She is adopted by the hunting cat Narknon, given the warhorse Sungold, taught to ride as the Hillfolk do, without a bridle or stirrups, and trained as a warrior. Having proven herself the best at the trials that test young people's horsemanship and martial skills, she is given Gonturan, the blue sword of Aerin herself. She joins the king's Riders as Corlath gathers an army and prepares to face the northerners.

Harry is not a tractable symbol of hope. Corlath expects the main thrust of the attack at one mountain pass, but Harry fears some of the Northerners will cross in the west, closer to the Outlander occupied regions. When Corlath refuses to consider that danger, Harry and two friends go to defend it, gathering a band of Hillfolk and some of the garrison of an Outlander fort, including her friend Colonel Dedham and her brother Richard, as they go. They find themselves facing, not a small force of Northerners, but the main army; the other attack is a feint. For a time they hold their own in bloody battle, but the inhuman sorcerer

Thurra is more than they can overcome. Driven by her Gift, Harry uses Gonturan to cause a landslide that seals the pass and buries most of the Northern army. Corlath's army has fought a hard battle as well, and the North is defeated. Harry shows them that *kelar* can be used to heal as well as kill, and saves many wounded. Corlath, who admits his potentially disastrous mistake, fears Harry will leave him for the Outlanders, but Harry stays to marry him, and her Outlander allies also find places among the Hillfolk of Old Damar. In time, through her efforts, diplomatic relations are established between her Homeland and Damar.

The Hero and the Crown (1984) won the 1985 Newbery Medal. It is Aerin's story, in a Damar very different from what it is in Harry's day, a rich agricultural land rather than desert and dry hills. Aerin is a first sol, royalty of the first rank, the king's beloved daughter but not his heir. Her dead mother was a Northern 'witch-woman' from beyond the mountains and Aerin is the only pale-skinned redhead in the kingdom. Aerin is loved by her cousin, first sola Tor, but more distant cousins torment her for her lack of Gift. Aerin adopts her father's lamed former warhorse Talat, teaching herself to fight, a skill that should be instinctive to one of royal blood but is only acquired by Aerin through hard work. She develops the bridleless technique of the Hillfolk of *The Blue Sword*. Aerin decides to begin hunting dragons, which are small but dangerous predators; she rediscovers an ancient formula for a fire-proof ointment. Her skill as a dragon hunter makes her father proud and wins the respect of the common people but is derided by the courtiers. Word of a real dragon, Maur, giant, ancient, and powerful, comes when the king is leaving to deal with a brewing rebellion and can spare no force to fight it. Aerin secretly goes alone to face Maur.

Aerin's battle with Maur is one of the great literary dragon fights, stirring and terrible. She is nearly killed, and though her burns heal in time, she remains ill in body and spirit. She finally slips away, seeking help from the immortal mage Luthe. He saves her from dying, but she is left 'not quite mortal'. She discovers that Damar's real enemy, the enchanter behind the Northern attacks and the dragon, is her mother's brother Agsded. Her own *kelar* turns out to be great, a legacy of the Northern ancestry that makes her, like Luthe, not entirely human.

To save Damar, Aerin goes to face her uncle in her second

great battle, bearing the blue sword Gonturan, joined by a pack of wild dogs and another of wild cats. Aerin's confrontation with Agsded is one of power and magic as well as swordsmanship. After defeating Agsded and a reunion with Luthe during which they become lovers, she takes the long-lost crown back to the City. Her people are engaged in a desperate battle against a demonic Northern army. Aerin leads a renewed defence and gains the victory, but her father is slain and the landscape of Damar itself changed by the magic unleashed. Tor and Aerin rebuild their kingdom, and though she loves and marries Tor, it is suggested that, being immortal as Tor is not, she will eventually rejoin her other love, Luthe.

The Blue Sword and *The Hero and the Crown* remain among the most enduringly popular fantasies, for children or adults, of the decade. Damar, whether Harry's arid land of the Hillfolk or the pastures and woods and wilds of Aerin's day, is underlain with casually-mentioned history and legend, tantalizing glimpses of a greater world that reinforce the impression of a real and living place. The cultures of both times are fascinating combinations of the familiar and the new, consistently and thoughtfully created. Harry and Aerin, complicated, not understanding even their own motivations some of the time, are thoroughly believable people both as restless, alienated girls and as struggling, driven champions. The stories contain action, psychological and emotional drama, and thoughtfulness, in plots that are satisfyingly traditional heroic coming-of-age stories, and, when they were written, daringly original in the path the heroes follow. They are thrilling and perilous tales in which victory, failure, glory, and tragedy all remain possible even in the end. The battles are gripping and the romance both tender and suggestive of deeply-felt passion (while being nothing to which a thirteen-year-old's mother should object). McKinley's prose, as much as her admirable heroes and plots, is what makes her work superlative. She writes with poetic balance and beauty, possessing a sure ear for the rhythms of English.

Rumours persist of a third Damar novel (there are even hints of it in Aerin's visions), and readers remain ever hopeful, but McKinley's website suggests she has wrestled with this third story for years and failed to come to grips with it in a manner satisfying to herself. However, some of her short stories and fairy-tale novels exist on the fringes of the world of Damar, mentioning either the kingdom itself, its legends, or aspects of its invented zoology.

McKinley has also written two collections of stories. *The Door in the Hedge* (1981) contains retelling of 'The Princess and the Frog' (or 'The Frog Prince') and 'The Twelve Dancing Princesses', as well as two original fairy-tales on traditional themes, 'The Stolen Princess' and 'The Hunting of the Hind'. All four stories bring an emotional complexity to the simple motifs they incorporate and feature women and men who quietly change their situation or their worlds. The stories in *A Knot in the Grain* (1995) take a similar approach, but are all original tales, although with traditional elements. In both 'The Stagman' and 'Touk's House', the young women, one a queen sacrificed to a monster by her usurping uncle, one a girl given like Rapunzel as the price for theft from a witch's garden, slowly realize where their hearts actually incline, and in the end find love with the 'monsters' rather than the princes, a theme McKinley also explored in the second of her two novels retelling 'Beauty and the Beast', *Rose Daughter*.

With Dickinson, she has co-written the short story collection *Water: Tales of Elemental Spirits* (2002). The six stories, three by each author, deal with encounters between humans and water beings of one sort or another. All are about people finding a place for themselves in the world, who transform themselves through encounters with water spirits benevolent or malign. Of particular interest to those who enjoy McKinley's two novels set in Damar is the final story, 'A Pool in the Desert'. Hetta, a young woman from modern 'Homeland', is a drudge in her tyrannical parents' home. She dreams of Damar, researches it on the Web, and finds it a former colony that has gained independence. She discovers that Zasharan, the man she visits in dreams and has come to love, existed long ago in Damar's past, some time between Aerin's day and Harry's. Through her garden pool, with the aid of a newt who either is itself a power existing in a pool in Damar's desert or is the agent of that power, she flees to Damar's past, overcoming, in the space of a paragraph, enough mentioned dangers for a novel, and the sand-god who has been her enemy since she first entered the desert in her dreams. Her sister, apparently able to resist their parents' assorted financial, emotional, and psychological tyrannies, eventually researches Damarian legend, to find Hetta became a noted (although legendary) bard.

Water is not McKinley at her best. The protagonists in the stories of both authors are more passive and reactive than willing to take charge of their own destinies. They wait quietly, acting only when forced to, rather than breaking out in deliberate action or in passion to effect change as an act of will, an approach observable in some of McKinley's later fairy-tale retellings, as well.

In *Sunshine* (2003), McKinley turns to a new branch of fantasy, and returns to writing of heroes who play an active role in precipitating and resolving events. Since vampires have become 'mainstream' fiction, and *Sunshine* is a vampire story, it is often found in plain 'fiction' rather than the fantasy section. *Sunshine* presents a rigorously developed alternative world in the aftermath of a war between humans and 'others', vampires, demons, fays, and were-beasts, who are not one unified force; some are not actually enemies of humanity. With its young hero, the baker Sunshine, taking passionate and sometimes violent charge of her own identity, her heritage of magic, and entering into a difficult alliance with a vampire in order to achieve, she hopes, a greater good, the book will appeal to teens as well as the adults.

Whether re-imagining fairy-tales or creating new heroes whose stories have the imaginative impact of old legends encountered for the first time, McKinley brings her characters and settings to vivid life. Her young women face the world and the situations they find themselves in with strength, courage, and humour; although they are often at odds with themselves or their apparent role in their societies, they work to open up new possibilities, rather than wallowing in self-pity or self-obsession. Her worlds have texture and detail that suggest greater landscapes and histories lie beyond the scope of the present story, just waiting to be discovered. The conflicts her characters confront are never simple; their internal and external struggles complement one another and throw their inner and outer lives into relief. The romantic element of her stories is always very satisfying; McKinley's female heroes never lose their selves in accepting a conventional happy ending. Her prose is elegant, balanced, and highly readable; she writes of subtle emotions and violent battle with equal deftness. The passivity or reactivity of some of her later protagonists makes books like *Rose Daughter* or stories such as 'A Pool in the Desert' weaker than her earlier works, but she remains one of the best of her generation, and the two novels set in Damar are deserving of a place among the classics of fantasies for teens.

David Eddings (b. 1931)

David Eddings is a prolific American fantasy author who grew up in the state of Washington, but lives in New York with his wife, Leigh, with whom he has co-written most of his later books. Eddings is an adult writer, but his first series, the *Belgariad*, and its continuation, the *Mallorean*, remain extremely popular with many young readers. Their narrative style, diction, and content are at a level appealing to teens and many pre-teen children, despite having always been published for adults.

The *Belgariad* consists of five books: *Pawn of Prophecy* (1982), *Queen of Sorcery* (1982), *Magician's Gambit* (1983), *Castle of Wizardry* (1984), and *Enchanter's End Game* (1984). They follow Garion, a naive boy growing up on a farm where his Aunt Pol is the cook. When enemies come seeking them, Garion, his aunt, the old storyteller Mister Wolf, and the smith Durnik, set off on the quest that will occupy them through five books. The Orb of Aldur, which protects the western lands from the evil god Torak, has been stolen. Garion soon learns his Aunt Pol and Mister Wolf are none other than the legendary sorceress Polgara and her father Belgarath, many thousands of years old. They are joined on their quest to retrieve the Orb by the courtly knight Mandorallen, the thief, spy, and prince, Silk, the strong-man Barak, and the proud and wilful princess Ce'Nedra, among others. Eddings uses stock characters made distinctive by physical description and a few broadly-drawn character traits, rather than creating people with any depth or complexity, but he does it well. They are shallow, but memorable.

In the course of their journey, Garion discovers that Polgara and Belgarath really are his relatives, many generations removed. He also is a sorcerer and the product of a long breeding program to blend the races of the various kingdoms, and is heir to the Rivan throne and the rightful guardian of the Orb. They travel through the different lands of the world, consciously and meticulously fulfilling the requirements of a prophecy about a confrontation with Torak. Each nation has a guardian deity, and the character of the inhabitants of each is shaped by that deity's attributes – some are devious, some avaricious, some blunt and boisterous, and so forth. Each culture has remained unchanged for thousands of years. Two prophecies, that of the Light and of the Dark, foretell the course of events, but with different hoped-for outcomes. By the end, Garion must confront the god Torak in a battle to the death, reclaim the Orb, and take his place as King of Riva.

The concluding series, the *Mallorean*, is also five books: *Guardians of the West* (1987), *King of the Murgos* (1988), *Demon Lord of Karanda* (1988), *Sorceress of Darshiva* (1989), and *The Seeress of Kell* (1991). Geran, the son of Garion and Ce'Nedra, is kidnapped by Zandramas, the Child of the Dark, for use in some ritual to give the Dark Prophecy supremacy in the world. Again, a band of friends travels through various lands, each with its dominant characteristic, attempting to decipher and meet the demands of their Prophecy of Light and rescue the child. Their success in bringing their prophecy to pass is due to the mysterious orphan Eriond. He is chosen by Garion to become the Child of Light, which is, Garion knows, the destiny for which Eriond was born. The Seeress of Kell chooses between Eriond and Geran, thus determining which prophecy triumphs. Eriond takes his place as the new god, patron of the human-sacrificing Murgos, who formerly worshipped Torak. He imposes reform on their society overnight, while Geran is restored to his parents. There is no free will, no individual free choice between good and evil in this world, either for the Murgos, whether worshipping Torak or Eriond, or for the innocent toddler Geran, who might have ended up a vessel for the Dark Prophecy.

With his wife Leigh, Eddings has written several books connected to the *Belgariad*. *Belgarath the Sorcerer* (1996) and *Polgara the Sorceress* (1997), although they cover events that happen before the *Belgariad*, are best read afterwards, since they take knowledge of events in those ten books for granted. *The Rivan Codex* (1999) is about the process of writing the series.

The *Belgariad* exerted an influence on American fantasy which lasted through the next decade, being the first really popular example of the type, greatly influenced by the tradition of medieval Romance, in which a youth, following a path laid out by destiny, sets out on a quest the end of which he does not know (usually lasting in modern series for numerous books of ever-increasing girth). In modern stories of this type, he (almost always he) is guided and pushed by a number of archetypal helpers, all of whom know more of his fate than he does and who take great pains to make sure the requirements of prophecy are met. They, not his own personality, choices, and actions, sometimes seem to be the force that puts him in the right place at the right time, to be recognized as fulfilling the demands of destiny. Eddings in particular has his human heroes function as pawns of powerful immortals and gods, who move them through the patterned requirements of the prophecy with no scope for free action. Their choices, their unique personalities, are not what govern the achievement or failure of their destinies, but the manipulations of more powerful beings to whom the hero is a tool (which could call into question their status as a hero at all, in books where such characters fail to struggle against or even question their fate). Eddings' first title makes it clear this is a deliberate philosophy on his part. The device has often been taken to excess in modern fantasy for both adults and children, functioning in lieu of the development of motive in character and complexity in plot. It also tends to belittle the potential effects of individual actions and choices.

Through these ten books, the outcome for which Garion and his friends work is not merely their own lives or deaths, or the fates of their kingdoms; it is the shape of the future of the world. Eriond's elevation to divinity as a merciful and all-loving god, and the departure of most of the national gods for other worlds, at least suggests the possibility that the static world is changing. The overall concern of the series, beyond the orderly fulfilment of prophecy, can be interpreted as the need to remake the world. Garion changes not only the human world, but the divine, a pattern existing in myth (where one generation of gods is often successor to an older, darker generation), but not common in modern fiction until humans had acquired godlike powers of destruction over their world, and began to need stories telling of godlike powers of restoration as well.

Tamora Pierce (b. 1954)

Pierce was born the eldest of three daughters, a self-proclaimed Pennsylvania 'hillbilly'. When she was eight, her parents moved to California. Her mother's alcoholism broke up the family, a messy divorce followed, and mother and daughters returned to Pennsylvania. All three were eventually estranged from her. This troubled childhood seems to have influenced Pierce's creative interests, in her portrayal of young female protagonists without family to support and encourage them, her desire to write stories offering girls a pattern of independence and self-assurance, and her heroines' aversion to formal romantic commitment and tendency to view it as limiting of the self. During a creative writing course, Pierce wrote a fantasy novel, satisfying the desire she, like McKinley, felt for such stories in which girls played the leading role. This never found a publisher as an adult work, but, after being told in censored form to the teenage girls in the group home where she worked, it became the basis for Pierce's first young adult series, *The Song of the Lioness* quartet.

The four books, *Alanna: The First Adventure* (1983), *In the Hand of the Goddess* (1984), *The Woman Who Rides Like a Man* (1986), and *Lioness Rampant* (1988) follow the development of a young hero, Alanna, in the kingdom of Tortall, a fairly generic medieval setting, which is, if meant to be realistic, poorly re-searched, and if meant to be invented, thin and undistinguished. Alanna, disguised as a boy, goes to court in her brother Thom's place to train for knighthood in a boarding- school atmosphere, while Thom studies sorcery. 'Alan' wins the respect of her fel-lows by 'his' refusal to be bullied, 'his' hard work, and 'his' de-termination to excel. Alanna becomes close friends with George, young master of the country's criminal underworld, and with Jonathan, heir to the throne. She goes through puberty, saves the prince from magical attacks with the help of the Mother God-dess, and after Jonathan learns her secret, becomes both his squire and his lover.

Once Alanna becomes a knight by passing her Ordeal, which consists of enduring illusions of her fears, she discovers evidence the king's nephew, Duke Roger, has been trying to kill the royal family with a magically-induced illness. While fighting him in single combat to prove the truth of her allegations, her corset is cut, revealing her as a woman in front of the entire court, but she succeeds in killing Roger. Reluctantly accepted by all as a lady knight, Alanna then travels to the desert, where she finds a place among the Bazhir tribes. She defeats a murderous, incompetent, and misogynistic shaman, taking his place and beginning to change the way the tribes treat their women by making two girls her apprentices. Jonathan and Alanna quarrel about marriage. When they part in anger, Alanna begins sleeping with George, who has always loved her.

She sets off wandering aimlessly, decides to find the legendary Dominion Jewel to take back to Tortall, and is joined on her quest by Liam, a martial arts master with whom she has a brief affair. They are also joined by Thayet, a refugee princess of Sarain, and Thayet's companion, the warrior girl Buri. Alanna fights the mountain elemental god to whom the jewel belongs; he lets her have it because he finds such encounters with mortals amusing. When they return to Tortall, it is to find that the king has died and Thom has raised Duke Roger from the dead. Roger's magic poisons Thom as the duke and his fellow conspirators plot treason. They attack during Jonathan's coronation. While her friends fight to protect the new king, whose connection with the land and the power of the Dominion Jewel enables him to suppress the earthquakes Roger is causing, Alanna confronts her old enemy. Roger is killed trying to call her sword, part of which he made, to him. Among the many other dead are Liam and Thom. In the end, Jonathan marries Thayet and George, pardoned, is made a baron, his proposal of marriage finally accepted by Alanna.

Pierce's other books, like her first series arranged into 'quartets', follow the same pattern of misfits aspiring beyond what they are allowed, and daring to pursue their desires. *The Immortals* quartet (1992-1996) is set in Tortall under Jonathan's rule. The hero is Daine, an orphan whose 'wild magic' has been awakened, allowing her to talk to animals. Through the course of the books Daine lives with a wolf-pack, adopts a baby dragon, discovers that her unknown father is a hunting god, finds love, and saves Tortall from invasion and the human and divine worlds from destruction by Chaos. The *Protector of the Small* quartet (1999-2002) is about a girl, Keladry, pursuing options Alanna made possible. She is openly, if grudgingly, admitted to training for knighthood and goes on to save Tortall from destruction.

The *Circle of Magic* quartet explores a different land from Tortall, in which four young people with unusual talents are brought together. The series begins with the book entitled *The Magic in the Weaving* in Britain, *Sandry's Book* in the United States (1997). It introduces four main characters, Sandry, whose power is expressed in weaving and in light, Tris, who can influence the weather, Daja, whose skill is with metals, and Briar, whose connection is with plants. The foursome are brought together to study magic and crafts at the Winding Circle Temple. In trying to save her friends and new community from an earthquake, Sandry weaves their four magics together, giving each new abilities to draw on and creating interferences and synergistic effects between their powers.

The Power in the Storm/Tris's Book (1998) sets the young mages the task of defending the damaged Winding Circle against magic-using pirates and treachery, focusing on exiled Tris and her family's invitation to return home. *The Fire in the Forging/ Daja's Book* (1998) has them travel with their teachers to investigate a drought and prevent a famine. Daja's smithcraft, affected by the combination of the four magics, creates a living iron vine, and the Traders to whom she is an outcast nonentity are forced to deal with her, trying to obtain it. Forest fire and the rivalry of a fire mage are added problems to be faced. In the end Daja wins the right to return to the Trader life, and so must choose whether to do so, or to continue as an artisan, to her people's way of thinking a demeaning profession among the despised non-Trader people. *The Healing in the Vine/Briar's Book* (1999) focuses on the only boy in the foursome, as Briar leads his friends in fighting an epidemic. This series is followed by another four books, *The Circle Opens* (2000-2003), in which the teens go out into the world having mastered a new kind of magic.

Pierce's plots are, on the whole, simple, the prose uncomplicated, and the characterisation broad rather than subtle. The influence of the 'teen novel' is strongly evident in the attention paid to issues like puberty and sexual attraction, which are often ignored or described in more emotional and less physical terms in other fantasies. The hero's problems in the books set in Tortall are usually resolved by supernatural intervention. The hero inevitably recognizes evil people and objects at first sight before any action reveals them to be so, and in the end, it turns out that any character not friendly to the hero is a villain – as she of course knew all along.

The *Circle of Magic* books gain in complexity over *The Song of the Lioness* and the other series set in Tortall in terms of both character and world, and the depiction of people's motives and inner lives grows in depth, making for a more satisfying story. The heroes do more to cause and to solve their own problems; bald coincidence, mystic promptings, and divine intervention are not used so lavishly. The non-Tortall series also spend more time developing the principles of the magic used, as well as the cultures in which the characters live and travel.

Pierce's books have a wide appeal and an ability to draw in 'reluctant readers' through their ease of reading. They are not challenging or demanding stories in terms of complexity of ideas or prose style. For that very reason, they continue to be extremely popular across a broad range of young readers, as well as appealing for their action-loving, usually female, heroes and their quick-paced plots.

Brian Jacques (b. 1939)

Brian Jacques grew up in working-class Liverpool. As a boy he developed an enthusiasm for literature, and worked as a merchant seaman after finishing school at fifteen. Eventually, he returned to Liverpool, and has worked as longshoreman, bus driver, policeman, and comic, among other things. While working as a truck driver, he wrote *Redwall* for the students at the Royal Wavertree School for the Blind. This became the first in a long series of novels. There are also two Redwall picture books, *The Great Redwall Feast* (1996) and *A Redwall Winter's Tale* (2001). Jacques has also written a short story collection, *Seven Strange and Ghostly Tales* (1991).

Jacques' first book was *Redwall* (1986). Matthias, a young novice mouse at Redwall Abbey, admires the legendary Martin the Warrior. When the ship-rat Cluny and his hordes invade Mossflower forest, the abbey becomes a refuge for the woodland folk. Riddles and a quest into the roofs of the abbey, where he becomes the prisoner of the insane King Bull Sparra of the sparrows, set Matthias on the trail of Martin's sword. He encounters a number of helpful and often comic allies: Warbeak the sparrow king's niece, the old 'British officer' type, Basil Stag Hare, the feuding friends Captain Snow the owl and vegetarian cat Squire Julian Gingivere, and the endlessly-squabbling Union of Guerrilla Shrews. He outwits and overcomes in battle deadly enemies, like Bull Sparra and Asmodeus the adder.

Cluny besieges the abbey, which puts up a valiant and well-planned defence against all attempts to scale or undermine the walls. This defence is successful until a refugee, whose family Cluny holds captive, opens the gates. The final confrontation between Matthias and Cluny takes place in the belltower, where wit and daring play as important a role as martial prowess in Matthias' victory over the rat. Matthias gives up a future as a monk to marry the mousemaid Cornflower and serve as Redwall's champion.

The second book, *Mossflower* (1988), tells of events leading to the founding of the Abbey, and of the arrival of the legendary Martin the Warrior in Mossflower forest. Mossflower is ruled by the tyrannical wildcat Tsarmina, who has murdered her father and imprisoned her brother, the virtuous Gingivere, ancestor of Squire Julian from the first book. (Such small connections run through all the series, helping to weave the stories into one history in the reader's mind.) Wandering warrior Martin is imprisoned, and when the mouse-thief Gonff is jailed with him, the two escape. Martin joins the resistance movement led by characters such as Gonff, Mask the otter master of disguise, and Abbess Germaine. After many adventures, a final campaign against Tsarmina takes place, involving a great feat of engineering which floods her castle, forcing her to face Martin, a battle in which she meets her death.

Subsequent stories in the series roam back and forth chronologically, sometimes returning to characters from previous books, sometimes exploring a new area of Redwall's history or that of the surrounding lands. They mix humour and action with considerations of the value of both honour and common sense, acknowledging the worth of the peaceful, contemplative, and charitable life demonstrated by the Abbey, as well as the need to defend it with force if necessary.

Jacques' prose is particularly suited to dramatic reading aloud, with frequent exclamations and excited interjections. The *Redwall* books are written in short chapters, with several threads of plot interlaced in the manner of some medieval romances, so that one character is always left hanging at a moment of crisis while another's story resumes, pulling along even reluctant readers, who might be daunted by the greater length of *Redwall* compared to many young children's novels. The cast of characters is always large, containing heroes and allies both wise and comic, villains and their thuggish henchmammals, many of whom the narrative follows at one point or another. Jacques' language is rich and varied; while those children who struggle chapter to chapter will be carried along by the action and suspense, he will not bore the demanding reader with over-simple diction or lack of story-complexity either. His battle scenes and sieges are realistic, with both the tactics and the characters' experiences carefully thought out; he is a craftsman here in particular, creating a consistent and credible realism in a medieval world of anthropomorphic animals. In battle's aftermath, there are horror and solemnity as well as excitement and triumph. Throughout the series, Jacques continues his attention to descriptive detail, embarked on in part to provide his first, sightless, audience with word-pictures, giving the *Redwall* world a vibrant texture and reality. With 2004's *Rakkety Tam*, the series extended to seventeen novels.

Jacques has also written two young adult novels based on the Flying Dutchman legend, *Castaways of the Flying Dutchman* (2001) and *Angel's Command* (2003). *Castaways of the Flying Dutchman* uses the story of the ship cursed to sail for eternity as its starting point. In 1620, a mute Danish boy, fleeing an abusive stepfamily, falls into Copenhagen harbour and is rescued by the crew of *Flieger Hollander*. He is given to the cook to work in the galley and named Neb by the crew, who are a gang of vicious, cruel thugs. The Dutch captain, Vanderdecken, is trying to get to Chile to collect a fortune in emeralds. The crew repeatedly attempts mutiny and murder, so after Vanderdecken's life is saved by Neb and Denmark, a dog the boy rescued, the captain makes them his guards. The ship is beset with storms while rounding Cape Horn, and the captain finally swears that nothing in heaven or on earth will stop him, and curses God. An angel appears to pronounce the ship's doom, to sail forever with a crew of undying men and ghosts. Neb and Den are washed overboard, and the angel tells them they will be unaging as well, but because of their innocence will travel the world helping people. Neb is given the gift of speech, and he and Den are able to communicate telepathically.

Washed ashore, boy and dog are taken in by Luis, an elderly South American shepherd. For three years they live with him, acquiring new skills and learning what it is to be loved and treated kindly. After Luis' death the angel tells them they must move on at the sound of a bell. In 1896, after more than two centuries of travel, the pair, now known as Ben and Ned, are in England. They help Winifred Winn, an elderly navy captain's widow, to save the village of Chapelvale from an industrialist who plans on demolishing it to quarry limestone. Ben and Ned protect her from a gang's bullying and lead a search, following riddling clues, for a medieval deed proving her family's ownership of the entire village. Again, a bell ringing signals it is time for Ben and Ned to leave. They cannot ever find a home. *Angel's Command* continues their adventures.

Castaways has a few historical inaccuracies, like the baled straw in the Victorian barn (an anachronism even more painful in Pierce's medieval world of Tortall, since one could attribute the Victorian bales to the hay press used when shipping fodder long distances, though such bales would be unlikely for local consumption). Even worse is the use of Old English, the name of the language used from around 500 to 1100 A.D., in describing the language of a sampler stitched in 1670. Nonetheless, the story is a solid piece of work. The concept of the immortal wanderers aiding others yet never able to find a home themselves is instantly engaging. Both Ben and Ned come across as at once lightheartedly young and soberly old and wise in experience and understanding, a difficult characterisation to achieve. The wise and innocent child or youth, who remains a virtuous person under horrible conditions that could be expected to drag him or her down to the cruelty and corruption of those around them, is an old motif in literature, not much used outside of fairy-tales or after the early twentieth century, and yet it has an enduring appeal. Ben is never in danger of becoming annoyingly sweet, a danger with this type of character; he remains a well-balanced and vulnerable human throughout his adventures, risking himself for people he cares about and causes he believes to be right.

In the eighties, the trend towards both long continuing adventures and worlds that grew in history through book after book established itself firmly as an aspect of fantasy for children as well as adults. *Redwall*, the *Belgariad*, and Tamora Pierce became identifiable 'brand names'. The growth of the hero's personal quest into a mission to save the kingdom, or the world, from destruction came more and more to be the dominant theme in fantasy, a trend with its roots in Tolkien, the Second World War, and the start of the Cold War. Eddings' Dark Prophecy will corrupt if not destroy the world, should it and not the Light Prophecy prevail in the end; McKinley's Damar could be overrun with the demonic armies of the North; in some of Pierce's books, the threat is not only to the political order, but to the whole way of life of Tortall, or to the gods themselves. In nearly all of these stories, even in Kaye's gentle fairy-tale of *The Ordinary Princess*, the heroes take control of their own fate, acting when those around them, older and supposedly wiser, fail to see the danger or to take action against it. Alternately, still more perceptive than their elders, they accept as natural what society condemns, and by standing firm change those around them. In Eddings, where the reverse is true, one can see the security of predestination, the reassurance that strong forces are at work to make sure all turns out as it should – an alternate reaction, possibly, to the same sense of powerlessness to effect change.

Perhaps the most significant development in the fantasy of the eighties, however, was the emergence of the female hero as questing warrior. Harry, Aerin, and Alanna gave girls something they had hungered for: Romance heroes who were women, riding out to save the kingdom and prove themselves. Though some writers of adult fantasy were already writing of similar heroes, it would be the nineties before the idea was common; by the twenty-first century some adult fantasy writers, mostly British, would create worlds in which male and female equality in the martial field was taken for granted by the characters and societies concerned.

XV
The Nineties, part one

By the nineteen-nineties, the uncertainties of the eighties had largely resolved themselves. Society in Great Britain and North America seemed stable and prosperous, the future assured. Nelson Mandela was elected president of South Africa in 1994, a headline which could only have been satire even a decade before. In Europe, East and West Germany were reunited, while the Baltic states were in the process of achieving independence. The Soviet Union under Gorbachev was liberalizing; a popular uprising foiled a hardline coup. The Soviet government fell apart, with Boris Yeltsin emerging as the leader after the Communist Party dissolved.

Not all world affairs were changes for the better. The disintegration of the USSR led to revolts and civil wars in various of its republics. Throughout the decade, there were civil wars along ethnic lines in what had been Yugoslavia and in African countries such as Rwanda. The euphemism 'ethnic cleansing', for forced displacement and genocide, was picked up by the media and used as if it were an acceptable description of such crimes, with no consideration of the implications of accepting the word 'cleansing' as appropriate rather than monstrous in such a context. After the Soviet withdrawal from Afghanistan, a civil war among the various American-armed factions which had fought the Soviets brought the extreme fundamentalist Taliban to power. Iraq invaded Kuwait in 1990, leading to the 1991 American-led Gulf War, a war most memorable for its blow-by-blow media coverage.

However, in Great Britain and North America, where the books under discussion were written, published, and primarily read, society as a whole was affluent, secure, and materialistic. Most people's major concerns were not world affairs, or the future, but their own well-being and material status. Electronic devices became a status symbol – the more you had, the more knowledgeable, up-to-date, and somehow in control you appeared to be. In 1990, academics and university students used desktop computers for writing and research, even if they did not own one themselves, and many businesses were beginning to use them for everything from communications to inventory control, but they were not yet part of the average household. By the middle of the decade, computers were almost as common as televisions, and as the speed of processors increased, people who needed or wanted to be on the cutting edge replaced them every year. Cell phones, fax machines, laptops, and personal organizers with more memory than the computers of 1990, were, by the end of the decade and the millennium, viewed as essential by a vast segment of the population. The internet had grown from a system called ARPANET, created in the seventies by the American DARPA (Defence Advanced Research Projects Agency) as a communications system meant to be invulnerable to nuclear attack through its ability to route messages by multiple paths, and from the similar NSF Net, established by the US National Science Foundation to link universities; internet usage now mushroomed. In the early nineties, university students were the only young people likely to have email addresses; by the end of the decade, email use had spread widely into the general population, until a few years into the twenty-first century, those who lacked email were the exception rather than the norm. Web-based accounts and public access terminals in places such as libraries and schools put email and the internet within the reach of nearly everyone. Elementary school children were routinely taught to use computers, if only to play games and develop co-ordination skills essential for manipulating the mouse, in some cases even before they could read. The World-Wide Web, established in 1990/91 by CERN (Centre Européane de Researche Nucléare) as a means of disseminating and sharing research data using HTML (hypertext mark-up language), became the prime research tool, source of both information and misinformation, for students and the general public.

In the nineties, fantasy for children was less inclined to have an evident focus on some central authorial concern than that of writers of the sixties to eighties (such as Dickinson, L'Engle, Alexander, or Pierce). Although books were written in which modern real-world children encounter ancient magic or supernatural conflicts, they were rarely as popular as, or of the quality of, those by Susan Cooper or Alan Garner. The influence of adult fantasy, now a mature genre in which great attention was paid to the development of detailed and cohesive secondary worlds, affected writing for children. Children's writing returned to epic or Romance themes more and more: quests, undertaken not by a visitor from the 'real' world but by an inhabitant of a secondary world or an imagined past, to save his or her self, nation, or world, with a detailed background of politics, religion, society, and culture, became far more common, though plots involving present-day, real-world heroes swept out of time or place continued their popularity. Traditional heroic fantasy, but in which the characters were animals, influenced perhaps by Richard Adams' non-fantasy *Watership Down*, the adult animal-fantasy *Duncton* books of William Horwood, and most of all by the success of Brian Jacques' *Redwall* series, became very popular. De la Mare's *The Three Mulla-Mulgars* was only about ninety years ahead of its time.

Fantasy remained a genre. People read fantasy and science fiction, or they did not. Though adult fantasy often made it to the best-seller lists, such works, even Tolkien's, were still not regarded as real literature by the 'mainstream' (though contemporary 'literary' writing is as much a genre as any other). However, by the end of the nineties, a combination of several factors had won fantasy more acceptance in the mainstream. The impending release of three movies based on *The Lord of the Rings* may have been one factor in this, but the sudden popularity of two children's fantasy series among adult, and mainstream, readers was the primary cause. Philip Pullman's *Northern Lights* trilogy, and most of all J.K. Rowling's *Harry Potter* (see Chapter XVII), did much to raise the mainstream reader's awareness and even acceptance of fantasy as a genre not for the 'weird', but for everyone.

O.R. Melling (b. 1956)

O.R. Melling (a pseudonym) was born in Ireland and moved to Canada with her family when she was a young child; she is one of ten siblings. She studied philosophy and Celtic studies as an undergraduate at the University of Toronto and obtained an M.A. in medieval history, travelling extensively before eventually returning to live in Bray, Ireland, with her daughter. As G.V. Whelan, Melling is a screenwriter and literary critic.

Melling's fantasies involve modern teens swept into the world of Irish myth and folklore. One of her earliest uses the story of the *Tain Bo Cuailnge* as its background. The *Tain*, like the Welsh *Mabinogion*, is a story from pre-Christian times preserved in medieval manuscript form. It is the story of Maeve of Connaught's invasion of Ulster, defended by the young hero Cuculann, in a war over a bull. In *The Druid's Tune* (1983), Canadian teens Jimmy and Rosemary are sent by their father to stay on their Uncle Patsy's small farm in Ireland. Spying on the strange hired man, Peter Murphy, they are pulled into a world of legend, where they are captured by Maine, Queen Maeve's son, just as the army is preparing for war. Love, battle, friendship, and the attempt to help reunite the several aspects of druid Peter Murphy make an action-filled adventure that is better than most stories of the sort where a journey through time involves modern children in heroic legend or mythology, although it is not as original in conception as Melling's later works.

The Singing Stone (1986) is likewise a journey through time and myth, but unlike the fairly conventional *Druid's Tune*, the main character is, in the end, revealed to have a good reason for her adventures in a mythological time. Kay Warrick has grown up a modern foundling, shuffled from foster home to foster home. Investigating megaliths in Ireland, she finds herself in Bronze Age Ireland, where she befriends Aherne, a young woman of the Tuatha de Danaan, the people of the goddess Danu. Fintan, an ancient mage, sets them the task of finding the four treasures of the Tuatha de Danaan. The young women's search involves them in the invasion of the Gaedil, destined supplanters of the Tuatha de Danaan. The people of Danu leave by means of the four treasures, to become the gods whose stories the Gaedil tell. Kay recognizes that she herself is a mage and a Druid. Aherne remains to marry Amergin, the new king. Fintan reveals to Kay that she is the daughter of her friends Aherne and Amergin, whom he stole, so that she would be able to return to help them in their youth. Like Fintan, Kay can move as she chooses through time. Unlike many stories of this sort, the rationale for Kay's central role in the affairs of another time is made part of the story, not merely an excuse to have a modern character for readers to identify with.

Melling's four-book series *The Chronicles of Faerie* turns from Irish mythology to Ireland's fairy folk-traditions. It gives a further degree of originality to the device of modern young people becoming involved in the hidden world of magic through its romances between fairies and mortals, and through the movement of people from one world to the other, not easily or lightly, but with real loss, danger, and irreversible change. Traditional stories abound in which romantic attachments between fairies and humans draw them from one world to the other, although it is rare for such affairs to have a happy ending. Melling ensures that they do, though not without the necessity of difficult choices and agonizing sacrifices. The first three books were reissued in one volume in 2002 as *The Chronicles of Faerie*; in 2004 all four books were reissued in one volume as *The Golden Book of Faerie* (though the series title remains *The Chronicles of Faerie*).

The first story, *The Hunter's Moon* (1993), has Canadian Gwen and her Irish cousin Findabhair hiking in Ireland, an Ireland in which the human and the fairy worlds coexist as parallel and sometimes intermingled realms. Findabhair is willingly carried off to be the fairy High King Finvarra's bride. Gwen pursues her cousin and the fairies around Ireland, struggling with the temptation to join them herself, arguing with Findabhair over her desire to abandon the mortal world. She learns that it is the year of the Hunter's Moon, when the Great Worm demands a living sacrifice. Gwen, along with new human friends who have a foot in the fairy world, must try to save her cousin, who is to be the sacrifice. Helped by Finvarra, they battle the Worm, but are defeated. The Worm demands Finvarra as his sacrifice instead and the Fairy King accepts this. When dawn comes the others find themselves back in the human world, their wounds healed. There they meet Finvarra, a human fiddler with no memory – the Worm claimed his immortality, and he must embark on a human life with Findabhair. *The Hunter's Moon* was revised for the 2004 reissue, with many episodes expanded, character motivations and interactions made more complicated and realistic, and details added which enrich the story; the prose, too, is more poetic (but never lush or overworked), more vivid and maturely confident, transforming an already good story into an excellent one.

In the second book, *The Summer King* (1999), another Canadian teen, Laurel, goes to Ireland, trying to come to terms with her twin sister Honor's death there in a hang-gliding accident. She discovers that for some, the afterlife and the otherworld may be the same. Honor is caught between the human world and the fairy, and to free her, Laurel must undertake a quest to find the Summer King, who has been missing for seventy years. He is required to light a ritual fire on Midsummer Eve, part of a chain of such fires which keep the human and the fairy worlds connected. Laurel has great difficulty accepting the reality of her mission, but undertakes it none the less. She is accompanied for much of her search by moody, troubled Ian. Fairies of various sorts from Irish traditional lore both help and hinder her, according to the traditional rules in which riddles and ritual play an important role.

The Summer King was imprisoned for shooting the mate of the King of the Eagles. Laurel discovers her friend Ian is an aspect of the Summer King, born as a human and intended to free him. When the two are brought together, they become one, and the Summer King's cruel, angry personality dominates. Only after a great battle and the capture of the Summer King is Laurel able to appeal to Ian to light the bonfire in order to maintain the connection between the worlds of faerie and humanity. She discovers, though, that it was the Summer King who killed her sister. Although the eagles forgive the king and Honor, dead in the mortal world, is free to become High King Midir's queen, Laurel does not forgive, even though Ian is able to overcome the crueller aspects of his nature as the Summer King. When he tries to leave the human world by drowning, Laurel's love wins out and she saves him. A revision of *The Summer King* for a new edition, similar to what was done for the revised edition of *The Hunter's Moon*, is also under way as of 2005.

The Light-Bearer's Daughter (2001) features a younger heroine, eleven-year-old Dana, who is having trouble coming to terms with her musician father's intention to move back to Canada. Honor, the fairy queen, sends Dana to carry a message to Lugh of Wicklow, the fairy king who is to be Midir's táinaiste, the king second in command to him. In return, Dana will be owed her heart's desire, which for her is the mother who disappeared without a trace seven years before. In the human world, a wood called Glen of the Downs is threatened by loggers and protected by activists; this is the darkness of which Dana must warn Lugh, as well as telling him of his new position. Along the way she learns about life, death, and personal darkness from boggles, a wolf, and a saint.

Dana succeeds in reaching Lugh and delivering her message. She is told the story of Lugh's wife, who was enchanted by a human musician's playing and forgot her fairy life to live with him and bear his child. Lugh believes Dana will be able to find his wife Edane, her mother, where he cannot. Edane, the Light-Bearer, is needed by the fairy realm to fight the darkness that is coming, the destruction of the Glen of the Downs, home to natural and fairy creatures. Dana's acceptance of herself restores light to her mother, literally and metaphorically, and light saves the woods. Lugh and his lost wife are reunited, while Dana is reconciled to the move to Canada, which now includes her father's fiancée, Aradhana.

The fourth novel, *The Book of Dreams* (2003) features a sullen, rebellious teenage Dana in Canada. Although other fantasy writers, most notably Charles de Lint, have brought aboriginal mythology into the landscape of Canadian fantasy, Melling's blending of immigrant and Native Canadian mythologies is outstanding in its successful integration of many traditions into a continuum of myth and folklore rooted in the natural and urban landscapes of Canada. Dana's quest to prevent servants of a nihilistic force that hates all life from severing the worlds of humanity and faerie (which will destroy both), takes her from coast to coast to coast, from Atlantic to Pacific to the Arctic. Dana resents having had to move to Canada, away from fairy-entwined Ireland, and to save Faerie she is forced to discover the magic inherent to Canada's landscape and peoples.

The Irish fairy lore at the heart of Melling's writing remains prominent, but Quebecois folklore, in the Loup Garou, a man cursed with wolf's shape, and the demon-propelled flying canoe that crashes when the name of God is called upon, are given a new life in Jean, Dana's werewolf boyfriend, and his spirit-canoe. There are Chinese guardian dragons in Toronto's Chinatown, the Hindu god Ganesh appears, the giant Fingal is living in

Cape Breton (a nod to the Stan Rogers song 'The Giant', which established him there) and is romancing the British sea-spirit Mother Carey. There are hard-partying goblins in Cape Breton, trolls in a parallel system of tunnels beneath Toronto's subway, and clans of fairies who emigrated with the Irish and are as Canadian as anyone else whose ancestors came over one or two centuries ago. Of central importance are the Old Ones, who are the spirits honoured by the aboriginal peoples. These are the great powers in the land called Turtle Island, the New World. There are not only ancient spirits out of Inuit and other native mythologies, but a modern Cree shaman and passing aboriginal heroes who might be ordinary men or might be semi-supernatural champions, caught between the mortal and the supernatural world, just as Dana and Jean are. Dana's quest for the Book of Dreams and the re-opening of the portals between the human world and Faerie takes her into the history of the human side of her family and requires, in the end, great sacrifice on the part of Dana and Jean. It returns to Melling's recurring theme, that the price for involvement in the Otherworld can be high, though the cost of ignoring it can be catastrophic. It is odd, and regrettable, that *The Book of Dreams* was not even shortlisted for the Governor-General's Award; it certainly deserved to be a contender.

The Chronicles of Faerie surpasses Melling's earlier works in innovation, in that the stories return to a traditional foundation for the intersection of the real and the imagined worlds – the drawing of humans into the fairy otherworld – and create something entirely new. Numerous stories send modern children through time or to take part in the action of familiar legend; fewer use a traditional folklore framework for human and magical interaction. Although the four novels are not a serial and each story can be read without reference to the others, they are connected both thematically and through overlapping characters. All are set in the present, draw in both Canadian and Irish characters, and feature girls as their heroes, setting off on quests in which success or failure has not only personal consequences, but ramifications for mortal and fairy worlds as well. All stress acceptance and reconciliation; good and evil, light and darkness, are not external abstracts, but are found within oneself.

Melling evokes the Irish landscape in loving detail. Her characters, both human and fairy, remain credible and true to their natures. Her teens are realistic and likeable people who embark on their adventures with determination and common sense. Melling shows them risking all that matters to them for what they see as a greater good, and in the process saving or finding the one they first set out for. They also gain a greater understanding of themselves and find friendship, love, and a renewed sense of family. Melling's fairies, wise and capricious, are not human in their motivations and desires and do not act to benefit either the human world or humans. They can be quite callous in their use of human agents, making any kindness or regard, as in all the traditional lore, a great boon, rather than something humans have the right to expect. Melling shows a particular skill for portraying the alien world-view of the fairies as both enticing and frightening to her human protagonists, keeping it consistent with the Irish fairy tradition that has them at once grand and comic, glamorous and grotesque.

Tanith Lee (b. 1947)

Tanith Lee was born in London and worked at a number of jobs, including waitressing and as a library assistant, before finding success as a writer. Her first books, published in the early seventies, were children's fantasy. In 1975, her first adult fantasy, *The Birthgrave*, was published. Lee spent most of the seventies and eighties as a highly-regarded writer for adults, known for an unconventional and creative fantasy. In the nineties, she created some exceptional books for teens, bringing her mature style to young adult books. She lives in Sussex with her husband, author John Kaiine.

Lee's early works for children and teens include stories both comic and serious. *The Dragon Hoard* (1971) is a heroic quest in search of a dragon's treasure, but though it goes through all the conventional motions, it does so with a whimsy that inverts the patterns of such stories. The fifty princes who set out to seek the treasure are naive and not particularly brave or intelligent, the monsters are generally amiable and misunderstood, and even the hero Jasleth blunders through mostly by being kind and lucky. The dragon, when they find it, is away at the dentist, the hoard unguarded. The most humorous element in the story is the wicked enchantress Maligna, whose birthday curse on Jasleth and his twin sister starts the whole adventure. Maligna has two postman-chasing wolves, a peevish toad familiar, and an ongoing feud with the serpent-drawn, fiery chariot for hire company. *The Dragon Hoard* is a light and frothy work, amusing but neither deep nor subtle. *Princess Hynchatti and Some Other Surprises* (1972) is a collection of short stories about questing princes and princesses in an equally light and humorous fairy-tale vein.

In *Prince on a White Horse* (1982), for older readers than *Hoard*, there is a similar lightness of tone in the narrative, but the story is not mere parody. A nameless prince finds himself in a place with no name. After being sent by Gemael the Red to kill a dragon, he learns he is the destined Deliverer who will save this illogical world from the Nulgrave that has broken through to devour it all into nothingness. The Nulgrave is despair, he learns. He revives a number of despairing people, triumphs over the Nulgrave by defying and denying it, and remembers that he is no prince at all, but an old man from our world, alone, poor, and now, in his world, dead. He sets out to restore the new world in which he has found himself by planting and building, with Gemael as his Lady. Although it wanders into the sort of word-silliness of which Lee is very fond, with its Beezles and Bezzles, *Prince on a White Horse* also has moments meant to provoke more serious thought, even offering themselves to outright allegorical readings, as when the prince, confronting the Nulgrave, persists in denying his own fear, fending off despair's power with humour and simple refusal to surrender to it.

East of Midnight (1977) is an example of Lee's more serious young adult fantasy of this period. The mind or soul of the runaway slave Dekteon is sent by his double, the sorcerer Zaister, into Zaister's body and world, switched with Zaister's own essence. In Zaister's world, women are the dominant sex. Zaister is the consort of the female king, Izvire, who represents the moon-goddess; the consort is sacrificed very five years. Dekteon has only a short time left until his sacrifice.

Unlike Zaister, Dekteon is not in awe of women. He is strong, a fighter, intelligent, and he also has gained Zaister's memories and knowledge of sorcery. By sorcery he sees Zaister's sufferings in the mines; Zaister, in Dekteon's body, has lost most of the sorcerous skills he counted on to save him from the slave's fate.

Dekteon sends one of the magical-mechanical servants, a Pallid, to save the dying Zaister. On the day of the sacrifice, Dekteon substitutes a disguised Pallid; Zaister never thought of actually defying the need for a sacrifice, only of finding someone else to die. After some effort, Dekteon persuades Zaister of his own power to effect change. The two return to their own bodies and their own worlds, but each retains many attributes of the other. Zaister, entering the city on the day the king is supposed to wed her new consort, begins a renewed relationship with his wife and daughter and an upheaval in the religion of the country. Dekteon, no longer a mere uneducated slave, is able to escape his past and start a new life in a new country.

Science fiction and fantasy examining gender roles was common in the seventies and early to mid eighties, a time when the feminism of the sixties and seventies had made such issues part of popular awareness. *East of Midnight* is part of that tradition, offering a clear-cut reversal of roles in a world where women rule and do not cry, and men never believe their own talents and inner strength equal to women's. Gender issues, though, are not the dominant theme. As in most of Lee's writing, that is the discovery of self and the search for personal fulfilment.

Two series which Lee wrote in the nineties were perhaps more widely read than her seventies young adult works like *East of Midnight*, not because her type of story had changed, but because the idea of what young adult fantasy could be had expanded. Her convoluted plots, *Oz*-like magic-driven mechanics, complicated personal relationships and psychology, and troubled but often redeemable families, were by the nineties less strange to the average teen reader; stories of her type had had time to become familiar.

The young adult novels *Black Unicorn* (1991), *Gold Unicorn* (1994), and *Red Unicorn* (1997) are the story of Tanaquil, who is the daughter of the erratic sorceress Jaive. They live in a large fortress in the desert, Jaive utterly involved in her magical experiments, Tanaquil bored and frustrated. She appears to have no magical skill, only a knack for fixing things. In the first book, Tanaquil is led by one of the peeves – cat-sized desert animals that live in and around the fortress and have begun to talk due to leakages of magic – to the bones of a long-dead unicorn. Tanaquil reassembles the skeleton, but it comes to life. She and the peeve follow it to Sea City, where she is befriended by Lizra, daughter of the city's ruler, Prince Zorander. Tanaquil discovers that Zorander is the father who abandoned her mother, and Lizra her half-sister. Tanaquil learns that the black unicorn she restored to life needs her to repair the gate through which it can return to its own world, a Perfect World, and that her ability to mend anything is a magical talent. She restores the gate for the unicorn and visits the Perfect World beyond, where lions do lie down with lambs. Horrified to discover that even her footprints blight the world, she returns home and destroys the gate.

In *Gold Unicorn*, Tanaquil is on her way back to her mother's fortress after a year's travelling. Tanaquil is captured by mercenaries in the service of the empress Veriam, who is conquering the world; Veriam turns out to be Tanaquil's half-sister Lizra. The empress' giant mechanical, steam-driven, gold-plated unicorn, a weapon of fear, does not work. Tanaquil is compelled to make it function and succeeds in doing so. During an attack by mousps (flying crosses between mice and wasps created by the magician Worabex), Lizra, Tanaquil, the peeve, and the mercenary commander Honj, who is Lizra's lover, fall into another world.

The gold unicorn, symbol of war, is a gate to a hell of unending war fought by creatures who rise from their graves every morning to fight again. Trapped there, Tanaquil and her companions escape only when Lizra allows herself to be courted by its demon-like emperor, winning permission to leave with skills of flattery and seeming-acquiescence she learned manipulating her cold, stupid, and proud father. By the end Tanaquil realizes that she and Honj have fallen in love. Lizra's sojourn in hell has given her a distaste for war and she gives up plans for further conquest. Inside the cold empress' shell, Lizra is still the lonely sister Tanaquil came to love, and she realizes that she cannot take Honj from her.

In *Red Unicorn* Tanaquil is back at the desert fortress, finding it less easy to resign herself to the loss of love than she hoped. She is miserable, while her mother and the magician Worabex are giddily in love and even the peeve has found a mate. Knocked out by a waterspout when Jaive and Worabex try to build a garden in the desert, Tanaquil finds herself in a green-skied world where no-one eats meat and giant wolf-like squirrels waylay travellers for nuts. Tanaquil is the double of Princess Ta-nakil, a sorceress around whom things often fall apart or ex-plode. The ruler is her sister, Sulkana Liliam, double of Lizra. And naturally, Liliam is supposed to marry Honj's double, the courtier Jharn, who loves Tanakil. Tanaquil's mending-sorcery does not come into play here, but she discovers she is nearly all-powerful and can do any magic she thinks of: walking through walls, changing her appearance, becoming invisible. Tanaquil and the peeve set out to prevent Tanakil's plan to poison her sis-ter, but in the end Tanakil herself stops Liliam drinking the poi-soned tea.

Tanaquil is able to consider her own life, seeing it reflected in this inverted world, and offers Tanakil advice. She must do the simple, straightforward thing, and tell Liliam about herself and Jharn. Liliam, Tanaquil has seen, actually loves another. Having offered Tanakil a better way to confront her problems, Tanaquil understands what the peeve has been trying to tell her: she is in-side a world of her own mind. She is actually lying insensible in bed, her mother, Worabex, and even her camel keeping anxious watch. Returning is easy, once she realizes it. Tanaquil knows she must take her own advice, and talk to Honj. She sets out to find him, and meets him coming to find her, summoned by a letter from Worabex. Word that Tanaquil was seriously ill spurred Honj to tell Lizra his true feelings, which relieved the empress, as she wanted to make a marriage alliance with an overseas king, the double of Liliam's true love, but did not want to hurt Honj by rejecting him. Freedom and love are possible for them all, because Tanaquil finally acted, not out of misery or anger, but seeking happiness and honest communication.

These are an outstanding example of young adult fantasy, funny, moving, inventive, and thought-provoking. Tanaquil's prickly and mutually frustrating relationship with her mother is utterly believable, as is her cautious love of the imperious half-sister she discovers. It takes her the course of three books to re-alize her mother does love her, and that long to recognize Jaive as a person needing love and friendship, as well. The peeve grows and changes too. From his initial demands for bones, through his growing vocabulary and ability to think, his convic-tion that 'aubergine' is a swear-word, his gleeful fights with as-sorted magical snakes, tomatoes, and fleas, he is more than a comic sidekick. His growing comprehension of the world echoes Tanaquil's; his childlike delight in the world is something she needs to remember to share.

Lee's other popular series of this era was the four-book *Wolf Tower* sequence, or as it was called in American editions, the *Claidi Journals*. The books, the first three of which were issued under different titles in the United States, are *Law of the Wolf Tower* (1998; US: *Wolf Tower*), *Wolf Star Rise* (2000; US: *Wolf Star*), *Queen of the Wolves* (2001; US: *Wolf Queen*), and *Wolf Wing* (2002). As in the *Unicorn* series, the hero is a teenage girl living in an isolated enclave surrounded by desert, a girl discontented with her lot but apparently powerless to alter it until an intrusion from outside, in the former series the fossil unicorn bones, in this a stranger, proves the catalyst for change.

In *Law of the Wolf Tower*, Claidi is maid to a cruel mistress in the House, a walled palace and garden in the desert called the Waste. The royalty spend all day in idleness broken by meaningless rituals, while slaves and servants do all the work. One day the House guards shoot down an approaching balloon and the attractive balloonist, Nemian, is imprisoned. The most ancient Old Lady of the house, to whom he was bringing a message, arranges his escape with Claidi. In her difficult journey across the desert Claidi falls in love with Nemian, but finds herself disillusioned almost at the same time. Nemian is self-absorbed, condescending, and alternately dismissive and ingratiating. Claidi is saved from being sacrificed in a village of bird-worshippers by people she views as bandits, a band of nomadic Hulta led by Argul, to whom she is very attracted.

Nemian and Claidi travel with the Hulta for a time, but when Argul is about to propose marriage, Nemian begs Claidi to come to his city with him, and his desperation persuades her. She realizes this is a mistake at once. The City is ruled by the family of Wolf Tower, which administers the bizarre Law. Nemian is already married and has no interest in Claidi; the Law demanded he bring her. Claidi is believed to be heir to an important position in the city. Argul and his friends rescue her, but first Claidi tries to destroy the dice-determined cruel Law of the City, forcing it to find a new way of life.

Wolf Star Rise begins as Claidi is kidnapped by balloon on her wedding day. She eventually ends up at a fantastical house, in an equally fantastic jungle across the sea. The rooms of the vast house move around, not magically but mechanically; one can be trapped in a room with no exit for days, or halfway up a stair when it suddenly breaks in two and goes whirling away. A trek to find the library becomes a five-day expedition, with supplies brought along on a cat-drawn sled. The only inhabitant is the moody young man Venn and his mechanical and genetically/magically engineered servants and friends, created, like the house and the jungle, which contains natural, mechanical, and engineered beasts, by his mother Ustareth, an exile from Wolf Tower. She is, under the name Zeera, Argul's dead magician mother. Claidi escapes back to Argul in the giant flying Wolf Star, an intelligent sky-ship called Yinyay, built by Ustareth.

In *Queen of the Wolves*, the Hulta have been led to believe that Claidi ran back to Nemian and the City, Argul has gone looking for her, and Claidi is not welcome among the nomads she thought were to be her new family. She sets out to find Argul, who has learned about his Wolf Tower ancestry. Claidi is taken prisoner by the ruler of Raven Tower, Princess Twilight Star. Twilight intends a breeding programme to create a super human, a 'queen of the wolves'. Argul and Claidi flee this fate.

Although they marry and can live safely in the flying tower or sky-ship Yinyay, in *Wolf Wing* their new life is less happy than they expected; Claidi believes Argul gave up something he needed, leadership of the Hulta, for her, and a distance grows between them. They decide to rescue Claidi's fellow slaves from the House, but find there has been a revolt and a new social order. Claidi, Argul, her friend Dengwi, Venn, Twilight's daughter Winter and her bodyguard Ngarbo are summoned to a continent inhabited by Ustareth, who is not dead after all. The individual journeys of the characters are a series of tests, but also an exploration of the sort of fantastic landscape Lee obviously loves creating. Sausage and mutton chop trees feed Claidi's dog, sandstorms deposit picnics assembled from atoms, and when a river threatens to drown them and flowers to tie them in its path, Claidi and Argul both discover great inherent powers and learn something about themselves and their relationship. The three couples are told by the scientist-magician that they are humans evolving new powers through nature, not engineering. Claidi is determined that whatever magician-like powers she may have, she must keep her connection to the things that matter in life. Her security in herself is symbolized by the resolution of the uncertainty over her name, which other characters keep assuming to be a shortened form of various names, or not to belong to her at all. Ustareth tells her that 'Claidi' on its own is an ancient word of that world, meaning a wolf on the wing.

The *Wolf Tower* books are written as a journal, which seems incongruous at first for a story of so much action, adventure, and mystery, but the style quickly comes to feel natural. Claidi writes in her stolen book whenever a moment of peace allows, and thus the first person narrative has an immediacy that would be more artificial if it were a story she was telling after it was all over. At the point when each episode is recorded, she does not know its import or connection to what will come. The journal itself becomes part of the plot, as various people read it, forge lying copies of it to mislead, and bug it to track her. The story contains many of the same motifs as the *Unicorn* trilogy: a hero struggling to find her own purpose in life, isolated castles in the desert, law-bound communities, living mechanical creatures, magical hybrid plants and animals, and even the impulse towards vegetarianism, a world where nothing has to kill to survive. The story in it does not, like so many, end with the heroes' marriage, as though that were the end of change and growth, but becomes in part an examination of settling into permanent partnership, and all the awkwardness and uneasiness, the difficulties and discoveries and compromises, that go with married life.

Lee creates worlds of exuberant strangeness, which are more in the tradition of L. Frank Baum's *Oz* than of anything else, a difficult approach to serious world-building and one which can make the reader's belief in the story harder to sustain. Lee succeeds, though, due to the internal consistency and attention to detail, the very realism of the whimsically unnatural she describes. The artificial creations and living mechanisms of her worlds are often a result of magic or futuristic science, or an art that is a blurring of the distinction between the two; this, again, recalls Baum, for whom magic and technology were, in *Oz*, two sides of the same coin. The psychological plausibility of Lee's characters reinforces the reality of the worlds in which they move. In all of Lee's books, the discovery of one's self is the thematic centre of the story, without any sacrifice of external conflict and drama, a combination which should have lasting appeal to teens and older children.

Patricia C. Wrede (b. 1953)

Wrede, the eldest of five siblings, was born in Chicago and studied biology at Carleton College in Minnesota. She received an M.B.A. from the University of Minnesota and worked as an accountant and financial analyst. Her first book, *Shadow Magic*, came out in 1982 and she began writing adult and young adult or children's fantasy full-time in 1985.

Wrede's *Enchanted Forest Chronicles* are in the tradition of Lang's *Pantouflia* books, Milne's *Once on a Time*, and Kaye's *The Ordinary Princess*. They play with the conventions of fairy-tales, but are not mere spoof of an established form; they tell a good story while having fun with an understood set of rules. The first book, *Dealing With Dragons* (1990), introduces Cimorene, a most improper princess with an interest in fencing, Latin, magic, and cooking. To avoid an arranged marriage, she volunteers to become the dragon Kazul's princess – having a princess to do one's cooking and cleaning is a status symbol among dragons. In between persuading princes she does not need to be rescued, Cimorene has a wonderful time. All is not well among the dragons, though. The dragon Woraug is plotting a coup with the help of two wizards, Zemenar and Antorell. He poisons the King of the Dragons, and with the wizards' help, plans to rig the contest by which the next king is chosen. In return, the wizards will be allowed unlimited access to some magical caves – wizards have no magic of their own, but store it in their staffs, which can suck the magic out of naturally magical things, like dragons and the Enchanted Forest. Cimorene and her friend Princess Alianora discover the plot; they also find a method of temporarily melting wizards *à la* Dorothy, which comes in handy. They foil the wizards and Woraug, Kazul becomes the next King of the Dragons (a title not determined by gender), Alianora marries a questing prince whom the two princesses rescued along the way, and Cimorene stays with Kazul as her Royal Cook and Librarian.

The next two books, *Searching for Dragons* (1991) and *Calling on Dragons* (1993) continue Cimorene's adventures. In the course of the second, the wizards attack the Enchanted Forest and kidnap Kazul. Mendanbar, King of the Enchanted Forest, comes looking for Kazul to get advice. After helping Cimorene unblock a drain with his magic sword, he joins her in a search for Kazul, once they borrow a malfunctioning flying carpet from a giant. Other characters encountered are a royal uncle who is a member of the men's auxiliary of the wicked stepmothers' society, Telemain the didactic magician, and the fire-witch Morwen and her cats. The wizards are defeated, Kazul rescued, and Cimorene and Mendanbar, having fallen in love, have a grand royal wedding, though Mendanbar keeps muttering that it would be easier to elope.

In the third book the wizards steal Mendanbar's enchanted sword, wrongly believing that its loss will enable them to absorb all the forest's magic. While the king remains behind to protect the forest, the pregnant Cimorene, Kazul, Morwen, and Telemain go in search of the sword. The entire Society of Wizards attacks the castle and seals the king inside. There is a spell on the king that can only be broken by the enchanted sword, which can only be used by the true heir of the kings. As he or she has not been born yet, they have a while to wait.

Talking to Dragons (1993) is told in the first person by Daystar, son of Cimorene. He knows nothing of his parents' history, not even his father's name. Cimorene has raised him in a cottage on the edge of the Enchanted Forest with all the proper things a hero needs: common sense, good manners, and an understanding of how fairy-tales work. When he is sixteen, she gives him the sword and sends him into the forest. After many adventures, and having acquired the hero's necessary band of comrades, Daystar reaches the castle, frees his father, and is reunited with both parents, while the king's allies defeat the wizards in a great battle.

Wrede plays with the traditions and sometimes the clichés of fantasy and fairy-tales, but never derisively. Those traditions are conformed to rigorously or turned on their heads, either way with great comic effect. A Rumpelstiltskin-type dwarf, for instance, is stuck with a house full of the children he has carried off, the giant and his wife are plagued by young men who show up, have a meal, and steal all their harps, a kindly but officially wicked uncle tries to lose a young prince in the forest with that nephew's eager assistance, and dragons prefer their princesses to cook Cherries Jubilee rather than serve as the entrées themselves. The stories are fast-paced adventures and are very well-written. The logic of the magic of the Enchanted Forest and the creatures that live in and around it is consistently and thoroughly worked out. Although characterisation, especially for the supporting cast, is shallow, as is often the case in a genre-spoof which presents character in terms of the archetypes of that genre, the main characters are engaging and full of life. The plots have a nice degree of complexity in the assorted adventures the heroes encounter as they pursue the main objective of their quests. What makes these outstanding most of all is their humour; Wrede writes good comedy, in both character and event.

Wrede has also written two children's or young adult fantasies set in a Regency England which has a Royal College of Wizards to research and oversee magic, the study of magic offered at Oxford and Cambridge, and a Ministry of Wizardry, which also undertakes some foreign service functions, as part of the government. *Mairelon the Magician* (1991) tells the story of Kim, a girl living on the streets of London as a thief. Kim is disguised as a boy and fears nothing so much as ending up in the brothels, once she becomes too old to pass as male. She is hired to break into a travelling magician's caravan and report on its contents. 'Mairelon the Magician' is not the marketplace entertainer he appears, but a real magician, a wealthy gentleman and former English agent in France, Richard Merrill. Kim is caught, but wins her captor's trust and joins Mairelon and his manservant Hunch in unravelling a plot involving some missing magical artefacts stolen from the College. Numerous other people are after the Saltash Bowl, which Mairelon has already recovered, and the still-missing Platter, including a criminal master known to and feared by Kim, a Bow Street Runner, and an organisation of harmless and boisterous would-be druids, who complicate the already convoluted plots, thefts, and counter-thefts of the several fake replicas of the Platter that are circulating. There are burglaries, an elopement, an incompetent highwayman, a murder, and a potentially deadly spell foiled by Kim before all is sorted out. Kim is discovered to have a natural talent for wizardry and is adopted by Mairelon as his ward, ending her days of poverty and fear.

In *The Magician's Ward* (1997) a year has passed. Kim is

making great progress in her studies of proper English and literacy, as well as all the other things necessary to becoming a wizard and a lady. Mairelon's very proper aunt, Mrs. Lowe, is determined to turn Kim into an acceptable young lady and find her a husband. His more flamboyant wizard mother decides that she needs more than that: Kim must have a coming-out Season to be presented to Society. The agony of paying calls and having dresses fitted is enlivened by her continued studies and a bungled burglary of their library. Kim and Mairelon investigate the mystery and begin to uncover a far worse crime. Mannering, a non-wizard, has found a way to link wizards in a spell which allows him to control and use their magic, but which can cause them to lose their minds as a result. Mairelon falls victim to Mannering. Kim, with some help from friends and unexpected allies, captures Mannering and saves the minds of Mairelon and the other wizards caught in the spell. Along the way, she realizes she loves Mairelon, the only man who sees her as herself. As the Royal College begins the delicate business of undoing Mannering's spell, Mairelon's powers are restored and Kim is sentenced to the grim task of shopping for a bridal wardrobe.

Wrede's two books about Kim and Mairelon are as much mystery as they are fantasy, and as mysteries, they are equally well done. The suspense is sustained throughout, while enough information is uncovered by Kim to give a satisfying sense of progress being made, even as the problem she must solve becomes more complex. The schemes of the various villains are always credible within the context of the story, as are the various false leads and tangents without which no mystery novel is enjoyable. Wrede's strength as a comic writer is apparent, though here it is more a comedy of character and contrast than the parody of genre conventions so evident in the *Enchanted Forest* books. The fantasy element itself, a ritualized magic of formal spells and long study, is well woven into the historical setting, which is ably portrayed by Wrede. The underworld slang used by Kim can be deciphered from the context and should not deter the average young fantasy reader, who is usually willing to embrace a new 'technical' terminology along with a new world. The books are also a rags-to-riches love story made more satisfying by the evolution of the teacher-guardian and student-ward relationship into a trusting friendship on both sides, before romance ever enters the picture.

The magical Regency world of the *Mairelon* stories actually appeared first in *Sorcery and Cecelia* (1988), co-written by Wrede and her friend Caroline Stevermer. Although an adult book at its first publication, *Sorcery and Cecelia* was reissued in 2003 with its full title, *Sorcery and Cecelia or The Enchanted Chocolate Pot: Being the Correspondence of Two Young Ladies of Quality Regarding Various Magical Scandals in London and the Country*, as a young adult book. This epistolary novel (i.e. written in the form of letters) began as a game: Wrede, as Cecelia, and Stevermer, as her cousin Kate, began exchanging letters in character, building the world and the plot as they went. According to their afterword, they did not plan out any of the details in advance and kept surprising one another with developments, although afterwards, when they realized they had created a novel, they edited, tidied, and worked out the chronology of events more carefully. Both authors succeed in giving their 'young lady of quality' an authentic-sounding manner in her letters. Kate, in London in the spring and summer of 1817, and her cousin Cecelia, left behind in the country, each encounter mysterious and possibly sinister intrigues, which only gradually are discovered to have a connection. Kate, mistaken by a mysterious, murderous woman for a male wizard in disguise, narrowly avoids death by chocolate pot, while Cecelia, trying to learn magic without her aunt's knowledge, discovers a neighbour is involved in evil and illegal branches of magic. As this novel owes something to the tradition of Jane Austen and those who later wrote romance novels set in her era, romantic entanglements also form an important part of the plot. An innocent girl is the focus of a charm that renders her irresistible to men; Kate enters into an engagement of convenience with a wizard they call 'the Mysterious Marquis', who is the subject of a conspiracy aimed at the stealing of his magic and vengeful murder; Cecelia is suspected by the Marquis' elegant and attractive friend of being an agent of his enemies. A sequel, *The Grand Tour* (2004), relates, through diary entries, another tale of magical conspiracy foiled, as Cecelia and Kate honeymoon on the continent with the husbands who provided the romantic interest in the first book. *Sorcery and Cecelia* displays Wrede's, and Stevermer's, talent for having fun with a genre's conventions, here, the twentieth-century 'Regency romance' novel. However, it is also a satisfying mystery set in a well-conceived and consistently portrayed alternate world. The slow unfolding of the plot, and the (realistic) plethora of friends and neighbours who find their way into the letters and only gradually take on identity for the audience, make this a book less likely to hold the attention of younger readers, even those who may have read and enjoyed Wrede's two Maire-lon books with the same setting, but its appeal to teens and adults is an enduring one. Caroline Stevermer has also written two young adult fantasies, *A College of Magics* (1994) and *A Scholar of Magics* (2004), set in a magic-rich alternate version of our own world at the end of the nineteenth century.

Wrede's characters are a particular strength of her books. They are not often complex and rarely face any great internal conflicts; their trials lie outside themselves. They are consistently believable: funny, self-aware, confident, curious, generous to those around them, and determined to do what is right to resolve situations where the danger is not to themselves, but to others, and from which they could easily walk away without becoming involved.

Robin Jarvis (b. 1963)

Jarvis was born in Liverpool; he studied graphic design and worked as an illustrator and designer of characters for television and advertising. His first books, the *Deptford Mice* trilogy, grew out of drawings of cartoonish mouse characters. The novels contain his own illustrations, a pleasing exception to the current trend away from including illustrations in children's novels.

The Dark Portal (1989) is the first in the *Deptford Mice* trilogy. Its main characters are Audrey Brown, a young mouse, and her friends and family. They live in an abandoned house, which has in its cellar the dreaded Grill letting on to the sewers. The story begins with Audrey's father's death. An evil force draws him through the Grill into the sewers, where he is captured and murdered, a sacrificial victim offered to their god Jupiter by the sewer rats. The rat fortune-teller Madame Akkikuyu has a vision in which Audrey destroys Jupiter, so Jupiter sets out to capture her. This is facilitated by Audrey, her brother Arthur, and her friends all running around the sewers looking for, at various times, the dead Mr. Brown, Audrey's 'mousebrass' talisman, and one another. They are captured, fight their way to freedom, and return to the house, always missing one or two of their party. Prophetic bats do their part to move things along, making dire warnings to which no-one pays much attention and introducing the country field-mouse, Twit, to Thomas Triton, the retired midshipmouse, who aids in the final battle. Audrey is captured by Madame Akkikuyu and taken for sacrifice. Jupiter, a grotesque, fire-breathing cat, is destroyed by Audrey's 'mousebrass', a talisman given each mouse when they reach adulthood. Hers is the anti-cat charm, given to her by the mouse god of spring and summer himself. Audrey throws it at Jupiter, who is knocked into the sewers and drowned by the spirits of his victims.

The Crystal Prison (1989) carries on immediately from *The Dark Portal*. Audrey's friend Oswald lies sick and dying from his sufferings in the sewers. The squirrel Starwife, an ancient and autocratic seer, summons Audrey and orders her to take the amnesiac Madame Akkikuyu into the country and live with her for the rest of the rat's life, to keep her from returning to evil. Audrey refuses, but the Starwife leaves her no choice, offering a cure for Oswald, with Audrey's compliance as the price. Oswald is cured, and Audrey, her brother Arthur, Akkikuyu, and field-mouse Twit travel to Twit's home field of Fennywolde. There, Akkikuyu wins the respect of the field-mice, while Audrey is regarded with suspicion by a religious fanatic.

The corn dolly Audrey makes for a celebration is destroyed by the Calvinist-like Isaac Nettle, but Madame Akkikuyu repairs it and gives it life by magic, guided by the tattoo in her ear, who calls himself Nicodemus. Akkikuyu, feeling rejected by Audrey, who refuses to let her share her sleeping-nest, follows Nicodemus' promptings back into evil ways, murdering birds for sorcery. The corn dolly begins stalking and murdering young mice, and Audrey is blamed. Though she is saved from hanging, Nicodemus still wants a sacrifice. Akkikuyu, glad the object of her obsession has been spared, happily plans to sacrifice another mouse girl. When the rat discovers that her tattoo is actually the spirit of Jupiter, planning to return to the world in her body, she flings herself into the waiting bonfire. The ritual is nevertheless completed and Jupiter's spirit returns, imprisoned in Akkikuyu's fortune-telling crystal. With the rat dead, Audrey is free to return to the city, but when a field-mouse breaks the crystal, Jupiter is freed, setting the scene for the conclusion of the trilogy, *The Final Reckoning* (1991), in which Jupiter's desire for revenge against the mice threatens the world with an unending winter. It contains the same degree of horror in the details of the story, the vicious and power-hungry evil on the part of the villain, and the combined helplessness and defiance on the part of the mice, which characterize the first two books.

A second trilogy, the *Deptford Histories*, continues to build the Deptford world. *The Alchymist's Cat* (1991) gives Jupiter's seventeenth-century origins. *The Oaken Throne* (1993) tells of war and betrayal among the squirrels, while *Thomas* (1995) relates an early adventure of Thomas Triton the midshipmouse and a conflict with worshippers of an evil snake. The *Deptford Mouselets* series follows, beginning with *Fleabee's Fortune* (2004), a story about the rats. Among other fantasy series by Jarvis are *The Wyrd Museum* and *The Whitby Witches*, each of which runs for several books and is similar to the *Deptford* series in pitting young people against evil forces, although the protagonists in these are human.

Jarvis' style is rich in descriptive detail, both charming and gruesome. His mouse societies are thoroughly realized. They have a religion that gives their communities cohesion, but which is also the subject of differing interpretations and even the cause of division. Their seasonal rituals are not only a factor in the creation of a believable reality, but become important parts of the story, demonstrating the values inherent in the way of life threatened by both Jupiter's lust for domination and Isaac Nettle's joyless interpretation of the Green Mouse.

As animal fantasy, the *Deptford Mice* books are rather different in approach from the stories of Jacques' *Redwall* (see Chapter XIV) or of Garry Kilworth's *Welkin* (XVI). Where Jacques created a medieval society of animals in which humans are never mentioned, even if they do exist, and Kilworth incorporated humans into his medieval and Victorian animal worlds, Jarvis' mouse, rat, and squirrel societies exist in modern and past England, living under and off of an unwitting human population. They are also, unlike *Redwall* or *Welkin*, less heroic fantasy than 'dark' fantasy, fantasy heavily imbued with the gothic or horror tradition. The overall atmosphere is one of fear-filled darkness where secret powers strive for dominance over the innocent. There is no ancient cosmological conflict enacted between rat and mouse gods as there might be in a traditional fantasy where divinities take a hand. Jupiter does not seem to have any desire to impose a new order on the world, and is not even one of the traditional rat gods, but a new one. He is motivated by greed, cruelty, and destruction for their own sakes. Acts of courage and self-sacrifice defeat him, and he is given renewed power by greed, self-interest, and ignorance. The heroes all exemplify the virtues needed to resist such a force. Though they themselves bicker and are sometimes selfish and thoughtlessly cruel, they risk their lives and make great sacrifices for their friends and their people.

Jarvis' *Deptford* stories are very graphic in their portrayal of violence and death. There is such a quantity of both that after a time, it begins to seem as though the intent is merely to shock for the sake of shocking; death loses any emotional impact, becoming mere physical gruesomeness. Characters are introduced only to provide bodies, a habit of horror movies and second-rate mysteries. There is no value placed on the lives that are lost, either for the characters who must endure suffering, loss, and death, or for the readers.

A disturbing aspect of *The Crystal Prison* is the suggestion that living with Akkikuyu in the country for the rest of her life is the right thing to do, the thing Audrey should do to be a good person. Through Akkikuyu's insistence on sharing Audrey's sleeping nest and the continual identification of Audrey's enforced friendship and her innocence with Akkikuyu's own youthful love affairs in the rat's memories, Akkikuyu's possessiveness and jealousy of Audrey takes on a tinge of sexuality disturbing in a relationship the young mouse has forced upon her. If this were a situation to be questioned and overcome by the heroes it would be a different matter; it becomes troubling because the Starwife's 'wisdom' in demanding this of Audrey, or her right to do so, is never questioned by anyone but Audrey, who appears 'wrong' and selfish for doing so. It is Madame Akkikuyu who, in the end, still appears the victim wronged by fate in the minds of the mice, although throughout the story it is her own choices that lead her to commit evil acts. Her relief at Audrey's last-minute escape does not stop her intending to sacrifice another mouse; she changes her mind about that not because she realizes it is wrong, but to spite Jupiter. Akkikuyu is no wronged innocent, and though she does have urges in that direction, is ultimately no repentant villain, yet in the end she is accepted as both. The story leaves the impression that if Audrey had given in to Akkikuyu, given her the utter slavish devotion the rat desired and the Starwife ordered, Akkikuyu would not have returned to evil – it is all Audrey's fault for defending herself against Akkikuyu's smothering, possibly sexual, attentions. Most children will read the *Deptford* books as horror or adventure stories and give such matters no consideration, and yet, the underlying implications of the characters' beliefs and actions deserve awareness and consideration on the part of readers.

Salman Rushdie (b. 1947)

Salman Rushdie was born in Bombay; he was educated in England and studied history at King's College, Cambridge. He worked in theatre, television, and advertising before finding success as a novelist with his second book, the Booker Prize winning *Midnight's Children* (1981), which is set in India and Pakistan in the years following India's independence. Like many of his books, it contains a degree of the fantastic while being classified as general literature rather than fantasy, and practises a sharp satire of politics and society. His fourth novel, *The Satanic Verses* (1988), which was deemed by some to mock Islam and particularly the prophet Mohammed through some of its characters and its quotations from the Koran, was banned in India and in numerous Muslim countries. Iranian religious leader Ayatollah Khomeini called for the deaths of Rushdie and his publishers; various bounties were offered. Rushdie was forced to go into hiding; the Norwegian publisher of the book and its Italian translator were wounded in attacks, while the Japanese translator was murdered. Over twenty people were killed during protests against the book in India and Pakistan. Although Iran eventually announced, in 1998, that the call for Rushdie's death had ended, a private foundation maintains a bounty in the millions for his death. Rushdie has been married three times, and lives in London and New York.

Rushdie's *Haroun and the Sea of Stories* (1990) is a fantasy equally enjoyable for children and adults, about the need for stories and free speech, and the danger of neglecting both. Haroun Khalifa lives with his father Rashid and mother Soraya in a nameless sad city in the country of Alifbey (Hindustani for 'alphabet', as an afterword about the names explains – those of many characters and places have significance). In the sad city, people eat glumfish and factories manufacture sadness. Rashid is a professional storyteller, but when the city's sadness seeps into their lives and Soraya leaves him for their neighbour, the fiction-deriding clerk Mr Sengupta, Rashid's storytelling abilities dry up. He sees no point to telling stories anymore. Rashid and Haroun travel with a cheerfully speed-obsessed mail coach driver to the Valley of K, where Rashid has been hired by politician Snooty Buttoo to charm the crowd at a rally. When Iff the Water Genie arrives to disconnect Rashid's subscription to the Story Water from the Great Story Sea, also called the Ocean of the Streams of Story, Haroun forces the Genie to take him to see the Walrus, the Grand Comptroller, so he can persuade them his father does not really want his subscription to Story Water cut off. They ride Butt the giant living mechanical Hoopoe, who bears a striking resemblance to Mr Butt the exuberant bus-driver, to the moon Kahani (which means 'story').

Kahani is divided into two lands, Gup, which has unending day, and Chup, where there is unending night. Its ocean is filled with streams of story which flow from the wellspring of stories in the neglected Old Zone of ancient tales, merging and mingling. However, it is being polluted, stories degraded. Rather than meeting the Walrus to discuss his father's case, Haroun ends up going with Butt, Iff, a Floating Gardener, and the talkative Plentimaw fishes to stop the pollution, while Rashid, who has travelled in a dream to Kahani, goes with the Guppee army to meet an invading army from Chup.

Chup is a land of silence and darkness, padlocked books and followers of the Cultmaster Khattam-Shud, who has gone from opposing stories to preaching against speech altogether; his most fanatical adherents sew their mouths shut. Chupwala Shadows have their own life, though they remain attached to those who cast them, but Khattam-Shud has found a way to separate his.

While he and his army have captured and plan to sacrifice to their idol the Guppee princess Batcheat, his Shadow is in the south, planning to destroy the Story Sea not only with poison, but by plugging the spring. Aided by the Chupwala warrior Mudra and his Shadow, who communicate with a language of gesture from Indian dance, Rashid and the Guppees battle Khattam-Shud's army, which is so used to silence and suspicion it has no unity, while the ever-debating Guppees can act for a common cause and are victorious.

Haroun is able to foil Khattam-Shud's Shadow. He uses the power of some wishwater he was given, along with a great deal of concentration and willpower, to set the moon Kahani rotating again, so that both lands experience night and day. Daylight melts the shadow-ship on which the poisons and the plug are being made and destroys the detached Shadows; it also melts the idol in the Chupwala city, which falls on the real Khattam-Shud. Mudra is chosen as president of Chup and a new era of peace and dialogue begins.

When Haroun and Rashid return, Haroun fears his father has dismissed it all as a dream, but at the rally, Rashid tells not the mindlessly happy story Snooty Buttoo requires, but the tale of Haroun and the defeat of Khattam-Shud's efforts to silence stories and discussion. The people, identifying the dictatorial Khattam-Shud with Snooty Buttoo, are stirred to rise up and drive him from their valley. When father and son return to their nameless city, it is raining happy endings, a gift from the Walrus. The citizens have remembered the city's name, Kahani; Soraya has realized that her infatuation with Sengupta was a mistake and has returned to her family.

Haroun can be read allegorically, as is obvious with sadness factories and a Sea of Stories, but it never works at only one level at a time. There are numerous puns and echoes of other stories, shadows of the landscape of Kashmir where Rushdie's family roots are, observations on art, society, language, democracy, and the responsibility of creators towards art. There are reflections of characters in other characters, which bind Alifbey and the moon Kahani together without ever being so simple as to have one merely a dream-duplication of the other. Khattam-Shud looks in his true form like the 'mingy' little clerk Sengupta, while the silly Princess Batcheat with her unbearable singing is an altered reflection of Soraya and her sweet voice, and the two un-quenchable Butts, Hoopoe and driver, share an enthusiasm that lifts Haroun's spirits in both worlds. As an adventure, *Haroun and the Sea of Stories* is filled with invention, action, and humour enough to hold the attention of any child; as an allegory, it does much more, though, in its consideration of the value and potential power of story-telling. It also bears comparison to Carroll's *Alice's Adventures in Wonderland* and *Through the Looking-Glass* in its fantastic creatures to be encountered, landscape to be explored, its witty word-play, and the author's obvious delight in language.

Eloise McGraw (1915-2000)

Eloise McGraw was born in Texas and lived in Oklahoma and Oregon; she was married and had two children. Her first children's book appeared in 1950. McGraw was primarily a writer of historical fiction, but was also one of those who continued Baum's *Oz* series. She won Newbery Honors for *Moccasin Trail* (1952), *The Golden Goblet* (1961), and for her last book, the children's fantasy *The Moorchild*.

The Moorchild (1996) takes the fairy traditions of the British Isles as its starting point, but in a very different way from Melling's work. McGraw's story is set in a small pre-industrial farming and fishing village on the edge of a moor in no particular place or time. The hero is a changeling, Saaski, raised as the daughter of Yanno the blacksmith and his wife Anwara. Her grandmother, Old Bess, the village wise-woman, recognizes that something is amiss with the colicky, screaming baby who hates iron, rowan, and St. John's wort, and whose eyes keep changing colour. Baby Saaski remembers her life before, as Moql, a 'youngling' of the Folk. It was a carefree existence as one of a swarm of youngsters living under a mound on the Moor. However, Moql never fit in there. She could not change her shape or become invisible, and was a danger to them all. Her father was a human man, lured into the mound by her mother for a brief period and sent away again, to find himself back in the human world after the passage of many years. Moql is changed with a human baby, which will be kept as a slave of the Folk.

Growing as a human baby, Moql gradually forgets her past, but as Saaski, she never fits into village life. She prefers to roam the moor and play unearthly tunes on her grandfather's bagpipes. The villagers begin to blame her for anything that goes wrong. Her only friends are the wandering tinker's boy, Tam, and eventually, Old Bess. The villagers, though, intend to burn her. Saaski begins to remember life in the Mound and comes up with a plan to rescue her parents' true daughter. The rescued child becomes a baby again, as she was when she was stolen. Tam and Saaski take her to Old Bess to be reunited with her parents, and set out travelling together.

The Moorchild could be called a quest for self; Moql does not belong with the Folk, nor Saaski with the villagers. The place she creates or finds for herself is with Tam, another youth without a home but a person at home in himself, as Saaski is not until she accepts the truth about her parentage and her nature, and out of love for the couple who raised her, risks her freedom to save their real child. The book is dedicated to 'all children who have ever felt *different*', and McGraw uses the fairy changeling tradition to tell a story of not fitting in that does not find its happy ending in compromise or concession. The hero does not learn to be like everyone else by making friends, and is not suddenly recognized as worthy by admiring or grateful peers after some acceptable triumph, the more usual patterns when 'being different' is the theme in a children's book. Instead, Saaski creates a life for what she is.

Rumiko Takahashi (b. 1957)

Rumiko Takahashi was born in Niigata, Japan, and studied at Japan Women's University. At the same time, she also studied at Gekiga Sonjuku, a famous school for the art of manga, one of the most important forms for print storytelling in Japan. By the end of the twentieth century, her work as a manga creator had made her one of the wealthiest women in Japan, a master of an artistic and literary form still largely dominated by men.

Manga are comics, or more accurately, graphic novels (that is, they are more along the lines of *Asterix*, *Tintin*, or Neil Gaiman's *Sandman*, in that they tell sustained stories in which all the considerations that would go into a novel come into play, rather than being a short strip aimed at a concluding quip). The form is used to publish both short stories and long serials, some of which have continued for years. Many series first appear a chapter at a time in weekly manga magazines, and are then republished in collections devoted to one title, containing anywhere from five to ten chapters per volume. There are manga representing every genre of fiction, from romance and sports stories to science fiction and fantasy. Manga in English translation existed, but were difficult to find in the nineties; by the early years of the twenty-first century they have become very popular, with a presence in most bookstores. Specialist publishers and at least one mainstream science fiction and fantasy company have made many of the more popular series available; in North America and Europe, manga with science fiction and fantasy elements are proving the most popular.

Although many manga creators are either writers or artists, Rumiko Takahashi is both writer and illustrator. Her first work was published in the seventies. In the nineteen-eighties, her first serials, the weekly *Urusei Yatsura,* a comedy with science fiction elements, and the monthly *Maison Ikkoku,* a realistic romance, appeared, both coming to a conclusion in the late eighties. She quickly became one of the most popular manga creators in Japan, and by the end of the nineties had several other series to her credit as well, including the extremely popular martial arts/fantasy/comedy *Ranma 1/2* (1987-1996). However, it is *Inuyasha* (also sometimes *Inu-Yasha*), which is Takahashi's most significant contribution to fantasy for children and teens.

Inuyasha, which began serial publication in the weekly *Shônen Sunday* in 1996, was first published in English in 1997. By the winter of 2005, the story had reached forty volumes in Japan, with English publication lagging behind at twenty. *Inuyasha,* subtitled 'A Feudal Fairy Tale', is the story of a modern teenage girl, Kagome, and a medieval half-demon. Kagome's family are the hereditary caretakers of a Shinto shrine. Kagome herself is the reincarnation of Kikyo, a priestess from five hundred years before, guardian of the Shikon no Tama, a jewel with the potential for great evil power, which Kikyo's guardianship purified. However, Kikyo was in love with Inuyasha, son of a human mother and a powerful dog-demon lord. Kikyo and

Inuyasha were tricked into believing each had been betrayed and attacked by the other; Kikyo died of her wounds and was cremated with the Shikon no Tama, while Inuyasha was left pinned to a tree by her arrow for fifty years, sealed away from the world. A demon seeking the Shikon no Tama drags Kagome five hundred years into the past through the shrine's ancient well; the jewel emerges from her body, is stolen by the demon, and shattered (by Kagome's arrow as she tries to shoot the demon) into numerous shards which scatter all across the land. Kagome frees Inuyasha, who at first believes she is his betrayer, Kikyo. Kikyo's little sister Kaede, now an elderly priestess, instructs Kagome and Inuyasha to find all the shards of the Shikon no Tama, since even a single piece of it is enough to give a demon vast power. Kaede gives Kagome some power over the initially-recalcitrant half-demon by means of a necklace, which allows her to restrain Inuyasha with the command 'Sit'. However, the partnership between Kagome and Inuyasha evolves into friendship and even attraction. On the quest the pair are joined by others: the orphaned fox-demon Shippo, the demon-exterminator Sango, and the amorous Buddhist monk Miroku.

In the course of their travels they encounter many demons and monsters, some created by Takahashi, others drawn from Japanese folklore and legend. Not all are malevolent; nor are all the humans friendly, or innocent victims of demonic attack. They find shards and lose them again, encounter witches, ghosts, warlords, peasant villagers, and forest-spirits. Kagome goes home through the well occasionally, frantic about all the school she is missing or having quarrelled with Inuyasha, but rarely stays long, returning to the past with first-aid materials, snack-foods, and eventually her bicycle; her grandfather invents increasingly improbable ailments to explain her long absences. Inuyasha's band discovers that amid all the chaos of demons trying to gain power through Shikon shards (which mirrors the human political instability of that period, when daimyo or feudal lords fought one another for ascendancy under an ineffectual shogunate), they have one most deadly enemy, the extremely powerful demon Naraku. Naraku murdered Kikyo, killed Sango's entire village and enslaved her brother's reanimated corpse, cursed Miroku's family, and now seeks to gather all the shards himself. Their hunt for Shikon shards turns into a pursuit of the elusive Naraku, while other stories weave in and out of that main plot. The wolf-demon Kouga's rivalry with Inuyasha for Kagome's affection, the awkward love triangle between Inuyasha, Kagome, and a resurrected Kikyo (who needs to keep capturing the souls of the dead to survive), Sango's desire to free her brother, even if it means his death, the complex relationship between Inuyasha and his human-hating half-brother Sesshoumaru (who has nevertheless restored to life and adopted Rin, a human girl), the simmering rebellion of one of Naraku's subordinates, and Kagome's family's cheerful connivance at her long absences in the past – all these add to the rich, multi-stranded nature of the story. There is action-filled battle, mystery, romance, tragedy, hope, and a great deal of humour, too, all in a well-researched setting depicting Ashikaga- or Muromachi-period Japan around the year 1500, with its society of peasant villages and feudal lords' wooden castles, scattered across a landscape of wild forest and mountain.

Inuyasha has all the elements that make good fantasy. Its folkloric and historical backgrounds form an integral part of the story, while its magic and supernatural are consistently portrayed. There is an independent tradition of fantasy literature in the East, going back to at least the Middle Ages and the Chinese epic *Journey to the West*, which was written in the form it still has today in the fifteen-seventies, but which existed in oral tradition and written legends much earlier. *Journey to the West*, a long quest undertaken by a small band of characters with various magical abilities, who encounter a seemingly unending succession of monsters on their way, has been an enduring influence on the fantasy tradition in China and Japan; its influence on *Inuyasha* in structure and spirit is very evident and reference is made to it in some episodes.

Takahashi is a master at conveying wry, ironic, or suddenly introspective facial expression with a few subtle lines, which adds the internal life to the dialogue that a novel's narrative would. As a result of their experiences, each of the heroes grows and changes in skills, confidence, and approach to dealing with others, while the villains are not motiveless evils, but are driven by greed for power, for control over others, by hunger for souls or human flesh, by loyalty to a lord or love or lust for some person. The many plot threads and the complex interrelationships of the major and secondary characters keep the story from ever becoming merely a mechanical exercise in encountering and defeating a string of enemies. *Inuyasha* has much to offer young fantasy readers, not least the freshness and unfamiliarity of its setting and supernatural elements to European and North American readers. However, with its strong characters, complex relationships, and occasional demand that the heroes pause to reassess their own assumptions and motivations, the appeal will not limited to the exotic setting, either. It should not be overlooked by those seeking out a good fantasy story merely because it is not a novel.

An *Inuyasha* anime (Japanese animation) of nearly 170 episodes has aired on television in Japan and has recently become available in North America; there have also been three movies. The anime adheres very closely to Takahashi's original manga.

XVI
The Nineties, part two

Philip Pullman (b. 1946)

Philip Pullman's father was in the RAF, so as a boy he lived in numerous countries around the world. He studied at Oxford, becoming a teacher; married with two sons, he still lives in Oxford. In addition to his fantasy for children and teens, he has written the *Sally Lockhart* books, a series of young adult adventures with a Victorian setting, and a number of other works for young people.

Count Karlstein (1982) is a children's book which uses the European folk tradition of a demonic huntsman. It is set in the wild forests and mountains of Switzerland in 1816. English orphans Charlotte and Lucy live with their uncle, Count Karlstein, in Castle Karlstein. To gain his title, the Count had made a bargain with Zamiel the Demon Huntsman; in return, he must provide a human victim on All Souls' Eve. Lucy and Charlotte are to be the huntsman's prey, but the maid Hildi overhears the plan and warns them to run away. Soon there are an unexpected number of allies for the girls; Hildi and her brother, the poacher Peter, the bluff and kindly coachman Max and his sweetheart Eliza, their old teacher Miss Davenport, Meister Haifisch the lawyer, and the conjurer Doctor Cadaverezzi. The sisters, unaware of those trying to help them, are pursued about the countryside by Karlstein's henchmen, while the thick-headed local police complicate the situation by arresting nearly anyone they lay their hands on. Lucy and Charlotte are finally found and a complicated plan is put into effect, whereby they will be given back to the Count, to be imprisoned in a hunting lodge for Zamiel. Peter is to defend them with a silver bullet, but it does not come to that. He defies Zamiel and declares the girls under his protection, and the demon, who does not harm true huntsmen, goes to claim the Count instead. The Count had murdered his brother to become the heir to Karlstein; Haifisch the lawyer has discovered the fate of the son of the previous Count. The infant was kidnapped, left in an orphanage, and had a varied career as a soldier and coachman. Max is the true Count Karlstein, and guardian of Lucy and Charlotte.

The structure of *Count Karlstein* is unusual for a children's book. The framework for the story is an attempt by various participants in the events to assemble their recollections, years later. Different characters tell their stories in greatly contrasting styles. Hildi, who carries the greatest part of the narrative, is the best story-teller, able to paint a well-rounded picture of events and surroundings, Lucy is emotional and dramatic in the manner of the gothic novels that are her favoured reading, Miss Davenport lecturing and practical, and the police reports completely ignorant of what is actually going on around them. *Count Karlstein* is a story both suspenseful and funny; the multiple narrative voices add to the humour through their conflicting interpretations of other characters and events, and also contribute to the mystery and suspense.

The Firework-Maker's Daughter (1995) is a short children's novel with a more conventional narrative. Lila, daughter of the firework-maker Lalchand, learns the art of firework-making from her father, but he feels this was a mistake on his part. A daughter should not be a firework-maker. Lila accordingly sets out to obtain Royal Sulphur from Razvani the Fire-Fiend, a journey necessary to becoming a master firework-maker. Lalchand is horrified when he finds she has gone; she does not know that one must also have magic water from the Goddess of the Emerald Lake, to survive the volcano's flames. Lila's friend Chulak and his charge Hamlet, the white elephant, undertake their own quest, to get the magic water and catch up with Lila. Both travellers have adventures along the way, with incompetent pirates who go through several other unsuccessful careers in the course of the story, hostile villagers, and a helpful goddess. When Lila reaches the fire-fiend's grotto, he only taunts her. She does not even know about the Three Gifts she should have brought him, and has none of the magic water. Nevertheless, she takes Razvani up on his challenge and tries to walk into his flames. Just in time Chulak and Hamlet arrive with the flask of magic water. The flames do not harm her. The fire-fiend tells her that royal sulphur does not exist and, that since she has come to him, she

366

must have brought the Three Gifts even though she does not know it. There is no time to ponder this, though, because Chulak has learned that Lila's father is to be executed for supposedly allowing the white elephant to escape from the city. They return to plead with the king for Lalchand's life, and the king decides that only if Lila wins a fireworks competition will her father be spared. Together, Lila and Lalchand create a display that wins the awe and admiration even of the other competitors. Lalchand apologizes for not trusting her and treating her as a true apprentice; he tells her the Three Gifts needed to reach Razvani were talent, courage, and luck, and the royal sulphur is simply the wisdom gained in the journey.

The Firework-Maker's Daughter is a fine adventure in the tradition of children's books in which a young person undertakes a quest to prove him- or herself. It has all the proper ingredients for such a story: good friends, obstacles to be overcome, revelations and discoveries, reunions and reassessments. Like *Count Karlstein*, there is a large element of humour, as well.

The books on which Pullman's enduring fame will rest, however, are the ones that make up the trilogy called *His Dark Materials*. The first, *Northern Lights* (1995) or in North America, *The Golden Compass*, won both the Carnegie Medal and the Guardian Award. The story continues in *The Subtle Knife* (1997) and *The Amber Spyglass* (2000), which won the 2001 Whitbread Book of the Year Award, the first time a children's book had done so. Although the series is written for young adults, in North America it was initially sold more often as adult fantasy. Like *Harry Potter*, it often showed up on adult bestseller lists. The new audience it brought to children's fantasy was not so much the non-fantasy reading teen, but the adult fantasy reader. It also attracted, due to the discussion it provoked in venues usually reserved for 'literary' works (such as Morningside on the CBC), the 'literary' reader generally embarrassed to admit to sampling 'genre fiction'.

Northern Lights is set in a world like our own, but lacking some of our technological advances and containing many more fantastic cultures and creatures, such as witches and intelligent, armoured polar bears. The most profound difference is in the daemons: people's souls, which exist in separate animal form. Children's daemons change shape at will, while those of adults have one permanent form. Lyra, a wild and somewhat belligerent girl, and her daemon Pantalaimon, live in Jordan College at Oxford. A complicated series of events puts her in possession of the alethiometer, a device which provides her with answers to questions by pointing to symbols Lyra is able to interpret. She discovers her father is the powerful and mysterious Lord Asriel and her mother the seductive and equally powerful Mrs. Coulter, each of whom has some secret intention concerning her. Lyra's friend Roger is kidnapped, and Lyra undertakes to rescue him, going into the north with a clan of gyptians who want to rescue their own stolen children. Mrs. Coulter, an agent of the Church, is involved in terrible experiments to sever children from their daemons, a process which leads to their deaths. The experiments are meant to find out some of the properties of Dust, mysterious particles that react differently around children and adults. The gyptians and witches succeed in the rescue, but Lyra and Roger end up on further adventures, learning more about the witches, meeting Iorek Byrnison, exiled leader of the armoured bears, and helping him to regain rule over his people. He in turn helps Lyra find Lord Asriel, to whom she believes she must deliver the alethiometer. Asriel, however, murders Roger and opens a way into another world. Lyra and her daemon enter the other world, planning to stop whatever Lord Asriel intends to do.

The Subtle Knife is set largely in our world. Will Parry's explorer father vanished when he was young; he looks after his unstable, paranoid mother alone. There are real enemies seeking his father's papers, though, and when they show up, Will entrusts his mother to his piano teacher and flees. Will meets Lyra, who is astonished at his lack of a daemon, but they discover their troubles are connected. They find a way to yet another world, where Spectres devour the daemons of adults and gangs of vicious children roam the towns. Will is identified as the next possessor of the subtle knife, which can cut anything, even windows between worlds. In our world, the scientist and former nun Dr. Mary Malone is researching Dust; she is told by rebel angels how to reach another world, where she must wait for Lyra and Will. The scientist-turned-shaman Stanislaus Grumman of Lyra's world turns out to be Will's father. He explains that every gain in human freedom and knowledge has had to be fought for against 'the Authority'. The rebel angels want human freedom and wisdom, the Authority they rebel against, human submission and obedience. Lyra is kidnapped, and Will sets out to save her.

The Amber Spyglass increases the suspense and mystery. Mrs. Coulter, warned that Lyra will be the new Eve of a new Fall, intends to kill her, but her maternal love is finally awakened and she keeps her in a drugged sleep instead. Will rescues Lyra, guided by rebel angels, who tell him the Authority, whom humans think is God, is not the Creator but only the first of the angels, who has deceived nearly all those who came after him into believing he was the Creator. When humans die, their ghosts go to a world that the angels describe as a prison camp. Lord Asriel plans revolution and a Republic of Heaven; he and Mrs. Coulter destroy the Authority's regent, Metatron, and lose their own lives, while Will and Lyra, separated from their daemons – Will's having emerged from within him – travel through the world of the dead. This is guarded by harpies, who, forced to feed on memories of wrong and wickedness, have become foul and terrible. True stories and good things nourish them, though. Will and Lyra win their co-operation in guiding the ghosts out into the universe where they can dissolve back into atoms as they yearn to do, in return for the ghosts sharing their true memories of good things learned and experienced in life. Along the way, unwittingly, they find and release the long-imprisoned and now senile Authority, who dissolves with great relief, free at last.

When Will and Lyra meet Dr. Malone, she shares with them the story of her loss of religious faith and the new life-affirming spirituality she has grown into. Will, Lyra, and their daemons learn that Dust, which is created by consciousness, the knowledge and wisdom which came with the Fall, leaks out into the abyss whenever the knife cuts a window in a world. Such a window also creates a Spectre, which feeds on Dust and on adult daemons. Without Dust, intelligent life in all the worlds will end. All the windows but one must be sealed, and no more can be made. That one must be left open to allow ghosts to leave the world of the dead.

Will and Lyra discover they love one another, but humans grow ill and die if they live in a world other than their own for long, and neither will let the other make that sacrifice. The angel Xaphania and Dr. Malone help them understand they must make the Republic of Heaven in their own worlds by how they live, and teach others to live with kindness, patience, and curiosity as well, always seeking wisdom. Once they have returned to their own worlds, Will breaks the knife and the angels begin sealing all the openings between worlds. Lyra, having grown up through experiencing an adult's intensity of love, has lost the ability to read the alethiometer, but can regain it through much work: what she understood instinctively in Innocence, she must regain through a lifetime of study in Experience.

His Dark Materials is complex, inventive, chilling, and thought-provoking. The underlying mythology is built on the Old Testament, the *Paradise Lost* of John Milton (1608-1674), and most of all, on the ideas and images of the longer works of the visionary poet and artist William Blake (1757-1827), which allude repeatedly to ideas of revolt against oppressive authority founded on received wisdom, human and spiritual, and cry out for renewal and revolution, a new dawn for the human spirit. The Spectres are in fact straight out of Blake, though Pullman concentrates only on their negative aspects, while the harpies appear to be developed from Blake's recurring characters, the Daughters of Albion, in their role in *Jerusalem* (Tristanne J. Connolly, pers. comm.). The underlying message of the book, and like some of the earliest children's fantasy novels it does have one, is the need to make a heaven on earth, or to use Blake's metaphor from his short poem 'Jerusalem', to build Jerusalem in England. The importance of living, not in fear of future damnation, but for the fullness of experience, love, and understanding, is what Lyra and Will learn and must teach in their own worlds. The series, though, is oddly humourless, compared with Pullman's other works such as *I Was a Rat!* (see Chapter IX) and *Count Karlstein*; reading *His Dark Materials*, one is never allowed to forget that behind it all lies a heavy weight of authorial intent, which by times threatens to suffocate the characters. It sometimes takes its intended message too seriously to allow a reader full immersion in the world.

Garry Kilworth (b. 1941)

Garry Kilworth was born in York and grew up in an RAF family during World War Two and the post-war years, living in numerous places around the world. He joined the RAF himself and served for seventeen years. Eventually he attended London University's King's College and studied English. Kilworth has written fantasy and science fiction for adults as well as historical novels and general fiction. He writes as Garry Douglas and F.K. Salwood as well. Kilworth is married and has two children.

Kilworth's children's books tend to be speculative fiction. Although he has written for children since the eighties, his *Welkin Weasels* series became his most widely-known work in the nineties. Very similar to Jacques' *Redwall* in conception, the *Welkin* books feature anthropomorphic animals living in societies that blend human and animal attributes. The first trilogy, *Thunder Oak* (1997), *Castle Storm* (1998), and *Windjammer Run* (1999) differs from most fantasies where animals live as if they are humans, by taking that situation and making it a central part of the story. In the medieval island of Welkin, the humans have all gone away, and some species of animals have acquired human-like intelligence, speech, and customs. The stoats have formed a feudal ruling class, while weasels are a servile underclass, and some prey species such as mice and voles remain unintelligent food-animals. The weasel Sylver and his outlaw band live in the forest, in continual conflict with stoats Prince Poynt and Sheriff Falshed. Welkin is mostly at or below sea level, protected by human-made dykes, which are beginning to erode. Sylver's friend, the stoat Lord Haukin, recognizes the danger, and little though they like the idea of humans, they realize that humans can both repair the dykes and free the weasels from stoatish oppression.

In *Thunder Oak*, Sylver's quest to find the humans begins. The humans left clues as to their whereabouts; the first of these is hidden at Thunder Oak. Sylver and his band must find the oak, so they set out searching for a great sea eagle eggshell with the only complete map of Welkin on it. They encounter animate statues and scarecrows, an animal Valhalla, and tribes of various animals, not all of whom want the humans to return. They are hunted by Sheriff Falshed and the fox assassin Magellan. By the end, their band has suffered losses and they have learnt only that the humans are in an enchanted sleep.

Castle Storm introduces new problems. Sylver and his band seek the castle to find another clue to the humans, but vast armies of rats led by the outcast stoat magician Flaggatis invade Welkin. The outlaws encounter warring societies of chivalric squirrels led by Pommf de Fritte and Clive of Coldkettle, a giant, weasel-eating dragonfly nymph, a stoat Grand Inquisitor, and ferret spies Rosencrass and Guildenswine. They find their next clue, while their friend Lord Haukin saves Welkin from the rats, demanding as his reward from Prince Poynt that Sylver be pardoned and made a lord when he returns from his quest.

In *Windjammer Run*, Sylver and his band follow the clue they found in the previous book to Dorma Island. They crew their ship with pine martens led by a Long John Silver take-off, the three-legged cook Short Oneleg, who believes they are looking for treasure. Sheriff Falshed pursues them, and so does Flaggatis. They run into problems at nearly every island they visit: giants, magic, attacks at sea, a Kraken, mutiny. When they reach Dorma Island, they must wake the humans and persuade them to return to Welkin. The humans left Welkin because the wars between north and south were destroying the land; a magic tune on the wind lured them away so the land could have peace. The human children persuade their reluctant parents they must return to repair the dykes, and a society of compromise between humans and animals is worked out.

Gaslight Geezers (2001), *Vampire Voles* (2002), and *Heastward Ho!* (2003) are set in a 'Victorian' Welkin ruled by the human child-queen Varicose. Nearly all the characters are descendants of ones in the first trilogy. Montagu Sylver is a noble who does not use his title and lives at 5A Breadoven Street, while Bryony Bludd, descendant of the first Sylver's companion Bryony, is a veterinary surgeon and his admiring confidante, Watson to his Holmes. Monty's cousin Spindrick Sylver is an anarchist, Jeremy Poynt is mayor of the muscalid side of the capital city, Muggidrear, and Falshed is chief of police. The characters all repeat the personalities and relationships of the first three books, except for Spindrick, who wants to destroy society so that animals will go back to living naturally. The first book plays with Monty as a Holmes-type detective figure; the second sends Monty and Bryony in pursuit of a master vampire, while Spindrick goes off as a colonial explorer in pursuit of a magic sleep-inducing soil to be used in his anarchistic disruption of society. The third sees all the characters heading east, playing with the culture of the Victorian explorers, to a confrontation with Monty's nemesis, the lemming Svetlana.

Kilworth's prose style in the *Welkin Weasels* books can sometimes be irritating; he will often repeat himself within paragraphs, recapping previous sentences for no apparent reason. The characters do not evolve at all, but simply act out their assigned traits, even when the plot might seem to be pushing them towards change. There is much physical humour and wordplay, and the characters move from crisis to crisis, each adventure revealing a new problem to be overcome. In the later 'Victorian' books, many elements are thrown in simply for the nudge-in-the-ribs reference to some nineteenth- or twentieth-century work of fiction. However, they contain the same blend of perilous adventure, mystery, pastiche, and slapstick humour as the early three, as well as the same tumble from crisis to crisis for the characters.

Among Kilworth's other writing for children, *Spiggot's Quest* (2002), the first of a series called *The Knights of Liöfwende*, stands out. It is set in Liöfwende, a faerie Britain populated by all the fairies of British folklore, boggarts, seelie, redcaps, pixies, tylwyth teg, and many more, as well as by immigrants from the continent, such as Scandinavian trolls, German kobolds, and Slavic leshies. Spiggot, a young boggart smith, is sent by his father to deliver a suit of armour to Cimberlin, fairy king of Northumberland. He travels with Kling, a Shetland pony-sized water rat who pulls the cart and makes wry comments on everything, particularly the lack of food and Spiggot's tendency to get sidetracked. On the way they find Jack, who has been thrown into faerie after a motorcycle accident.

Spiggot, Jack, and Kling encounter many dangers, some of which are of their own making. Jack's ignorance of faerie leads him to offend people without realizing it and commit acts that no sensible fairy would, such as drinking from a stream that gives him a fish's head. He escapes death at the hands of some toad-like creatures only because of his own embarrassing webbed toes, and is given the gift of a toad-tongue, which fortunately wears off after a while, though in the meantime he cannot stop himself consuming large numbers of flies and beetles. He persuades Spiggot to buy Kling back, after the boggart has sold the rat for a magic crossbow, but then he himself sells Spiggot to the revolting Redcap as a steed in return for golden guineas to buy his way home, though he later repents and rescues the boggart.

Not all their problems are their own fault. Something is amiss in faerie: armies are on the march, malevolent creatures from below ground are emerging, ancient trees are dying. To get past a skagg, an underground creature with sword-blades of bone instead of hands, Spiggot puts on the king's armour and defeats it in battle. They run afoul of King Mallmoc's tyrannical ulcugga, who enslave both humans and other fairies to work in their mines and forges, and rescue Rosamund, a medieval girl who found herself in Liöfwende after leaping from her tower window with a broken heart. When they reach Cimberlin's court, the king is outraged that a lowly boggart has worn his armour. Jack's pleading that Spiggot acted to protect him and Rosamund, and his skill with sleight of hand, win the king's favour. Spiggot is made a knight-errant of the king, with Jack and Kling as his squires, and despatched on a quest to send the underground creatures ravaging the land back where they belong, the plot of the next book, *Mallmoc's Castle* (2003).

Spiggot's Quest has all the strengths of the *Welkin* books, continuous action, slapstick humour, mystery, a band of companions with enough friction to be funny, and a world where the fantastic is ever-present. It also features two heroes, Spiggot and Jack, who are capable of learning and growing as they travel, and a friendship between the four travellers that strengthens through the book. The great variety of British fairies is revelled in and used with great inventiveness as Spiggot and his friends make their roundabout way from Rutland, through the Midlands to the Welsh border, and up to Yorkshire and Northumberland. Oddly enough, given that these are works by a mature author written within the same few years, the actual style of *Liöfwende* is a noticeable improvement over that of *Welkin*; the redundancies are gone, making the prose flow much more smoothly.

Dave Duncan (b. 1933)

Scottish-born Dave Duncan lives with his wife in Calgary, Alberta and Victoria, British Columbia. Duncan worked as a petroleum geologist before turning to writing fantasy and science fiction, primarily for adults. Duncan's *King's Blades* series of adult fantasy novels, *The Gilded Chain* (1998), *Lord of the Fire Lands* (1999), *Sky of Swords* (2000), *Paragon Lost* (2002), and *Impossible Odds* (2003) is set in the kingdom of Chivial and neighbouring countries. The main characters in these adult novels are all 'King's Blades', champion knights magically bonded as protector to the king or one of his lords.

In his young adult *King's Daggers* trilogy, Duncan takes Stalwart, a young musician trained as a Blade but not yet bound, and Sister Emerald, a member of the White Sisters who are trained to detect magic, as his heroes. *Sir Stalwart* (1999), *The Crooked House* (2000) and *Silvercloak* (2001), take place in a detailed world that is technologically anywhere between the late medieval period and the seventeenth century, except for a lack of gunpowder. There is a carefully-constructed and consistent system of magic and plenty of swashbuckling action. Throughout the trilogy, Stalwart and Emerald work undercover, ensuring the King of Chivial's safety at great risk to themselves.

In the first book, King Ambrose's attempts to end corruption among the various magical orders has resulted in assassination attempts. Stalwart is secretly made a Companion of the King's Blades, also called the Old Blades. Publicly, he is driven in disgrace from Ironhall, the school where Blades are trained. Emerald is apparently thrown out of the White Sisters, also in disgrace. The Old Blades are using Emerald as bait – a former White Sister is just what the assassins may want. Emerald is kidnapped by the insane sorcerer Doctor Skuldigger, as planned, while Stalwart, apparently a lowly carter and musician, is also captured to be a subject in magical experiments to create monstrous chimeras. They are imprisoned in a marsh-surrounded and chimera-guarded village, but Stalwart has a sword hidden in his archlute (an instrument popular in the seventeenth and eighteenth centuries, with a much longer neck than an ordinary lute), and the two of them escape, having killed most of Skuldigger's thugs. The king jokingly names Stalwart and Emerald 'the King's Daggers'.

The Crooked House sends Stalwart and Emerald to investigate a mysterious death. With Stalwart's friend the Blade-in-training Badger, they investigate a gang of sorcerers. Badger, though, is actually the youngest son of the family which led the last rebellion in Nythia, once independent and now part of Chivial. The leader of the sorcerers, Owen, is his only surviving brother, and Badger has sworn to kill the king. Stalwart and Emerald unravel another sorcerous plot to kill the king while Badger wrestles with conflicting loyalties.

In the concluding book, Emerald goes in disguise as a boy to the Blades' training school of Ironhall, where she endures the traditional abuse meted out to the newest boy. A legendary assassin, Silvercloak, has been hired by Skuldigger to kill the king, and it is thought he will strike at Ironhall. At a crucial moment, Stalwart is refused admittance to Ironhall by those who still believe he is a runaway, while Emerald and the king are trapped on the battlements by Silvercloak. Stalwart climbs the castle wall to reach them and outwits the assassin, turning his magic against him. This time, both Emerald and Stalwart receive public recognition for their deeds.

The *King's Daggers* books are full of action and suspense, growing up, politics, intrigue, and, in Emerald and Stalwart, likable heroes with a great deal of courage, intelligence, and personal integrity. The series brings the detailed world-building and story-complexity of quality adult fantasy to a book for younger readers. There is a hint of romance, in Sir Fury's admiration of Emerald and Stalwart's embryonic jealously, but it does not overshadow the stronger friendship of mutual trust, confidence, and dependence which has developed between Stalwart and Emerald on their missions. Older readers may also enjoy Duncan's works for adults, although in his adult books he has an occasional tendency to revert to elements of weak, formulaic fantasy, and present his female characters as set types, devoid of any individual personality: the cheerful trollop, the spunky girl, the overbearing wife, and the suffering abused woman, eager to turn to the hero for consolation in her husband's absence. None of the female characters in his adult books have the satisfying wholeness of Emerald. In his young adult trilogy, though, Duncan offers a well-rounded cast of characters and stories filled with action and intrigue.

Louise Cooper (b. 1952)

Louise Cooper, who lives with her husband in Cornwall, England, was born in Herefordshire and wrote prolifically while still a student. Her first novel was published when she was twenty, but real success came with her *Time Master* trilogy set in the world of Chaos and Order: *The Initiate* (1986), *The Outcast* (1986), and *The Master* (1987). The *Time Master* books form an adult fantasy series which is also enjoyed by young adult readers. She has since written two more adult trilogies, *Chaos Gate* (*The Deceiver*, *The Pretender*, *The Avenger*, 1991-92) and the grimmer *Star Shadow* (*Star Ascendant*, *Eclipse*, *Moonset*, 1994-95) set in the same world. Her eight-book *Indigo* series (1988-93), about the travels of a young woman made immortal and charged with remedying the ills caused by demons she released into the world, will also have great appeal to teen fantasy readers. By the late nineties, however, Cooper was concentrating on writing children's books, usually fantasy or supernatural thrillers.

Cooper's writing for children and young adults, like Tanith Lee's work of the nineties, builds on the sorts of stories she has written for adults. Whether secondary world fantasy or real-world stories into which the supernatural intrudes, they feature convincing settings and young heroes who work their way through unsettling mysteries with the help of loyal friends to save themselves from some supernatural peril.

Her children's series *Creatures*, for beginning readers, contains numbered books, from *Creatures 1: Once I Caught a Fish Alive* (1998) to *Creatures 9: Here Comes a Candle* (2000). The titles are all phrases familiar from nursery rhymes or fairy-tales. The stories are spooky tales of children who encounter unnatural or supernatural animals: malevolent fish and birds, ghostly cats, mysterious dogs, and a computer virus spider that wants to escape the computer, are among the 'creatures' featured in these. Another children's series for quite young readers begins with *Sea Horses* (2003). Intended to span four books, it features a destructive spirit in the form of a horse, inadvertently released by Tamzin, who must find a way to remedy the evil she has unleashed. For older children, *Hunter's Moon* (2003), is a ghost story set in Norfolk, in which cousins Gil and Jonas must resist and fight a seven-centuries dead witch who drains the life from red-haired children, to save Gil's sister from dying and free the witch's ghostly stepchildren, murdered by her and still in her power.

A five-book young adult series of gothic stories, *Dark Enchantments*, consists of unrelated short novels about girls who encounter dark and dangerous supernatural forces, often connected to a love story, their own or someone else's. All but one of these books were reissued shortly after the first publication with a different title: *Hounds of Winter/Heart of Ice* (1996/1998), *Blood Dance/Heart of Stone* (1996/1998), *Firespell/Heart of Fire* (1996/1998), *The Shrouded Mirror/Heart of Glass* (1996/1998), and *Heart of Dust* (1998). Like her adult works, this series has become unaccountably hard to find.

Two of Cooper's young adult series from around the turn of the century demonstrate her strengths. The first of these, her young adult trilogy *Daughter of Storms* (1996), *The Dark Caller* (1997), and *Keepers of Light* (1998) is set in the world of her *Time Master* books, where the seven gods of Chaos and their counterparts of Order have been engaged in endless conflict throughout the ages. This story happens two hundred years after the end of *The Master*, in the Age of Equilibrium, when balance is maintained between the two antagonistic divine forces. This is not a world in which gods exist for the benefit of humanity; the gods are neither omniscient, omnipotent, nor particularly concerned with individual lives. Humans are supposed to sort out their own problems, and the gods, though they may offer advice, take a hand only when the balance of power or the structure of their universe is threatened.

In *Daughter of Storms*, Shar Tillmer is sent by her uncle Thel to join the Sisterhood, a nun-like order, even though she would prefer to become an Initiate of the Circle. Circle Adepts live in an ancient castle on the Star Peninsula and are magic-wielders as well as the religious leaders of the world. Shar uncovers evidence of a conspiracy against the High Initiate, the Circle's leader. Thel is the leader of the conspiracy, and Shar, who has great and unusual powers due to the circumstances of her birth, is a valuable tool for him. The plotters plan to murder the High Initiate during an eclipse of the two moons, when the barriers between the mortal world and the elemental planes are weak.

Shar is to be used as the medium to summon and control a dangerous sixth-plane elemental to commit the murder. Compelled to summon the elemental for Thel, Shar resists and calls on the god Yandros instead, saving herself.

In *The Dark Caller*, Shar runs away from the castle to join a woman she believes to be Giria, her mother. Giria, long supposed to be a drowned suicide, is with the Keepers of Light, a religious group devoted solely to Order. Shar has various adventures trying to find proof that the woman claiming to be her mother really is such, and finally decides to trust her. Shar's friends, the young Initiate Hestor and the ex-bandit Kitto, find evidence that elementals from the sixth plane are active, seeking revenge against Shar for foiling them before. They run into great dangers trying to find and help Shar, and make matters worse by keeping information from the High Initiate. Even though two of the gods become involved, it is Shar's own great power finally breaking loose that frees her from the hellish sixth plane.

In *Keepers of Light*, Shar's fame and extraordinary talents have gone to her head. The Circle Initiates are experimenting with the use of the Maze, an ancient part of the castle that allows instantaneous travel, the use of which has long been forgotten. Shar's illicit experiments reveal the possibility of travelling in time as well as space; she decides to go back and kill her uncle, Thel, before he can murder her parents. In the course of her experiments she enters the Chaos Gate that joins the mortal and divine realms, becoming trapped among the planes. Tarod of Chaos and Ailind of Order, both gods of Time, discover too late that Shar's ignorant meddling has cut them off from the mortal world, and that her damage to the Chaos Gate and Time could spread throughout the world. When their worshippers briefly stabilize the gate, the two gods of Time enter the mortal world to seal the Gate. They have no interest in rescuing Shar, since everything was entirely her fault. Only when a follower of Order pleads for the Chaos-devoted Shar is she rescued and pardoned by the gods. Her punishment is to be sent to the Keepers of Light for a time, to learn some discipline and self-restraint among the adherents of Order.

These are excellent examples of the use of a secondary world created for adult fantasy in a book for young people. The impression that a complex world, with its geography, culture, religion, and history underlies the story is maintained, without the detail ever becoming overwhelming. The relationships between Shar and her friends, the young men Hestor and Kitto, the competition and jealousy as well as the loyalty and affection, are convincingly portrayed. The adults are not merely dull-witted obstructions, as is sometimes the case when teen heroes have to be freed to act. Here, the adults do have the intelligence and strength to be involved; what they often lack, through circumstances or deliberate withholding on the part of the teens, is information. This enables them to be brought in when it is realistically necessary, while leaving the young heroes to take the central active role. Shar, rather than starting as a flawed character who must improve through the course of the books, begins as an innocent, a victim who manages to take control of her own destiny. Having done that, she develops dangerous negative traits – arrogance, over-confidence, self-justifying slyness, even a willingness to attempt murder – which she must repent of and learn to combat, coming to understand the consequences to both others and herself. Throughout, she remains a sympathetic character though, one whose adventures will be followed with even more anxiety as to the outcome, when she begins to become her own worst enemy.

Teens who have enjoyed these may want to track down Cooper's nine adult books set in the world of Chaos and Order (although the *Star Shadow* trilogy might be considered more suitable for older teens due to the brutality of the rulers of the world in that era). On the other hand, adults wishing for more of Cooper's Chaos and Order should find the trilogy about Shar an engrossing chance to revisit Tarod and the castle on the Star Peninsula.

Cooper's three-part story *Mirror, Mirror*, published for older children or teens in numbered volumes as *Breaking Through* (2000), *Running Free* (2000), and *Testing Limits* (2001), is something very different. It begins with fifteen year-old Angel Ashe, who lives in Zone Bohemia, Birmingham, Eurostate 8, with her 'prime parent' Soho. This world is one of utterly commercialized technology, where nothing, not even breakfast, education, or medicine, is free of interactive advertising. Angel is miserable, a misfit continually galled by her society and her self-absorbed, trend-obsessed mother. Soho arranges an eighteen-month period of 'Societal Adequacy' for her, a 'Pairing' – that is, an arranged marriage which Angel cannot legally refuse. Running away from the party at which she has found this out, Angel stumbles through a sculpture of mirrors and water into another world, and her adventures begin.

Angel finds herself in a world she believes to be the past because of its superstition and lack of technology, but it is actually an alternate reality that seems like a comic nightmare of New Age sentiment. There she is hailed as a 'Spirit Childe', but befriended by the orphan Winter, who has figured out a little about the mirror-sculpture hidden behind a waterfall, through which Angel entered this world. He and Angel try to make it work again without success. The villagers expect her to cure them by magic when an epidemic strikes; Winter falls ill, but Angel finally makes the gateway work and takes them both to her world. Angel invents a story of abduction and, for Winter, amnesia, and becomes an instant celebrity, something Soho takes full advantage of. Overwhelmed by constant media exploitation, Angel and Winter plan to flee back to Winter's world with drugs to cure the epidemic. Angel has persuaded Soho to buy the mysterious mirror and water sculpture for her. However, Pye, a stranger with very strange manners, shows up, saying the sculpture is his, and dangerous. Angel, Winter, and Twinkle, her robotic 'Therapet' cat, flee through the sculpture.

In *Running Free*, Angel, Winter, and Twinkle have arrived in a world very like Winter's, but more suspicious and violent. They are condemned to death, but escape using the tireless robot cat to break out of their prison. They find a world that is a variation on Angel's, as well as one where everyone lies compulsively, and one, most like our reality in the behaviour of its people, where the mirror-sculpture is in a spaceport near a nuclear-war devastated Birmingham, from which ships leave for colonies in space with little more fuss than jets crossing the Atlantic. Eventually they are found by Pye, the creator of the sculptures or gates, just as they are choking to death in a poisoned, dead world. Pye has created a home for himself in an uninhabited reality, and has gathered various odd creatures into his household, including the intelligent butler dog Gregory. He offers to take on Angel and Winter as apprentices. Though Winter is happy to be wanted, Angel feels she should go back to her mother. When she does, though, she finds herself only another commercial asset, a means to fame and wealth through her 'celeb' status. With great difficulty, she manages to return to Pye's world.

In the conclusion of the story, *Testing Limits*, Pye, Angel, and Winter discover that someone is using Pye's gates to kidnap famous people from different realities. Soho is one of the missing. The culprit is Tertia, a genetically altered person from Pye's world, a sociopathic, telekinetic adult in a child's unaging body. She has created her own fantasy world, where the captive celebrities are forced to act out various roles for her amusement. Tertia captures Angel and stakes her out to be struck by lightning; escaping that fate, Angel, Winter, the compulsive liar Suuu, and Pye try to outwit Tertia in her own games. She is finally trapped and exiled to an isolated place where she can do no harm, and the kidnap victims returned to their own dimensions, most believing they have been part of some confusing publicity event. Angel must cope with Soho's indifference and refusal to believe she really is her missing daughter, who was not loved and never mourned. At least Angel has created her own home and loving family with Pye and Winter.

Mirror, Mirror is more than just an adventure through possible realities or an ironic examination of various trends in contemporary society, though as the latter in particular it also has much to offer. One role of speculative fiction is to call attention to the real world by taking elements of it to extremes, drawing attention by sharp light and shadow to something already present, and *Mirror, Mirror* does this with glee. However, it is most of all Angel's search for love, acceptance, and a sense of her own identity and worth, her ultimate coming to terms with the guilt she feels for not surrendering herself to being the daughter her mother wants, which makes for a story that will resonate with many young people. Her recognition that she must value herself and live her own life with those who love her for herself makes a strong conclusion to the series.

Although she has received little attention as a fantasy writer for and about teens, Louise Cooper deserves more recognition in the field for her innovative, richly textured world-building and realistic, sympathetic characters. She creates stories with intriguing, suspenseful plots, in which engaging young protagonists grow to meet extraordinary challenges.

Terry Pratchett (b. 1948)

Terry Pratchett was born in Buckinghamshire. He sold his first short story at the age of thirteen, and left school to work as a journalist when he was seventeen. He later worked as a press officer for the Central Electricity Generating Board. His first novel was a children's fantasy, *The Carpet People* (1971/1992); his fourth was the first *Discworld* book. Pratchett has been called Britain's best-selling living novelist; *Discworld* books invariably top bestseller lists. He received an O.B.E. in 1998. He is married, has one daughter, and lives with his wife Lyn in Wiltshire.

As a children's author, Pratchett belongs mostly to the nineties, although it must be pointed out that children are avid readers of the *Discworld* books, which began appearing in 1983 with *The Colour of Magic*. By 2004's *Going Postal* the series had reached thirty-three novels, including the lavishly illustrated (by Paul Kidby) short novel, *The Last Hero* (2001) and three children's books. There are also semi-non-fiction works: *Nanny Ogg's Cookbook* (1999), *The Science of Discworld* (2000), and *The Science of Discworld II: The Globe* (2002), the latter two books co-written with scientists Ian Stewart and Jack Cohen, intermingling *Discworld* episodes with discussions of science and the humanities to form a good introduction to current knowledge about our universe and our selves. In addition, there are assorted plays and graphic novel adaptations, diaries, guidebooks, and maps.

Pratchett's very first novel, *The Carpet People*, is hard to find in its original 1971 edition. However, a revised version was published in 1992. Pratchett's foreword to this explains that his ideas of what fantasy should be had changed greatly since its original publication; he writes that fantasy was for him no longer about battles and kings, but about avoiding the need for both. He ended up revising *The Carpet People* extensively to accord with these ideas, calling the 1992 version a collaboration with himself.

The Carpet People is set in a carpet, a vast landscape to its microscopic inhabitants, with cities, villages, warring cultures, monsters, barbarians, cows, and horses. The forests are the carpet fibres, some cultures mine for varnish in a chair leg and use it to make their artefacts, a match is an escarpment and a penny a towering highland. Aside from their size, the characters are human; they hunt, build fires, and experience day and night, although at an incongruously rapid rate at odds with what must be going on in the room the carpet occupies, since Fray, the legendary destructive force of nature which causes all their upheavals and the near-fall of a civilization, is the passing of a vacuum cleaner. The story is the journey of a tribe of Munrungs, lead by the prosaic chieftain Glurk, his brother Snibril, and the wise man Pismire, after their village is destroyed by the terrible whirlwind and earthquake of Fray. They encounter numerous dangers, but worst are the tunnelling mouls, who have taken over the country of the barbarian warrior-king Brocando and are methodically devouring his people. The Munrungs help him defeat the mouls, but when they reach Ware, the capital city of the empire to which they belong, mouls are there too, destroying from within. Glurk, Snibril and their friends, including the exiled General Bane, drive the mouls from the city and then lead the defence against an attacking moul army. They are losing until the wights, peaceful and confusing people who remember the future, join the battle. In the end, the emperor who allowed the mouls in has vanished and Bane, assumed to be in charge, is considering a new federation rather than an empire. Snibril sets out to see the Carpet, riding his white horse in proper heroic fashion.

Many of Pratchett's continual themes and concerns show up in the revised *Carpet People*, issues of individual responsibility prime among them. Snibril is similar to many of his heroes, idealistic and common-sensical at once, straightforward to the point of apparent naiveté, wryly ironic, passionate about justice, simple kind behaviour between people, and the need for individual action. The characters are not among Pratchett's most memorable, seeming pale copies of *Discworld* 'types' for whom they are more likely the prototypes, trial runs of traits and characteristics he would later develop more fully. It is, however, an enjoyable tale of a quest for safety that turns into a heroic struggle to save a way of life against a nihilistic enemy.

Pratchett's next books for children were a more considered utilisation some of the ideas he first experimented with in *The Carpet People*. The trilogy consisting of *Truckers* (1989), *Diggers* (1990), and *Wings* (1990) was also published in one volume as *The Bromeliad* (1998). Here the heroes are nomes, tiny people about four inches high who live much faster than humans – eight or ten years is a lifetime. In the first book, a small community of nomes lives in a bank near a highway. Most of their community has been killed by predators or the dangers of encroaching human development; the hero Masklin does not even realize it is possible to die without being eaten or squashed. Only some old folks, and young Masklin and Grimma, survive. Finding food is hard with only one man to do the hunting, winter is coming, and a fox digs out their den, eating two of the old folks before Masklin and Grimma can drive it off. Masklin realizes they have to leave; they stow away in the back of a truck and end up in a town, at a department store. There they discover they are not the only nomes in the world; the Store hosts a thriving civilization. The Store nomes, on the other hand, do not believe in the outside world. Like Mary Norton's *Borrowers*, they live off what human society can provide, and their clans, named after their departments, feud like Italian renaissance city-states. The religion of the Store nomes is based on the benevolent Arnold Bros (est. 1905), who built the Store for the benefit of nomes.

The Thing, a small black cube which is the outside nomes' most sacred possession, although no-one remembers why, wakes up and begins to talk. It can tap into the electrical fields of the Store's wiring, interpret the slow drone of human speech, and contains a great deal of information about the world. Fifteen thousand years have passed since it was last active. It tells them it is the 'Flight Navigation and Recording Computer', and discovers that the words mean nothing to Masklin. Nor does the concept of interstellar travel, or the word 'planet'. Masklin tells the Thing, when it asks for instruction, that they want to go home and be safe, a problem it at once begins to work at solving.

When Masklin and Grimma learn the Store is going to be demolished, they once again face the task of stirring an unwilling and frightened population to move, only this time, there are thousands of them. However, with the help of many others, this is accomplished. Scouts find an old quarry, and a complicated method whereby teams of many nomes can drive a truck is developed by Dorcas the engineer. Eventually, and not without many difficulties, protests, and near-rebellions, the nomes evacuate the Store, having learned, after a fashion, to work together for a common cause, and to concede that women are intelligent too – the priest-caste Stationeri have previously insisted that women cannot learn to read, because their brains will overheat.

In *Diggers*, their new life, in which people are not divided into clans and Grimma is teaching all children to read, is disrupted when the quarry is reopened. A newspaper informs them that a person they come to think of as 'Grandson Richard, 39', grandson of 'Arnold Bros' who built the Store, is going to be attending the launch of his corporation's new communications satellite in Florida. Masklin wants to steal a satellite to get all the nomes back to the Ship in which they long ago came to Earth. The Thing has much explaining to do about space, oxygen, and vacuum, but suggests that if it gets close enough to the Ship, it can control it. Masklin and some friends set out for Florida, while Grimma and Dorcas are left to plan and enforce an evacuation from the quarry to a nearby barn.

A religious fanatic delays the evacuation until they are trapped by snow, but Grimma inspires Dorcas with her plan to fight the humans. They damage equipment and vehicles and even take a prisoner for a time, but there are too many humans. Dorcas and his young assistants repair an old excavator, and the nomes flee the quarry in it, smashing trucks and leaving chaos behind them. Police cars pursue; there appears to be an eclipse. A huge shadow settles over them and from it descends a floating platform on which is, not Masklin, but a bromeliad in a pot, with frogs living in the flowers – something Grimma had told Masklin she wanted to see, and to which she had compared the narrow life she was forced to live.

Wings follows the adventures of Masklin, the Thing, Gurder, and Angalo, as they stow away on the Concorde, an adventure in itself. Once in North America, they meet more nomes, led by the woman Shrub. These nomes travel widely, riding wild geese. They help the travellers reach NASA's Cape Canaveral, where the English Nomes get close enough to the launch pad for the Thing to transmit a programme to the satellite the shuttle is about to take into orbit. When in orbit, the television satellite transmits to the hidden ship as the Thing instructed. After revealing himself to humans to get the Thing near electricity again, being mistaken for a newly-arrived alien, and escaping with the help of Grandson Richard, Masklin joins his friends in the Ship. They collect a bromeliad and frogs for Grimma, and then Grimma and the rest of the English nomes, before setting off to explore the universe, which contains, the Thing says, whole planets populated just by nomes.

The nomes' adventures in travel are hilarious, hair-raising, and thought-provoking, while the comedy (and terror) of the assorted vehicular thefts is laugh-out-loud funny. Masklin and Grimma, like most of Pratchett's main characters, are deeply thoughtful people with a clear and often unexpected perspective on the world. Even his characters who are familiar 'types' – bloody-minded, indomitable, complaining old grannies or obsessive enthusiasts lost in the wonders only their imaginations can see – seem at once people more true and real than many one meets every day. The story itself leads the reader to pause and consider what used to be called 'the human condition'. In the nomes, we see ourselves; in their observations and misinterpretations of human behaviour, we see the unexpected comedy and pathos of human nature: the humans gather around the Ship's ramp, waiting for some pronouncement of alien wisdom from the stars, while the actual alien scurries unnoticed between their feet, intent only on getting aboard.

The Bromeliad actually deserves to be called science fiction, since the nomes are aliens and there is no magic – it contains nothing supernatural at all, in fact. However, a story of tiny people hijacking human vehicles somehow ends up being called fantasy, and the identification between nomes and gnomes makes this inevitable.

Although there is no actual connection between the two series, the town of Blackbury, the location of the nomes' Store, is also the setting of Pratchett's three children's books about Johnny Maxwell, a boy whose imagination affects reality. These books are what one young reader has called more 'normal' than Pratchett's other books. They feature a human hero in the real world of the early nineties, with a slightly more conventional supernatural or element of unreality.

The first, *Only You Can Save Mankind* (1992), centres on a computer game with the title of the novel. The player is the last defender of humanity against the attacking alien ScreeWee fleet. But the ScreeWee keep sending Johnny messages offering to surrender, and the manual says nothing about such a scenario.

Johnny, sick and stressed about the ongoing disintegration of his parents' marriage and the (first) Gulf War, finds himself in a fighter confronting ScreeWee, accepts their surrender and is then responsible for escorting them safely home. The lizard-like ScreeWee Captain insists he observe the Geneva Convention. Other players continue to attack the fleet, so Johnny must defend them against human players, assuming he is dreaming and yet not quite believing it, experiencing every destruction of another fighter as real, with all the attendant terror and guilt. The Gunnery Officer stages a mutiny, arresting the Captain and resuming the fighting, which will result in the complete annihilation of the ScreeWee, who are very poor fighters. In the real world, Johnny tracks down Kirsty, another player with whom he has managed to communicate. Kirsty is a bright, lonely, abrasive girl, who enjoys killing game-aliens and calls herself Sigourney. Meeting her proves to Johnny that somehow everything to do with the ScreeWee is real. He persuades her she can join him, and that night, she does. She and Johnny, on the alien flagship, rescue the Captain, but Kirsty's imagination begins to shape things as well, making the ScreeWee less like four-armed newts and more like the predatory aliens of the movie *Alien*. Johnny, Kirsty and the Captain retake the ship, imprisoning the murderous Gunnery Officer. The Gunnery Officer follows the rules of Kirsty's imagination. He escapes, attacks the Captain, and is going to kill Johnny. Kirsty finds herself unable to fire her gun, finally experiencing this as reality. It is Johnny who does fire, when no other choices are left. He and Kirsty leave in the escape pod she imagines, as the ScreeWee fleet crosses the Border which announces Game Over, safe from human attack forever.

Johnny and the Dead (1993) begins when Johnny discovers he can see and talk to the dead in an old cemetery, which has been sold by the local council to a giant consolidated company as a location for a factory. When the dead discover their peaceful cemetery is threatened, they expect Johnny to do something about it. He and his friends fail to find anyone famous buried there, though they do learn about a 'Pals battalion' from Blackbury, a group of men who enlisted together during the First World War and were nearly all killed on the Somme four weeks later. Johnny reflects on the war, youth, and death, but is no closer to saving the cemetery. The dead, their horizons expanded by Johnny's gift of a radio, learn to travel as energy, embarking with unquenchable enthusiasm on continued existence. Though Johnny rallies public opinion to save the cemetery, the corporation which has bought it begins to destroy it anyway, planning to blame Hallowe'en vandals. Johnny and his friends prevent this, but the dead themselves try to destroy the place, since they no longer need it. Johnny persuades them of what he has himself realized: it is the living who need it to remind them of their past.

Johnny and his mother are living with his withdrawn grandfather in *Johnny and the Bomb* (1996). Johnny becomes obsessed with Paradise Street, which was bombed during the Second World War. When he and his friends find the time-travelling bag lady Mrs. Tachyon unconscious, Johnny ends up having to look after her trolley of mysterious black squishy bags and her insanely vicious cat Guilty while she is hospitalized. She has been injured by the explosion of a bomb, back in 1941, while scavenging from the just-destroyed pickle factory, and has taken herself forward to a time where the National Health Service will look after her. Bags of time, Johnny realizes, are what she has in her trolley, and his own concern with the 'Blackbury Blitz' lands him, Kirsty, Wobbler, Bigmac, and Yo-less in the past. Bigmac is arrested as a spy, and although they manage to rescue him, when they return, Wobbler does not. They have affected the future; Wobbler's encounter with an evacuee boy who was running away to London made the boy change his mind; the boy remained in Paradise Street and was one of the casualties. He was also Wobbler's grandfather. In the present, Johnny and his friends are found by an elderly, wealthy man, Sir John, who tells them he is Wobbler. Trapped in the past, he made a fortune by knowing which trends were going to catch on, investing in burger bars and computers. None the less, Sir John would rather grow up in the present.

Eventually Johnny, still obsessed with Paradise Street, finds a way to change things. A series of mechanical problems and miscommunications prevented the air-raid siren warning of the approaching bombers that night. Johnny decides they must make sure the warning gets through. They cannot persuade the man in charge of the look-out post to believe an attack is coming, but the young aircraft spotter Tom joins them in their desperate effort to reach the siren at the police station and sound the alarm.

The bombs fall, but everyone on Paradise Street is safe. Back in the present, Johnny's grandfather, who would never talk about his war experience, is happy now to tell how he got a medal for running two miles in an unbelievably short time to sound the air-raid siren.

All three Johnny Maxwell books blend the fantastic with the everyday realism of a group of friends instantly recognizable as thirteen-year-olds one quite possibly knows, hanging out and having long, rambling debates about the most serious and non-sensical of topics. The stories contain the subtle irony that is one of Pratchett's distinguishing traits as well as a wry realism. Pratchett's characteristic concerns translate well to a real world setting: individual responsibility towards both oneself and others, self-deception, and the rarity of a person who can see through all the clutter, delusion, and conventions of everyday existence to at least a closer approximation to the truth of how people think, believe, and act. Johnny, like Masklin of *The Bromeliad* or Carrot in the *Discworld* books, is a wise innocent. He is not such a naive innocent as George MacDonald's Diamond – it is Kirsty, not Johnny, who is naive in her dogmatic view of the world – but nonetheless something akin. He sees the world, wrongs and injustices that are ignored and the euphemisms that hide truths of death, destruction, and responsibility; he believes in what he sees, even when he does not understand it, rather than in what he is told he is seeing. The fantastical experiences he has stand as metaphoric enactments of the things that trouble him: war, death, the past, the future.

The Amazing Maurice and His Educated Rodents (2001) is a *Discworld* book for older children or teens, which won the Carnegie Medal. The Discworld (which is flat, and travels through space on the backs of four elephants standing on a giant turtle) is a secondary world that Pratchett originally created par-tially as a spoof on the role-playing-game-influenced, unliterary imitations of Tolkien that abounded in the seventies and early eighties. It rapidly became much more, increasing in complexity and seriousness while never losing its profoundly comic nature. Most very long series exhaust themselves, while the Discworld and its cast of major characters keep growing in literary finesse. Many teens and younger children are avid readers of Discworld books, but *The Amazing Maurice* was the first written specifically for the juvenile audience.

The character 'Amazing Maurice', with his educated rodents, is first mentioned in passing in *Reaper Man* (1991), where the wizards complain of the con man's activities in Ankh-Morpork and neighbouring cities. Whether or not Pratchett had a story idea even at this time, ten years later Amazing Maurice appeared in a book of his own, no con man but a con cat, with a troupe of literate rats and a piper in tow. The rats and Maurice have been 'Changed', gaining speech and intelligence, by wizards' rubbish. Maurice, using the rats and a young musician, Keith, whom he calls 'the stupid-looking kid', is trying to make a fortune. They inflict a plague of rats on a town, Keith hires himself out as a piper, the rats follow him out of town, and they move on to the next. In the town of Bad Blintz they run into trouble. There is already, supposedly, a plague of rats, and a near-famine in the town. With the help of the mayor's daughter, Malicia Grim, they discover that the two ratcatchers who are oppressing the town, stealing food and extorting money, have hundreds of caged rats in cellars and tunnels, where they starve them to make them more vicious for cruel ratting contests. The most deadly enemy, though, is a creature the rat-catchers made out of eight rats knotted together at the tail. This is the abominable, telepathic rat-king called Spider. It can control the normal rats and is driven entirely by hatred of humans and desire to dominate all rats and the world. Only Dangerous Beans, the weak, near-blind thinker, is able to resist the rat-king's influence over other minds, its terrorizing and its persuasions, perceiving clearly that behind the rat-king's talk of representing all rats lies a disregard for everything except its own power. Maurice sacrifices his own life (luckily as a cat, he has several to spare) in killing the rat-king, and sacrifices another for the fatally-wounded Dangerous Beans' sake. The mayor of Bad Blintz is quick to adapt to a town shared with intelligent rats. Maurice sets off travelling again on his own, and at the end, is recruiting a new 'stupid-looking kid' for a new scheme.

The Amazing Maurice and his Educated Rodents has some very sombre moments, and the heroes face much realistic pain, loss, and cruelty before the end. The complex psychology of the characters – Maurice's long-simmering guilt over having been Changed by eating one of the talking rats when he was only an ordinary cat, Dangerous Beans' loss and restoration of faith and hope in the future, practical Darktan's near-apotheosis in the trap – makes the book more likely to be appreciated fully by teens and older children than by the very young. It is a work for children to read when they themselves decide they are ready, not, despite talking animals, plenty of humour and a happy ending, a book to read aloud to very small children.

The Wee Free Men (2003) is another Discworld book for children and teens, featuring witches and the pictsies, who are tiny, blue-tattooed, hard-drinking, quarrelsome, 'braid Scots' speaking, cattle-raiding pixies. Nine-year-old Tiffany Aching, a farmer's daughter who is also a witch, sets off into fairyland with the pictsies, her late grandmother's book on sheep diseases, and her weapon of choice, a cast-iron frying pan. She intends to save her annoying baby brother and, as an afterthought, the baron's son, from a fairy queen in a world where dreams can be stronger than reality and just as deadly. Aside from the wonderful and unforgettable Nac Mac Feegle clan of pictsies, whose warriors are led by Rob Anybody, Tiffany is also accompanied on her mission by a toad who was once a lawyer. Among the monsters she encounters are the dromes, which spin webs of dreams and devour those caught in them. The queen's entire world is a parasitic one, which creates nothing of its own and can only take from others; this does not make it weak. Only by insisting on the reality of herself and her place in the world does Tiffany face down the queen in the end, reducing her, briefly, to what she really is as well. Along the way Tiffany learns a great deal about both herself and her shepherd grandmother, and about the uses, abuses, and responsibilities of power.

A Hat Full of Sky (2004) continues Tiffany's story a year or so later. Tiffany leaves home to learn witchcraft from Miss Level, who is one woman inhabiting two bodies. Tiffany's great power attracts the attention of a hiver, an ancient force from the beginning of time; her ignorance of much of what she does with her power leaves her vulnerable, and she is possessed. The hiver does not so much control her as suppress all her normal self-control. Tiffany becomes arrogant, utterly self-obsessed, and terribly dangerous, acting on the assumption that if you have power, you should use it to get what you want. Granny Weatherwax, the most powerful of the Discworld witches and a central character in a number of other books in the series, and Rob Any-body, chief of the pictsie clan for which Tiffany is the official hag (or witch), attempt to help her save herself, but the struggle is not without great risk to everyone involved. Though the hiver is forced out of Tiffany, it still hunts her; to save those gathered at the festive witch trials, she relies on her understanding of both the hiver and herself to communicate with it and take it into the desert that is the beginning of death, for the peace and silence it seeks. Trapped there, she meets Death, another popular Disc-world character, and is shown the way out by Granny Weather-wax. Tiffany earns the respect of Granny as well as of the young apprentice witches who had mocked her when she first went to stay with Miss Level, but realizes that being a powerful witch means continually having to make difficult choices and con-stantly subjecting one's motives to scrutiny.

Like all the *Discworld* books, *Amazing Maurice*, *The Wee Free Men*, and *A Hat Full of Sky*, emphasize more than any other theme the power and necessity of individual integrity and action, even and especially in the face of evil, which is always an utterly mortal thing, arising not from any divine or demonic force but from people's choices, actions, and wills. This theme also domi-nates all of Pratchett's other writing for children. Pratchett is not only incredibly prolific, funny, and an excellent prose stylist, but occasionally wise as well.

The nineties saw fantasy for children increase in complexity, in part but not solely because adult writers such as Terry Pratchett, Louise Cooper, Dave Duncan, and Tanith Lee were turning skills acquired in writing long novels set in detailed secondary worlds to juvenile works. After the maturation of adult fantasy during the course of the eighties, it was now shaping children's fantasy, just as the juvenile literature of earlier generations had influ-enced the adult genre. The expectation of depth and complexity in secondary world fantasy meant that even lighter or simpler tales, like the *Enchanted Forest Chronicles*, *The Moorchild*, *Spiggot's Quest* or *The Firework-Maker's Daughter*, took place against a background of greater texture and colour than a similar story might have been felt to require in, for instance, the fifties. Rushdie's *Haroun*, though it moves by times into the realms of allegory or of fable, offers complexity and internal consistency in its depiction of the moon Kahani; it is not simply a landscape of metaphor, but an interconnected world where that landscape is crucial to the actions of the characters, the development of the societies or of that world, and hence to the working of the plot. Fantasy using animals as its characters demanded new societies and cultures for those animals – Jarvis' mice, Kilworth's weasels and stoats – another example of the desire for fully realized secondary worlds, even if those worlds, like Jarvis', are recognizable as a variation on our own. Stories set in worlds more recognizably ours, Melling's Ireland and its intertwined Faerie, Pratchett's Blackbury of Johnny Maxwell and the nomes, Wrede's alternate Regency London, are developed with equal care and attention to carrying the audience to a specific world, a place and time, known or previously unknown to them.

Plots such as Melling's, of teens drawn into magical adventures from lives in the ordinary world, Wrede's Pygmalian orphan-makes-good or literary fairy-tales of the Enchanted Forest, and Rushdie's whimsy-filled lesson, provided familiar patterns to the general children's book audience. However, writers like Pratchett, Lee, Cooper, and Pullman required of their readers a greater familiarity with the traditions of secondary world fantasy, a willingness of the audience to accept another world, and to make the effort to assimilate that new world into the imagination. One of the greatest powers of speculative literature, whether fantasy or science fiction, is its freedom to explore possibilities beyond our reality, the 'what-ifs' and 'if ... thens' that lead not only to the fantastic, but to new ways of viewing ourselves and our world. All speculative fiction writers do this to varying degrees; in the nineties, among children's writers, the interest in exploring further afield from reality, often with the intent to examine specific themes and issues of human nature, began to dominate over tales set in worlds recognizably founded on cultures, histories, or mythologies of our own.

However, just as children's fantasy was becoming a more complex and specialized genre, with an audience becoming more segregated, as adult audiences of science fiction and fantasy are at least perceived to be, Rowling's 1997 *Harry Potter and the Philosopher's Stone* brought in a broad, 'mainstream' audience, both adult and juvenile. The long-term effect of this on the shape of children's fantasy remains to be seen, but in the short term, in the years around the turn of the century, it changed the popular perception of children's fantasy, and brought in a new readership, some at least of whom may be enticed to explore further into the genre.

XVII
Into the Twenty-First Century

It is difficult to examine the impact on history and the 'mood of the times', on young people's development or on writers' imaginations, of events while they are still news, without the broader vision allowed by distance. The twenty-first century began without the popularly-predicted chaos of the millennium bug, a computer programming flaw that was largely corrected before the event. It did begin with violence, with the terrorist attacks on the United States of September 11, 2001, the ensuing American overthrow of the Taliban government of Afghanistan, further terrorist bombings in Bali and Madrid, and the controversial American detention of prisoners declared not to be prisoners of war and thus not protected by the Geneva Convention, as well as the also-controversial American-inspired and -led war on Iraq in 2003. What these world events may come to mean for young readers, how they may affect what children seek in their fiction, or what they impart to the compost out of which story-tellers create (to borrow a metaphor from Tolkien as paraphrased by Carpenter, *Biography* 182), it is too soon to speculate.

However, it is safe to suggest that these first years of the twenty-first century have seen an upsurge of interest in fantasy in the English-speaking world, and probably an increase in fantasy in all of European children's literature. Part of this is due to the maturation of adult fantasy literature through the eighties and nineties, with writers creating complex worlds, mythologies, and histories, as well as philosophies and characters capable of equal complexity and evolution, adopting the literary standards of Tolkien rather than merely imitating the superficial aspects of his work. Part, around the turn of the millennium, was the popularity of the extremely long, fat, serial, by authors such as Robert Jordan, which appeared in general bestseller lists and generated reviews and discussion of such series in weekend papers, where non-fantasy readers could not help but notice. For a time, part was no doubt due to the three movies based on *The Lord of the Rings* in 2001-2003, which, through high-quality effects and epic spectacle, as well as celebrated actors, received much attention and drew in an audience far beyond those who knew the book.

A little-acknowledged facet of the current 'respectability' of fantasy is the use of fantasy or supernatural elements in many television shows, although these are usually disguised as science fiction, considered more 'real' than mere fantasy. Mystic relics of ancient cultures, communication with animals, telepathy, as well as ghosts, vampires, witches, heroes and villains with 'special' powers, and prophetic dreams, all rub shoulders with aliens, space travel, parallel universes, and possible human futures, on both the science fiction and cartoon speciality channels, and even on 'mainstream' networks. Such elements are also offered with little apology in allegedly realistic sitcoms and dramas. All this, whether done well or poorly in terms of internal credibility, originality, and consistency, has created a climate where the trappings of fantasy are less alien, and therefore less 'unbeliev-able', to that general reader who dips occasionally into fantasy but does not usually plunge wholeheartedly into another world, the reader unwilling or unable to make the imaginative leap to other possibilities. Fantasy, to such a reader, has become a less foreign and difficult terrain, and they may venture farther in than they otherwise would, leaving the easy known world for the new with less reluctance, because they recognize a few of the superfi-cial landmarks. They may dare to read a more demanding fan-tasy, because television has told them the fantastic is acceptable, and not just for the weird quiet kid in the back row.

Part of fantasy's new popularity, and more importantly, its acceptability, is due to children's fantasy, particularly Philip Pullman's *His Dark Materials* and J.K. Rowling's *Harry Potter.* Pullman has been discussed previously, as an author of the nine-ties, which is arguably where Rowling also belongs. Her first four books appeared from 1997 to 2000. The series of seven re-sumed again in 2003, but the impact and repercussions of *Harry Potter* are likely to shape expectations of children's fantasy in the early twenty-first century more than it had time to in the nine-teen-nineties. Rowling is a young author with, potentially, a long career ahead of her; hence she is discussed as an author of the twenty-first century.

J.K. Rowling (b. 1965)

Joanne Rowling grew up near Bristol and later near Chepstow, the oldest of two sisters. She studied French at Exeter University and later worked for Amnesty International, beginning *Harry Potter* while enduring a long train trip in 1990. She taught English in Portugal, married, and moved to Edinburgh with her infant daughter after a divorce. There she set out to finish what would be the first *Harry Potter* book. She was working as a French teacher when the book was published. The American rights were sold to Scholastic for an advance of over $100,000, enabling Rowling to turn to writing full time. Rowling married Neil Murray in 2001 and with him had a son and a second daughter; she lives in Scotland.

Harry Potter is perhaps more likely than most other children's fantasy to be known in detail to the adult for whom this survey is intended. However, since it may be only the familiarity of *Alice's Adventures in Wonderland*, assembled from passing references and the flotsam of popular culture, it will be treated like the rest, and the main points of the plot summarized here.

Harry Potter and the Philosopher's Stone (1997; published in the US as *Harry Potter and the Sorcerer's Stone*) begins with the baby Harry, survivor of a magical attack that murdered his parents, being left on the doorstep of his mother's sister and her family. The Dursleys are Muggles – ordinary, non-magical people – and are deeply ashamed of their magical in-laws. Though the wizarding world celebrates its liberation from the tyranny of Lord Voldemort, who terrorized it until his mysterious disappearance during the attack on the Potters, Harry grows up suffering deprivation and abuse from the Dursleys. Only when he is accepted into Hogwarts, a school for witches and wizards, does he discover that, in the wizarding world, he is both wealthy and famous as the only survivor and somehow the overthrower of Voldemort. He makes both friends and enemies at Hogwarts. Chief among the former are the half-giant groundskeeper Hagrid, Ron Weasley, and Hermione Granger. Among the latter are snobbish and vicious Draco Malfoy, whose parents were supporters of Voldemort, and the Potions master, Snape.

Harry and his friends discover that the formula for unending life, the philosopher's stone, is hidden in a forbidden part of the school, and that those who want Voldemort to return are planning to steal it. Harry, Ron, and Hermione overcome the various traps and riddles that guard it. Only Harry makes it through to the end, where he discovers the enemy is the timid Defence Against Dark Arts teacher, Quirrell, whose body Voldemort has parasitized. Harry outwits Quirrell and Voldemort to save the Stone from them, but is in danger of being killed when Dumbledore saves him.

In *Harry Potter and the Chamber of Secrets* (1998), Ron's younger sister Ginny falls under the power of an enchanted diary which contains a version of a copy of the young Tom Riddle, who grew up to be Voldemort. Ginny is compelled by Riddle to release the basilisk immured in the hidden Chamber of Secrets. The Chamber was built by Salazar Slytherin, one of Hogwarts' founders, a wizard who despised Muggles and wizards with Muggle parentage. After the basilisk attacks Hermione and several other students (by various lucky chances only petrifying them, literally), Hagrid is blamed and taken away (without any kind of trial) to Azkaban, the wizards' prison, while Dumbledore loses his position as headmaster. Harry and Ron figure out how to reach the Chamber, attempting to rescue Ginny, who is going to be used by Riddle to take on new life. With the help of a sword brought by Fawkes, Dumbledore's phoenix, Harry fights and kills the basilisk, is poisoned by it in the process, and is saved by the phoenix's tears. He destroys the diary-Riddle, the petrified students are restored, Hagrid is freed from prison and Dumbledore returns to set to rest Harry's doubts about his own virtues, reassuring him that although he may have some of the attributes that the founder of the dark-inclined Slytherin House admired, his own actions and choices determine what he is.

The main story in *Harry Potter and the Prisoner of Azkaban* (1999) is the escape of a dangerous murderer from Azkaban prison. Sirius Black is supposed to have been a follower of Voldemort. He was also Harry's godfather and the friend who supposedly betrayed Harry's parents to Voldemort. The Ministry of Magic believes Black is now after Harry. Dementors, the grey-cowled creatures who guard the wizards' prison of Azkaban, are sent to guard the schoolgrounds, though Dumbledore refuses to allow them in. The new Defence Against Dark Arts teacher, Professor Lupin, helps Harry learn to counter the effect of the Dementors, who suppress all joy and pleasure by their presence and who can kill by sucking out a person's soul.

Though Hermione and Ron are at odds over the ongoing attempts of her new cat, Crookshanks, to eat Ron's rat Scabbers, the friends work together trying to save one of Hagrid's hippogriffs, condemned to death for biting Draco Malfoy. In one complicated night, they discover that Black is an 'animagus', capable of taking the form of a dog, that he is hiding out near the school, that Lupin is a werewolf, and that the rat Scabbers is another animagus, Peter Pettigrew. All three were friends of Harry's father. It was Pettigrew, not Black, who betrayed the Potters and committed the murders for which Black was imprisoned. Black is captured by Snape, Pettigrew escapes, and the Dementors are summoned to suck out Sirius Black's soul. Harry and Hermione, after much very broad hinting by Dumbledore, find a way to save both Buckbeak and Black using Hermione's time-turner. The usual quandary presented by such a time-travel device, the desire to go back and change some climactic tragedy of a character's life (such as the murder of Harry's parents), never seems to occur to Harry, much less tempt him. Harry worries that he was wrong to save Pettigrew's life when Black and Lupin wanted to kill him; Dumbledore assures him it was the right thing to do and may have unintended consequences.

The plot of *Harry Potter and the Goblet of Fire* (2000) is long and convoluted, but it centres on the wraithlike Voldemort's attempt to create a new body for himself. His spell to do so requires a little of Harry's blood; to get this, he embarks on one of the most needlessly complex of all supervillain schemes. In the Triwizard Tournament, three champions representing the three schools of Hogwarts, Beauxbatons, and Durmstrang compete in hazardous tasks. Only the older students are allowed to put their names in to compete; one from each school is magically chosen. Harry's name is chosen as well as Cedric Diggory's for Hogwarts, even though Harry is too young and did not enter his name. Harry succeeds in the first two tasks, helped by his friends, who aid him with research, and by others who contrive to give him hints.

The third task is to reach the Triwizard Cup in the centre of a maze filled with magical creatures. Harry and Diggory help one another and take the Cup together. However, the Cup has been turned into a 'Portkey'. A Portkey is any object, enchanted so that it carries a person touching it to a preset place. The Cup takes them to a graveyard where Voldemort is preparing his spell to return to life. Cedric is killed, Harry captured, and a drop of his blood used in the spell. To prove that Harry is less powerful than he is, Voldemort frees the boy and challenges him to a wizard's duel. Harry manages to hold off Voldemort, helped by ghostly 'echoes' of those murdered with Voldemort's wand. He reaches the Portkey, taking himself and Cedric's body back to Hogwarts, where he is kidnapped by one of Voldemort's followers and rescued by Dumbledore.

The strength of this particular story lies in its portrayal of the muddles of adolescent romance, which begin to trouble the characters' lives. This aspect is very convincingly and unsentimentally portrayed throughout. Harry has a crush on Cho Chang, who is going out with Diggory; Hermione's friendship with Bulgarian Quidditch star Viktor Krum is rather more than friendship on his part, while her irritation with Ron hides stronger feelings, as presumably must Ron's sudden dislike of his former sports hero Krum. The book's major flaw lies in its plot.

Harry Potter and the Goblet of Fire is weak in the logic at the core of the story. The entire central storyline of the Triwizard Tournament and Harry's exceptional situation as a fourth participant is contrived by the villains to get him in a position to touch the Triwizard cup. Anything can be made into a Portkey. Harry's winning of the cup is difficult, and generally regarded as unlikely. Numerous methods, simpler and less likely to go wrong, could have been adopted by Voldemort to get Harry to touch a Portkey to take him to the location of the ritual. The villains could far more easily have gained access to his book, his bedroom slippers, or his broomstick, to make a Portkey they wanted Harry, and Harry alone, to touch, rather than using the prize in a dangerous contest Harry was not supposed to be able to enter and which is barely within his ability to win on his own. The whole thing jars against common sense. A scheme so open to failure, so unnecessarily complicated, seems a very bad tactic from a villain who has not previously demonstrated such poor planning. It tips one out of the story, into awareness of the author's intentions in assembling the plot, which is an indication that those intentions have not been fulfilled in a manner internally consistent within the book. The two main streams of the plot, Harry's participation in the tournament and Voldemort's desire for Harry's blood, are harnessed together in a manner that is ill-conceived and artificially contrived. This is unlikely to lessen most young readers' enjoyment, although those to whom it occurs, and there will be some even among young readers who have an innate sense of the necessity of internal logic for a story, will find it a far weaker book than the first three, less conducive to total immersion because less believable.

The series' fans were left frustrated by the long gap before the publication of the next book, *Harry Potter and the Order of the Phoenix*, in 2003. When it appeared, it followed the pattern of the earlier works, though it was once again longer than the last. It is also a much stronger book than *Goblet of Fire*, lacking the weak internal logic and awkward forcing of the plot that marred the fourth book. Harry has become an angry, frustrated teen, passively inviting fights with his bullying cousin, feeling resentful of his exclusion from the secret resistance group led by Dumbledore, the Order of the Phoenix. The Order is dedicated to fighting Voldemort's spreading influence in the wizarding world. Like the rest of that world, Hogwarts begins to experience the first steps towards a fascist regime, with a government-appointed overseer reporting on evidence of incorrect beliefs. Harry is revealed to be the subject of a prophecy; he will destroy Voldemort, or Voldemort him. Lured into a trap at the Ministry of Magic, he and his friends in turn become bait for the adult members of the Order, and Sirius Black is killed. Once again, Dumbledore arrives in time to save Harry and rescue what can be rescued from the situation. The sixth in the series, *Harry Potter and the Half-Blood Prince*, followed in July 2005.

Harry Potter and the Philosopher's Stone was very popular from the first in Britain, but the publication of the third book was turned into a media event by the publisher Bloomsbury, its release to bookstores handled like sensitive government information, generating a frenzy among young readers. North America began to read Rowling more slowly; *Philosopher's Stone* was available, although not well known, from the beginning in Canada, while the first book was published for the United States in October of 1998 as *Harry Potter and the Sorcerer's Stone* – 'philosopher' apparently being considered too difficult a word for

American children. Exposure on an American television show resulted in a sudden *Harry Potter* craze. By 1999, they were *the* books that everyone, child and adult, was reading, even those who had never touched a fantasy novel before. Bloomsbury even issued the book with a more sombre cover as an 'adult edition', and continues to do so for each new instalment of the series.

The first three books all won the Smarties Award, which is voted for by children from a shortlist chosen by a panel of adult judges. The fourth was awarded a Hugo, one of the most prestigious science fiction awards, which is voted for by attendees at the World Science Fiction Convention; the closest it had ever previously come to going to a children's author is the multi-Hugo winning Robert A. Heinlein, who wrote science fiction for both adults and teens.

The success of the books meant that Rowling had the financial power to oversee the production of the movies based on them – she could afford to refuse contracts that did not offer sufficient artistic control, as most authors cannot. Thus the movies follow the plots of the books fairly closely. The very popularity of the *Harry Potter* books generated difficulties for Rowling. Nancy K. Stouffer, an American who had self-published a children's book set in a thinly-conceived post-apocalyptic, nuclear-mutant future, *The Legend of Rah and the Muggles* (1984), and a separate series of activity books featuring a character named Larry Potter, accused Rowling of plagiarism. Rowling, her American publisher (Scholastic US), and Warner Bros, which was producing the movies, sued Stouffer, seeking the cessation of her public accusations. Stouffer then went to court herself with a counterclaim of infringement of copyright. She was found by the judge to have altered documents and lied to support her case. The accusations of plagiarism against Rowling were proven groundless, and Stouffer was both fined and ordered to pay part of the defendants' costs (BBC News).

The audience for *Harry Potter* is broad. It is fantasy, and attracts the fantasy audience by offering an alternate vision of our world, one with a secret parallel society hidden within. Its fantastic trappings are those familiar in popular culture – witches and wizards in pointy hats, incantations and potions – and so it draws in the non-fantasy reader who might baulk at being asked to encompass imaginatively an utterly new world. At the same time it is the story of the suffering orphan, another enduringly popular motif with appeal to a wide range of tastes.

It is also part of the tradition of the school story, well over a century old. There is the new boy/girl, thrown into the new society of the school and rising to be a leader within that society, moving year by year from child towards adult. There are the best friend, as well as the outcast revealed to have valuable abilities who becomes a friend, the bullying enemies, the enemy teacher, the understanding and allied teacher, and many other elements that are almost mandatory in the school story genre. Even children, not given to articulating much literary analysis beyond likes and dislikes, seem to recognize *Harry Potter*'s kinship to Enid Blyton in both the school story aspect, and perhaps even more, in the theme of friends foiling adult villainy through peril-filled adventures that must be conducted largely below the level of adult radar (a formula which is mocked in Pratchett's *Amazing Maurice* – it isn't over till there's tea and buns). Unlike the situation commonly found in Blyton's adventure stories, a few of the adults around Harry do often seem to have an intimation of what he and his friends are up to, and offer unsubtle help and hints.

The series is marked by humour, with a great deal of slapstick. In its portrayal of Harry's enemies minor or major, from thuggish, obese Dudley Dursley, greasy and often irrational Professor Snape, or timid and treacherous Peter Pettigrew, it makes frequent resort to farce and caricature. In addition to the broadly-drawn characters, situational comedy is predominant, as in the Dursleys' attempts to flee the barrage of letters announcing Harry's admission to Hogwarts, Harry and Ron's drive to school in a flying car, posturing incompetent Gilderoy Lockhart, or Professor Trelawney's affected predictions of death and disaster. Hermione's attempt at activism for house-elf rights despite the usual house-elf love of subservience and self-abasement offers broad irony.

Rowling's skill in balancing these elements has resulted in a book capable of sustaining interest among very diverse people, to whom those elements appeal in differing degrees. She makes Harry a character in whom everyone can see something of themselves; he is, actually, rather neutral and passive, more reactive than active. For the audience, he functions as a mirror for imaginative identification, without many strong characteristics of his own to intrude, which is particularly noticeable in a book where most people are defined by a few clearly-depicted traits. Harry has no deep driving passions, no (as of book five) great internal struggles or temptations. Few critical events are his initiative; in general he reacts to things happening to him, initiating action himself only as a last resort. Few problems or events are even his fault, until the end of *Order of the Phoenix*. His failure then to unwrap Sirius' gift of a magic communicating mirror leaves open the possibility that had he done so, he would have been able to contact Sirius and thus not have falsely believed his godfather a prisoner, a belief which led to Harry's rushing into ambush in a rescue attempt and Sirius' death in trying in turn to rescue Harry. This is a tragic fault rather than a large and active mistake; a fit of sulkiness causes the entire chain of events. His sins are minor: disobedience to school rules and an excessive amount of eaves-dropping, which is somehow never deliberate (until the fifth book, when it is initiated by other characters). The latter thus becomes less a wrongdoing on the character's part or a deter-mined effort to acquire vital knowledge and instead, in their cu-mulative effect, a weak plot contrivance. Harry is a decent, average sort of person, moved to anger in defence of his friends or his parents' memory, heroic and determined to do the right thing when necessary, but not defined either negatively or posi-tively by any desire for revenge, or any apprehension of grave *general* injustice in the disturbing embryonic fascism of the wizarding world (present even in the first book). He is very much an Everyman, not an exception, into whom the audience can project their own child and teen selves. In this universality of application lies part of his universality of appeal.

Rowling is not a deep nor a subtle writer; she does not incite much reflection on the human condition or offer those insights into people and possibilities that make one go back to ponder. Her attempts at such are usually heavily explicated, as with the Mirror of Erised in *Philosopher's Stone*, which shows one's deepest wishes, or Harry's ability to create a protective Patronus, given power by his love for his dead father, in *Azkaban*. The Dementors are, as an embodiment of the effects of depression, her most successful venture into metaphoric representation. Even they become more crude or blunt in their poetic workings,

though, through the defences against them: chocolate to counteract the deadening effect of their presence and wand-cast creations of white light, powered by memory of joy, to drive them
away. They remain, though unsubtle, very effective and frightening as both creatures and symbols. This lack of subtlety in
symbolic and philosophic content contributes to the wide appeal
of the series; it is not entirely too shallow for those who prefer
some complexity of thought in their stories, and not too difficult
for those who do not.

The fourth book, *Goblet of Fire*, was criticized by some because it was dark and tragic – a character died. This was hardly
an innovation in children's literature, although death is now less
likely to be presented in fantasy set in the modern, more-or-less
real world like *Harry Potter* than in a story where it is at the remove of a heroic age or a grander and more terrible and splendid
world. Much of the criticism aimed at the existence of this death
must be simply due to those critics having actually read little
children's literature. Death did not used to be an event foreign to
children's books. Only relatively recently has death been either
omitted from children's literature or made the sole focus of the
story, something not to be discussed with children except under
special circumstances, with no admission that death, loss, and
grief are eventually a part of real life for everyone. *The Hobbit*,
The Lion, the Witch and the Wardrobe, *The Silver Chair*, *The
Wind on the Moon*, *The Golden Compass* and its sequels, *The
Bromeliad*, *The Deptford Mice* trilogy, *Redwall*, *Amazing
Maurice and His Educated Rodents*, and the first *Welkin Weasels*
trilogy, all have characters, major or minor, likable or not, who
die as part of the story. The only difference is that *Harry Potter*
is more clearly and all at once our world, our time, and our own
species.

Rowling's world is apparently not far enough removed from
the real for some critics to feel safe in encountering death there.
It is possible this may also be true for some young readers. As
with any death of a well-developed character in a book read by
children, the reaction of the individual child varies. But books
are not television. Images are not instantaneously forced into the
mind. It is easy for readers to put them down and leave them, to
not absorb the images that are beyond what they want to take in
– children, left to themselves, will read what they are emotion-

ally ready for. Books are a secure environment in which to explore the boundaries of emotion, to expand one's experience on the imaginative level. What they are not ready to tolerate or digest, most young readers will skip or set aside. Condemning *Goblet of Fire* for the death of Cedric or *Order of the Phoenix* for that of Sirius Black is misguided.

An unusual feature of the *Harry Potter* series is that the books are written for an audience that increases in age as the characters do. *Goblet of Fire* and *Order of the Phoenix* will be read by some quite young children, but are more likely to be read by older ones, due to their length and their darker tone. This is not unique. Ransome's *Swallows and Amazons* series tends to deepen in its portrayal of character and the challenges taken on by the children as they age and their skills increase; within fantasy, *The Lion, the Witch and the Wardrobe* is written for a younger audience than is *The Last Battle*. However, in recent years, series have tended to be regarded, not as something to work one's way through over time, but as a set to be collected, with each book, although adding new history, plot, and character development, providing the same level of experience. Rowling does not aim to do this, and criticism of her failure to do so is again misguided. The youngest readers must be allowed to grow into the later books at their own pace.

Rowling's role in the history of children's fantasy literature is an important one, although more for the impact *Harry Potter* has had on the popularity of the genre than for its purely literary merits. The prose style of *Harry Potter* is only average in quality; the series brings little new to the genre in content or approach. What Rowling has done, because of the unprecedented mass media attention focused on her books, is attract the interest of many readers who previously overlooked or disdained fantasy, and engender a state where a preference for fantasy is not regarded as a little peculiar or suspect. *Harry Potter* itself is a thoroughly engaging, highly entertaining series, with a magical sub-culture vividly-evoked through a wealth of memorable detail; it will remain a children's classic even after the current popular frenzy has ebbed.

Kenneth Oppel (b. 1967)

Oppel was born in Port Alberni, British Columbia, and grew up in Halifax, Nova Scotia, and Victoria, BC. His first book, *Colin's Fantastic Video Adventure* (1985) was published while he was still a teen. He studied English at the University of Toronto and still lives in Toronto with his wife and children.

Oppel's most familiar works are three fantasies about bats, but he has written other speculative fiction for children and teens, such as the science fiction *Dead Water Zone* (1992). In this, a teenager from the privileged suburbs goes looking for his sickly, genius brother in the slums on the harbour, the 'dead water zone' where the water gives people exceptional strength, but slowly kills them. *The Live-Forever Machine* (1990) is another novel for young readers with a science fiction theme. Oppel also writes picture books.

Silverwing (1997), *Sunwing* (2000), and *Firewing* (2002), however, are fantasies that follow the pattern of traditional quests, except that the hero is a young bat. In *Silverwing*, Shade is a bat who one day breaks the ancient law and stays out until dawn to see the sun. The mythology behind the conflicts in the book tells of a war between birds and beasts in which bats took no part; they were exiled to the night when peace was made. They believe the spirit Nocturna has promised them that someday they will return to daylight. Shade's home is destroyed because his colony refuses to give him up to punishment by the owls. As they migrate south, Shade gets lost and meets Marina, a bat exile. They fall in with Goth, a giant meat-eating jungle bat who has escaped from a lab and begun a new war between birds and bats. Shade and Marina have many narrow escapes with bats and rats on their way south, realizing nearly too late that Goth is not only a meat-eater, but a cannibal.

In *Sunwing* the war between bats and the owl-led birds continues. Shade's colony ends up in a human building they cannot escape, a place that initially seems a bat paradise, but which Shade and Marina discover to be a centre where bats and owls are fitted with explosives and devices to direct them to targets. Shade overcomes this control and allies with other escaped bats and an owl prince, Orestes. Meanwhile, Marina seeks Shade with the help of a rat army; Goth, king of the jungle bats, sets about sacrificing one hundred hearts to his god, Cama Zotz. If this is accomplished, a coming eclipse will mean the death of the sun, the release of Zotz from the Underworld, and the defeat of Nocturna, Zotz's sister. Rats, bats, and owls unite to fight Goth, and one of the human explosive discs is used to destroy the jungle bats' stronghold. Through Orestes' and Shade's pleading with their elders, a truce is declared.

Firewing continues the story with Shade's son, Griffin, who finds himself in the underworld, ruled by Cama Zotz and inhabited by dead bats, most of whom fail to realize they are dead. Some, who do realize they have died, believe there will be a better afterlife presided over by the goddess Nocturna. As he travels through the underworld, Griffin is hunted by the dead Goth, who wants to use his life force, and helped by a dead bat from his own colony, Luna. Shade pursues his son as well, hoping to rescue him before he joins the dead.

Oppel's bat stories are full of dangers, horrors, narrow escapes, and friendship. His young bats come across as human teenagers rather than bats in their emotions, slangy speech, and mannerisms. Because of this, the books seem more in the tradition of *Redwall* or of Robin Jarvis' *Deptford Mice* (with which they have other similarities in their sacrifice-demanding evil gods and human societies unaware of parallel animal ones), than of *Watership Down*, in presenting 'human' animals, despite Oppel's effort to have his bats live as non-anthropomorphic animals, without technology or human-like culture. Oppel devotes much attention to creating the reality of his bat world; he avoids mentioning colours, as he points out in an afterword, and his attention to the sound-world of bats makes for interesting novelty. The idea of bat history preserved in echo chambers that hold a sound, needing only to be repeated once a year to endure, is a unique piece of magic. As the mythology of the bats' world becomes more predominant, the fantasy element grows stronger, until in the third book the conflict between the divinities becomes the primary force shaping the plot. There is little depth to Oppel's characters, good or evil. The mythological aspect, so crucial to the plot, is not brought to life with any intensity of belief on the part of the characters or any vivid detail, never losing that 'assembled from stock parts' feel; the evil of the meat-eating bats in particular lacks any convincing motivation, their religion seeming more something sketched in to give Goth an excuse for his psychopathy than anything in which he and his followers actually believe.

Oppel turned to a human protagonist for *Airborn* (2004), which won the 2004 Governor-General's Award for children's literature. *Airborn* is set in an alternate version of our own world, one in which most intercontinental shipping is carried by airships using not hydrogen or helium, but the fictitious mango-scented gas hydrium. Matt Cruse is a cabin boy on the luxury airship *Aurora*; his ambition is to work his way up to captain. Matt's relationship with the ship is strongly emotional; his father served on her until his accidental death, and Matt feels closest to his father in the air, to the point that being on land evokes in him a kind of phobic reaction.

Matt's adventures start when he is instrumental in rescuing a dying balloonist. A year later, that explorer's wealthy grand-daughter, Kate de Vries, boards *Aurora* for a flight to Australia. Kate has her grandfather's diary, which records observations of batlike, flying panthers she and Matt come to call cloud cats. Kate, whose ambition is to become a scientist, hopes to observe them for herself and bring back proof her grandfather's wits weren't deserting him. Despite the social gulf between them, Matt and Kate become friends. The *Aurora* is boarded and plundered by the murderous pirate Szpirglas, whose base for his black airship has never been found. Damaged in the aftermath of the encounter, the *Aurora* is wrecked on an uncharted island near where Kate's grandfather observed the cloud cats. While the crew makes repairs, Kate and Matt find a cloud cat skeleton, and then a cat with a damaged wing. They also discover, too late to avoid capture, that the island is Szpirglas' base. Captured, they escape, and with the help of another young crewman, Bruce, sneak back onto the pirate-occupied *Aurora* and try to get her airborne. Their fight to overcome the pirates and free the crew and passengers is one of outstanding high drama and tragedy.

Airborn works on many levels. It is not just a tale of adven-ture and fantastic discovery, but a story of two young people hampered in their ambitions by the restrictions of society. The world has changed since the early days of airships and it is no longer easy to work one's way through the ranks; the companies prefer their officers to have the certification of the Parisian Airship Academy, and the tuition puts such training out of the reach of working-class youths. Although women can attend university, it is not considered quite the proper pursuit for a young lady, and Kate's parents have no sympathy for her ambitions. Both Matt and Kate must go to great lengths to pursue their goals, while Bruce, whose father owns the airship company, seems to have been given the opportunities they both want, yet has no driving passion and does not know what he wants out of life; his murder at the hands of the pirates means he never has the opportunity to find out. Kate achieves success in her mission to prove the cloud cats real and wins her parents' permission to attend university, but recognizes that to much of the scientific community and in the popular eye, she is more of a novelty act, not to be taken seriously, her cloud cat skeleton and slides suspected of being faked. She still has much to prove, to win the respect of the field she has chosen to enter. Matt, on the other hand, is able to attend the academy, thanks to reward money offered for the pirates. The delicate beginning of romance between Kate and Matt is handled with great naturalness and humour, a fact of their friendship and a part of its tensions. The most critical moment of Matt's development, though, occurs as he falls from the ship, landing on the tailfin and surviving a final confrontation with Szpirglas, more by luck and the chance intervention of predatory cloud cats than anything he does himself. It is then that he finally accepts the reality of his father's death, and it is this moment that starts the healing of his grief, enabling him to feel whole and at home on the ground as well as on the *Aurora*.

Airborn offers a convincing and well-realized world, in which young protagonists confront and overcome great challenges and dangers, while moving into maturity. In *Airborn*, more than in the *Silverwing* trilogy, one gets the sense of a real world vaster than the scope of the story, in which much more remains to be explored. The characters in this latest work have a greater depth and reality as well. This all suggests that Oppel is a writer only now hitting his stride, from whom readers can expect many more impressive fantasies.

Cornelia Funke (b. 1958)

Funke was born in Dorsten, Westphalia, in Germany She studied education and illustration, going on to become first a professional illustrator and then an author as well, writing picture books and children's novels, and establishing herself as a popular and very prolific author for young people in Germany through the late eighties and nineties. Her success spread to Britain and North America following the translation of her children's fantasy *Herr der Diebe* (2000) into English as *The Thief Lord* in 2002. Her novels usually feature her own illustrations. Funke lives near Hamburg with her husband and children.

The Thief Lord is set in modern Venice. The action revolves around two orphaned runaways, Prosper and his little brother Bo. They have fled to Venice, which their mother always described to them as a place of wonder and beauty, to avoid an aunt who wants to adopt Bo because of his angelic appearance, but intends to send Prosper away to boarding school to be rid of him. Prosper and Bo have joined a gang of street children who live in an abandoned cinema. Their leader is the mysterious Thief Lord, Scipio, a boy who claims to be a master thief, but actually only steals antiques from his own house. The plot also follows closely the doings of private detective Victor Getz, hired to find Bo. Scipio is not actually a thief, but the unloved son of a wealthy man; when the Thief Lord is commissioned to steal the wing of a wooden merry-go-round lion from a photographer, Ida, Scipio decides to attempt real burglary. The gang rejects him when they discover his deception; they are caught breaking in to Ida's house, but find in her an unexpected ally. She wants to see the merry-go-round to which the wing belongs, and helps them follow the mysterious Conte who wants it. The merry-go-round is magical; riding on it can make a person younger or older, depending on the direction. The Conte and his sister turn themselves into children, Scipio turns himself into an adult, and Barbarossa, the greedy dealer in antiques and stolen goods, is turned into a small boy while trying to merely lose a few years. He also breaks the merry-go-round, so that no-one is able to change themselves back. Aunt Esther, who has kidnapped Bo and become completely disillusioned with him, is tricked into adopting Barbarossa, while Ida takes in Prosper, Bo, and Hornet,

412

the one girl in the gang. The other two go back to the hardship and freedom of Venice's streets and canals, while Scipio, trapped as an adult, becomes Victor's partner. The story admits both the positive and negative aspects of childhood and maturity; neither Scipio nor the Conte are entirely happy with the bargain they have made, much as they had thought they desired it. Scipio, at least, does eventually make a contented life for himself as an adult.

Funke's next book to be translated was *Tintenherz* (2003), which appeared in English the same year titled *Inkheart*. In this, Meggie discovers that her bookbinder father Mo is able to read characters out of books, setting them loose in the real world when he reads aloud. His talent also led to her mother being trapped in a book, long ago. When characters who escaped from the book on that occasion re-enter their lives, Meggie and Mo find themselves in the midst of a dangerous adventure, travelling with the ambiguous Dustfinger, pursued by the villainous Capricorn, who enjoys causing pain and suffering and is trying to prevent anyone returning him to the book. Eventually Meggie and Fenoglio, the author who wrote *Inkheart* (the book within the novel) and created Capricorn and his world, are able to defeat Capricorn. Held captive, Meggie is forced to use the talent she has inherited from her father to read life out of the book, but takes control of the story through additions Fenoglio has made. She is unable to read the sentences in which Capricorn, originally an antihero who survived despite his cruel deeds, is killed, but Mo takes over and brings the scene to life, killing Capricorn. When Meggie, her father, and her rescued mother return to live at her great-aunt's house, along with a number of fairies, trolls, and other creatures brought to life from books, Meggie decides to become an author, believing that is where true power in words lies.

Children's books in which characters from other books come to life in the 'real world' of the story and take part in the action have had a place in fantasy for a long time. Nesbit's *Wet Magic* (1913), for instance, has as its climax a battle in which good and villainous characters from storybooks and history take part. Most of the book-characters who enter Meggie's world are from the book-within-the-book *Inkheart*, but Tinker Bell from *Peter Pan* also makes a minor appearance. Each chapter begins with a quotation from some other work of fiction. The fictional world from which Capricorn and Dustfinger have come is never glimpsed in any of the powerful beauty and terror it is claimed to possess, though. The grounds for Dustfinger's homesickness for it despite the tragic fate that is supposed to await him in the penultimate chapter, and Meggie's mother's lingering wistfulness for that world, are never shown, only stated. Funke can claim a power for Fenoglio's created world, but she fails to create a reality as compelling as that to which the characters are responding; the depth of wonder and horror she claims for Fenoglio's *Inkheart* is not actually conveyed. The cruelty and brutality of Capricorn and his henchmen, the pathos of Dustfinger's love for Meggie's mother, remain mechanical, resulting in, for some readers, not only failure to believe in the reality within Meggie's world of Capricorn and Dustfinger, but in a lack of belief in Meggie's story at all. Doubling the layers of literary belief Funke attempts to instil only has the effect of drawing attention to the artificiality of the story's world, because the fiction within the fiction lacks reality even within the outer layer of story.

Funke is more successful when she lets her fantastic stand on its own. Her next book to appear in English, *Dragon Rider* (2004), was one of her earlier children's novels, *Drachenreiter*, originally published in 1997. The book begins with Firedrake, a young silver dragon, and his brownie companion Sorrel setting off on a quest to find a legendary valley in the Himalayas where dragons can live without interference from humans. His home valley in Scotland is about to be dammed and turned into a reservoir. Somewhere in Europe, they acquire Ben, a homeless boy living in an abandoned factory. They are helped by a cartographer-rat, and his aviatrix niece, and hunted by Nettlebrand, a golden dragon created by a medieval alchemist. Although Nettlebrand cannot fly, he can travel magically from any body of water to another, however small. Nettlebrand lives only for the pleasure of hunting and killing true dragons. His homunculus servant Twigleg joins Firedrake, Ben, and Sorrel as a spy, but finds himself becoming attached to Ben. They meet and are helped by a characters ranging from Professor Greenbloom, a human archaeologist who researches fabulous beasts in his spare time, Greenbloom's wife and daughter, Indian dragon-expert Dr. Zubeida Ghalib, a sea serpent, Tibetan monks, and meet other creatures helpful or dangerous, such as a genie and a roc. In the dragons' hidden valley, they find that the dragons have retreated entirely from the world, becoming encased in stone. Only one, Maia, remains. With the help of Ben, Sorrel, and a mountain brownie, Firedrake and Maia melt Nettlebrand. The remaining dragons are woken, Firedrake heads home to lead his people to the safety of the valley, and Ben finds a home with the Greenblooms.

Funke's *Inkheart* and *Dragon Rider* are similar to the books of Eva Ibbotson in their focus on children without families or in families that have suffered disruption, who encounter magical creatures portrayed in a broadly-drawn and often comic manner in an otherwise real-world setting. However, Funke brings much more detail to her settings and circumstances. *The Thief Lord* also focuses on unwanted children who find a place to belong in the end, although its magic is less anticipated; it surprises when the story turns from being straight, imaginative yet realistically-possible adventure to fantasy, halfway through the book. It is also a magic presented as more unexpected to the characters; the transforming merry-go-round is a singular, mysterious magic artefact within an otherwise realistic modern Venice.

Funke's humour lies mostly in the characters and their interactions; it is broad and clowning rather than subtle. Her horror and villainy are likewise blatantly portrayed, rather than being anything the characters (and readers) have to discover and come to recognize. Her stories of children on their own in a world where magic lies largely-unnoticed just under the everyday, of gathering a loyal band of friends in pursuit of some goal while being pursued by a villain who will go to any lengths to harm them and prevent them succeeding, have many elements in common with Ibbotson and Rowling. They attract the young readership that is looking for a story that, while not necessarily deep in its portrayal of character or world, is filled with action, excitement, and the possibilities and consequences of magic entering the here and now.

Neil Gaiman (b. 1960)

Gaiman was born in England and began his career there writing comic books, most notably the *Sandman* supernatural horror series of 75 issues, which won numerous awards in its field through the nineties. He has written other comics and graphic novels for an adult and teen audience, screenplays and radio scripts based on these, as well as scripts unconnected to his own stories. He also writes short stories and adult novels. The fantasy novel *Good Omens* (1990) – a funny and thought-provoking story of an angel, a devil, a very engaging bicycle-riding eleven-year-old Antichrist named Adam, and the end of the world, co-written with Terry Pratchett – will, like Pratchett's *Discworld* and Gaiman's *Sandman*, be eagerly read by teens, though that group was not the main intended audience. Gaiman lives in Minnesota with his wife and three children.

As a children's writer, Gaiman attracted sudden attention with the novel *Coraline* (2002), illustrated by David McKean. (It is easy to imagine it accompanied by the art of the late Charles Keeping.) Coraline Jones and her parents move into a flat in an old house. The other flats are occupied by a pair of retired actresses and their pack of Highland terriers, and an elderly man who claims to be training a mouse circus. There is also an aloof black tomcat. The old man passes on a warning from the mice against 'going through the door', while the actresses, Miss Spink and Miss Forcible, read in the tea leaves that Coraline is facing great danger, and give her a stone with a hole through it, which they say might help. Coraline keeps hearing odd noises and seeing shadows; she unlocks a door that she knows has been bricked up and finds a corridor beyond, leading to another version of the house. There she finds a disturbing couple with black button eyes, who claim to be her other mother and father. The other mother wants Coraline to stay with them forever, and keeps trying to sew black buttons onto her eyes.

Coraline flees back to her own world, but finds her parents gone. After a kindly policeman offers no better help than to advise hot chocolate for nightmares, Coraline realizes rescue is up to her. She returns to the other flat, where the actresses' stone helps keep the other mother's will from dominating her. She meets the ghosts of three children killed by the other mother long ago, trapped, their own names forgotten. The other mother fed on their vitality and has hidden their souls somewhere; they hope Coraline, if she can free her own parents, can also find their souls and allow them to pass on to whatever lies beyond death.

Taking the cat's advice, Coraline challenges the beetle-eating other mother to a game, setting freedom for herself, her parents, and the dead children if she wins, against staying willingly and having buttons sewn into her eyes, if the other mother does. The game proposed by Coraline is to find her parents and the souls of the children. She discovers that looking through the hole in the actresses' stone reveals the souls as vital, glowing sparks of colour. When she finds the third child's soul, the other mother closes the ways out of the alternate house, trapping Coraline and the cat. Coraline manages to seize the snow-globe that holds her parents, trick the other mother into opening the door, and escape with the rescued souls. The next morning her parents remember nothing. In a dream, the children whose souls she rescued warn Coraline that the other mother is still a danger; her animate hand is in Coraline's house, looking for the key to the connecting passage. Coraline lays a trap for the hand, ending its threat to the house.

Coraline is not a 'lesson' story, not one of those books meant to blandly teach that one's parents really do love one even if they cook chicken with prunes and refuse to buy green gloves – Coraline already knows this perfectly well, and defies the other mother by saying so. *Coraline* cannot be distilled to anything so mundane as a simple instructional tract. It is about fear and courage and exploration. The nightmarish nature of Coraline's adventure is not conventional popular culture horror. The images – the other mother who becomes more and more inhuman and spiderlike until she is nothing but a hand, the other father who reverts to a giant doughy grub, the old man composed of rats, and the sewn-on black button eyes – are more chilling for being the sort of thing that inhabit real nightmares: loss, things that are just disturbingly off, expanded versions of our own house in which we become lost and trapped. Although frightening, Coraline's encounters with fearsome things lead to considered action on her part, not despair or mindless terror; they are always within her ability to cope, and her ability expands as she confronts and surmounts each danger. Even when all seems hopeless, she and the reader rediscover hope, getting up and going on, encouraged by cats and ghosts, memory of her parents, and unwillingness to surrender. She is an indomitable hero who, like Lewis Carroll's

Alice, may indulge in a brief bout of tears but always thereafter sets briskly about finding her way through fear and darkness, alien worlds and dead ends, with common sense, courtesy, intelligence, and courage to aid her.

Garth Nix (b. 1963)

Australian Garth Nix was born in Melbourne and grew up in Canberra. After obtaining a bachelor's degree at Canberra University, he worked at a number of jobs, including editing and marketing, and served in the Australian Army Reserve, turning to full-time writing in 2002. He lives in Sydney, Australia, with his wife and son.

Even Nix's early works show his ability to create detailed secondary or alternate worlds, interesting and engaging characters both strong and vulnerable, and plots in which neither tension nor balance between desperate struggle and hope of success is lost. *The Ragwitch* (1990) is a fantasy which begins in modern Australia and quickly moves to another world. The main characters are eleven-year-old Paul and his older sister Julia. While exploring a beach, Julia finds a ragdoll, which possesses her. When the Ragwitch-dominated Julia transports herself back to the witch's own world, a terrified Paul follows to rescue her, finding himself in the island Kingdom, where several races of vicious monsters from the North threaten the peaceful southern cantons. Paul is lost and frightened; Julia was always the leader and the one he looked up to. However, he meets people willing to help him on his way, most the sort who by quiet example demonstrate courage, wisdom, and joy in life, and many quite comic eccentrics.

In the Kingdom's past, the Ragwitch was a human witch who sought magic in the Nameless Realm, for use in a war against invading creatures of the North. The evil of the Nameless Realm possessed her and she conquered the Kingdom herself as the North-Queen, turning those she overcame into Glazed-Folk, utterly possessed tools with no remnant of their former self, a forerunner of ideas Nix would develop in *Sabriel* and *Shade's Children*. The North-Queen was expelled to another world, where she made herself a new, indestructible body, that of the

Ragwitch. Paul travels to seek help from the four Elementals, the beings who represent Earth, Air, Fire, and Water, accompanied by Leasel the hare and Quigin, a young apprentice Friend of Beasts, one who talks to animals. Paul's quest is not a simple one. The Kingdom is engulfed in war as the Ragwitch's armies invade, and the Elementals are not all benevolent. At the same time, Julia is fighting the Ragwitch from within. Forced to witness horrible deeds through the witch's eyes, she nevertheless resists, and in the landscape of the Ragwitch's mind and memory she finds allies, two people of the past trapped as she is, and a rowan tree spirit who entered the witch willingly to aid them.

Paul finally meets the Patchwork King, the supernatural king of dreams and magic, and is permitted to ask for a spell. He resists the temptation to be sent back to his own world safely, and asks for a way to destroy the Ragwitch; the Patchwork King forges the gifts Paul was given by the Elementals into a weapon. While Julia and her friends fight within the Ragwitch's mind, Paul seeks her out on the battlefield. He wounds her, but when she speaks in Julia's voice he hesitates to kill her. Julia briefly manages to take control of the witch and between the two siblings, she is killed and the Kingdom saved. Paul is led back to his own world by the Patchwork King, bleakly believing Julia dead, but the King also leads Julia back from the afterlife where her three friends now are. The siblings find themselves on the beach together, their experiences and new friends not forgotten, but solemnly and affectionately treasured.

The Ragwitch contains the elements of traditional quests, but like all such stories when done well, does not make Paul's encounters with helpers and advisors, which form the backbone of the narrative, simplistic, nor his success automatic. Though the Master of the Air is stern yet kind and the Earth Lady forthright and friendly, Paul barely escapes the mercurial Water Lord with his life, and the Fire Queen is chaotic, whimsically demanding, and leaves him permanently scarred. The temptation he faces when he meets the Patchwork King — to save himself and his sister and abandon those fighting a losing war in the Kingdom — is not a trivial one. He has no guarantee he will survive killing the Ragwitch and knows Julia will likely die with her; he has no guarantee his attempt to kill her will succeed. Paul's determination that he must try comes from knowing that the people and

419

animals of the Kingdom have fought for him, and that Julia herself would believe choosing to destroy the witch was the right choice, even at the cost of her own life. The two quests, Paul's to seek help from the Elementals, and Julia's to keep her self from being absorbed into the Ragwitch, are interlaced. Once Paul and Julia are both in the Kingdom, each chapter has a double title, and contains events experienced by Julia and by Paul at around the same point in the story. Although marketed as a young adult novel in North America, with a paperback cover suggesting it is more horror than fantasy, *The Ragwitch*, with its determined eleven-year-old hero, is quite readable for pre-teens of even average reading levels, and the violence of battle, the tragedy and pathos of possession and death, are only what is appropriate to a fantasy examining such serious themes. It does not contain the often gratuitous gruesomeness of teen horror novels.

A far more frightening book is the excellent young adult novel *Shade's Children* (1997). It is set in a near future in which seven Overlords, humans from another dimension who regard this world's inhabitants as mere animals, have caused all adults to vanish. Children are raised in barracks in the empty city, their bodies harvested for minds to run cyborg creatures in the Overlords' ritualistic battle game. Shade, the computer-stored and hologrammatically-present personality of a scientist, trains the surviving feral children as his army, with the aim of eventually destroying the Overlords, but Shade himself becomes a tyrant, betraying the children he began fighting for. His personality becomes fragmented and in the end that version closest to the man he once was helps the last two free survivors of his band, Ella and Drum, to destroy the devices that have brought the Overlords to the world, though at the cost of their own lives, willingly sacrificed. Two more of the group, Ninde and Gold-Eye, captured and about to be executed, do survive, the foresighted Gold-Eye seeing a future in which the world is free and children grow up to raise families of their own, society restored.

In *Shade's Children*, both imagined future and alternate dimension technologies take the place of magic, making it more properly science fiction than fantasy, but many of Nix's themes and concerns are the same as in his fantasies. There are parallels in the motifs, particularly with *Sabriel*, in the young people well-trained but alone in a deadly and dangerous world, charged not only with their own survival but with saving that world. They face not mere death: loss of free will and enslavement as a tool of the enemy is a constant, horrifying danger. Along with the *Sabriel* trilogy, *Shade's Children* stands among his best works to date.

Nix also writes for younger readers. His six-book series *The Seventh Tower* features short books, short chapters, and rapid, cliff-hanger action, all collectively appealing to children newly embarking upon novels or, since the story the series tells is not one obviously aimed only at 'little kids', those older children whose reading skills are below average for their age. *The Seventh Tower* never descends to over-simplification in language, character, or plot, and will be appropriately challenging for new novel readers, encouraging them to expand their vocabularies while not intimidating them. The six volumes, *The Fall* (2000), *Castle* (2000), *Aenir* (2001), *Above the Veil* (2001), *Into Battle* (2001), and *The Violet Keystone* (2001), tell one serial story.

The heroes, Tal and Milla, live in a world of perpetual darkness maintained by the Veil, which cuts off the sun's light and protects the world from dangerous creatures from Aenir, a world or dimension of magical beings. Tal is one of the Chosen, the aristocracy of the society that lives in the vast Castle. Chosen lives are both precarious and luxurious; there is constant competition for status and social position, and the risk of demotion, but they are supported by the slavelike Underfolk and have no need to do any real work themselves. Seven towers of the Castle reach up beyond the Veil into the sunlight. All light and warmth in the Castle comes from sunstones, coloured jewels that are also used by the Chosen for magic. These are recharged atop the towers. When Tal's father disappears with the family's primary sunstone, Tal has no way to enter the magical world of Aenir on the day he must do so to bind a Spiritshadow to himself, becoming an adult. Spiritshadows are creatures of Aenir, bound, often unwillingly, to serve Chosen, replacing their own shadows. Without accomplishing this, he will be demoted to Underfolk. Various attempts to gain a sunstone by legitimate means fail, so Tal climbs a tower to steal one. He is driven off by Spiritshadows, falls, and is carried by the wind out onto the wasteland of ice and snow that covers the rest of the world. There he is captured by a band of warlike Icecarls, who travel the ice in ships and sledges, following rivers of gigantic Selski, the animals which provide their food and building materials. Each group is ruled by a Crone, and the Crones keep in touch with one another telepathically.

A prophecy sends Tal and the aspiring Shield Maiden Milla, bound together by oaths and a 'blood brotherhood' ritual, back to the Castle, where they encounter numerous dangers, all gradually revealed to be part of one conspiracy against the entire world. Tal and Milla enter Aenir, where to save their lives Tal binds Spiritshadows to them, an act which is an abomination to Milla. Back in the Castle, their mission is complicated by a brewing rebellion of renegade Underfolk calling themselves the Freefolk. Tal obtains the lost Violet Keystone, which is the symbol of imperial rule. With the empress dead, its possessor is regarded as emperor and is able to control many of the magical devices in the Castle. The keystone is split by his eccentric if not outright mad great-uncle Ebbitt, and is shared with Milla. The Icecarl warrior, though, returns to warn the Crones of the danger to the world from forces in Aenir, and to commit suicide by 'going to the ice' because of the Spiritshadow bound to her. However, she and her Spiritshadow come to terms with one another and Milla is sent back to the Castle as War-Chief of an army.

Tal is captured, his half of the Violet Keystone stolen by the Chosen Sushin, who has been an enemy of Tal's family all along, and Tal himself is tortured. Through his skill with sunstones he is able to free himself, and his sometime enemy, the rebel Crow, comes to help him. Sushin is being controlled by the shape-changing dragon Sharrakor, who wants the Veil shut down so he can lead an invasion from Aenir. Eventually Tal, Milla, Crow, and Ebbitt enter Aenir, where they have friends; not all the creatures there are malevolent or allies of Sharrakor. They free their Spiritshadows, since they are determined that they will establish a new order without oppression and slavery. Tal's and Milla's former Spiritshadows continue to help them, though, as they finally confront Sharrakor. He is destroyed, though Crow loses his life in the process. Back in the Castle, the Violet Keystone is restored and Tal becomes emperor of all the people of the Castle, not just the Chosen. He institutes, not without difficulties, a new society that is not founded on exploitation of most of the population. Along the way, Tal's father has been rescued and the inventive and occasionally bizarre worlds of the Castle, the ice, and Aenir are explored in intriguing detail.

Although copyright in the series is actually held by Lucasfilm rather than Nix, the story is his; it is not a novelization of some prepared plot or script. According to an interview on the series website, Nix was invited to write the books and given a few ideas that George Lucas had suggested as a foundation to start from: a particular style of architecture and a sunless world were the main ones. Tal and Milla's numerous adventures, separately and together, show them growing in skills, maturity, authority, and confidence. The improbable situation of the world and the sunless societies of the Castle and the Icecarls are portrayed with meticulous attention to internal consistency and credibility.

Another very worthwhile series for younger readers by Nix, *The Keys to the Kingdom*, begins with *Mister Monday* (2003) and *Grim Tuesday* (2003), and continues with *Drowned Wednesday* (2005), with four more days to follow. Written for a slightly higher reading level than *The Seventh Tower*, this series follows the adventures of Arthur Penhaligon in a near-future world of killer influenza outbreaks and draconian quarantine laws. In the first book, Arthur, near death from an asthma attack, is given a key which grants him entry to, and power within, the House, a vast edifice existing outside the everyday world, built by the Architect of creation and now controlled by Her stewards, who have become corrupt and self-serving. Guided by an escaped fragment of the Architect's imprisoned Will in the form of a small frog and helped by Suzy Turquoise Blue, a human girl from the seventeenth century, Arthur has to survive the schemes of Mister Monday and his minions in order to claim his place as a mortal Heir of the Architect. His main desire, though, is to find a cure for the plague Monday has unleashed on his city. By the end, Arthur has taken Monday's place and returned to his own world with a cure for the magical plague, but a confrontation with the other stewards of the House looms.

Grim Tuesday continues the next day, as Arthur is summoned back to the House to deal with a plot by Grim Tuesday to gain the First Key and depose Arthur as Master of the Lower House. Again, his family and friends are threatened in his own world while he struggles against powerful enemies in a dangerous, un-familiar landscape. Arthur avoids capture by disguising himself as one of Grim Tuesday's endentured Denizens, mining the Pit from which Tuesday extracts Nothing to make the various products he sells to other parts of the House. Tuesday has, literally, undermined the House and endangered its existence, but his greed is boundless. Arthur escapes with Suzy's help and the two, aided by Tom, the mysterious Mariner who is enslaved by Tuesday but acts against him whenever possible, voyage in a Sunship to find the second part of the Will. Nithlings threaten every part of his quest, but in the end Arthur defeats Grim Tuesday, gains mastery of the Second Key, and prevents Nothing from leaking through Tuesday's Pit and destroying all of creation. He has barely returned home, with a broken leg and a return of severe asthma, before Lady Wednesday summons him back to the world of the House, leading to *Drowned Wednesday*.

By this third book, it seems clear that the seven Trustees of the Will have fallen into the seven deadly sins or vices of Catholic theology, Monday surrendering himself to sloth and Tuesday to avarice, while Wednesday, who rather than threatening Arthur seeks his aid, has been cursed with an insatiable appetite that threatens all life in her realm within the House – gluttony in the extreme. Nix's storytelling mastery does not seem likely to falter as the series continues its exploration of the exotic and novel landscape of the House and of Arthur's difficult role as the Architect's Heir.

Nix's most outstanding works to date, however, are the three young adult fantasy novels in the trilogy beginning with *Sabriel* (1995). The world in which these stories are set is one of the most original in recent fantasy. There are two main countries in which the action takes place, the Old Kingdom to the north and Ancelstierre south of it. The two are divided by the Wall, which is not mere stone but a work imbued with great magic. South of the Wall, Ancelstierre maintains the Perimeter, a defensive line of trenches, barbed wire, and dugouts. Ancelstierre is a parliamentary democracy, socially and technologically in the equivalent of the first decades of the twentieth century. It may even be some version of our world, because English is a subject in schools, Roman numerals are mentioned, and Shakespeare alluded to in passing, though it appears to share neither geography nor history otherwise.

The Old Kingdom is a very different place. Things not hand-made disintegrate or fail to function; Charter Magic, worked through understanding and use of the Charter Marks (symbols that make up the Charter that describes the world), is used by Charter Mages. The Old Kingdom is a dangerous place. Free Magic, unbound, dangerous, and often malevolent, is opposed to Charter Magic. Worse, there is no safety even in dying. Death is a vast river along which the spirit must travel before reaching the final gate and release into true death. On the journey, the Dead spirit is vulnerable. It can be enslaved and used by necromancers, with the individual's self completely forgotten and only a hunger for Life remaining. Necromancers can reanimate corpses with Dead spirits or use such spirits to create even more powerful creatures. In the past, such corrupt magic was opposed by the royal family and the Abhorsen, who like a necromancer can enter Death and compel the Dead with seven named bells, each with its particular power and significance. The Abhorsen's duty is to combat Free Magic creatures, necromancers, and the Dead.

When *Sabriel* begins, the Old Kingdom has experienced two centuries of anarchy and terror. The royal family is long dead, murdered by Kerrigor, a renegade prince who became a necromancer and then a Free Magic creature. People live in terror of the Dead; society has descended into lawlessness and local tyranny. Sabriel, a schoolgirl in Ancelstierre, is the daughter of the Abhorsen; when a magically-made Sending brings her the Abhorsen's bells and sword, she knows her father is trapped in Death, and crosses the Wall to save him. Her companion on her quest is Mogget, a Free Magic creature bound to the service of the Abhorsens by a collar of Charter Magic. He appears to be a small, sardonic, white cat; in his own form he is a creature of white fire, full of hatred for the Abhorsens. Along the way, Sabriel rescues Touchstone, the illegitimate son of the last Queen, a berserker, and the only survivor of the royal blood, who has been trapped on the edge of Death since Kerrigor's betrayal.

Sabriel, Touchstone, and Mogget survive encounters with the Dead and find the Abhorsen, but are ambushed by Kerrigor. The Abhorsen, taking a final leave of his daughter, sends Sabriel and Touchstone to find and destroy Kerrigor's mortal body, hidden in Ancelstierre near the Perimeter, while he and Mogget in his demonic, unbound form attack Kerrigor's spirit, using the Abhorsen's seventh bell, which casts all who hear it into Death.

In Ancelstierre, Sabriel and Touchstone have the help of Ancelstierran soldiers and Sabriel's schoolmates, some of whom are Charter Mages, as they try to open Kerrigor's coffin while besieged by the Dead. Many lose their lives in this battle, before Sabriel is able to bind Kerrigor.

In *Lirael: Daughter of the Clayr* (2001), the next generation provides the main characters. Sabriel is the Abhorsen, Touchstone is the king and her husband, and together they have devoted their lives to restoring the Old Kingdom. The story begins with teenage Lirael, born one of the brown-skinned, blond-haired Clayr, who live in a vast communal complex tunnelled into mountain and glacier in the north. Their lives are dominated by the Sight, visions of possible futures they see in the ice. Lirael, though, is an orphan and an oddity, white-skinned and black-haired. She never acquires the Sight, the mark of adulthood among the Clayr, which leaves her feeling so incomplete she contemplates suicide. Some of the older Clayr recognize her emotional problems and assign her an adult's role as an Assistant Librarian in the vast and even dangerous Library (in which standard equipment issued includes a dagger). Lirael's explorations into forbidden parts of the library lead to encounters with dangerous Free Magic creatures, which she learns to defeat. She also tries to create a Charter Sending, a magically-formed pet dog, as a companion. What she gets is something else entirely: a very independent and intelligent creature of combined Free and Charter Magic, who announces that she is the Disreputable Dog. The Dog takes over Lirael's education, leading her over the course of several years to stretch her considerable magical abilities and knowledge, and to cease wallowing in self-pity. Eventually, Lirael discovers she is a Remembrancer, one who sees the past rather than the future. When the Clayr send her on a long journey to a region from which they know great danger of some sort is coming, she encounters, fights, and escapes from the necromancer Hedge in Death, and learns from Dog a great deal about the cosmology of the world and the origins of the Charter; readers will gradually come to realize that the Disreputable Dog herself is one of the Seven great powers who formed the Charter, after whom the Abhorsen's bells are named.

Meanwhile, Touchstone and Sabriel have gone on a secret diplomatic mission to the capital of Ancelstierre, trying to persuade the right-wing government there to stop sending refugees from a distant war over the border into the Old Kingdom, where they disappear – used, Sabriel fears, by some necromancer to create an army of Dead. Their daughter Ellimere, heir to the crown, is regent, while their son Sameth, though supposed to be the Abhorsen-in-Waiting, is physically and psychologically scarred by a disastrous encounter with the necromancer Hedge, so that he cannot face returning to Death or continuing his studies. He runs away to rescue his Ancelstierran friend Nicholas Sayre, who came to the Old Kingdom to pursue a scientific investigation but has fallen victim to an ancient evil. Sam is joined by Mogget, hunted by the Dead, and rescued by Lirael. Lirael and Sameth discover that they are aunt and nephew; her father was the last Abhorsen and she, not Sam, is the Abhorsen-in-Waiting, to Sam's great relief.

In *Abhorsen* (2003), the story concludes. The book begins with a shock: the apparent deaths of Sabriel and Touchstone when their car is blown up by a bomb in the Ancelstierran capital. Only many chapters later do readers learn they survived and escaped north to Sabriel's old school. Sam discovers the beginning of self-acceptance as Lirael has, realizing that his talent for making things is a legacy of the blood of the Wallmakers, another aspect of the Charter, but he and Lirael are unable to rescue Nicholas. He is possessed by a sliver of a great evil power, Orannis, whose aim is nothing less than the destruction of all life in the world. Orannis was long ago divided and bound in the form of two metal hemispheres, which his servant Hedge is trying to reunite, using Nick's scientific knowledge. Lirael and Sam, with a large force of Ancelstierran Perimeter Scouts, go to do what they can to prevent the hemispheres from being reunited in Ancelstierre. Nick fights to retain his own self and will. At the edge of the final gate in Death, Lirael uses her skills as an Abhorsen and Remembrancer to see how Orannis was originally bound, since even Mogget and the Dog, who were both present, have forgotten. As more kinsfolk and allies arrive, Lirael directs them all through the ritual to rebind Orannis. It nearly fails; only when Mogget, freed by Sam, chooses to join them, is Orannis bound so that Lirael can destroy him, though she knows the price will be her life. The Dog, though, saves her by taking the full impact of Orannis' vengeance on herself.

The story concludes with restoration and renewal, as Nicholas encounters the Dog in Death; she sends him back into life, to Lirael. During the course of the three books readers have learnt the names and titles of the Abhorsens' bells, which are named after the Seven who made the Charter; the Dog is, appropriately for a character who is the cheerful epitome of dogginess, Kibeth, the Walker, and in the very end she is walking, not down the river to the final gate, but along the border between Life and Death.

A collection of short stories set in the Old Kingdom, *Across the Wall*, followed in the summer of 2005. It contains a dozen stories previously published individually and difficult to find elsewhere, and a parody of the 'choose your own adventure' type of book so popular with young readers in the early eighties. All of the stories add to Nix's rich Old Kingdom world and are paired with some supplementary commentary by the author. One of the longer stories, which takes up the adventures of Nicholas Sayre six months after the end of *Abhorsen*, was also published as a novella entitled *The Creature in the Case* to benefit World Book Day 2005 in the UK and Ireland; it was made available to schoolchildren in return for World Book Day tokens worth £1. Like *Harry Potter*, *Sabriel* and its sequels have been reissued in 'adult' editions.

Nix's world of the Old Kingdom can be very dark, with not even death an escape from oppression or suffering. This view of death as a potentially hazardous journey which a spirit must undertake is one found in many cultures. Some traditions have regarded the dead, even beloved family members, as potentially hostile powers, hungry for life, needing to be appeased or constrained. These are not bizarre or alien fears to the human psyche. Neither does Nix treat such ideas, even the shambling, decomposing bodies of reanimated Dead enslaved by necromancers, as the mere special effects of horror shows. His world is rich, varied, and complex, and the nightmare is part of it, showing the darkness that is opposed by the values of life for which the characters are willing to fight and die, but for which they would rather live. Even Mogget, who abstained from the original conflict with Orannis and from the creation of the Charter, comes to value life through his enforced existence as a physical being, choosing in the end to fight; his reasons – fish, sunshine, mice – are comically feline, but underscore that such simple pleasures and small joys are a significant part of what makes living worth fighting for and life in general worth saving.

Nix's heroes are convincingly portrayed, as complex, self-indulgent and yet truly troubled teens capable of maturing, and as young people taking on adult duties and responsibilities, discovering themselves in the process. They experience guilt and failure as well as growth and victory, but in the end surmount their self-defeating emotions and go on. The Disreputable Dog and Mogget are particularly endearing characters, utterly credible animals, while at the same time they are wise in their various ways, powerful, and mysterious. The world itself is described with great attention to literary belief, while the actual stories are complex, suspenseful, and bear a second reading, minor details taking on greater significance in hindsight. There appears to be scope for more stories set in this world; allusions to other histories abound.

Nix is a writer of great imagination, power, variety, and depth. Whether writing for beginning readers, children, or teens and adults, he creates highly original worlds, rich in texture and history; his characters, human and non-human alike, are psychologically believable, complex and always fascinating, his heroes sympathetic even when behaving at their worst and admirable when they rise to meet the challenges of true heroism. His cosmologies and systems of magic and the supernatural are internally consistent, fully integrated into the worlds of which they are a part, and original in both conception and detail. *Sabriel* and its sequels in particular ensure that Nix will be regarded, in the future, as one of the greats of his generation of writers of fantasy for young people.

It is difficult to judge what shape fantasy is taking in this first decade of the twenty-first century. There is a tendency, quite probably due to the influence of adult secondary world fantasy, for books to become longer, more complex in both background and plot. Series rather than single books look likely to continue their domination, in part because the creation of a detailed world, with history, cosmology, religion, societies, and a geography extending off the edges of the book's map, leads naturally to the expansion of story beyond the constraints of a single novel, and generates for the author new stories, as the world takes on in-

creasing reality. However, writers like Cornelia Funke demonstrate that the tradition of Nesbit remains very appealing.

Certainly 'the *Harry Potter* phenomenon' has had a great impact, raising awareness of children's fantasy and contributing to
its influence on popular culture. Whether the general public interest created by *Harry Potter* will endure, and create new readers for less 'accessible' fantasy – such as secondary world
fantasy, which requires a greater imaginative effort in the reader
unused to moving beyond the real world – remains to be seen.

A notable aspect of this increased attention has been the reissuing of classics of children's fantasy from the nineteenth and
twentieth centuries by both major and smaller publishers. Recognition of the growing market for juvenile speculative fiction
has also resulted, at least in North America, in the reissuing, by
publishers such as Tor and Del Rey, of some adult fantasy and
science fiction in versions repackaged for younger readers.
These are not abridged editions; they usually appear in trade paperback form, with longer volumes subdivided, and bright, presumably 'child-friendly' covers. Robert Jordan's lengthy *Wheel of
Time* series, Terry Brooks' *Sword of Shannara* and Orson Scott
Card's science fiction *Ender* books, proven popular with teens in
their original format, are examples of this repackaging. The
question might be asked: is it teens and pre-teens who fail to
browse through library and bookstores shelves for stories they
are ready to read, not daring to explore and expand their range,
or adults who discourage them from doing so by excessively su-
pervising their reading or continually telling them, 'You can't
read that, it's too hard/too old for you'? One overhears this comment in bookstores rather too often, as parents pull their children
away from the adult fantasy and science fiction shelves and back
to the juvenile section.

A drawback of the increased popularity of fantasy is its
adoption by television shows as a mere veneer, particularly, the
equation of fantasy with 'New Age' mysticism. When used without attention to internal consistency and credibility, without any
effort to make the 'rules' by which the fantastic functions internally logical, the supernatural becomes mundane and expected,
creating a reliance on it as a prop rather than an inherent element
of the story. It may also blur the boundaries of fantasy and reality by blending real world stories, pseudoscience ('the aliens built

the pyramids, because humans just couldn't possibly do something so complicated'), and the New Age magic (or 'magick') of crystals and hodge-podges of pantheons.

A literary fantasy world should do much more; by presenting a fantastic created with care and deliberation, that fantasy element, large or small, is at once more credible within the story and can lead to a consideration of reality, of how the world really is, and how it can be changed. Good literary use of the improbable and impossible, however fantastic, cultivates the ability to think. The popularity of fantasy and its perceived profitability has begun to result in books being written in which fantasy elements are used as in television, just tossed in, as easy toys and background with no serious effort put into creating a world capable of inducing what Coleridge called 'willing suspension of disbelief' (*Biographia Literaria* 442) or what Tolkien termed 'literary belief' (*Tree and Leaf* 36). This clutter of mediocrity can obscure the good fantasy on the shelves and risk turning off someone sampling the genre for the first time. In the end, though, it is the good, the internally-consistent, the literary in which all elements work together to tell a story, that will endure in the reader's mind and survive through many re-readings, editions, and generations.

XVIII
Conclusion: '... wide and deep and high ...'

Children's fantasy literature, as we have seen, has a long history, and its rightful domain is, as Tolkien wrote of fairy-stories, 'wide and deep and high and filled with many things' (*Tree and Leaf* 9). There is no theme which cannot be explored in fantasy, no reach of the human imagination closed to it; there are many possibilities which can be given richest and most satisfying fulfilment, as fictional reality or through metaphoric presentation, in fantasy alone. Fantasy has its origins in some of the oldest stories still preserved and enjoyed today; every culture's earliest recorded works tend to be those which contain the elements of fantasy, whether written down four thousand years ago, or a mere one thousand, works such as the *Epic of Gilgamesh*, the *Iliad* and the *Odyssey*, and *Beowulf*. Specifically juvenile fantasy as literature (that is, as written rather than oral stories), can be said to have begun not as a genre rigidly cut off from 'the mainstream', nor as something for children alone, but in the fairy-tale collections meant for adult entertainment or scholarly perusal. These fairy-tales became children's literature, as did the fantastic stories of the chapbooks, which told of Arthur and Robin Hood and Jack the Giant-Killer. The fantastic, returning slowly to respectability after a period of mistrust of anything perceived to be doctrinely misleading or distracting (not yet wholly behind us), entered literary writing for children, as the belief that the sole function of children's stories was to instruct and inform weakened. By the second half of the nineteenth century, some of the most important writers for children, people like George MacDonald and Lewis Carroll, were writing children's books in which fantasy provided the foundation of the tale. E. Nesbit pioneered stories which related the adventures of contemporary children with inconvenient magical objects and creatures, while Andrew Lang and his many assistants brought the myths, legends, and folktales of the world to children through his *Fairy Books*.

In the first half of the twentieth century Walter de la Mare and L. Frank Baum created heroic and secondary world fantasy for children, while most authors continued primarily in Nesbit's pattern, focusing on child protagonists whose lives were enlivened, but not threatened or transformed, through encounters with the fantastic. Tolkien, and to a lesser extent his friend Lewis, changed the face of fantasy, taking the creation of secondary worlds to new heights, writing fantasy in which the conflict is epic in scale and the fate of peoples or a world hangs in the balance. Tolkien also recalled to the attention of writers and readers, or in many cases introduced for the first time, the vast imaginative depths of British and northern European myth and legend, while Lewis brought the sensibilities of medieval Romance to stories of children interacting with the fantastic.

Others followed the example of Tolkien and Lewis in writing for children. Stories of ordinary children encountering magic for adventures whimsical or instructive, or child-heroes in the centre of more serious adventures involving fantastic elements, were joined by tales of young people in imagined worlds living stories in the patterns of heroic legend, medieval Romance, or folktale quest. Other stories, also influenced by Tolkien and Lewis, were built on the idea of ancient supernatural forces still lurking beneath the mundane modern world, involved in conflicts that, by fate or chance, drew in modern young people.

Children's fantasy rose and fell in popularity through the twentieth century. It was up around the end of the nineteenth century, but in decline between the wars. *The Hobbit* and *The Chronicles of Narnia*, though almost instantly established as classics of children's literature, did not immediately spawn a revival of interest in those aspects of fantasy which Tolkien and Lewis had brought to the fore. Time was needed for their influence to be digested by a new generation of writers. Fantasy was popular again in the seventies and oddly less so in the eighties, at a time when adult fantasy was increasing in both popularity and quality; it then rocketed to a surprising pitch of respectability in the late nineties.

At least two factors were involved in this most recent upsurge of interest. The obvious one was the media attention devoted to J.K. Rowling, which made certain no-one could miss the existence of the *Harry Potter* books. A less obvious factor was the increase over the last three decades of the century in serious attention to the creation of internally cohesive realities in fantasy, fantasy in which the fantastic is not merely whimsy, window-dressing, or there for comic effect. From Diana Wynne Jones and Lloyd Alexander to Philip Pullman and Garth Nix, the body of 'serious' fantasy — serious as in taken seriously as art by its creators — grew and influenced others, both writers and readers; one could say a critical mass of modern children's fantasy was reached. The growing popularity and hence 'respectability' of adult fantasy throughout the nineties has also played a role in drawing attention to children's fantasy. Even without that attention, though, many authors would still be writing fantasy for children and teens, and many children and teens would still be reading it. Fantasy has been an enduring part of writing for children for a very long time and though its popularity may once again ebb, it will always remain.

Through the past two centuries or so, children's fantasy has reflected the beliefs and the needs of the societies in which it was written, just like any other form of literature. It has offered instruction in religion, morality, and science, demonstrating the philosophical or didactic concerns of the authors. It has been playful, thought-provoking, and has opened up new vistas to young imaginations. It has suggested alternate possibilities in life and thought. It has shown visions of worlds where the individual, however young or apparently powerless, can effect change. For people living in a highly industrialized, homogenized society, it has sometimes offered worlds where individual craft and creation still have value, where every village is, at least for subsistence, self-sufficient, and every person a craftsman. On the other hand, it has often used magic to supply the many conveniences of banished industrial technology, or has blithely inserted numerous peasants and servants to deal with the delving and spinning required to support the more nobly-placed heroes, and left those workers faceless.

Fantasy has offered relief and escape from the weight of the present, from the anxieties and fears of the real world. As part of that antidote, it has told stories of problems solved, heroes made, and kingdoms saved, at times when real problems seemed insoluble, when young people were powerless to affect the outcome of situations of personal or global significance and were overwhelmed by the threats looming in the world around them. Perhaps most importantly of all, fantasy has held a mirror to the real world, one that has, by concentrating light and deepening shadows, served to emphasize good and evil, right and wrong, wisdom and folly, so that they might be recognized more clearly when encountered in life.

Bibliography

Anderson, Eric. 'Harry Spells Danger'. *The Philadelphia Trumpet.* Edmond, Oklahoma: Philadelphia Church of God. Sept./Oct. 2000. 26-27.

Annals of English Literature, 1475-1950. 2nd. Ed. Oxford: Oxford UP, 1961.

BBC News. '"Evil" Harry Potter attacked by parents'. news.bbc.co.uk/1/ hi/education/47513.stm. Oct. 13, 1999.

—. 'School bans Harry Potter'. news.bbc.co.uk/1/hi/education/693779.stm. 29 March, 2000.

—. '"Satanic" Harry Potter books burnt'. news.bbc.co.uk/1/hi/entertainment/arts/1735623.stm. 31 December, 2001.

—. 'Emirates ban Potter book'. news.bbc.co.uk/1/hi/entertainment/arts/1816012.stm. 12 February, 2002.

—. 'Rowling wins Potter plagiarism case'. news.bbc.co.uk/1/hi/entertainment/arts/2268024.stm. 19 September 2002.

—. 'Russia rejects Potter ban'. news.bbc.co.uk/1/hi/education/2617103.stm. 3 December, 2002.

—. 'Australian college bans Potter'. news.bbc.co.uk/1/hi/entertainment/arts/3038434.stm. 2 July, 2003.

—. 'Author jailed over sex charges'. news.bbc.co.uk//1/hi/england/north_yorkshire/3683343.stm. 4 May, 2004.

Beaty, Susan. 'Eleanor Farjeon'. *This England.* Spring 1989. 38-42.

Beowulf and The Fight at Finnsburg. 3rd. Edn. Ed. & Introduction Frederick Klaeber. Lexington, MA: Heath, 1950.

Bingham, Jane, and Grayce Scholt. *Fifteen Centuries of Children's Literature: An Annotated Chronology of British and American Works in Historical Context.* Westport, Conn.: Greenwood Press, 1980.

Briggs, Julia. *A Woman of Passion: The Life of E. Nesbit.* New York: New Amsterdam Books, 1987.

Brogan, Hugh. *The Life of Arthur Ransome.* London: Hamish Hamilton, 1985.

Cameron, Eleanor. *The Green and Burning Tree: On the Writing and Enjoyment of Children's Books.* Boston: Little, Brown and Co., 1969.

Carpenter, Humphrey. *J.R.R. Tolkien: A Biography.* London: George Allen & Unwin, 1977.

—, and Christopher Tolkien. Eds. *The Letters of J.R.R. Tolkien*. Boston: Houghton Mifflin, 1981.

—, and Mari Prichard. *The Oxford Companion to Children's Literature*. Oxford: Oxford UP, 1984.

—. *Secret Gardens: A Study of the Golden Age of Children's Literature*. London: Allen and Unwin, 1985.

—. *The Inklings: C.S. Lewis, J.R.R. Tolkien, Charles Williams, and Their Friends*. London: HarperCollins, 1997.

Chrétien de Troyes. *Arthurian Romances*. Trans. & Ed. William W. Kibler. Harmondsworth: Penguin 1991.

Coleridge, Samuel Taylor. *Biographia Literaria*. 2 Vols. 2nd. Edn. New York: George P. Putnam, 1848.

Connolly, Tristanne J. *William Blake and the Body*. Basingstoke: Palgrave Macmillan, 2002.

Crouch, Marcus. *The Nesbit Tradition: The Children's Novel in England, 1945-1970*. Totowa, NJ: Rowman and Littlefield, 1972.

Egoff, Sheila A. *Worlds Within: Children's Fantasy From the Middle Ages to Today*. Chicago: American Library Association, 1988.

Ensor, R.C.K. *England, 1870-1914*. Oxford History of England Vol. XIV. Oxford: Oxford UP, 1936.

Frye, Northrop. *Anatomy of Criticism: Four Essays.*. New York: Atheneum, 1968.

Garth, John. *Tolkien and the Great War*. London: HarperCollins, 2003.

Geoffrey of Monmouth. *The History of the Kings of Britain*. Trans. Lewis Thorpe. Harmondsworth: Penguin, 1966.

Gerstner, Hermann. 'Nachwort'. *Ausgewählte Kinder- und Hausmärchen*. Stuttgart: Philipp Reclam, 1981.

A Gest of Robyn Hode. Eds. & Introduction Stephen Knight & Thomas H. Ohlgren.
http://www.lib.rochester.edu/camelot/teams/gestint.htm &
http://www.lib.rochester.edu/camelot/teams/gest.htm .

Glennon, Lorraine. Ed. *The 20th Century*. North Dighton, MA: JG Press, 2000.

Green, Roger Lancelyn. *Tellers of Tales*. 2nd Edn. Leicester: Edmund Ward, 1953.

Hearn, Michael Patrick. 'Introduction'. *The Victorian Fairy Tale Book*. New York: Pantheon, 1988.

Hunt, Peter. Editor. *Children's Literature: An Illustrated History*. Oxford: Oxford UP, 1995.

Jones, Diana Wynne. *Official Diana Wynne Jones Website*. "Autobiography". http://www.leemac.freeserve.co.uk/autobiog.htm. Jan. 2005.

Ker, W.P. *Epic and Romance: Essays on Medieval Literature*. 2nd. Edn. London: Macmillan, 1926.

Laȝamon: Brut. Vols. I & II. EETS O.S. 250 & 277. Eds. G.L. Brook

& R.F. Leslie. Oxford: Early English Text Society, 1963, 1979.

Lattimore, Richard. 'Introduction'. *The Iliad of Homer*. Trans. Lattimore. Chicago: University of Chicago Press, 1951.

Le Morte Arthure. EETS E.S. 88. Ed. J.D. Bruce. Oxford: Early English Text Society, 1903.

Lewis, C.S. *An Experiment in Criticism*. Cambridge: Cambridge UP, 1961.

Locke, John. *Some Thoughts Concerning Education*. Eds. John W. & Jean S. Yolton. Oxford: Clarendon, 1989.

Luke, David. 'Introduction'. *Jacob and Wilhelm Grimm: Selected Tales*. Harmondsworth: Penguin, 1992.

Lynn, Ruth Nadelman. *Fantasy Literature For Children and Young Adults: An Annotated Bibliography*. 4th. Edn. New Providence, NJ: Bowker, 1995.

Malory, Sir Thomas. *Le Morte Darthur*. 2 Vols. Ed. Janet Cowan. Harmondsworth: Penguin, 1969.

—. *Works*. Ed. Eugène Vinaver. 2nd. Edn. Oxford: Oxford UP, 1971.

Medlicott, W.N. *Contemporary England, 1914-1964, with epilogue 1964-1974*. Longman History of England Vol. XI. Harlow: Longman, 1976.

Meigs, Cornelia, et al. *A Critical History of Children's Literature*. New York: Macmillan, 1953.

Milne, Christopher. *The Enchanted Places*. Harmondsworth: Penguin, 1976.

Morte Arthure. EETS O.S. 8. Ed. E. Brock. Oxford: Early English Text Society, 1865.

Of Arthour and of Merlin. Vol. 1. EETS O.S. 268. Ed. O.D. Macrae-Gibson.Oxford: Early English Text Society, 1973.

Philip, Neil. Ed. *The Penguin Book of English Folktales*. Harmondsworth: Penguin, 1992.

Prince, Alison. *Kenneth Grahame: An Innocent in the Wild Wood*. London: Allison & Busby, 1994.

Le Roman de Brut de Wace. 2 Vols. Ed. Ivor Arnold. Paris: Société des anciens textes français, 1938-40.

Rumble, Thomas C. 'Introduction'. *The Breton Lays in Middle English*. Detroit: Wayne State University Press, 1965.

Sanders, N.K. 'Introduction'. *The Epic of Gilgamesh*. 3rd. Edn. Ed. & Trans. Sanders. Harmondsworth: Penguin, 1972.

Scott, Sir Walter. 'Introduction to the Monastery'. *The Monastery*. Waverley Novels Vol. XVIII. Edinburgh: Robert Cadell, 1832.

Shippey, T.A. *The Road to Middle-earth*. 2nd. Edn. London: HarperCollins, 1992.

Shippey, Tom. *J.R.R. Tolkien: Author of the Century*. London: HarperCollins, 2000.

Taylor, A.J.P. *English History, 1914-1945*. Oxford History of England

Vol. XV. Oxford: Oxford UP, 1965.

Tolkien, J.R.R. 'On Fairy-Stories'. *Tree and Leaf.* 2nd Edn. London: Unwin Hyman, 1988. (Also in *The Monsters and the Critics*, 1983/1997; originally delivered as a lecture in 1939 and published in *Essays Presented to Charles Williams*, Oxford: Oxford UP, 1947.)

—. 'A Secret Vice'. *The Monsters and the Critics and Other Essays.* Ed. Christopher Tolkien. London: HarperCollins, 1997.

Vinaver, Eugène. 'Introduction'. *Malory: Works.* 2nd. Edn. Oxford: Oxford UP, 1971.

Watson, J. Steven. *The Reign of George III, 1760-1815.* Oxford History of England Vol. XII. Oxford: Oxford UP, 1960.

Wheatley, Henry B. Ed. *Merlin.* 4 Vols. EETS O.S. 10, 21, 36, 112. Oxford: Early English Text Society, 2000, 2005. (unaltered two-volume reprint of 1865, 1866, 1867, 1899).

Woodward, Sir Llewellyn. *The Age of Reform, 1815-1870.* 2nd. Ed. Oxford History of England Vol. XIII. Oxford: Oxford UP, 1962.

Zipes, Jack. 'Once There Were Two Brothers Named Grimm'. *The Complete Fairy Tales of the Brothers Grimm.* 2nd. Edn. New York: Bantam, 1992.

—. 'A Note on the Translation'. *The Complete Fairy Tales of the Brothers Grimm.* 2nd. Edn. New York: Bantam, 1992.

Index

Fairy Tales of Ireland, 33
fairy-tales, 10, 13-25, 31-36, 39-45,
48, 51-56, 61, 63-64, 66-68, 75, 86,
91, 94, 97-100, 121, 131, 134, 144,
147, 152-162, 171-81, 186, 225,
237, 290-93, 300, 310, 314, 318-
19, 329-40, 347-48, 377, 432
fairy-tales, literary, 16, 38, 44-45, 48,
54, 62, 64, 68, 84, 97, 101, 157,
159, 160, 291, 299-300, 318, 330,
347, 394
Fall, The (Seventh Tower), 421
Famous Five, 94
Far Pavilions, The, 299
Farjeon, Eleanor, 97-101, 121, 160-
62, 166, 237
Farmer Giles of Ham, 131-34, 165
Farmer, Penelope, 155
Farthest Shore, The, 255, 258
fascism, 114, 128, 402, 405
Father Christmas Letters, The, 132
*Faun and the Woodcutter's Daughter,
The*, 159
fauns, 144, 159
Fellowship of the Ring, The, 125
feminism, 256, 294, 298, 323, 330,
341
fifteenth century, 184-85, 202, 362
fifth century, 203
Figure in the Shadows, The, 307
Final Reckoning, The, 354
Finland, 42, 139-40
Finn Family Moomintroll, 140-41
Finn Mac Cool, 32-3, 168
Finnish (language), 119
'Fir Tree, The', 40
Fire and Hemlock, 287
Fire in the Forging, The. See *Daja's
Book*
'Fire-Bird, the Horse of Power and the
Princess Vassilissa, The', 34
Fires of Merlin, The, 216
Firespell. See *Heart of Fire*
Firewing, 408-09
Firework-Maker's Daughter, The,
366-67, 393
First Two Lives of Lukas-Kasha, The,
242-43
First World War, 34, 69, 71, 79, 92-5,
98, 101, 113, 116-17, 119, 135,

142, 149, 155, 157, 181, 282, 388
Five Children and It, 71-2, 76, 117,
156
Five of Us – and Madeleine, 75
Fleabee's Fortune, 354
folklore, 31, 36, 40, 80, 109, 111, 152-
53, 177, 215, 225, 236-37, 246,
271, 273, 312, 334-38, 359, 362-
65, 373
folktales, 10, 15, 17, 21, 26-31, 35-6,
39-42, 54, 62, 121, 159-60, 163,
166, 181-82, 222, 432-33
'Fool of the World and the Flying
Ship, The', 34
'Foolish Wishes, The', 19
Ford, H.J., 26
Forgotten Beasts of Eld, The, 276
Foundling, The, 238-39
fourteenth century, 19, 184, 186, 197,
209
France, 15-16, 19-23, 26-27, 30, 101,
120, 142, 144, 159, 184-85, 251-52
Fraser, Antonia, 207-209
Frederick Warne (publisher), 109
*French Legends, Tales, and Fairy
Stories*, 159
Froissart's Chronicles, 188
Frye, Northrop, 297
Funke, Cornelia, 412-15, 430
Fur Magic, 271
Further Adventures of Nils, The. See
Wonderful Adventures of Nils, The
Gaiman, Neil, 360, 415-18
Garden Behind the Moon, The, 189
Garner, Alan, 134, 166, 222-28, 240,
246, 271, 333
Garth, John, 135
Gaslight Geezers, 372
genies, 292, 415
Geoffrey of Monmouth, 183-84, 194,
198, 201, 203, 214
Gereint and Enid, 190, 201
German Hero-Sagas and Folk-Tales,
159
German Popular Stories, 24
Germany, 15, 21-7, 43, 62, 144, 151-
52, 159, 189, 300-01, 303, 331,
373, 412
Gest of Robyn Hode, The, 186-87, 218
Ghost in the Mirror, The, 307

Thomas, Edward, 98
Thousand and One Nights, The, 30, 292
Three Mulla-Mulgars, The, 86-8, 134, 155, 333
Three Royal Monkeys, The. See *Three Mulla-Mulgars, The*
thrillers, 93-4, 116, 197, 202, 230, 238, 250, 306, 377
Throme of the Erril of Sherril, The, 276
Through the Looking-Glass, 55-8, 94, 359
'Thumbelina', 40
Thunder Oak, 371
Tibet, 253
Tim Rabbit, 112
Time Cat, 238
Time Master trilogy, 377-78, 380
Time of the Ghost, The, 281, 286
time-travel, 9, 73-4, 80, 112, 154-55, 228, 234, 308, 334, 362-63, 379, 389, 400
'Tinder Box, The', 40
Tintenherz. See *Inkheart*
Tintin, 360
Toad of Toad Hall (play), 85
Toad Triumphant, 85
Told Again, 86
Tolkien and the Great War, 135
Tolkien Reader, The, 132
Tolkien, Christopher, 130
Tolkien, Edith (Bratt), 119, 130
Tolkien, J.R.R., 10-11, 25, 48, 68, 94, 98, 103, 116, 117-135, 137, 142-44, 146, 155, 162, 165-66, 222, 246, 249-50, 258, 298, 330, 333, 390, 396, 431-33
Tombs of Atuan, The, 255-56
Tom's Midnight Garden, 154-56
Tor (publisher), 68, 430
'Touk's House', 318
Tower at Stony Wood, The, 277
'Tower, The', 31
toys, 9, 18, 40, 96, 106, 111, 132, 221, 431
Traveller in Time, A, 112-13, 116, 155
Travers, P.L., 111
Trease, Geoffrey, 195-97
treasure, 14, 65, 74-5, 87, 106-09,

115, 121-23, 149-50, 153, 225, 234, 269, 308, 334, 339, 361, 372
Treasure of Alpheus Winterborn, The, 308
Tree and Leaf, 11, 132-33, 431-32
'Tree of Justice, The', 81
Tris's Book, 325
Tristan, 201
Tristan and Iseult, 168, 201
Trojan War, 108, 164, 168
Trolley to Yesterday, 308
trolls, 27, 41, 121, 123, 338, 373, 413
Trotsky, Leon, 34
Truckers, 384
Tuatha de Danaan, 334
Tulku, 253
Turkey, 26
twelfth century, 81, 149, 184, 187
'Twelve Dancing Princesses, The', 173, 318
'Twelve Wild Geese, The', 32
twentieth century, 7, 70, 79, 85, 91, 112-13, 117, 137, 154, 157-58, 162, 166-67, 181, 187, 222, 234, 282, 293, 299, 303, 329, 360, 424, 430, 433
twenty-first century, 76, 194, 238, 281, 330, 332, 361, 396-97, 429
Twilight of Magic, The, 102
Two Towers, The, 125
'Ugly Duckling, The', 39-40
Unendliche Geschichte, Die. See *Neverending Story, The*
unicorns, 226, 229, 237, 341-444
United Arab Emirates, 12
United States, 12, 46, 136-37, 152, 219, 221, 248, 258, 281, 293, 295-96, 331, 396, 402
'Uraschimataro and the Turtle', 28
urban fantasy, 309, 312
Urusei Yatsura, 361
Uttley, Alison, 112-13, 155
Vampire Voles, 372
vampires, 262, 319, 372, 397
van Dyne, Edith. *See* Baum, L. Frank
Vanity Fair, 44
Vengeance of the Witch-Finder, The, 308
Vesper Holly, 238
Victorian era, 26, 46-7, 51, 54, 59, 61,

About the Author

K.V. Johansen has Master's Degrees in Medieval Studies (Toronto) and English (McMaster). The author of a number of children's books, she held the 2001 Eileen Wallace Research Fellowship in Children's Literature from the Eileen Wallace Collection at the University of New Brunswick. She also received the 2004 Frances E. Russell Award for research in children's literature from the Canadian section of IBBY, the International Board on Books for Young People.

Other Books Published by Sybertooth Inc.
www.sybertooth.ca/publishing/

Stalin vs Me
Volume IX of the Bandy Papers
by three-time Leacock Medal winner Donald Jack
ISBN 0-9688024-7-8 (trade paperback)

The Moss Diary
Vital Statistics, Springhill, Nova Scotia, 1918-1976
2nd edn. with update, genealogical data 1977-2000
Compiled by the Springhill Heritage Group
ISBN 0-9688024-3-5 (cd-rom)

Highlights in the History of Children's Fantasy
Twelve Short Pieces Originally Published in *Resource Links*
by K.V. Johansen
ISBN 0-9688024-6-X (e-book)

Printed in the United States
48108LVS00003B/4